BUSINESS TENANCIES

BUSINESS TENANCIES

Russell Hewitson

LLB, Solicitor, Principal Lecturer in Law,
Northumbria University, Consultant
with Harvey & Marron Solicitors

Cavendish
Publishing
Limited

London • Sydney • Portland, Oregon

First published in Great Britain 2005 by
Cavendish Publishing Limited, The Glass House,
Wharton Street, London WC1X 9PX, United Kingdom
Telephone: + 44 (0)20 7278 8000   Facsimile: + 44 (0)20 7278 8080
Email: info@cavendishpublishing.com
Website: www.cavendishpublishing.com

Published in the United States by Cavendish Publishing
c/o International Specialized Book Services,
5824 NE Hassalo Street, Portland,
Oregon 97213-3644, USA

Published in Australia by Cavendish Publishing (Australia) Pty Ltd
45 Beach Street, Coogee, NSW 2034, Australia
Telephone: + 61 (2)9664 0909   Facsimile: + 61 (2)9664 5420
Email: info@cavendishpublishing.com.au
Website: www.cavendishpublishing.com.au

British Library Cataloguing in Publication Data
Hewitson, Russell
Business tenancies
1 Commercial leases – England
2 Commercial leases – Wales
I Title
346.4'20434

Library of Congress Cataloguing in Publication Data
Data available

ISBN 13: 978-1-859-41897-0
ISBN 10: 1-85941-897-X

1 3 5 7 9 10 8 6 4 2

Printed and bound in Great Britain

For Andrea and Dominique

CONTENTS

TABLE OF CASES

TABLE OF STATUTES

TABLE OF STATUTORY INSTRUMENTS

INTRODUCTION

Since 1 October 1954, business tenancies have been subject to the protection of Part II of the Landlord and Tenant Act 1954. The policy behind the 1954 Act is to protect the goodwill of a tenant who has spent time building up a business. It does this by first granting a business tenant security of tenure; secondly, ny entitling a business tenant to apply to the court for a new tenancy; and thirdly, by entitling a business tenant who is unable to renew its tenancy to the payment of compensation. In addition, Part I of the Landlord and Tenant Act 1927 gives a business tenant the right to carry out improvements and to obtain compensation for them.

Until last year, the 1954 Act statutory regime had remained largely unchanged since its introduction. However, 2004 saw the implementation of substantial reforms which broadly followed recommendations made by the Law Commission in 1992. Chief amongst these is that instead of having to apply to court for an order excluding security of tenure, a tenant now receives advance notice that the 1954 Act is not to apply to the tenancy together with a 'health warning' drawing attention to the implications of the 1954 Act not applying to the tenancy. The reforms also streamline the renewal process and generally make the system fairer for both landlords and tenants; for example, it is now possible for a tenant to apply for an interim rent. New forms have also been issued and the Civil Procedure Rules 1998 have been altered to provide specifically for the 1954 Act court procedures.

In writing this book, I have attempted to produce a work which will be a first point of reference for a practitioner on a day to day basis. I have therefore tried to analyse both the law and practice to produce a useful consideration of both the statutory provisions and the wealth of case law.

I would like to thank the staff of Cavendish Publishing Limited for their support. However, any errors which remain are my responsibility alone.

Finally, my thanks to Andrea, Dominique, Moyra and Don for their love, support and encouragement during the writing of this book.

The law is as stated at 1 January 2005.

CHAPTER 1

WHAT IS A BUSINESS LEASE?

Under the provisions of Part II of the Landlord and Tenant Act 1954 (the 1954 Act), a tenant who has a business lease will be entitled to a new tenancy provided the landlord does not establish a statutory ground of opposition and the tenant takes certain procedural steps laid down in the 1954 Act. For a business lease to be protected in this way by the 1954 Act, it must comply with the requirements contained in s 23(1) of the 1954 Act. If it does not, then it will not be protected.

1.1   SECTION 23(1)

Section 23(1) of the 1954 Act provides that Part II of the 1954 Act:

> ... applies to any tenancy where the property comprised in the tenancy is or includes premises which are occupied by the tenant and are so occupied for the purposes of a business carried on by him or for those and other purposes.

Section 23 has been amended by the insertion of s 23(1A) and s 23(1B) as follows:

> (1A) Occupation or the carrying on of a business –
>
> (a) by a company in which the tenant has a controlling interest; or
>
> (b) where the tenant is a company, by a person with a controlling interest in the company,
>
> shall be treated for the purposes of this section as equivalent to occupation or, as the case may be, the carrying on of a business by the tenant.

> (1B) Accordingly references (however expressed) in this Part of this Act to the business of, or to use, occupation or enjoyment by, the tenant shall be construed as including references to the business of, or to use, occupation or enjoyment by, a company falling within subsection (1A)(a) above or a person falling within subsection (1A)(b) above.

Thus, for the protection of the 1954 Act to apply:

(a) there must be a tenancy of premises;

(b) at least part of the premises must be occupied by the tenant; and

(c) the occupation must be for the tenant's business purposes.

In addition, the tenancy must not be one of those types of tenancies which are excluded from protection (see Chapter 2).

1.2   A TENANCY

The first requirement under s 23(1) of the 1954 Act is that there must be a tenancy before the 1954 Act will apply. 'Tenancy' is defined in s 69(1) of the 1954 Act as being a:

> ... tenancy created either immediately or derivatively out of the freehold, whether by a lease or underlease, by an agreement for a lease or underlease or by a tenancy agreement or in pursuance of any enactment (including this Act), but does not include a mortgage term or any interest arising in favour of a mortgagor by his attorning tenant to his mortgagee ...

This definition includes:

(a) tenancies;

(b) sub-tenancies (see 1.2.3);

(c) tenancies created by the 1954 Act;

(d) tenancies created by any other Act;

(e) agreements for tenancies;

(f) agreements for sub-tenancies; and

(g) tenancies by estoppel (see 1.2.5).

It does not include:

(a) mortgage terms;

(b) licences (see 1.2.1);

(c) tenancies at will (see 1.2.2);

(d) leases of rights of way (*Land Reclamation Co Ltd v Basildon District Council* [1979] 2 All ER 993, CA);

(e) occupation under a management agreement (see 1.2.4);

(f) leases of chattels (*Mirabeau Ltd v Sheckman* [1959] EGD 133);

(g) situations where the tenancy has ceased to exist, for example where the tenancy has been terminated by the tenant serving a notice to quit or where it has been forfeited by the landlord (but see 4.1 for the situation where the tenant seeks relief from forfeiture).

1.2.1 Licences

The 1954 Act does not apply to licences and it is therefore important to determine whether an agreement which calls itself a licence does in fact grant the occupier a licence, or whether, instead, it grants the occupier a tenancy. The leading authority on this point is the House of Lords' decision in *Street v Mountford* [1985] AC 809, where it was held that there will be a tenancy if the agreement confers exclusive possession for a term at a rent. Whilst this decision related to residential premises, in practice it applies equally to commercial premises (*London and Associated Investment Trust plc v Calow* [1986] 2 EGLR 80; *Dresden Estates Ltd v Collinson* (1987) 55 P & CR 47, CA; *Venus Investments Ltd v Stocktop Ltd* [1996] EGCS 173; *National Car Parks Ltd v Trinity Development Co (Banbury) Ltd* [2001] EWCA Civ 1686; (2002) 2 P & CR 18, CA; *Pankhania v Hackney London Borough Council* [2002] EWHC 2441; [2002] NPC 123). It did not matter in *Street v Mountford* that the agreement called itself a licence and that the occupier had agreed not to have any protection under the Rent Act 1977. The key factor is whether the occupier had been granted exclusive possession.

Lord Hoffmann, in *Bruton v London & Quadrant Housing Trust* [1999] 3 All ER 481, HL, said (at 485):

> The decision of this House in *Street v Mountford* [1985] AC 809 is authority for the proposition that a 'lease' or 'tenancy' is a contractually binding agreement, not referable to any other relationship between the parties, by which one person gives another the right to exclusive occupation of land for a fixed or renewable period or periods of time, usually in return for a periodic payment in money. An agreement having these characteristics creates a relationship of landlord and tenant to which the common law or statute may then attach various incidents. The fact that the parties use language more appropriate to a different kind of agreement, such as a licence, is irrelevant if upon its true construction it has the identifying characteristics of a lease. The meaning of the agreement, for example, as to the extent of the possession which it grants, depend upon the intention of the parties, objectively ascertained by reference to the language and relevant background. The decision of your Lordships' House in *Westminster City Council v Clarke* [1992] 2 AC 288 is a good

example of the importance of background in deciding whether
the agreement grants exclusive possession or not. However, the
classification of the agreement as a lease does not depend upon
any intention additional to that expressed in the choice of
terms. It is simply a question of characterising the terms which
the parties have agreed. This is a question of law.

Whilst the presence of rent is not essential to the creation of a
tenancy (see *Ashburn Anstalt v Arnold* [1988] 2 All ER 147, CA;
and s 205(1)(xxvii) of the Law of Property Act 1925), in *Onyx
(UK) Ltd v Beard* [1996] EGCS 55 it was held that the absence of
a provision for the payment of a rent indicated that the
arrangement was not a commercial one and raised the question
of whether it might be construed as a licence, rather than as a
lease.

It may be possible for an owner of premises to avoid
granting an occupier exclusive possession by reserving itself
rights in the agreement. The effect of this will depend on the
construction of the reservations in all the circumstances of each
case and it is clear that to deny exclusive possession the
reservations must be extensive. In *Dresden Estates Ltd v
Collinson,* the agreement which was described as a 'licence'
provided that the owner of the property ('the licensor') could
move the occupier ('the licensee') to any other part of its
property. It was held by the Court of Appeal that the occupier
was not granted exclusive possession and there was a licence.
In *Shell-Mex and BP Ltd v Manchester Garage Ltd* [1971] 1 All ER
841, CA and *Esso Petroleum Ltd v Fumegrange Ltd* [1994] 2 EGLR
90, CA, two cases relating to agreements to occupy petrol
stations, it was held that exclusive possession had not been
granted because the agreements provided that the occupiers
would not interfere with any of the owner's employees or
agents in the exercise of the owner's rights of possession. In
both these cases the reserved rights were wide-ranging; for
example, in *Esso Petroleum Ltd v Fumegrange Ltd* the licensor
reserved control over the physical layout and the way in which
the business was to be run, and consequently the reservation of
more limited rights by an owner, such as a mere right of entry
or access as in *Addiscombe Garden Estates Ltd v Crabbe* [1957] 3
All ER 563, CA, will not deny exclusive possession.

In *National Car Parks Ltd v Trinity Development Co (Banbury)
Ltd* the court had to decide whether an agreement described as
a 'licence' was a lease and thus protected by the 1954 Act. The
agreement granted the right to occupy premises as a car park,

required the occupier to manage and administer the premises, laid down regulations for the conduct of the occupier's business, allowed the owner 40 car spaces at no charge and provided for three months' notice of termination. The occupier had to pay a percentage of 'net profit' for the use of the car park. The court decided that exclusive possession had not been granted and that the agreement was a licence. The regulation as to how the occupier should run its business and the fact that the owner could potentially use the premises itself for parking its cars meant that exclusive possession had not been granted. Whilst the label which the parties chose to put on the agreement was not conclusive, it did carry some weight.

In *Hunts Refuse Disposals Ltd v Norfolk Environmental Waste Services Ltd* [1997] 3 EG 139, CA, an agreement granting an exclusive right of access to part of a working quarry (which was still being used as such) to use that part as a rubbish tip, was held to be a licence on the basis that it was not expected that someone given a right to tip rubbish was to have exclusive possession.

In the light of the case law it is suggested that, rather than rely on attempting to avoid the protection of the 1954 Act by the use of a licence, use should be made instead of the contracting out provisions in s 38(4) of the 1954 Act (see 2.2). However, although risky, the use of a licence may be considered in the following situations:

(a) where there is genuinely no grant of exclusive possession, such as an agreement for 'a shop within a shop', or where the occupation is limited to only part of a day or week;

(b) where the grantor has no power to create a lease (*Wroe v Exmos Cover Ltd* [2000] 15 EG 155, CA);

(c) where a prospective tenant is allowed into occupation pending completion of the lease. In any event, if it was found that a licence was not created, this situation would give rise to a tenancy at will and so would still be outside the protection of the 1954 Act (see 1.2.2).

1.2.2 Tenancies at will

The 1954 Act does not apply to tenancies at will whether arising expressly or, more commonly, by implication of law. The Court of Appeal in *Hagee (London) Ltd v AB Erikson and Larson* [1975] 3 All ER 234 held that an express tenancy at will was not within the 1954 Act and a similar decision was reached by the House of Lords in *Wheeler v Mercer* [1957] AC 416 in relation to a tenancy at will arising by implication of law.

The classic situations in which tenancies at will arise are:

(a) where a prospective tenant is allowed into occupation of the premises pending completion of the negotiations for the lease (*Javad v Aqil* [1991] 1 WLR 1007, CA; *Adegbulu v Southwark London Borough Council* [2003] EWHC 1930; (2003) 2 P & CR D20);

(b) where a tenant holds over after the expiry of the contractual tenancy (*Cardiothoracic Institute v Shrewdcrest Ltd* [1986] 1 WLR 368; *London Baggage Co (Charing Cross) Ltd v Railtrack plc* [2000] L & TR 439); and

(c) where a prospective tenant is allowed into occupation under the terms of an agreement for lease, unless the circumstances are such that a periodic tenancy was intended instead (*Hamerton v Stead* (1824) 3 B & C 478 at 483; *Braythwaite v Hitchcock* (1842) 10 M & W 494 at 497).

The Court of Appeal in *Hagee (London) Ltd v AB Erikson and Larson* said that in any other situations the court must look very carefully at the terms of the agreement, as a tenancy which is described as a tenancy at will but is in fact on the proper construction of the agreement either a periodic or fixed term tenancy will be upheld as such.

In *Walji v Mount Cook Land Ltd* (2002) 1 P & CR 13, CA, the continued occupation of the tenant following the service of a s 25 notice and where the parties had negotiated an agreement subject to contract was considered to be under a quarterly periodic tenancy and not a tenancy at will.

When granting a tenancy at will, it should be remembered that it must be determinable at the will of either party; in other words, the landlord and the tenant must be able, at all times during the tenancy at will, to require the tenant to leave the premises. In addition, a tenancy at will must not be granted for a fixed term.

1.2.3   Sub-tenancies

The definition of a tenancy in s 69(1) specifically includes a sub-tenancy and the Court of Appeal in *HL Bolton (Engineering) Co Ltd v TJ Graham and Sons* [1959] 3 All ER 90, CA confirmed that a sub-tenant will be protected by the 1954 Act. An unlawful sub-tenant will also be protected where, for example, the head landlord's consent to the granting of a sub-tenancy has not been obtained in accordance with the lease (*D'Silva v Lister House Development Ltd* [1970] 1 All ER 858). In this situation, the only remedy which the head landlord can take is to forfeit the headlease, which will in turn bring the sub-tenancy to an end. However, what would be the position if the head landlord lost the right to forfeit, or the sub-tenancy had been granted on, say, the day before the expiry of the term thus giving the head landlord no real chance to forfeit? The head landlord will then be bound by the sub-tenancy which will be protected by the 1954 Act. In these situations the head landlord would be best advised to oppose the grant of a new sub-tenancy under s 30(1)(c) of the 1954 Act (see 8.3). As to how a landlord can discover whether there are any sub-tenancies, see 6.2.2.

In *Parc Battersea Ltd v Hutchinson* [1999] 2 EGLR 33, the term of the sub-tenancy was equal in length to the term of the tenancy and so amounted to an assignment of the tenancy. As the original tenancy had been contracted out of the 1954 Act, the 'sub-tenant' was also unprotected.

1.2.4 Management agreements

Premises may be occupied under a management agreement whereby the owner of the business allows the occupier to run the business. In this situation will the manager be able to claim protection under the 1954 Act? The answer depends on the terms of the management agreement. If the management agreement goes beyond mere management and gives the manager the right to carry on his own business in the premises, then it will be caught by s 23 and a tenancy will arise. A tenancy arose in *Wang v Wei* (1975) 119 Sol Jo 492 where a restaurant owner granted someone a management agreement to run the restaurant and inject capital into the business. Similarly, a tenancy arose in *Dellneed Ltd v Chin Ltd* (1987) 53 P & CR 172, where a young, inexperienced man was allowed to run a restaurant on his own account under supervision by means of a *Mai Toi* agreement (an agreement common in the Chinese community providing for table use or table rent) which expressly provided that it did not create a tenancy. In this case the circumstances of the agreement did not follow the parties' true intention, which was for the occupier to run its own restaurant business with the benefit of the owner's equipment, name and goodwill.

1.2.5   Tenancies by estoppel

The concept of a tenancy by estoppel is the product of 'the fundamental principle of the common law which precludes a grantor from disputing the validity or effect of his own grant' (*per* Millett LJ in *First National Bank plc v Thompson* [1996] Ch 231 at 237). This principle prevents both the landlord and tenant from denying that the grant did not create the tenancy which it purported to create, notwithstanding that the landlord's title was defective so that, as against third parties, he could create no interest in it. Lord Hoffmann in *Bruton v London & Quadrant Trust* said (at 488):

> ... it is not the estoppel which creates the tenancy, but the tenancy which creates the estoppel. The estoppel arises when one or other of the parties wants to deny the ordinary incidents or obligations of the tenancy on the ground that the landlord has no legal estate. The basis of the estoppel is that, having entered into an agreement which constitutes a lease or a tenancy, he cannot repudiate that incident or obligation.

It was held in *Bell v General Accident Fire & Life Assurance Corp Ltd* [1998] 1 EGLR 69, CA that a tenancy by estoppel is a tenancy for the purposes of the s 69(1) definition. In this case a tenancy was granted by a company which was a member of the same group of companies as the owner of the building. The tenant and its assignee believed that the grantor was the owner of the building and that the tenancy which had been granted was protected by the 1954 Act. In subsequent court proceedings, it was agreed by the parties that the tenancy was one arising by estoppel but whether the 1954 Act applied was in dispute. It was argued that it was not a tenancy created either immediately or derivatively out of the freehold as the grantor did not own the freehold. The Court of Appeal decided that such tenancies were within the 1954 Act as it was not possible to discern in either the policy, the scheme or the detailed provisions of the 1954 Act any legitimate reason why such a tenancy which affected premises occupied by a tenant for business purposes should be excluded from the protection of the 1954 Act. On this basis, the landlord, within s 44 of the 1954 Act (see 4.3.2.1), was the grantor, rather than the owning company as it was the owner of the fee simple by estoppel.

An attempt to establish a tenancy by estoppel and so bring an occupation within the 1954 Act failed in *Wroe v Exmos Cover Ltd*, as the occupier had not acted to his detriment in reliance on any representation made to him. The occupier had occupied a room in a building for business purposes under an agreement which described itself as a licence. In addition, the grantor was not permitted under the terms of its own lease to grant tenancies of part of the building. The grantor wrote to the occupier enclosing a s 25 notice (see 4.3) and indicating that the grant of a new tenancy would be opposed under s 30(1)(g) of the 1954 Act (see 8.7). The matter proceeded thereafter on the basis that there was a tenancy but the trial judge decided that the occupation was under a licence and not under a tenancy. The Court of Appeal agreed as it was impossible to say that the occupier remained in occupation in reliance on the letter or to hold that, in following through with the statutory renewal procedure, the occupier was acting to his detriment in reliance on any representation made to him. As Chadwick LJ put it: 'The most that can be said is that the respondent made a procedural mistake.'

1.2.6 Time share leases

Although uncommon in relation to business premises, time share or discontinuous leases can sometimes occur; for example, where a number of consultants share a consulting room and each has a lease which gives each of them the right to use the premises for a particular time each week. Such a lease is capable of being a tenancy (*Smallwood v Shepherds* [1895] 2 QB 627), but what is not clear is whether the 1954 Act will apply to such a lease and, if it does apply, how it will operate (see Duddridge, R and Brown, J, 'Continuing the discontinuous?' (1998) 18(2) Rent Review and Lease Renewal, for a detailed discussion of the possibilities).

1.3 PREMISES

1.3.1 What constitutes 'premises'?

The requirement that 'the property comprised in the tenancy is or includes premises' will normally be satisfied where buildings or land or both are occupied by the tenant. Examples of what have been held to constitute premises include:

(a) gallops let for training and exercising racehorses (*Bracey v Read* [1962] 3 All ER 472);

(b) a field used for running a livery stables and riding school (*Watkins v Emslie* [1982] 1 EGLR 81, CA);

(c) former brick pits used as a gun club (*Botterill v Bedfordshire County Council* [1985] 1 EGLR 82, CA);

(d) an 'eggshell' within a building where the tenancy just comprised the internal skin of the walls and no load-bearing structures were included (*Pumperninks of Piccadilly Ltd v Land Securities plc* [2002] EWCA Civ 621; [2002] 3 All ER 609, CA).

A lease of a right of way will not be a tenancy of premises (*Land Reclamation Co Ltd v Basildon District Council* [1979] 2 All ER 993, CA), but where such a right (ie, an easement) is included in a lease of a building or land which is occupied for the purposes of a business, the right will be protected by the 1954 Act (*Nevill Long and Co (Boards) Ltd v Firmenich and Co* (1984) 47 P & CR 59, CA). Where a right in a protected lease merely amounts to a licence, eg to advertise signs on the outer walls of a building, it will not be protected by the 1954 Act; however, it may be included as a lease term on renewal (*Re No 1 Albemarle Street* [1959] 1 All ER 111, CA).

The requirement in s 23(1) of the 1954 Act that the property 'includes premises' means that the 1954 Act may apply to premises which are used for both residential and business purposes.

1.3.2   The 'holding'

The 1954 Act refers throughout to 'the holding'; for example, in s 32 of the 1954 Act the property to be included in the new tenancy is the holding, and the word is used in some of the grounds of opposition in s 30(1) of the 1954 Act. Section 23(3) of the 1954 Act defines 'the holding' as:

> … the property comprised in the tenancy, there being excluded any part thereof which is occupied neither by the tenant nor by a person employed by the tenant and so employed for the purposes of a business by reason of which the tenancy is one to which this Part of this Act applies.

Prima facie, the holding will consist of the whole of the premises comprised in the tenancy. So long as the tenant occupies part of these premises for business purposes, the holding will include the rest of the premises which the tenant occupies for any other purpose, eg, residential purposes. The holding also includes any parts of the premises occupied by the tenant's employees in the business because of which the tenancy is protected by the 1954 Act, but not any parts of the premises occupied by the tenant's employees in another of the tenant's businesses.

The holding will not include:

(a) any part of the premises which is sub-let to a third party (unless it is the case that the tenant can be said to remain in occupation of that part for business purposes: see 1.4.2.1);

(b) any part of the premises which is unoccupied; and

(c) any part of the premises which is occupied by a third party.

The extent of the holding is to be determined on the date on which the order for the grant of the new tenancy is made (s 32(1) of the 1954 Act).

1.4   OCCUPATION

In order for a tenancy to be protected by the 1954 Act the premises must be occupied by the tenant. The leading case on the meaning of 'occupation' is *Graysim Holdings Ltd v P & O Property Holdings Ltd* [1995] 4 All ER 831, where Lord Nicholls, who gave the judgment of the House of Lords, said (at 835):

> As has been said on many occasions, the concept of occupation is not a legal term of art, with one single and precise legal meaning applicable in all circumstances. Its meaning varies according to the subject matter. Like most ordinary English words, 'occupied', and corresponding expressions such as occupier and occupation, have different shades of meaning according to the context in which they are being used ...

and

> In Part II of the 1954 Act 'occupied' and 'occupied for the purposes of a business carried on by him' are expressions employed as the means of identifying whether a tenancy is a business tenancy and whether the property is part of the holding and qualifies for inclusion in the grant of a new tenancy. In this context 'occupied' points to some business activity by the tenant on the property in question. The 1954 Act seeks to protect the tenant in his continuing use of the property for the purposes of that activity. Thus the word carries a

connotation of some physical use of the property by the tenant
for the purposes of his business.

Lord Nicholls was of the opinion that this test will be a good
starting point but will not provide an answer in all cases. Whilst
the issue in question will usually be one as to who is in
occupation of the premises where there are competing claims,
occasionally there will be cases where the issue will be whether
the property is occupied by the tenant at all. This latter issue
will be considered first.

1.4.1   Is the property occupied by the tenant at all?

A situation may arise where it is necessary to decide whether
the property is in fact occupied at all by the tenant; in other
words, the property appears at first sight to be empty. In such a
case the extent of the tenant's presence or exercise of control in
all the circumstances of the case must be carefully examined. In
Hancock and Willis v GMS Syndicate Ltd [1983] 1 EGLR 70, CA,
Eveleigh LJ said (at 72) that:

> The words with which we are concerned import, in my
> judgment, an element of control and user and they involve the
> notion of physical occupation. That does not mean physical
> occupation every minute of the day, provided the right to occupy
> continues. However, it is necessary for the judge trying the case
> to assess the whole situation where the element of control and
> use may exist in variable degrees. At the end of the day it is a
> question of fact for the tribunal to decide, treating the words as
> ordinary words in the way in which I have referred to them.

In *Bracey v Read*, the tenant was treated as being in occupation
of land used for gallops for racehorses, although this point was
conceded in the case. In *Wandsworth London Borough Council v
Singh* (1991) 62 P & CR 219, CA, the local authority was held to
occupy a small park, even though its employees only visited the
park infrequently. Its parks manager or one of his assistants
visited the park when passing and sub-contractors visited about
once a fortnight for about 32 weeks every year for horticultural
work. It had shown more than merely passive management and
had exercised a sufficient degree of presence, maintenance and
control. Ralph Gibson LJ in *Wandsworth London Borough Council
v Singh* (at 227) reiterated the trial judge's summary of the
relevant principles as follows:

> (i) 'Occupier' is not a term of art, nor does it have a precise
>   legal or technical meaning.

(ii) The word must be given its natural and ordinary meaning in the context of the 1954 Act.

(iii) To occupy premises necessarily involves physical occupation of, or presence in, the premises by the tenant.

(iv) It is not possible to determine whether a tenant is in occupation of premises for section 23 of the 1954 Act by itemising the circumstances found to be present in individual cases where a tenant was held in fact to be in occupation for that purpose and by then determining how many or how few of those circumstances are present in the instant case. Nevertheless the authorities show that certain elements have been treated as capable of amounting to 'occupation' namely:

(a) physical presence by the tenant;

(b) the exercise of control over those using the premises;

(c) the provision of services by the tenant which require him to be physically on the premises;

(d) the time and attention devoted by the tenant to the activity carried on.

And at 229 and 230 he summarised the position as follows:

If it is shown that the tenant, having possession of the premises and having given to no person the right to exclude the tenant from any part of the premises or to limit the tenant's access thereto, is by himself, his servants or agents physically present on the premises to such extent and exercising control of them to such extent as would reasonably be expected having regard to the nature of the premises and the terms of the tenancy, and is so present and exercising control for the purposes of the business or activity carried on by the tenant, then for my part it would seem likely at least that an observer, knowing the facts and applying the ordinary and popular meaning of the phrase 'occupation for the purposes of a business or activity', would hold that tenant to be in occupation.

1.4.1.1 Seasonal occupiers

A problem with occupation can arise where the tenant has a seasonal business, for example, where the premises are situated in a summer holiday resort and the tenant does not occupy the premises during the out-of-season period. In such a situation, the tenant will usually be held to be in occupation for the whole of the year (*Artemiou v Procopiou* [1965] 3 All ER 539, CA), unless the thread of continuity of business occupation has been broken as happened in *Teasdale v Walker* [1958] 3 All ER 307, CA. In this case the tenant granted a sub-tenancy of the premises, intending to recommence its business the following season, but was held not to be in occupation for the purposes of the 1954 Act.

It is worth noting that in *Artemiou v Procopiou* Salmon LJ said (at 545–46):

> ... it seems clear to me that anyone who goes into occupation of business premises in which a seasonal business is carried on is occupying them all the year round for the purposes of the business; if not, it is difficult to see for what other purpose he would be occupying them during the out-of-season months.

1.4.1.2   Involuntary break in occupation

Another problem area arises where the tenant has had to cease occupation because of something over which it has no control, for example where the premises have been destroyed by fire or where the tenant has to vacate in order to allow the landlord to carry out repairs. In this situation the tenancy will remain protected by the 1954 Act, provided the tenant continues to exert and claim the right to occupy the premises (*Morrison Holdings Ltd v Manders Property (Wolverhampton) Ltd* [1976] 2 All ER 205, CA; *Demetriou v Poolaction* [1991] 1 EGLR 100, CA).

In *Morrison Holdings Ltd v Manders Property (Wolverhampton) Ltd*, the tenants were forced to stop trading because of a catastrophic fire in the adjoining premises. They required the landlord to reinstate and expressed a desire to resume trading as soon as they were able to. The landlord demolished and reconstructed the premises and the tenants were held to be entitled to a new tenancy. Scarman LJ said (at 210):

> I would put it in my own words as follows: in order to apply for a new tenancy under the 1954 Act the tenant must show either that he is continuing in occupation of the premises for the purposes of the business carried on by him, or if the events over which he has no control have led him to absent himself from the premises, if he continues to exert and claim his right to occupancy ... in *I & H Caplan Ltd v Caplan (No 2)* [1963] 2 All ER 930, [1963] 1 WLR 1247 the temporary absence which did not destroy the continuity of occupation was absence at the volition of the tenant. In the present case the absenting by the tenants of themselves from the premises after the devastating fire was not their choice, but was brought about by the state of the premises created by the fire ...

The question of whether the tenant was in occupation was considered in *Flairline Properties Ltd v Hassan* [1999] EGLR 138. The premises in this case had been rendered unusable following a fire on 16 April 1995. On 29 September 1996, the tenant subsequently took a lease of nearby premises and resumed business. The lease of the damaged premises expired on 24 March 1997. The landlord argued that the tenant was not in occupation and that it was therefore entitled to possession. The tenant contended that he intended to reoccupy once the premises were reinstated and that this was evidenced by the retention of the key, storage of equipment there and a genuine intention to return. The tenant's case was upheld by the court. Interestingly, the judge said that the tenant should have communicated the intention to the landlord or its agent, although he went on to point out that such communication was strictly unnecessary. It was also made clear that the tenant's intention to reoccupy was not analogous to the intention required under s 30(1)(f) of the 1954 Act (see 8.6.2).

In *Webb v Sandown Sports Club Ltd* [2000] EGCS 13, in deciding the tenant's intent, the court decided that the natural inference from the circumstances was that the tenant had intended to quit the premises and so was no longer in occupation. Following service of a s 25 notice in which the landlord stated it would oppose a new tenancy under s 30(1)(g) of the 1954 Act (see 8.7) and a subsequent threat from the landlord to terminate a licence to use certain facilities, the loss of which would render it impossible for the tenant to operate his business on the premises, the tenant had advertised his intention to relocate his business. Once alternative premises had been found, the tenant ceased trading and removed almost all of his stock from the premises. Fifteen days later he returned to collect the remaining stock and three days after that served a notice discontinuing his application for a new tenancy. In proceedings to decide whether the tenant was entitled to compensation under s 37 of the 1954 Act (see Chapter 10), it was held that the natural inference to be drawn from the tenant's final visits to the premises was that he intended to quit.

1.4.1.3 Voluntary break in occupation

If the tenant voluntarily leaves the premises it is necessary to decide whether the thread of business continuity has been broken. If it has, then the tenant will no longer be in occupation for the purposes of the 1954 Act. The question of whether the thread has been broken is one of fact, so that a break whilst the tenant goes on holiday or where the tenant vacates in order to allow urgent structural repairs to be carried out will not mean that the thread is broken. However, where the tenant gives up occupation in order to move to more desirable premises, the thread may be broken (see *Aspinall Finance Ltd v Viscount Chelsea* [1989] 1 EGLR 103). A borderline case is *I & H Caplan Ltd v Caplan (No 2)* [1963] 2 All ER 930, where for some months, whilst their right to a new tenancy was being litigated, the tenants ceased trading and vacated the premises. Once they had succeeded in obtaining a new tenancy they resumed trading. Cross J held that the thread of continuity was not broken. He said (at 938):

> I think it is quite clear that a tenant does not lose the protection of Part II of the Landlord and Tenant Act 1954, simply by ceasing physically to occupy the premises. They may well continue to be occupied for the purposes of the tenant's business although they are de facto empty for some period of time. One rather obvious example would be if there was a need for urgent structural repairs and the tenant had to go out of physical occupation in order to enable them to be effected. Another example is that which the Court of Appeal had to deal with in *Teasdale v Walker* ([1958] 3 All ER 307, [1958] 1 WLR 1076). There premises were only occupied during discontinuous periods: they were closed and empty in the winter and only used in the summer. On the other hand, as the Court of Appeal pointed out, a mere intention to resume occupation if a new tenancy is granted will not preserve the continuity of the business user if the thread has once been definitely broken.

In *Bacchiocchi v Academic Agency Ltd* [1998] 2 All ER 241, CA, the court had to decide whether a tenant who voluntarily vacated the premises twelve days before the end of the term was still in occupation for the purposes of the 1954 Act during the whole of the tenancy (the outcome of this question was crucial to the tenant's claim for statutory compensation – see Chapter 10). It was held that the tenant was in occupation as the thread of continuity had not been broken. According to Simon Brown LJ (at 249):

> … whenever business premises are empty for only a short period, whether mid-term or before or after trading at either end of the lease, I would be disinclined to find that the business occupancy has ceased (or not started) for that period

provided always that during it there exists no rival for the role of business occupant and that the premises are not being used for some other, non-business purposes. That to my mind is how Pt II of the 1954 Act should operate in logic and in justice.

However, it was conceded by Simon Brown LJ that if premises were left vacant for months, the court would be readier to conclude that the thread of continuity had been broken. The decision in this case is difficult to reconcile as the tenant had ceased trading, had vacated the premises and had handed the keys to his solicitor. However, despite all this he was still held to be in occupation for the purposes of his business!

1.4.2 Who is in occupation where there are competing claims?

The situations where there may be competing claims and which need to be considered here are where the premises are occupied by:

(a) sub-tenants;

(b) the tenant's agent or manager; and

(c) the tenant's employee.

1.4.2.1 Occupation by sub-tenants

Will a tenant who sub-lets the whole or a part of the premises still be in occupation for the purposes of the 1954 Act? Clearly, if the whole of the premises have been sub-let, the sub-tenant will be the one in occupation, not the tenant, and so will be entitled under the 1954 Act. However, what if the tenant only sub-lets a part or parts of the premises? In this situation, if the tenant retains part of the premises for its own business use, then it will be in occupation of that part and the sub-tenant will be in occupation of the part which has been sub-let.

However, the tenant may be in the business of sub-letting the premises with the exception of common or communal parts for either business or residential use. The principles to be applied in this situation have been laid down by the House of Lords in *Graysim Holdings Ltd v P & O Property Holdings Ltd*. In this case the tenant held a 21-year lease of premises which it had fitted out as a market hall containing 35 market stalls, each of which it sub-let. Each stallholder had his own key to secure his stall. The tenant managed the market and provided heating,

lighting, rubbish collection and an attendant who opened and
closed the market. The House of Lords held that the tenant was
not in occupation of the premises and that the only persons
who were entitled to claim a new tenancy under the 1954 Act
were the market traders. It was not possible for there to be dual
occupation of the premises which had been sub-let.
Consequently, a business tenant and its sub-tenant cannot both
enjoy protection under the 1954 Act in relation to the same
premises. As has already been seen (at 1.4): 'The 1954 Act seeks
to protect the tenant in his continuing use of the property for
the purposes of that activity. Thus, the word carries a
connotation of some physical use of the property by the tenant
for the purposes of his business.' So where the tenant's business
involves allowing others to use the premises for their business
purposes, it will be a matter of fact and degree as to just who is
in occupation for the purposes of the 1954 Act.

It is, however, clear from this decision that in certain
situations a business tenant may still be in occupation for the
purposes of the 1954 Act where it has sub-let part of the
premises. In order to succeed, it must be established that the
tenant has reserved rights over the sub-let premises which are
so extensive that it remains in occupation. Whether the reserved
rights will be sufficient will be a matter of degree. As Lord
Nicholls said (at 836d):

> The degree of presence and exclusion required to constitute
> occupation, and the acts needed to evince presence and
> exclusion, must always depend upon the nature of the
> premises, the use to which they are being put, and the rights
> enjoyed or exercised by the persons in question.

It is now clear that, where a sub-tenancy has been granted, the
sub-tenant will be in occupation for the purposes of the 1954
Act. However, the answer is not as clear-cut where the occupier
holds under a licence. In this situation, the rights reserved by
the tenant may be sufficient to allow it to retain protection
under the 1954 Act. This can be illustrated by considering two
cases which were referred to by Lord Nicholls in *Graysim*.

The first of these decisions, which he treated as being
confined to its own facts, was *Lee-Verhulst (Investments) Ltd v
Harwood Trust* [1972] 3 All ER 619, CA. In this case the tenant of
a house let furnished rooms in it and provided services to the
occupants of these rooms, including the provision of bedding,
daily cleaning, provision of light meals if required, the use of a

payphone and the sorting of the post every day. In addition, it retained keys to the rooms and reserved the right to visit them at all reasonable times. In view of the extent of these services and the degree of control which they gave the tenant, it was held that the tenant occupied the whole of the house for its business purposes. In the second case, *Bagettes Ltd v GP Estates Co Ltd* [1956] 1 All ER 729, CA, the sub-lettings were of unfurnished residential flats and the tenant only provided hot water for the sub-tenants and cleaned the common parts. Consequently, the tenant did not remain in occupation for business purposes of the sub-let flats (see also *Linden v Department of Health and Social Security* [1986] 1 WLR 164).

The reasoning in *Graysim* was applied by the Court of Appeal in *Bassari Ltd v Camden London Borough Council* [1998] EGCS 27, CA. A six-storey building had been sub-let by its tenants as follows – the basement and ground floor had been sub-let to a hairdresser whilst the upper had been sub-let to residential sub-tenants. The tenant argued that it was in occupation of the whole of the premises as there was not sufficient evidence that the physical occupiers of most of the building were tenants and that it was using one of the rooms in the building, referred to as 'room six', solely for the purposes of sub-letting. The Court of Appeal dismissed the tenant's appeal on the basis that the occupiers had exclusive possession. Whilst evidence that the tenant had offered various services was adduced, it had not been suggested that those services were being supplied or had been supplied. Neither had the tenant reserved a right of entry nor retained keys. The court was satisfied that the position was not the same as in *Lee-Verhulst (Investments) Ltd v Harwood Trust*. So far as the use of room six was concerned, there was no evidence to show that this had been used by the tenant to run its business but, even if it had, the tenant would only have been entitled to a new tenancy of that room and this would then destroy the very business which the tenant was supposedly running from it.

1.4.2.2 *Occupation by the tenant's agent or manager*

Where the premises are occupied by the tenant's agent or manager the tenant may still be in occupation for the purposes of the 1954 Act. Clearly, the arrangement between the tenant and the agent or manager is relevant. If this goes further than allowing the agent or manager to run the tenant's business and is, in fact, a sub-lease, the tenant will lose its protection. In *Pegler v Craven* [1952] 1 All ER 685, CA, Jenkins LJ said (at 687):

> The conception of 'occupation' is not necessarily and in all the circumstances confined to the actual personal occupation of the person termed the occupier himself. In certain contexts and for certain purposes it obviously extends to vicarious occupation by a caretaker or other servant or by an agent.

Denning LJ also confirmed that premises could be occupied by an agent or manager in *Cafeteria (Keighley) Ltd v Harrison* (1956) 168 EG 668, CA. However, in this case, as the tenant had not actually appointed a manager, there was no intention to occupy and the landlord was entitled to possession.

A tenant which is a limited company may be in occupation even though its business is being managed by another company (*Ross Auto Wash Ltd v Herbert* (1978) 250 EG 971).

The decision in *Pegler v Craven* was applied in *Teasdale v Walker* [1958] 3 All ER 307, CA, where a management agreement was held to be a sham. It alleged that the occupier was the tenant's manager and that the tenant was the employer. However, on the facts, the manager's salary consisted of all of the profits except £750 a year, the manager could run the business in whatever way he chose, the manager paid for all goods used in the business and was liable for all outgoings. From this case it is clear that consideration must be given to whether:

(a) the tenant retains control over the way in which the business is run;

(b) the tenant has a financial interest in the business;

(c) the tenant is liable for the whole or part of the business outgoings; and

(d) the tenant has a right to reclaim the premises.

1.4.2.3 Occupation by the tenant's employee

Where the premises are occupied by the tenant's employee, then this will be treated as amounting to occupation by the tenant (*Chapman v Freeman* [1978] 1 WLR 1298, CA).

1.4.3 Occupation by beneficiaries under a trust

Where a tenancy is held by the tenant on trust, occupation by all or any of the beneficiaries under the trust for their business will be treated for the purposes of the 1954 Act as being equivalent to occupation by the tenant (s 41(1) of the 1954 Act). It has been established that the phrase 'beneficiaries under the trust' means persons who are entitled to occupy the premises as a consequence of their beneficial entitlement (*Frish Ltd v Barclays Bank Ltd* [1955] 3 All ER 185, CA; *Carshalton Beeches Bowling Club Ltd v Cameron* [1979] 1 EGLR 80, CA; *Meyer v Riddick* [1990] 1 EGLR 107, CA). The effect is that the tenancy will be protected by the 1954 Act. Notices under the 1954 Act must be served on the trustees, and the trustees must make any application to the court for a new tenancy.

Where property is held on trust not for individuals but for public charitable purposes, it is submitted that s 41(1) of the 1954 Act will not apply as such trusts will not have any beneficiaries who can take advantage of that statutory provision. In *Methodist Secondary Schools Trust Deed Trustees v O'Leary* [1993] 1 EGLR 105, CA, Sir Christopher Slade felt that the operation of s 23 of the 1954 Act in such situations 'may give rise to knotty problems'. Additionally, Lord Denning MR, in *Parkes v Westminster Roman Catholic Diocese Trustee* (1978) 36 P & CR 22, CA, took the view that s 41(2) of the 1954 Act (see 8.7.3.1) does not apply to a charitable trust and it is submitted that this view should also apply to s 41(1) of the 1954 Act. Where the charity is itself in occupation, it will have the protection of the 1954 Act.

1.4.4 Partnerships

There are special provisions relating to partnerships in s 41A of the 1954 Act. These apply where:

(a) a tenancy is held jointly by two or more persons; and

(b) the property comprised in the tenancy is or includes premises occupied for the purposes of a business; and

(c) the business (or some other business) was at some time during the existence of the tenancy carried on in partnership by all the persons who were then the joint tenants or by those and other persons and the joint tenants' interest in the premises was then partnership property; and

(d) the business is carried on (whether alone or in partnership with other persons) by one or some only of the joint tenants and no part of the property comprised in the tenancy is occupied, in right of the tenancy, for the purposes of a business carried on (whether alone or in partnership with other persons) by the other or others.

The joint tenants who for the time being carry on the business are referred to in s 41A of the 1954 Act as the 'business tenants' (s 41A(2) of the 1954 Act).

Thus, where the tenancy is held in the joint names of two or more partners and is occupied by the partnership for its business purposes, the 1954 Act applies to the tenancy. A problem arises, however, when one or more of the tenants leaves or retires from the partnership, leaving the remaining tenants together with other partners and notices are required to be served under the 1954 Act. In this situation, s 41A(3) of the 1954 Act provides that the remaining tenants can make a s 26 request for a new tenancy (see 5.1) and can give notices under s 27(1) and (2) of the 1954 Act (see 5.2). Such a document must state that it is given by virtue of s 41A and must set out the facts by virtue of which the persons giving it are the business tenants (s 41A(3) of the 1954 Act). There is no need for the absent tenants to be brought into the equation.

In addition, s 41A(4) of the 1954 Act allows a landlord to serve a s 25 notice (see 4.3) by giving it to the business tenants and, again, there is no need for the absent tenants to be brought into the equation.

An application to the court for a new tenancy may be made by the business tenants (s 41A(5) of the 1954 Act), and the court may order the grant of a new tenancy to them or to them jointly with other members of the partnership (s 41A(6) of the 1954 Act). The court may also order that the grant of the new tenancy be made subject to the satisfaction, within a time specified by the order, of such conditions as to guarantors, sureties or otherwise as appear to the court equitable, having regard to the omission of the other joint tenants from the persons who will be the tenant under the new tenancy (s 41A(6) of the 1954 Act).

The business tenants are entitled to recover any amount payable by way of compensation under s 37 or s 59 of the 1954 Act (s 41A(7) of the 1954 Act).

1.4.5   Group companies

Where the tenant is a member of a group of companies, but the property is occupied by another member of the same group, then that occupation is treated for the purposes of s 23 of the 1954 Act as being occupation by the tenant (s 42 of the 1954 Act). In addition, an assignment from one member of a group of companies to another will not be treated as an assignment to another tenant (s 42(2)(c) of the 1954 Act). By virtue of s 42(1) of the 1954 Act, two companies will be members of the same group if either one of the companies is a subsidiary of the other or both are subsidiaries of a parent company or the same person has a controlling interest in both companies ('subsidiary' is defined in s 736, Companies Act 1985, as amended by s 144 of the Companies Act 1989: see Appendix 8).

If a group company occupies under a sub-lease granted to it by another member of its group, will its occupation be protected as a sub-tenancy so that it will be entitled to claim the protection of the 1954 Act rather than the granting company? It is submitted that this will not be the case because the occupation stems from the fact that the occupier is a group company and not a sub-tenant. This view is supported by Evershed MR (at 195) in *Frish Ltd v Barclays Bank Ltd*.

1.4.6   Occupation by a company owned by the tenant

Occupation or the carrying on of a business by a company in which the tenant has a controlling interest amounts to occupation or the carrying on of a business by the tenant (s 23(1A) of the 1954 Act). Similarly, where the tenant is a company, occupation or the carrying on of a business by a person with a controlling interest in the tenant amounts to occupation or the carrying on of a business by the tenant. A person has a controlling interest in a company if, had he been a company, the other company would have been its subsidiary, and 'company' and 'subsidiary' have the meanings given by s 735 and s 736 of the Companies Act 1985 respectively (s 46(2) of the 1954 Act).

1.5   BUSINESS

It is not sufficient for the tenant merely to occupy the premises; they must be 'occupied for the purposes of a business carried on by him or for those and other purposes'. This does not mean that the business must be carried on on the premises, merely that they must be occupied for that purpose (*Bracey v Read*; *Hunt v Decca Navigator Co* [1972] EGD 331). In *Methodist Secondary Schools Trust Deed Trustees v O'Leary*, Sir Christopher Slade said (at 108):

> Though they may perhaps be rare, it is possible to conceive cases where a tenant occupies premises 'for the purposes of a business carried on by him or for those and other purposes' ... without actually carrying on a business on the premises. To postulate a hypothetical case, let it be supposed that a hotelier employs a chef at a very high wage, but for exceptionally long hours, and requires him, as a condition of his employment, to live in a cottage situated very near the hotel, of which cottage the hotelier is tenant, because this is the only practical way to ensure that the chef will be able to perform properly his onerous duties in the hotel ... I see no reason why the hotelier-tenant should not be able to assert that the chef is occupying the cottage for the purposes of his business. On the other hand, I would see no grounds for saying that that hotelier is carrying on his business in the cottage, because the chef himself would be using the premises solely as his own private residence and would not be performing any of his chef's duties in the cottage.

In *Methodist Secondary Schools Trust Deed Trustees v O'Leary*, a school caretaker was carrying on his employer's business by living in a house adjoining the school as he was required to be on call there (but, in the event, the 1954 Act did not apply – see 1.5.6).

'Business' is defined in s 23(2) of the 1954 Act as including 'a trade, profession or employment and includes any activity carried on by a body of persons, whether corporate or unincorporated'. This definition distinguishes between a tenant who is an individual and one which is a body of persons, such as a club, a partnership or a company. The effect is that an individual must be carrying on a 'trade, profession or employment' in order to be protected whereas a body of persons merely has to carry on 'any activity'.

It is not necessary to prove either an intention to profit or an ability to distribute any profits in order for a business to be protected (*Hawkesbrook Leisure Ltd v Reece-Jones Partnership* [2003] EWHC 3333; [2004] 2 EGLR 61).

1.5.1   Where the tenant is an individual

An individual must carry on an activity which amounts to a 'trade, profession or employment'. In *Abernethie v AM & J Kleiman Ltd* [1969] 2 All ER 790, CA, it was held that this did not include a person who gratuitously ran a spare-time activity in his own home. It will always come down to a question of degree and so, in *Lewis v Weldcrest Ltd* [1978] 3 All ER 1226, CA, the taking in of lodgers was not a 'trade, profession or vocation' in view of the number of lodgers, the size of the premises and the sums and services involved.

1.5.2   Where the tenant is a body of persons

In the case of a tenant which is a body of persons, it will be sufficient that the tenant's use amounts to 'an activity'. This has been given a wide meaning by the courts and has been held to include:

(a) a members' tennis club (*Addiscombe Garden Estates Ltd v Crabbe* [1957] 3 All ER 563, CA);

(b) the running of an NHS hospital (*Hills (Patents) Ltd v Board of Governors of University College Hospital* [1955] 3 All ER 365, CA);

(c) the provision of a community centre (*Parkes v Westminster Diocese Trustee*);

(d) the supply of residential accommodation in connection with medical education (*Groveside Properties Ltd v Westminster Medical School* (1983) 267 EG 593, CA); and

(e) the maintenance of a park by a local authority (*Wandsworth London Borough Council v Singh*).

The Court of Appeal did, however, impose a limitation on the meaning of 'activity' in *Hillil Property and Investment Co Ltd v Naraine Pharmacy Ltd* [1979] 2 EGLR 65, CA. It was decided in this case that the activity in question must be correlative and similar to a 'trade, profession or employment'. Consequently, in this case, the casual dumping of rubbish at the demised premises by contractors during the fitting out of other premises was held not to amount to an 'activity'. Megaw LJ said (at 67):

The word 'activity' connotes some general use by the persons occupying, and not some particular, as it were casual, operation such as was being carried out by the contractors here in using [the premises] as a temporary dumping ground for spoil from the other buildings.

The cases in which the word 'activity' in section 23(2) have been considered appear to have been cases where that which has been recognised as being an 'activity' is such a thing as a lawn tennis club, occupying for the purpose of its activities as a members' club; and other similar instances. Although the activity is something which is not strictly a trade, a profession, or an employment, nevertheless, being an 'activity' for this purpose it must be something which is correlative to the conceptions involved in those words. In my judgment the learned judge in the county court was quite right in not paying regard to the provision as to 'includes any activity' for the purposes of his judgment. He does not appear to have referred to it, and I think rightly so. However, that is not the end of the matter, because the definition in sub-section (2) is, '"business" *includes* a trade, profession or employment and includes any activity ...'. So the mere fact that what was being done is not properly to be called an 'activity' is not the end of the matter. We still have to look to see, and the learned judge had to look, as he did look, to see, whether what was being done in [the premises] could properly be described as leading to the conclusion that [the premises] was occupied by the tenants for the purposes of a business carried on by the tenants. That is a question of fact and degree, depending upon the evidence in the particular case.

There is no requirement that the tenant must be carrying on its business in order to make a profit (*Hawkesbrook Leisure Ltd v Reece-Jones Partnership*).

1.5.3   Sub-letting premises

The sub-letting of the premises by the tenant can amount to a 'business'; however, this is subject to the occupation test laid down in *Graysim Holdings Ltd v P & O Property Holdings Ltd* (see 1.4.2.1).

1.5.4   Mixed use premises

It is permissible for the premises to be used for both business and residential purposes and for the tenancy to be protected by the 1954 Act. This will occur where the business use is the significant purpose of the occupation. The test to be applied was laid down in *Royal Life Savings Society v Page*; *Cheryl Investments Ltd v Saldanha* [1979] 1 All ER 5, CA as being whether the business activity is a significant purpose of the tenant's occupation or merely incidental to the residential occupation. This will ultimately be a question of fact.

Thus, in *Royal Life Savings Society v Page*, a doctor who occasionally saw patients at his flat did not occupy the flat for business purposes but, in *Cheryl Investments Ltd v Saldanha*, a tenant who had a telephone, typewriter and files in the flat and who frequently received business visitors there did occupy for business purposes.

The test was subsequently applied in *Gurton v Parrott* [1991] 1 EGLR 98, CA, where the tenant of a dwellinghouse converted some outbuildings into dog kennels. The use of these was held to be merely incidental to her residential use. It was also applied in *Wright v Mortimer* (1996) 28 HLR 719, CA, where an art historian's use of his flat for writing was merely incidental to his residential use.

In *Tomkins v Basildon District Council* [2002] EWCA Civ 876; [2002] 3 EGLR 33, CA, the lease provided for both business and residential purposes and the tenancy was protected by the 1954 Act. The tenant subsequently ceased the business use and the landlord then treated the tenancy as a residential one. However, the landlord was later able successfully to terminate the tenancy under the 1954 Act as there had been no contractual variation of the user clause in the lease and business use had remained the permitted use.

1.5.5 The business must be carried on by the tenant

As has already been seen, it is well established that the business must be carried on by the tenant. There are two statutory exceptions to this rule, as follows.

1.5.5.1 Tenancies held on trust

Where a tenancy is held on trust, the carrying on of a business by all or any of the beneficiaries is treated as being the business of the tenant for the purposes of s 23(1) of the 1954 Act (s 41(1) of the 1954 Act).

1.5.5.2 *Associated companies*

The conduct of a business by one member of a group of companies of which the tenant company is a member is construed as the conduct of the business of the tenant (s 42(2)(a) of the 1954 Act).

1.5.6   Business use in breach of a covenant in the lease

Where the business use is being carried on by the tenant in breach of a prohibition in the terms of the tenancy not to use the premises for business purposes, the 1954 Act will not apply (s 23(4) of the 1954 Act). The only exceptions to this rule occur where either the immediate landlord or his predecessor in title has consented to the breach or the immediate landlord has acquiesced in the breach.

The usual type of prohibition which is caught by s 23(4) of the 1954 Act is a covenant in a lease not to use the premises for business purposes. However, such a prohibition, if not expressly included in the lease, may be implied, as in *Methodist Secondary Schools Trust Deed Trustees v O'Leary*, where there was a covenant in the lease whereby the tenant was 'to use the demised premises for the purpose of a private residence in single occupation only'. The Court of Appeal decided that the effect of this covenant was to prohibit business use and the 1954 Act did not apply.

If the lease does not contain a prohibition not to use the premises for business purposes, but does include a prohibition against using the premises for a specified use, eg, 'not to use as a solicitor's office' or, alternatively, a covenant to use only for a specified use, eg, 'to use as a solicitor's office', then the 1954 Act will apply, despite the premises being used as a solicitor's office in the first example or for some other use in the second example.

The prohibition must subsist 'under the terms of the tenancy' and so s 23(4) of the 1954 Act will not apply if the parties have varied the terms of the lease so that a business use which was prohibited is now allowed, or where the prohibition is subject to a precondition which has not yet been fulfilled. If the prohibition is contained in a headlease but not in a sub-lease, then s 23(4) of the 1954 Act will have no application to the sub-lease (*D'Silva v Lister House Development Ltd*).

Business use will not prevent the 1954 Act from applying where there has been consent or acquiescence. The meaning of both these terms was considered in *Bell v Alfred Franks and Bartlett Co Ltd* [1980] 1 All ER 356, CA. It was said that 'consent' involves more than merely standing by without objecting to the breach and requires a positive, demonstrative act. This act may be written, oral or by conduct. 'Acquiescence' involves a passive failure to do anything about the use once it is known about. In *Methodist Secondary Schools Trust Deed Trustees v O'Leary*, Megaw LJ thought it was clear that the landlord could not be said to have acquiesced in the breach 'unless he knew of the facts which gave rise to the breach'.

CHAPTER 2

PARTICULAR EXCEPTIONS WHERE THE 1954 ACT DOES NOT APPLY

In the following situations the 1954 Act will not apply:

(a) agricultural holdings (see 2.1.1);

(b) mining leases (see 2.1.2);

(c) service tenancies (see 2.1.3);

(d) tenancies not exceeding six months (see 2.1.4);

(e) agreements for the renewal of a tenancy (see 2.1.5);

(f) where a public interest certificate has been issued under ss 57 and 58 of the 1954 Act (see 2.1.6);

(g) where the court has made an order for a new tenancy but the tenant has had the order revoked (see 2.1.7);

(h) licences (see 2.1.8);

(i) tenancies at will (see 2.1.9);

(j) tenancies which have been excluded from the protection of the 1954 Act (see 2.1.10).

There are, in addition, some miscellaneous exclusions which are listed at 2.3.

2.1 THE EXCEPTIONS

2.1.1 Agricultural holdings

By virtue of s 43(1)(a), the 1954 Act does not apply to agricultural holdings which have their own statutory regime contained in the Agricultural Holdings Act 1986. Section 69(1) of the 1954 Act provides that 'agricultural holding' has the same meaning for the purposes of the 1954 Act as in s 1(1) of the Agricultural Holdings Act 1986. This defines 'agricultural holding' as:

> ... the aggregate of the land (whether agricultural land or not) comprised in a contract of tenancy which is a contract for an agricultural tenancy, not being a contract under which the land is let to the tenant during his continuance in any office, appointment or employment held under the landlord ...

and a contract of tenancy is a contract for an agricultural tenancy:

> if, having regard to –
>
> (a) the terms of the tenancy,
>
> (b) the actual or contemplated use of the land at the time of the conclusion of the contract and subsequently, and
>
> (c) any other relevant circumstances,
>
> the whole of the land comprised in the contract, subject to such exceptions only as do not substantially affect the character of the tenancy, is let for use as agricultural land.

The definition of 'agricultural holding' allows mixed use, eg, agricultural use combined with business use and, where this occurs, a decision has to be made as to whether the land is an agricultural holding or not. The three factors set out in (a), (b) and (c) above are used to determine the answer to this question. It is clear that the substantial use of the land is important (*Manson v Bound* (1954) 164 EG 377). If the tenancy appears to satisfy both regimes then it will be excluded from being protected under the 1954 Act and will be protected as an agricultural holding (*Short v Greeves* [1988] 1 EGLR 1, CA).

Since 1 September 1995, the 1986 Act has not applied to new lettings to new tenants. Instead, the Agricultural Tenancies Act 1995 provides that the tenancy will be a 'farm business tenancy'. The 1954 Act does not apply to such a tenancy (s 43(1)(aa) of the 1954 Act). 'Farm business tenancy' is defined in s 1 of the 1995 Act (see Appendix 12).

2.1.2   Mining leases

The 1954 Act does not apply where the land is let under a mining lease (s 43(1)(b) of the 1954 Act). By virtue of s 46, the definition of 'mining lease' is contained in s 25(1) of the Landlord and Tenant Act 1927, which states:

> ... a lease for any mining purpose or purposes connected therewith, and 'mining purposes' include the sinking and searching for, winning, working, getting, making merchantable, smelting or otherwise converting or working for the purposes of any manufacture, carrying away, and disposing of mines and minerals, in or under land, and the erection of buildings, and the execution of engineering and other works suitable for those purposes.

In *O'Callaghan v Elliott* [1965] 3 All ER 111, CA, it was held that the 1954 Act did not apply to a lease granted for the extraction of sand and gravel.

2.1.3   Tenancy granted in consequence of employment

The 1954 Act does not apply to a tenancy which, first, has been granted to a tenant because the tenant was the holder of an office, appointment or employment from the landlord and which, secondly, will continue only for as long as the tenant holds that office, appointment or employment (s 43(2) of the 1954 Act). Where such a tenancy is granted after the commencement of the 1954 Act, ie, 1 October 1954, it must be in writing and must express the purpose for which it was granted. If it does not, then the 1954 Act will apply and the tenant will be protected.

2.1.4   Tenancies for six months or less

Section 43(3) of the 1954 Act provides that the 1954 Act does not apply to a tenancy which is granted for a term certain not exceeding six months (see 2.2.1 for a discussion of 'term of years certain'). Such a short-term tenancy can therefore be very attractive to a landlord. However, there are two exceptions to this rule, as follows:

(a) where the tenancy contains a provision for the renewal or extension of the term beyond six months from its beginning (s 43(3)(a) of the 1954 Act); and

(b) where the tenant has been in occupation for a period which, together with any period during which its predecessor in the business, if any, was in occupation, exceeds 12 months (s 43(3)(b) of the 1954 Act). The tenant's occupation must be as a tenant under a fixed term tenancy or a periodic tenancy. However, the occupation of any predecessor in the business may not necessarily have to have been as a tenant, and may have been as a freeholder or a licensee (*Cricket Ltd v Shaftesbury plc* [1999] 3 All ER 283).

The exception in s 43(3)(b) of the 1954 Act will, in the case of a tenant just starting up in business, allow up to three successive tenancies to be granted, provided they are each for less than six months in length as, by the time the last one is granted, the tenant will not have been in occupation for 12 months.

A tenancy which on its expiry is outside the 1954 Act by virtue of s 43(3) of the 1954 Act cannot be retrospectively revived and brought within the 1954 Act by a subsequent period of occupation as a tenant at will, licensee or trespasser (*Cricket Ltd v Shaftesbury plc*). Thus, a tenant who has been occupying premises for less than 12 months as a tenant and who then remains in occupation under a tenancy at will or a licensee or as a trespasser cannot acquire the protection of the 1954 Act once there has been occupation for 12 months. The only way a tenant would be protected would be where, say, a periodic tenancy had been created after the short-term tenancy had expired. By way of example, suppose that a tenant is allowed to occupy premises from 26 November 2005 until 30 April 2006 and, shortly before that period expired, a similar agreement is entered into for the period from 1 May 2006 until 30 September 2006. At the end of this second agreement, the tenant remains in occupation as a tenant at will, while it negotiated with its landlord for the grant of a lease. These negotiations break down and the landlord purports to terminate the tenant's right to occupy with effect from 9 December 2006. Following *Cricket Ltd v Shaftesbury plc*, the tenant will not be protected by the 1954 Act as it has not been in occupation for a period exceeding 12 months because of its continuing occupation as a tenant at will after the expiry of the second agreement.

2.1.5 Agreements for the renewal of tenancies

By virtue of s 28 the 1954 Act will not apply once the parties to a lease have agreed that the tenant will be granted a new tenancy. The following points about such an agreement must be borne in mind:

(a) the agreement must be a binding and enforceable one (*RJ Stratton Ltd v Wallis Tomlin and Co Ltd* [1986] 1 EGLR 104, CA). Consequently, it must comply with s 2 of the Law of Property (Miscellaneous Provisions) Act 1989;

(b) the agreement must be made between the landlord and the tenant. In *Bowes-Lyon v Green* [1961] 3 All ER 843, HL, it was held that this must be the landlord under s 44(1) of the 1954 Act (see 4.3.2.1);

(c) the agreement must be for the grant of a 'future tenancy' to commence from a date to be specified in the agreement;

(d) the future tenancy must be of the holding (see 1.3.2), or of the holding together with other land. It cannot be of only part of the holding;

(e) the tenant must protect the agreement in case the landlord should dispose of the reversion; otherwise the buyer from the landlord will not be bound by the agreement (see *RJ Stratton Ltd v Wallis Tomlin and Co Ltd*). In unregistered land the agreement should be protected by registering a Class C(iv) land charge against the name of the landlord. Where the title is registered the agreement will usually be protected without any registration as an overriding interest under the Land Registration Act 2002, but consideration should be given to entering either an agreed notice or a unilateral notice on the register;

(f) if the negotiations for the agreement are being conducted on a 'subject to contract' basis the tenant must still protect its rights under the 1954 Act, eg, by applying to the court for the grant of a new tenancy which in *Solomon v Akiens* [1993] 1 EGLR 101, CA the tenant failed to do and so lost the right to a new tenancy when the landlord withdrew from the negotiations for a new tenancy.

The effect of an agreement being made under s 28 of the 1954 Act is that the current tenancy will come to an end on the date specified in the agreement for the new tenancy to start. Until this date the current tenancy is not protected by the 1954 Act. The new tenancy will, of course, be protected once it starts.

2.1.6 Where a public interest certificate has been issued

There are provisions in ss 57 and 58 of the 1954 Act relating to the determination of tenancies on grounds of national security and public interest. By virtue of ss 60, 60A and 60B of the 1954 Act, these provisions apply as well to premises where the landlord is the Minister of Technology, the Urban Regeneration Agency, the Welsh Development Agency and the Development Board for Rural Wales.

2.1.7 Where the court has made an order for a new tenancy but the tenant has had the order revoked

Once the court has made an order for a new tenancy, the tenant may apply for it to be revoked (see 9.7). If such an application is granted, the 1954 Act will not apply to the current tenancy. Instead, it will continue under s 36(2) of the 1954 Act for such period as the court may specify (see 9.7).

2.1.8   Licences

The 1954 Act does not apply to licences (see 1.2.1).

2.1.9   Tenancies at will

The 1954 Act does not apply to tenancies at will (see 1.2.2).

2.1.10   Tenancies which have been excluded from the protection of the 1954 Act

The parties to a new lease may agree to contract out of ss 24–28 of the 1954 Act so that the lease will not be protected by the 1954 Act. Such an agreement is *prima facie* void under s 38(1) of the 1954 Act. Prior to 1 June 2004, the parties in such a situation were required to apply to the court for an order authorising their agreement to exclude the 1954 Act. However, since 1 June 2004 this requirement has been replaced by a notice procedure and there is no longer any need for the court to be involved (see 2.2).

2.2   CONTRACTING OUT

Since 1 June 2004 an agreement by the parties to a proposed lease to contract out of security of tenure will be valid under s 38A of the 1954 Act provided:

(a) the tenancy is to be granted for a term of years certain;

(b) the landlord has served on the tenant a notice in the form, or substantially in the form, set out in Sched 1 to the Regulatory Reform (Business Tenancies) (England and Wales) Order 2003 (SI 2003/3096); and

(c) the requirements specified in Sched 2 to the Regulatory Reform (Business Tenancies) (England and Wales) Order 2003 (SI 2003/3096) have been met (see Appendix 17).

Failure to follow these procedures will render the agreement void and will mean that the tenant will have the right to renew the lease.

2.2.1 'Term of years certain'

The tenancy must be granted for a 'term of years certain', and so the parties cannot agree to exclude any other type of tenancy such as a periodic tenancy. In *Re Land and Premises at Liss, Hants* [1971] 3 All ER 380, it was held that a term of one year or more, as well as a term for a fixed period of less than one year, was included in the expression. However, in *Nicholls v Kinsey* [1994] 1 EGLR 131, CA, a tenancy for 12 months and thereafter from year to year was not a 'term of years certain' for the purposes of s 38(4). In *Metropolitan Police District Receiver v Palacegate Properties Ltd* [2000] 3 All ER 663, CA, a tenancy granted for five years and 'thereafter determinable by six months' prior written notice on the part of the landlord ...' was a 'term of years certain' for the purposes of s 38(4) of the 1954 Act.

A fixed term tenancy containing a break clause is a 'term of years certain' for the purposes of s 38(4) of the 1954 Act (*Metropolitan Police District Receiver v Palacegate Properties Ltd*). Pill LJ said (at 670):

> The term must be construed in the context of the Act. Section 69(1) defines 'notice to quit' as meaning a notice to terminate a tenancy (whether a periodical tenancy or a tenancy for a term of years certain) given in accordance with the provisions (whether express or implied) of that tenancy. In the context of a term of years certain, the only notice to quit which can be given is a right to break. The statutory meaning of notice to quit covers a notice exercising a break clause and clearly contemplates that a fixed term tenancy determinable by such a notice is still a term of years certain.

Pill LJ also expressed preference for the opinion of Diplock LJ in *Scholl Manufacturing Co Ltd v Clifton (Slim-Line) Ltd* [1966] 3 All ER 16, CA, who said:

> Under the common law, apart from surrender or forfeiture, a tenancy may come to an end by effluxion of time, if for a term of years certain, or by notice given by the tenant to the landlord or by the landlord to the tenant, if a periodic tenancy, or a tenancy for a term of years certain subject to a break clause.

2.2.2 Form of notice

Section 38A(3)(a) of the 1954 Act provides that the notice must be in the form, or substantially in the form, set out in Sched 1 to the Regulatory Reform (Business Tenancies) (England and Wales) Order 2003 (see Appendix 17 for a copy of the form). The form of notice contains a prominent 'health warning', drawing the tenant's attention to the consequences of contracting out of security of tenure.

It is anticipated that difficulties could arise where the notice served by the landlord is not exactly the same as the prescribed notice in Sched 1; for example, it might not contain all the required information or may have been completed incorrectly. Will such a notice be 'substantially in the form' set out in Sched 1? In such a situation, existing case law on defective s 25 notices will be relevant (see 4.3.1).

2.2.3   Procedural requirements

The procedural requirements in relation to the service of the notice and the subsequent action to be taken by the tenant are contained in Schedule 2 to the Regulatory Reform (Business Tenancies) (England and Wales) Order 2003.

The landlord should serve the notice on the tenant not less than 14 days before the earlier of either the tenant entering into the tenancy, or becoming contractually bound to enter into the tenancy. The tenant, or a person authorised to do so on his behalf, must, following receipt of the notice, make a declaration in the form, or substantially in the form, set out in para 7 of Sched 2 (see Appendix 17). This declaration confirms that the tenant has received the notice, read the health warning and accepts its consequences. A copy of the notice must be attached to the declaration. A reference to the notice and the declaration must then be contained in or endorsed on the lease.

If it is not possible for the landlord to give the tenant at least 14 days' notice, the notice can still be given before the tenant enters into the tenancy, or becomes contractually bound to enter into the tenancy, but the tenant, or a person authorised to do so on his behalf, must then make a statutory declaration in the form, or substantially in the form, set out in para 8 of Sched 2 (see Appendix 17) confirming that the tenant has received the notice, read the health warning and accepts its consequences. A copy of the notice must be attached to the statutory declaration. A reference to the notice and the statutory declaration must then be contained in or endorsed on the lease.

A detailed note of the chronology of the procedure should be kept for use in the event of a later dispute.

The agreement to contract out of security of tenure, or a reference to the agreement, must also be contained in or endorsed on the lease.

2.2.4   The effect of excluding ss 24–28 of the 1954 Act

The effect of excluding ss 24–28 of the 1954 Act is that the tenant has no security of tenure under the 1954 Act, nor any right to compensation. The tenancy will not be protected under any other statutory scheme such as the Rent Act 1977, the Housing Act 1985 or the Housing Act 1988 as strictly it is still a tenancy to which the 1954 Act applies; all that has been excluded are the provisions of ss 24–28 of the 1954 Act.

2.2.5   Form of agreement to be contained in an excluded lease

Pursuant to a notice dated .... served by the landlord on the tenant under the provisions of section 38A of the 1954 Act and a declaration/statutory declaration made by the tenant dated .... pursuant to Schedule 2 to the Regulatory Reform (Business Tenancies) (England and Wales) Order 2003 (SI 2003/3096), the parties agree that the provisions of sections 24–28 inclusive of the 1954 Act are to be excluded in relation to the tenancy created by this lease.

2.3   MISCELLANEOUS EXCLUSIONS

The following miscellaneous tenancies are excluded from protection:

(a) tenancies of land in a designated dockyard granted to a dockyard contractor (s 3(2) of the Dockyard Services Act 1986). The dockyards which may be so designated are Rosyth and Devonport;

(b) tenancies of land and premises designated under the Atomic Weapons Establishment Act 1991 granted to a contractor (para 3 of the Schedule to the Atomic Weapons Establishment Act 1991). The premises which may be designated are those which formed part of the Atomic Weapons Establishment on 25 September 1991;

(c) concession leases under the Channel Tunnel Act 1987 granted by the Secretary of State to persons constructing and/or operating the Channel Tunnel (s 16(2) of the Channel Tunnel Act 1987);

(d) new leases of flats granted under s 56 of the Leasehold Reform, Housing and Urban Development Act 1993 (s 59(2) of the Leasehold Reform, Housing and Urban Development Act 1993);

(e) tenancies to which s 31 of the Railways Act 1993 applies;

(f) leases of the Royal Naval College, the Dreadnought Seamen's Hospital and the Devonport Nurses' Home where the lease is granted under s 30 of the Armed Forces Act 1996;

(g) Public private partnership leases within the meaning of s 218 of the Greater London Authority Act 1999;

(h) a tenancy of land granted by the Secretary of State for the purposes of a detention centre contract under s 149(3) of the Immigration and Asylum Act 1999.

CHAPTER 3

CONTINUATION OF TENANCIES

3.1   THE CONTINUATION

A tenancy to which the 1954 Act applies will not end on its contractual term date but will be continued until it is terminated in accordance with the 1954 Act (s 24(1) of the 1954 Act). This continuation may be excluded in advance by the parties (see 2.2).

3.2   METHODS OF TERMINATION

The methods of termination which are authorised by the 1954 Act can be divided into those applicable at common law and those under statute.

3.2.1   Common law methods

Section 24(2) of the 1954 Act provides that a tenancy which is protected by the 1954 Act may be brought to an end by any of the following methods:

(a) surrender (see 4.2);

(b) forfeiture (see 4.1);

(c) notice to quit given by the tenant (see 5.5);

(d) forfeiture of a superior lease;

(e) notice to quit served by a mesne landlord on the superior landlord.

3.2.2   Statutory methods

If a tenancy has not been ended by one of the common law methods of termination, it will only come to an end if it is terminated by one of the following methods:

(a) a s 25 notice given by the landlord (see 4.3);

(b) a s 26 request made by the tenant (see 5.1);

(c) a s 27(1) notice given by the tenant (see 5.2.1);

(d) a s 27(2) notice given by the tenant (see 5.2.2);

(e) where agreement has been reached under s 28 of the 1954 Act for a future tenancy (see 2.1.5).

3.3   THE TERMS OF THE CONTINUATION TENANCY

Once the contractual term has passed, the tenancy will continue until it is terminated in accordance with the 1954 Act. It is the common law tenancy which is continued under s 24 of the 1954 Act and, as it is an estate in land, this continuation tenancy may be assigned by the tenant or forfeited by the landlord for breach of covenant. As Lord Denning MR said in *Cheryl Investments v Saldhana* [1978] 1 WLR 1329, CA:

> It is not a personal privilege of the tenant. It is a piece of property which he can assign or dispose of to a third person provided that it was not prohibited by the terms of the contract. And he may give it up on proffering notice to the landlord.

In *Berthon Boat Co Ltd v Hood Sail Makers Ltd* [2000] 1 EGLR 39, the parties entered into a collateral agreement at the same time as the lease, which provided that the tenant would pay the landlord commission 'throughout the term of the lease or any lease substituted therefor'. The court held that the tenant was liable to pay the commission during the continuation tenancy as the continuation tenancy came within the meaning of 'substituted'.

The terms of the continuation tenancy are the same as those of the contractual tenancy, with the exception of those terms dealing with termination.

3.3.1   Rent

The rent payable during the continuation tenancy will be that payable under the contractual tenancy. This is subject to the landlord's right to apply for an interim rent under s 24A of the 1954 Act (see 3.5). To avoid having to apply for an interim rent, a landlord could include in the lease a provision allowing for a rent review on either the penultimate or last day of the contractual term. This review will then take place in accordance with the rent review provisions in the lease, rather than s 24A of the 1954 Act. This is particularly useful in view of the decision in *Willison v Cheverell Estates Ltd* [1996] 1 EGLR 116. In that case, it was held that the landlord who had brought the contractual term to an end early by serving a break notice shortly before a rent review date could not implement the rent review during the continuation tenancy as the rent review date was calculated by reference to a specified period of 'the term'. In this context, 'the term' meant the contractual term only and did not include the continuation tenancy as well. In order to have been able to enforce the rent review 'the term' would have had to have been defined to include the statutory continuation specifically.

The person liable to pay the rent during the continuation tenancy is the tenant in whom the estate is currently vested. In leases granted before 1 January 1996, it was open to the original parties to agree in the lease that the original tenant would remain liable for the rent during the continuation tenancy or, alternatively, for the landlord and any assignor to agree similar terms on assignment. In *Herbert Duncan Ltd v Cluttons* [1993] 4 All ER 968, HL, this was achieved by stating that the term included the continuation period. In the absence of such agreement the original tenant is not liable for the rent during the continuation period (*City of London Corp v Fell* [1993] 4 All ER 968, HL). Such liability will not, however, extend to the payment of any interim rent, unless this is allowed by the construction of the agreement. In *Herbert Duncan Ltd v Cluttons*, the absence of specific reference to the interim rent in the covenant to pay rent meant that the former tenant was not liable for such rent. For leases granted after 1 January 1996, the position is governed by the Landlord and Tenant (Covenants) Act 1995 and, consequently, only the current tenant will be liable.

3.3.2   The premises

The premises comprised in the continuation tenancy are the same as those contained in the contractual tenancy. This means that where part of the premises has been sub-let, the tenant will continue to be the sub-tenant's immediate landlord. It should also be noted that, where such a sub-lease has been granted for a term longer than the headlease, the sub-lease will not take effect as an assignment by operation of law (*Skelton (William) and Son Ltd v Harrison and Pinder* [1975] 1 All ER 182).

3.3.3   Guarantors

A guarantor will only be liable under the guarantee to pay the rent due under the tenancy and not for any interim rent, unless the guarantee clearly provides for this (*Junction Estates v Cope* (1974) 27 P & CR 482; *A Plesser and Co v Davis* [1983] 2 EGLR 70).

3.3.4   Fixtures

The tenant's right to remove tenant's fixtures continues during the continuation tenancy (*New Zealand Government Property Corporation v HM & S Ltd* [1982] 1 All ER 624, CA). The tenant is also entitled to continue to use the landlord's fixtures (*Poster v Slough Estates Ltd* [1968] 3 All ER 257).

3.4   THE EFFECT OF THE TENANT CEASING TO OCCUPY DURING THE CONTINUATION TENANCY

3.4.1   Fixed term tenancies where no s 25 notice or s 26 request has been served

If the tenant ceases to occupy the premises for business purposes during the continuation tenancy the tenancy will still continue until the landlord brings it to an end by giving the tenant not less than three nor more than six months' notice in writing under s 24(3)(a) of the 1954 Act. Should the lease provide for the landlord to be able to serve a notice to quit, then s 24(3)(a) of the 1954 Act also allows the tenancy to be brought to an end by this method.

Should the tenant resume business occupation after notice under s 24(3)(a) of the 1954 Act has been given, this will not affect the validity of the notice (*Teasdale v Walker* [1958] 3 All ER 307, CA).

3.4.2   Fixed term tenancies where either a s 25 notice or s 26 request has been served

If the tenancy is being continued, and either a s 25 notice or a s 26 request has been served but the date specified in the relevant notice or request for termination has not yet passed and the tenant ceases to occupy for business purposes, the tenancy will come to an end on the date specified in the notice or request. It may, however, be possible for the landlord in such a situation to bring the tenancy to an end earlier than this by serving a notice under s 24(3)(a) of the 1954 Act.

3.5 INTERIM RENT

Where a tenant has applied for a new tenancy, s 64 of the 1954 Act (see 7.18) provides that the current tenancy will not come to an end until three months after the proceedings have been concluded. As a result, the tenant could by various means extend the period of continuation and, during this time, would continue to pay the rent reserved by the lease which would usually be less than the current market rent. To counter any unfairness which this may cause to the landlord, the Law of Property Act 1969 introduced into the 1954 Act a provision in s 24A which allows the landlord to apply for an interim rent which will be higher than that paid under the lease. Section 24A was wholly repealed on 1 June 2004 and replaced by a new provision.

3.5.1 Application for an interim rent

Interim rent under s 24A of the 1954 Act is only payable whilst 'the tenancy continues by virtue of section 24'. Consequently, an application cannot be made for interim rent to be paid where the tenancy continues pursuant to either s 28 or s 36(2) of the 1954 Act (see 2.1.5 and 9.7).

Either a landlord or a tenant may apply to the court at any time after service of a s 25 notice or the giving of a s 26 request for a determination of an interim rent (s 24A(1) of the 1954 Act). There is no requirement that an application has been made for a new tenancy under s 24(1) of the 1954 Act. Neither party may make an application if the other has made an application and has not withdrawn it (s 24A(2) of the 1954 Act); nor can the court entertain an application if it is made more than six months after the termination of the relevant tenancy (s 24A(3) of the 1954 Act).

Once a landlord has made an application for an interim rent, it will take effect as an election to treat the tenancy as having been determined, notwithstanding the fact that the appropriate statutory notice was defective (*Bristol Cars v RKH Hotels* (1979) 38 P & CR 411, CA). An application for an interim rent will not fail merely because the tenant's application for a new tenancy has been withdrawn or discontinued (*Michael Kramer and Co v Airways Pension Fund Trustees Ltd* (1976) 246 EG 911, CA); nor will it fail where the landlord assigns the reversion (*Bloomfield v Ashwright* (1983) 47 P & CR 78).

A landlord must ensure that it does not overlook its application for an interim rent if the application is adjourned. In *Arora v Bose* (1998) 76 P & CR D1, CA, the interim rent application was adjourned. The hearing for the new tenancy took place four years later. The landlord did not have the interim rent application restored and an interim rent was therefore refused.

3.5.1.1 *In which court should the application be made?*

An application for interim rent may be made in either the High Court or the county court (s 63(2) of the 1954 Act). In practice, the application will be made in the county court (PD 56, para 2.2).

3.5.1.2 *Application where proceedings for a new tenancy or for termination have been commenced*

Where proceedings have already been started for the grant of a new tenancy or the termination of an existing tenancy, PD 56, para 3.17 provides that the claim for interim rent should be made in those proceedings by:

(a) the claim form;

(b) the acknowledgment of service or defence; or

(c) an application on notice under CPR Part 23.

Any application under s 24D(3) of the 1954 Act (see 3.5.6) should be made by an application on notice under CPR Part 23 in the original proceedings.

3.5.1.3 *Application where no proceedings for a new tenancy or for termination have been commenced*

Where no proceedings have been started for the grant of a new tenancy or the termination of an existing tenancy, the claim for interim rent should be made under CPR Part 8. In addition to the matters required to be included in the claim form by Part, the claim form must include details of:

(a) the property to which the claim relates;

(b) the particulars of the current tenancy, including the date, the parties and the duration, and the current rent (if not the original rent);

(c) every s 25 notice or s 26 request given or made;

(d) if the tenancy has been terminated, the date and mode of the termination; and

(e) if the tenancy has been terminated and the landlord has granted a new tenancy of the property to the tenant:

   (i) particulars of the new tenancy, including the date, the parties and the duration, and the rent; and

   (ii) in a case where s 24C(2) of the 1954 Act applies but the claimant seeks a different rent under s 24C(3) of the 1954 Act, particulars and matters on which the claimant relies on as satisfying s 24C(3) of the 1954 Act (see 3.5.5)

An application for an interim rent which is not issued by the court, even if this is because of an error by the court, has not been made and there is no power for the court to backdate the application (*R v Gravesend County Court ex p Patchett* (1993) 26 EG 125). The claim form must be served within four months of issue (CPR 7.5(2)); however, it was said in a pre-CPR case that the application must be served promptly (*Coates Bros plc v General Accident Life Assurance Ltd* [1991] 1 WLR 712).

3.5.2   The date from which an interim rent is payable

Interim rent is payable from the 'appropriate date' which where the landlord has served a s 25 notice is the earliest date of termination that could have been specified in the s 25 notice, or where the tenant has made a s 26 request is the earliest date that could have been specified in the s 26 request as that date from which the new tenancy is to begin (s 24B(2) and (3) of the 1954 Act).

3.5.3   The court's discretion

The court has a discretion to order an interim rent as s 24A(1) of the 1954 Act provides that the court 'may' order payment of an

interim rent. In *English Exporters (London) Ltd v Eldonwall Ltd*
[1973] Ch 415, Megarry J said that the discretion contained in
the previous version of s 24A would normally be exercised in
favour of the landlord (confirmed by the Court of Appeal in
Charles Follett Ltd v Cabtell Investment Co Ltd (1987) 283 EG 195,
CA).

3.5.4   Amount of the interim rent

There are two different methods for determining the amount of
the interim rent payable by the tenant. The first method, which
is in s 24C of the 1954 Act, applies where a new tenancy of the
whole of the premises is granted and was never opposed by the
landlord. The other method is contained in s 24D of the 1954
Act and applies in every other case.

3.5.5   Amount of the interim rent where a new tenancy of the whole premises is granted and the landlord did not oppose renewal

Section 24C of the 1954 Act provides for the method of
determining the interim rent where a new tenancy of the whole
of the property has been granted (whether as a result of an
order for the grant of a new tenancy or otherwise) and:

(a) the tenant was in occupation of the whole of the property
comprised in the lease when the landlord served his s 25
notice or the tenant made his s 26 request; and

(b) the landlord's s 25 notice stated that he was not opposed to
the grant of a new tenancy or the landlord did not serve a
counternotice in response to the tenant's s 26 request.

In this case, the interim rent will be the same as the rent payable
under the new tenancy (s 24C(2) of the 1954 Act). However, this
will not be the case if either the landlord or the tenant can
establish one or both of the two qualifications in s 24C(3) of the
1954 Act. These are that:

(a) rental market conditions have changed significantly since
the date when the interim rent became payable; and

(b) the terms for the new lease have changed significantly from
those in the old lease.

These qualifications are not mutually exclusive and so a party
can rely on both of them.

In practice, as the interim rent will in most cases be the same as the rent payable under the new tenancy, a tenant will have no incentive to delay the determination of an interim rent.

3.5.5.1   A substantial difference in the market rent

The first situation is where the landlord or the tenant shows to the satisfaction of the court that the rent payable under the new tenancy differs substantially from the 'relevant rent' (s 24C(3)(a) of the 1954 Act). The 'relevant rent' is defined as the rent which the court would have determined under s 34 of the 1954 Act (see 9.4.2) to be payable under the new tenancy if the new tenancy had started on the 'appropriate date' (see 3.5.2).

Where either party proves that there is a substantial difference, then the interim rent will be the relevant rent, that is the s 34 market rent on the assumption that the new tenancy had started on the appropriate date (s 24C(5) of the 1954 Act). For the interim rent payable where either party proves that there is both a substantial difference in the market rent and a substantial change in the rent because of a change in terms, see 3.5.5.2.

3.5.5.2   A substantial change in the rent because of a change in terms

The landlord or the tenant may show to the satisfaction of the court that the terms of the new tenancy differ from the terms of the continuation tenancy to such an extent that the rent payable under the new tenancy is substantially different from the rent which the court would have determined under s 34 of the 1954 Act (see 9.4.2) as payable under a tenancy which started on the same day as the new tenancy and whose other terms were the same as the continuation tenancy (s 24C(3)(b) of the 1954 Act).

In order to succeed under this qualification, a party must therefore show that:

(a) there is a difference between the terms of the continuation tenancy and the terms of the new tenancy; and

(b) the rent determined for the new tenancy would be substantially different if the terms of the new tenancy were the same as the continuation tenancy.

If a party proves that there is a substantial difference in the rent because of a change in terms, then the interim rent will be the rent which is reasonable for the tenant to pay whilst the tenancy continues under s 24 of the 1954 Act (s 24C(6) of the 1954 Act). In determining this interim rent, the court must have regard to the rent payable under the terms of the continuation tenancy and the rent payable under any sub-tenancy of part of the property comprised in the continuation tenancy but, otherwise, sub-ss (1) and (2) of s 34 of the 1954 Act apply to the determination as they would apply to the determination of a rent under s 34 of the 1954 Act if a new tenancy of the whole of the property comprised in the continuation tenancy were granted to the tenant by a court order and the duration of the new tenancy were the same as the duration of the new tenancy which is actually granted to the tenant (s 24C(7) of the 1954 Act).

3.5.6   Amount of the interim rent in any other case

Section 24D of the 1954 Act provides for the method of determining the interim rent in any other case; for example, where the landlord has opposed, whether successfully or not, the grant of a new tenancy, or where a new tenancy is refused. In these situations, the interim rent will be the rent which is reasonable for the tenant to pay whilst the tenancy continues under s 24 of the 1954 Act (s 24D(1) of the 1954 Act). In determining this interim rent, the court must have regard to the rent payable under the terms of the continuation tenancy and the rent payable under any sub-tenancy of part of the property comprised in the continuation tenancy but, otherwise, sub-sections (1) and (2) of s 34 of the 1954 Act apply to the determination as they would apply to the determination of a rent under s 34 of the 1954 Act if a new tenancy from year to year of the whole of the property comprised in the continuation tenancy were granted to the tenant by a court order (s 24D(2) of the 1954 Act).

This method is essentially the same as the method prior to 1 June 2004 and means that the court must:

(a) determine a rent for a hypothetical yearly tenancy disregarding the matters in s 34(1) and (2) of the 1954 Act (see 9.4.2);

(b) have regard to the rent payable under the current tenancy;

(c) have regard to the rent payable under any sub-tenancy of part of the property comprised in the continuation tenancy; and

(d) determine a rent which it would be reasonable for the tenant to pay.

In practice, the yearly basis for the hypothetical tenancy has the effect of producing a rent which is less than that determined under s 34 of the 1954 Act for the new tenancy.

In determining the interim rent, the court is required to have regard to the rent payable under the terms of the current tenancy. This gives the court a discretion to cushion the tenant from the harshness of moving suddenly from paying the rent under the current tenancy, to having to pay the market rent (*English Exporters (London) Ltd v Eldonwall Ltd; Baptist v Masters of the Bench and Trustees of the Honourable Society of Gray's Inn* [1993] 2 EGLR 159). A cushion does not have to be provided in every case, but only where it is needed to protect the tenant (*Halberstam v Tandalco Corp NV* [1985] 1 EGLR 90, CA; *Dept of the Environment v Allied Freehold Property Trust Ltd* (1992) 45 EG 156). When deciding the amount of the cushion it may be relevant to consider the length of the continuation period and, the longer the continuation tenancy, the less the cushion will be (*French v Commercial Union Life Assurance Co plc* [1993] 1 EGLR 113, CA).

As a result of the cushion, the interim rent under s 24D of the 1954 Act will in practice be lower than the rent payable under the new tenancy. The amount of the cushion is for the judge to decide in each case and the differences in the discounts allowed can be seen in the case law. In *Regis Property Co Ltd v Lewis and Peat* [1970] 3 All ER 227, a discount of 33% was allowed. In *English Exporters (London) Ltd v Eldonwall Ltd* a discount of 6.6% was allowed where the lease had been granted three years before the introduction of s 24A of the 1954 Act and the tenant had an expectation that the lease would continue at a low rent for some time. A 10% discount was allowed in the cases of *Janes (Gowns) Ltd v Harlow Development Corp* [1980] 1 EGLR 52, *Ratners (Jewellers) v Lemnoll* [1980] 2 EGLR 65, *Boots the Chemist v Pinkland* [1992] 2 EGLR 98, and *Amarjee v Barrowfen Properties* [1993] 2 EGLR 133). Finally, a 50% discount was allowed in *Charles Follett Ltd v Cabtell Investment Co Ltd*, although it is suggested that this was an exceptional case and should be confined to its own facts (*per* Nourse LJ in *French v Commercial Union Life Assurance Co plc*). It is not easy to reconcile these cases as each turns on its own facts.

If either an order for a new tenancy is revoked under s 36(2) of the 1954 Act (see 9.7), or the landlord and the tenant agree not to act on the order, and an interim rent has been determined under s 24C of the 1954 Act, then the court, on the application of either party, can determine a new interim rent under s 24D of the 1954 Act without the need for a further application under s 24A of the 1954 Act (s 24D(3) of the 1954 Act).

3.5.7   Effect of disrepair

In *Fawke v Viscount Chelsea* [1980] QB 441, the Court of Appeal held that where the premises are in disrepair due to non-compliance with the landlord's repairing covenant, a differential interim rent could be ordered. The effect of this was that, whilst the premises are in disrepair, a lower interim rent was payable. This would then be increased to an amount previously determined once the premises are put into repair.

3.5.8   When is the interim rent to be paid?

The interim rent is payable as soon as it has been determined by the court. Interest will be payable on the interim rent from this date. If the lease contains a provision that interest on rent is not payable until, say, 14 days after rent becomes due, then interest on the interim rent will not be payable until a similar period has elapsed after determination by the court of the interim rent. It would seem that a court can award statutory interest under the Administration of Justice Act 1982 if this is claimed by the landlord.

CHAPTER 4

TERMINATION BY THE LANDLORD

This chapter considers the methods which a landlord may use to bring a tenancy to an end. Under s 24 of the 1954 Act a landlord may terminate a tenancy protected by the Act in any of the following ways:

(a) forfeiture for breach of covenant (see 4.1);

(b) surrender (see 4.2);

(c) notice under s 25 of the 1954 Act (see 4.3). In practice, this is the usual method of terminating a tenancy under the 1954 Act; and

(d) notice under s 24(3) of the 1954 Act where the tenancy is continuing and has ceased to be one to which the Act applies (see 4.4).

4.1   FORFEITURE FOR BREACH OF COVENANT

A landlord may bring a tenancy to an end by forfeiture where the lease contains a provision allowing this and there are grounds for exercising the right. A landlord's right to forfeit is expressly preserved by s 24(2) of the 1954 Act. Once a landlord has forfeited, the tenant will lose all protection under the 1954 Act, unless forfeiture can be avoided by the tenant making a successful claim for relief. It should be noted, however, that the court can grant relief in respect of a 1954 Act protected tenancy, even after the contractual term has come to an end by effluxion of time and the tenancy is continuing under s 24 of the 1954 Act (*Cadogan v Dimovic* [1984] 2 All ER 168, CA). In addition, a tenant may apply to the court for the grant of a new tenancy up and until the landlord's forfeiture action and any counterclaim for relief have been finally disposed of (*Meadows v Clerical Medical and General Life Assurance Society* [1980] 1 All ER 454).

4.2   SURRENDER

A tenancy can be ended by a surrender, either actual or by operation of law.

4.2.1 When does surrender occur?

Surrender always requires the agreement of both the landlord and the tenant. Where there are joint tenants, all of them must join in, or acquiesce in, the surrender (*Hounslow London Borough Council v Pilling* [1994] 1 All ER 432, CA).

Surrender can occur either by deed, or impliedly by operation of law and the following situations give examples of where this can occur:

(a) where the tenant vacates the property and returns the keys to the landlord who then accepts them. This was acknowledged in *Proudreed v Microgen Holdings plc* [1986] 12 EG 127, CA. However, if there are no other acts evidencing an intention by the landlord to resume possession and the tenant's return of the keys can be explained by some other intention, eg to accept a surrender once a new lease has been granted, there will be no surrender.

(b) where the tenant accepts another tenancy of the property, as in *Gibbs Mew plc v Gemmell* [1999] 01 EG 117, CA, where the tenant's acceptance of a tenancy at will surrendered the existing tenancy which was continuing under the 1954 Act;

(c) where the landlord changes the locks or relets the property to someone else (*R v Croydon London Borough Council* [1996] 18 HLR 493);

(d) where the tenant vacates and hands the keys to a guarantor following payment by that guarantor of outstanding rent arrears (*Filering v Taylor Commercial Ltd* [1996] EGCS 95, CA);

(e) where parties deal with an estate in land in such a way that a lease must have been brought to an end so that the superior dealing can take place (*Allen v Rochdale Borough Council* [1999] 3 All ER 443).

4.2.2 Agreements to surrender

Any agreement to surrender a tenancy is void unless it satisfies s 38A of the 1954 Act (s 38(1) of the 1954 Act). Section 38(1) also applies to any agreement which 'purports to preclude the tenant from making an application or request under' the 1954 Act. This has the effect that agreements which prevent the tenant from applying to the court for a new tenancy or making a request under s 26 of the 1954 Act for a new tenancy are also caught by this rule as 'purports to' has been construed as being equivalent to 'has the effect of' (*Joseph v Joseph* [1966] 3 All ER

486, CA). Section 38(1) of the 1954 Act does not apply to surrenders by operation of law.

Whilst s 38(1) of the 1954 Act renders any agreement to surrender void, the actual surrender itself will be valid.

An absolute prohibition on assignment or sub-letting in a lease but which allows the tenant to offer instead to surrender the lease back to the landlord should it wish to assign or sub-let, will not be caught by s 38(1) of the 1954 Act, but any subsequent agreement to surrender will be caught (*Allnatt London Properties Ltd v Newton* (1983) 265 EG 601, CA). Thus, the effect of such a clause is that the tenant is bound by an absolute bar on assignment or sub-letting.

The parties to a lease can enter into a valid agreement to surrender if they comply with s 38A of the 1954 Act. The requirements are the same as those in relation to an agreement to contract out of the 1954 Act and are as follows:

(a) the landlord must serve a notice on the tenant containing a health warning. This must be in the form, or substantially in the form, set out in Sched 3 to the Regulatory Reform (Business Tenancies) (England and Wales) Order 2003 (SI 2003/3096) (see Appendix 17); and

(b) the requirements specified in Sched 4 to the 2003 Order are met (s 38A(1) of the 1954 Act).

Schedule 4 to the 2003 Order provides that:

(a) the notice containing the health warning should be served on the tenant not less than 14 days before 'the tenant enters into the agreement to surrender or (if earlier) becomes contractually bound to do so'. However, it is possible for it to be served within the 14 day period;

(b) the tenant, or someone on his behalf, must make a declaration before he enters into the agreement to surrender or (if earlier) becomes contractually bound to do so (see Appendix 17) The form of the declaration will vary depending on whether or not the landlord's notice containing the health warning is served at least 14 days before the relevant date. If it is not, then the declaration must be by way of a statutory declaration. In either case, a form of the notice containing the health warning must be reproduced at the end of the declaration, which, where the notice is served less than 14 days before the relevant date, must be a statutory declaration;

(c) a reference to the notice containing the health warning and a reference to the declaration or statutory declaration made by the tenant must both be contained in or endorsed on the instrument containing the agreement to surrender.

4.3 NOTICE UNDER SECTION 25

The usual method which a landlord will use to terminate a tenancy protected under the 1954 Act will be the service of a notice under s 25 of the 1954 Act ('a s 25 notice'). Such a notice can be used to terminate:

(a) a fixed term tenancy on or after the contractual term date;

(b) a tenancy pursuant to a break clause;

(c) a periodic tenancy; and

(d) a tenancy which is continuing pursuant to s 24 of the 1954 Act.

In order to terminate a tenancy validly, a s 25 notice must satisfy the following conditions:

(a) it must be in the prescribed form (see 4.3.1);

(b) it must be given by or on behalf of the landlord (see 4.3.2);

(c) it must be given to the tenant (see 4.3.3);

(d) it must state the date on which the tenancy is to end (see 4.3.4);

(e) it must state whether the landlord is opposed to the grant of a new tenancy to the tenant and, if so, it must specify one or more of the grounds in s 30(1) of the 1954 Act as the ground or grounds for the landlord's opposition (see 4.3.5);

(f) if the landlord is not opposing the grant of a new tenancy, it must set out the landlord's proposals for the new tenancy (see 4.3.6); and

(g) it must relate to the whole of the premises comprised in the tenancy (see 4.3.7).

There is no longer a requirement for the tenant to notify the landlord as to whether or not he is willing to give up possession. This means that a landlord will not receive any formal indication of the tenant's intentions. To counter this, a landlord can force the issue by applying to the court for the renewal of the tenancy (s 24(1) of the 1954 Act). If the tenant does not intend to renew, then he should make this clear to the landlord in order to avoid the matter proceeding further and incurring legal and court costs.

4.3.1   The s 25 notice must be in the prescribed form

Section 25(1) provides that the s 25 notice must be in the prescribed form. There are two prescribed forms: Forms 1 and 2 in Sched 2 to the Landlord and Tenant Act 1954, Part 2 (Notices) Regulations 2004 (SI 2004/1005) (see Appendix 16). Form 1 should be used where the landlord is not opposed to the grant of a new tenancy, whilst Form 2 should be used where the landlord is opposed to the grant of a new tenancy.

Prior to 1 June 2004 there was only one prescribed form which was contained in the Landlord and Tenant Act 1954 Part 2 (Notices) Regulations 1983 (SI 1983/133), as amended by the Landlord and Tenant Act 1954 Part 2 (Notices) (Amendment) Regulations 1989 (SI 1989/1548). This notice was required to state whether the landlord would oppose any application for a new tenancy and, if so, upon which of the grounds mentioned in s 30(1) of the 1954 Act, by inserting into the notice the appropriate s 30(1) paragraph letters. It is possible that a situation could arise where a form prescribed by the 1983 Regulations is served after 1 June 2004. This old form of notice would be invalid, applying the decision in *Sabella Ltd v Montgomery* [1998] 1 EGLR 65, CA as it will not provide the tenant with the substance of the information required by the new forms.

4.3.1.1 Use of a form 'substantially to the same effect'

The 2004 regulations allow a landlord to use a form 'substantially to the same effect' in lieu of the prescribed form (the previous 1983 Regulations referred to a form 'substantially to the like effect'). In practice, it is usual to use either a preprinted version of the prescribed form purchased from law stationers, or an in-house produced form. However, difficulties can arise where the form used is not exactly the same as the prescribed form in that it does not contain all the prescribed information (see 4.3.1.2) or, alternatively it does contain all the prescribed information, but has been completed incorrectly (see 4.3.1.3). In either case, this may render the notice invalid.

4.3.1.2 The effect of omitting prescribed information

Where some of the prescribed information has been omitted, the test which is to be applied in deciding if the notice is valid or not is whether the notice gives 'the proper information to the tenant which will enable the tenant to deal in a proper way with the situation, whatever it may be, referred to in the statement of the notice' (*per* Barry J in *Barclays Bank Ltd v Ascott* [1961] 1 WLR 717). If it does not, then it will not be valid. This test was subsequently approved by the Court of Appeal in the cases of *Tegerdine v Brooks* (1977) 36 P & CR 261, *Morrow v Nadeem* [1986] 1 WLR 1381 and *Bridgers v Stanford* [1991] 2 EGLR 265. This is an objective test which involves comparing the form served with the prescribed form and identifying any differences between them. If there are differences, then the court must consider whether the two notices are still substantially alike and a difference can only be ignored if the information in the notice is the same as that contained in the prescribed form. The central question is whether a reasonable recipient would have been misled by the notice served.

The problems which can arise when the prescribed form is not used are illustrated in *Sabella Ltd v Montgomery*. In that case the Court of Appeal had to consider whether a s 25 notice was valid. The notice which was served on the tenant was different from the form prescribed by the 1983 Regulations in the following respects:

(a) it did not contain the 'act quick' warning notice, which is contained in a box and states the following:

> Important. This notice is intended to bring your tenancy to an end. If you want to continue to occupy your property you must act quickly. Read the notice and all the notes carefully. If you are in any doubt about the action you should take, get advice immediately, eg from a solicitor or surveyor or Citizens' Advice Bureau.

(b) grounds (f) and (g) to para 4 of the notes were omitted;

(c) paras 5–9 were omitted;

(d) the 'time warning' in the notes which states as follows:

> Warning to Tenant
> If you do not keep to the time limits in note 2, you will *lose* your right to apply to the court for a new tenancy.

was not enclosed within a box. This particular omission was held to be irrelevant.

The landlord argued that, on the facts, the notice was substantially the same as the prescribed form, as the matters omitted were not significant. This followed the decision of Dillon LJ in *Morris v Patel* [1987] 1 EGLR 75, where a s 25 notice which omitted the 'act quick' warning notice was held to be valid, as the tenant did consult solicitors and did take the necessary action within the statutory time limits. Dillon LJ appeared to suggest that a court may disregard an omission if the consequences of the omission turn out to be negligible. The court in *Sabella Ltd v Montgomery* decided that this proposition was not good law, and Aldous LJ said (at 68):

> Dillon LJ had earlier drawn attention to the absence in the notice of the 'Act Quick' warning notice. He said that its absence had not had any consequences since the plaintiff had consulted solicitors and had taken the appropriate steps according to the timetable required by the Act. That was an observation which was applicable to that case, but should not be understood as meaning that the fact that a recipient had not been misled was relevant. What has to be compared is the notice and the form, and the fact that a recipient may or may not have consulted solicitors is irrelevant. If the notice is not the same as or substantially to the same effect, it is invalid and it cannot be saved by establishing that the recipient did not suffer any prejudice. Further, I do not read the judgment as a decision that the 'Act Quick' warning notice is irrelevant and can be omitted. For the reasons which I give later in this judgment, I believe it is an important part of the form and any notice which omits it is not substantially to like effect as the form.

The Court of Appeal accepted that it was established that:

(a) it does not matter whether the recipient is misled or prejudiced by any omission or difference between the notice which is served and the prescribed form (see *Sun Alliance and London Assurance Co Ltd v Hayman* [1975] 1 WLR 177, CA). Thus, if the notice which is served would mislead the recipient in the same way as the prescribed form, it will still be valid;

(b) omissions or differences which are irrelevant to the recipient in question can be disregarded. This means that if the notes which explain the grounds of opposition are not included, it will not matter provided that the landlord is not opposing the renewal (*Tegerdine v Brooks*).

As Aldous LJ stated (at 67):

> The regulations make it clear that the actual form must be used
> or a form substantially to like effect. Thus, the comparison to
> be made is between the notices served and the form, and it is
> immaterial that any addition or omission had no material effect
> upon the actual recipient. Once the differences have been
> ascertained, then the decision as to whether the two are
> substantially to like effect will depend upon the importance of
> the differences rather than their number or amount. Section 66
> points to what is important, namely informing the recipient of
> his rights and obligations under the Act. It follows that a
> difference can only be disregarded when the information given
> as to the particular recipient's rights and obligations under the
> Act is in substance as effective as that set out in the form.
> Matter that is irrelevant to the recipient's rights or obligations
> may be omitted as in such a case the notice has given to the
> recipient information substantially to like effect as that in the
> form. That statement of the law, I believe, is clear from the Act,
> the regulations and authorities.

Consequently, the notice in *Sabella Ltd v Montgomery* was held to
be invalid. The 'act quick' warning notice was an important
part of the prescribed form and its omission will be fatal to the
validity of a notice as:

> It gives the recipient an important explanation of his rights and
> obligations, namely that the notice is intended to bring the
> tenancy to an end and, if the recipient wanted to continue to
> occupy the property, he should read the notes and act quickly.
> That is just the sort of information that section 66(2) envisages
> as being in the form that would be prescribed. (*Per* Aldous LJ
> (at 68))

In addition, the omission of the notes was also of relevance as
some of them related to a ground of opposition which the
landlord had relied on in the notice. The fact that the landlord
did not later rely on that particular ground was of no
consequence.

Given the easy availability and widespread use of
preprinted s 25 notices, it is difficult to understand how the s 25
notice in this case contained the omissions it did. This decision
clearly reinforces the need for those s 25 notices which are
produced by practitioners themselves as 'in-house forms' to be
thoroughly checked before being used.

4.3.1.3   When will an incorrectly completed notice be valid?

A statutory notice may have been incorrectly completed or may contain an error. The test which is to be applied in determining whether such a notice is valid or not was that laid down by Goulding J in *Carradine Properties Ltd v Aslam* [1976] 1 WLR 442 as being whether '… the notice is quite clear to a reasonable tenant receiving it? Is it plain enough that he cannot be misled by it?'. This was subsequently approved and followed by the Court of Appeal in *Germax Securities Ltd v Spiegal* (1978) 37 P & CR 204 and *Bridgers v Stanford*. It has also been approved by the House of Lords in relation to break notices in *Mannai Investment Co Ltd v Eagle Star Life Assurance Ltd* [1997] 3 All ER 352, HL. The effect of the test in practice is that the court will ignore a minor error in a notice, but not serious ones which would mislead the tenant.

In *Mannai Investment Co Ltd v Eagle Star Life Assurance Ltd* the tenant had served two break notices under the terms of two leases, each notice having a termination date of 12 January 1995. Each of the leases provided that it could be brought to an end 'by serving not less than six months' notice in writing … such notice to expire on the third anniversary of the term commencement date'. The correct date was in fact 13 January 1995. The House of Lords, by a majority, decided that it was obvious to a reasonable recipient with knowledge of the leases that the notice contained a minor misdescription and that the tenant was seeking to bring the leases to an end on 13 January 1995.

Whilst the notice in *Mannai Investment Co Ltd v Eagle Star Life Assurance Ltd* was a contractual one, nevertheless the test applies equally to statutory notices such as those served under the 1954 Act. This was initially confirmed by Peter Gibson LJ in *York v Casey* [1998] 2 EGLR 25, CA, a case involving a notice under s 20 of the Housing Act 1988, which contained an incorrect date for the end of the tenancy in question. In actual fact, it purported to describe the tenancy as ending before it started. It was held that this error was obvious or evident and that, nevertheless, the s 20 notice read in its context was sufficiently clear to leave a reasonable recipient in no reasonable doubt as to its terms (see also *Andrews v Brewer* [1997] 30 HLR 203, CA). An example of a notice which did not satisfy the test is *Clickex Ltd v McCann* [1999] 2 EGLR 63, CA, again a case dealing with a notice under s 20 of the Housing Act 1988. The notice specified that the tenancy would be for six months from 21 December 1995. This date was also specified in the tenancy agreement but was subsequently altered in that document to 8 January 1996, that being the date on which the tenancy actually started. The Court of Appeal decided that the error in the notice was not obvious or evident and so did not satisfy the first part of the test; nor did it satisfy the second part as, when it was read in the context of the tenancy agreement, it could not be said that a reasonable recipient would be left in no reasonable doubt as to the terms of the notice (see also *Panayi v Roberts* [1993] 25 HLR 421, CA). The *Mannai* test has now been applied in the context of the 1954 Act by the Court of Appeal in *Garston v Scottish Widows' Fund and Life Assurance Society* [1998] 3 All ER 596, CA, where Nourse LJ (at p 598) acknowledged that '[i]n the company of the man on the Clapham omnibus, the officious bystander and the man skilled in the art there has now been established the reasonable recipient, a formidable addition to the imagery of our law'.

It should be noted that the *Mannai* test may not always come to the assistance of the tenant. In *Lemmerbell Ltd v Britannia LAS Direct Ltd* [1998] 3 EGLR 67, CA, a lease had been granted to LAS Direct Ltd (Direct). Sometime later the landlord was advised that employees of the Life Association of Scotland (Life) would be using the premises. The landlord was also advised that both Direct and Life were subsidiaries of the same company. No assignment took place from Direct to Life. A break notice was later sent to the landlord under the terms of the lease which stated that Life was the successor in title to Direct. This defect as to the identity of the tenant could not be cured by the application of the *Mannai* test, as the notice did not contain a mere slip that was obvious to the reader when read in context. The reasonable recipient of the notice could not know, in the absence of proof of an assignment, whether Life was the tenant. It was not obvious that there was an error in the name of the tenant, nor who the actual tenant was, nor whether the sender of the notice was authorised by Direct to give the notice. It was impossible to cure the defect. Peter Gibson LJ said (at 71) that:

> The present case seems to me to bear little resemblance to the type of error addressed in *Mannai*. There, words containing a mere slip, obvious to the reader of the notice when read in context, were construed as meaning what they were plainly intended to mean. In the present case there is no equivalent error: the break notice is not merely given on behalf of Life

rather than Direct but contains the explanation as to why it was so given, *viz* Life was the successor in title to Direct. I find it impossible to see how, in these circumstances, it is permissible to construe the break notice as given on behalf of Direct.

In *Trafford Metropolitan Borough Council v Total Fitness (UK) Ltd* [2002] EWCA Civ 1513; (2003) 2 P & CR 2, CA, it was held that a two-stage test is to be applied when deciding whether a notice complies with the requirements of a statutory provision. The first stage involves a true construction of the notice. The second stage involves comparing the contents of the notice with the statutory requirements. The notice will be invalid if it does not contain the relevant requirements; it cannot then be saved under the *Mannai* test.

4.3.1.4 Examples of defects which have not invalidated a s 25 notice

The following are examples of defects in s 25 notices which have not rendered the notice invalid:

(a) failure to date the notice: *Falcon Pipes Ltd v Stanhope Gate Property Co Ltd* (1967) 204 EG 1243;

(b) failure to refer to a year in the date in the notice for the termination of the tenancy: *Sunrose v Gould* [1961] 3 All ER 1142, CA;

(c) where the notice contained the wrong termination date but the covering letter made it clear what date was intended: *Germax Securities Ltd v Spiegal*;

(d) failure to delete the part of the notice which stated that the landlord would not oppose an application for a new tenancy where the landlord specified a ground of opposition: *Lewis v MTC (Cars) Ltd* [1975] 1 All ER 874, CA;

(e) misdescribing the landlord as 'Norfolk Square No 2 Ltd' when the correct name was 'Norfolk Square Hotels No 2 Ltd': *M & P Enterprises (London) Ltd v Norfolk Square Hotels Ltd* [1994] 1 EGLR 129;

(f) failure to refer to a small part of the premises: *Safeway Food Stores Ltd v Morris* [1980] 1 EGLR 59;

(g) failure to sign the notice but the covering letter made it clear that the notice was served on behalf of the landlord: *Stidolph v American School in London Educational Trust* (1969) 20 P & CR 802, CA;

(h) omission of some of the grounds of opposition prescribed notes where the landlord was not opposing renewal: *Tegerdine v Brooks*;

(i) failure to set out in full the wording of the ground of opposition relied upon: *Bolton v Oppenheim* [1959] 3 All ER 90, CA; *Biles v Caesar* [1957] 1 All ER 151; *Philipson Stow v Trevor Square Ltd* [1981] 1 EGLR 56; and *Housleys Ltd v Bloomer-Holt Ltd* [1966] 2 All ER 966, CA. It should be noted that this type of defect should not now arise, as the full wording of the ground of opposition no longer has to be included in the notice; only the appropriate paragraph of s 30(1) is now required;

(j) use of an out-of-date form which showed an incorrect rateable value in relation to the county court jurisdiction: *Bond v Graham* [1975] 2 EGLR 63; *British Railways Board v AJA Smith Transport Ltd* [1981] 2 EGLR 69; *Sun Alliance and London Insurance Co Ltd v Hayman* [1975] 1 All ER 248, CA;

(k) serving a tenant with two s 25 notices together, one opposing renewal and the other not opposing renewal. The former was invalid as it failed to specify a ground of opposition. The second notice was valid. However, both notices were held to be invalid as they were inconsistent with each other: *Barclays Bank plc v Bee* [2001] EWCA Civ 1126; [2002] 1 WLR 332, CA.

4.3.1.5 Examples of defects which have invalidated a s 25 notice

The following are examples of defects in s 25 notices which have rendered the notice invalid:

(a) stating the landlord to be someone who was not the landlord: *Morrow v Nadeem*;

(b) service of a notice by the assignor of the reversion after the reversion had been assigned: *Yamaha-Kemble Music (UK) Ltd v ARC Properties Ltd* [1990] 1 EGLR 261;

(c) failure to name all of the joint landlords: *Pearson v Alyo* [1990] 1 EGLR 114, CA; *Smith v Draper* [1990] 2 EGLR 69, CA;

(d) stating that the landlord would not oppose the grant of a new tenancy if the tenant could find a guarantor without stating a s 30(1) ground: *Barclays Bank Ltd v Ascott.*

4.3.1.6 What should a landlord do if the s 25 notice is defective?

If, after serving a s 25 notice, the landlord discovers that it is defective in some way, eg, it has been incorrectly served or it contains an error, the s 25 notice cannot be withdrawn. Instead, consideration should be given to serving a fresh s 25 notice. If the error is a minor one, a decision may be taken that there is no need to take such action, although this is potentially dangerous. Where the error is serious, the landlord should serve a new s 25 notice on the tenant. This new s 25 notice should be served 'without prejudice' to the validity of the original s 25 notice. If the original s 25 notice later turns out to be invalid, this second s 25 notice will then come into play (*Keith Bailey Rogers and Co (A Firm) v Cubes Ltd* (1975) 31 P & CR 412; *Smith v Draper* [1990] 2 EGLR 69, CA).

4.3.1.7 What should a tenant do if the s 25 notice is defective?

If the tenant considers that the notice which has been received contains an error, the tenant should not treat this as rendering the s 25 notice invalid and so ignore it and do nothing. The error may turn out to be a minor one which does render the notice valid, or, alternatively, the tenant may be treated as having waived the error or may be estopped from later relying on it when arguing that the notice is invalid (see 4.3.1.8). In such situations the tenant's right to a new tenancy will have been lost. This risky strategy of doing nothing is illustrated by *Sabella Ltd v Montgomery*, where it led to the tenant being temporarily evicted from the premises.

The best course of action for a tenant faced with a possible defective notice is to apply to the court under s 43A of the 1954 Act (within the time limit for applying to the court for a new tenancy – see 7.3) for both a declaration that the s 25 notice is invalid and for a new tenancy. If such an application is not made, it could be argued by the landlord that the tenant has waived the right to contest the validity of the notice (*British Railways Board v AJA Smith Transport Ltd*).

If the tenant receives a defective s 25 notice but does not take issue with it and applies to the court for a new tenancy, then the court can treat the s 25 notice as being valid (*Keepers and Governors of the Possessions Revenues and Goods of the Free Grammar School of John Lyon v Mayhew* (1997) 17 EG 163, CA).

If the tenant (or the landlord, for that matter) is intending to object, such action must be taken at an early stage and it has been said that it is:

> ... most desirable in cases under [the 1954 Act] where time may be an important consideration, that parties who wish to take objection to the form or validity of the proceedings should act promptly and not reserve objections ... until proceedings have been on foot a matter perhaps of months ... (*Per* Jenkins LJ in *Tennant v London County Council* (1957) 121 JP 429)

4.3.1.8 Waiver and estoppel

A recipient of an invalid notice may decide to waive the defect, or elect not to pursue the point, so as to cure the invalid notice. Both waiver and election in this context are very similar. A party may also be estopped from challenging the invalidity of a notice.

Waiver and election

Lord Diplock in *Kammins Ballrooms Co Ltd v Zenith Investments (Torquay) Ltd* [1970] 2 All ER 871, HL said (at 894) that there were two types of waiver. The first type, he said, arose 'in a situation where a person is entitled to alternative rights inconsistent with one another. If he has knowledge of the facts which give rise in law to these alternative rights and acts in a manner which is consistent only with his having chosen to rely on them, the law holds him to his choice, even though he was unaware that this would be the legal consequence of what he did'. The second type, he said, which 'debars a person from raising a particular defence to a claim against him, arises when he either agrees with the claimant not to raise that particular defence or so conducts himself as to be estopped from raising it'.

The effect of a party waiving a defect or electing not to pursue it is that he or she will lose the right subsequently to object to the validity of the notice.

Examples of defects which can be waived include:

(a) a notice not being signed (*Tennant v London County Council* (1957) 121 JP 429, CA);

(b) a notice addressed to only one joint tenant (*Norton v Charles Deane Productions* (1969) 214 EG 559);

(c) a notice containing the wrong date for termination (*Bristol Cars v RKH Hotels* [1979] 2 EGLR 56, CA);

(d) a notice which incorrectly names the landlord (*Morrow v Nadeem*);

(e) a notice in the wrong prescribed form (*Keepers and Governors of the Possessions Revenues and Goods of the Free Grammar School of John Lyon v Mayhew*).

In *Stevens & Cutting Ltd v Anderson* [1990] 1 EGLR 95, CA, Stuart-Smith LJ said (at 97) that election arose as follows:

> A party may be deprived of the right to pursue a certain course of conduct if, when faced with two alternative and inconsistent courses of action, he chooses one rather than the other and his election is communicated to the other party. It is, however, now established that before he can be said to have elected, the party electing must know not only of the facts giving rise to the right but that he has the right.

In this case the tenant applied too early for a new lease. The landlord did not take issue with this as it only became aware of the defect after negotiations for a new lease had broken down. There was thus no election by the landlord. However, in *Keepers and Governors of the Possessions Revenues and Goods of the Free Grammar School of John Lyon v Mayhew*, the tenant knew that the landlord had used the wrong form, but carried on as if it were valid. A later challenge to the validity of the notice was unsuccessful as the service of a counternotice operated as a waiver of the defect.

Estoppel

A party may be estopped from challenging the validity of a notice where it has made a representation of fact, and the other party has relied on it to its detriment. In the case of a defective notice, there can be no estoppel unless the recipient has represented that the defect in the notice is not going to be pursued (*Kammins Ballrooms Co Ltd v Zenith Investments (Torquay) Ltd*). Detrimental reliance will not be presumed, but it can be inferred from the circumstances, so that the landlords in *Keepers and Governors of the Possessions Revenues and Goods of the Free Grammar School of John Lyon v Mayhew* suffered detriment by incurring lawyers' and surveyors' fees. They also refrained from serving a fresh notice in the correct form. As they did this on the faith of the tenant's representation that he was treating the notice as valid, it was plainly unconscionable for the tenant to take the point subsequently that the notice was defective.

4.3.2　The s 25 notice must be given by or on behalf of the landlord

A s 25 notice can only be given by the 'landlord', as defined in s 44(1) of the 1954 Act. Such a landlord is referred to in Sched 6 to the 1954 Act as 'the competent landlord' and is not necessarily the immediate landlord. A notice which is served by someone who is not the competent landlord will be invalid, as happened in *Yamaha-Kemble Music (UK) Ltd v ARC Properties Ltd*, where the assignor of the reversion served a notice following completion of the assignment of the reversion. For the possibility that such a defect could be waived, see 4.3.1.8. A notice may be served by a duly authorised agent of the landlord (*Tennant v London County Council; London County Council v Farren* [1956] 1 WLR 1297, CA).

The landlord's name should be stated in the notice, otherwise the notice will be invalid (*Morrow v Nadeem*).

4.3.2.1　The competent landlord

The starting point in deciding who will be the competent landlord is s 44(1) of the 1954 Act. This provides that the competent landlord will be the person who owns an interest in the property which is an interest in reversion expectant (whether immediately or not) on the termination of the relevant tenancy, and which is either:

(a) the fee simple; or

(b) a tenancy which will not come to an end within 14 months by effluxion of time and where no notice has been given to terminate it within that 14-month period or any further time by which it may be continued pursuant to s 36(2) or s 64 of the 1954 Act,

and which is not itself in reversion expectant (whether immediately or not) on an interest which fulfils the above conditions.

The time for determining the identity of the competent landlord is the date of service of the s 25 notice, and the 14-month period is taken from this date.

Someone who fulfils these conditions is estopped from denying that he does not fulfil them, notwithstanding that he has no title to the property (*Bell v General Accident Fire & Life Assurance Corp Ltd* [1997] EGCS 174, CA).

In other words, the competent landlord will be the person who has the freehold reversion, where the lease is a headlease, or the person who holds a lease with at least 14 months left to run and which is the immediate reversion to the tenancy in question. Problems identifying the competent landlord can arise where part of the premises are sub-let. The situation is best illustrated by way of an example. Suppose that the following events occur:

2000   Lease of premises granted by L, the owner of the fee simple, to T for a term of 10 years from 1 January 2000.

2005   Sub-lease of the whole of the premises granted by T to ST for a term of four years from 1 January 2005.

2009   T wishes to serve a s 25 notice on ST.

In this example, T can only serve a s 25 notice on ST if T is the competent landlord. The first question to ask is whether T is the owner of the fee simple. Clearly T is not, so the next question to ask is whether T has a tenancy with less than 14 months unexpired. As the whole of the premises have been sub-let, T will not be protected by the 1954 Act (see 1.4.2.1) and its lease will therefore expire either by effluxion of time or by notice to quit. As T's lease has entered its last 14 months T cannot be the competent landlord in respect of ST. The next person up the chain must now be considered. This is L, and the same questions must be asked of L as were asked of T to establish if it is the competent landlord. As L is the owner of the fee simple it will be the competent landlord.

However, what if T had only sub-let part of the premises to ST and had continued to occupy the remainder for its business purposes? T's lease will now be protected by the 1954 Act and can only be brought to an end under the 1954 Act. In this situation, T will be the competent landlord until either a s 25 notice or a s 26 request is served to bring T's lease to an end within 14 months. If this occurs, then L will be the competent landlord.

In order to discover what interest a party has in the premises, a s 40 notice should be served on them (see 6.2).

The competent landlord cannot merely have an equitable interest in the property, but must have a legal estate. In *Pearson v Alyo* Nourse LJ said that: 'The sub-section is concerned only with legal owners. The Act would be unworkable if it were otherwise.' However, in *Shelley v United Artists Corp Ltd* [1990] 1

EGLR 103, CA, the Court of Appeal held that a specifically enforceable option to take a new lease could be added to the end of the lease in order to allow the tenant to remain as the competent landlord. It was also held in this case that a landlord which serves a s 25 notice represents that it is the competent landlord and, if it later ceases to be the competent landlord, it must correct this representation; otherwise, it may give rise to an estoppel which will defeat any claim that the tenant has taken proceedings against the wrong landlord.

It is clear that the competent landlord may change during the renewal process (*XL Fisheries Ltd v Leeds Corp* [1955] 2 All ER 875, CA). Should this happen, the new competent landlord must be made a party to any proceedings under the 1954 Act (*Piper v Muggleton* [1956] 2 All ER 249, CA and *Rene Claro (Haute Coiffure) v Hallé Concerts Society* [1969] 2 All ER 842, CA). Where the competent landlord serves a s 25 notice and, within two months of service, a superior landlord becomes the competent landlord and gives the tenant notice (this must be in the prescribed form, which is Form 6 of the Landlord and Tenant Act 1954, Part 2 (Notices) Regulations 2004 (SI 2004/1005) (see Appendix 16)) that the s 25 notice is being withdrawn, the s 25 notice no longer has effect and the new competent landlord may serve a fresh s 25 notice (Sched 6, para 6 of the 1954 Act).

Any notice given by the competent landlord to terminate the relevant tenancy will bind the interest of any mesne landlord, notwithstanding that he has not consented to the giving of the notice (Sched 6, para 3 of the 1954 Act).

If the competent landlord's interest in the property comprised in the relevant tenancy is a tenancy which will come or can be brought to an end within 16 months (or any further time by which it may be continued under either s 36(2) or s 64 of the 1954 Act) and the competent landlord gives to the tenant under the relevant tenancy a s 25 notice to terminate the tenancy or is given by the tenant a s 26 request:

(a) the competent landlord shall forthwith send a copy of the notice to his immediate landlord; and

(b) any superior landlord whose interest in the property is a tenancy shall forthwith send to his immediate landlord any copy which has been sent to him (Sched 6, para 7 of the 1954 Act).

A landlord which receives a copy s 25 notice or s 26 request is under a duty to pass it on to his own landlord, even if he has an interest which is not limited to 16 months.

Where the competent landlord has given a s 25 notice to terminate the relevant tenancy and, within two months after the giving of the notice, a superior landlord:

(a) becomes the competent landlord; and

(b) gives to the tenant notice in the prescribed form (see Appendix 16) that he withdraws the notice previously given,

the s 25 notice shall cease to have effect, but without prejudice to the giving of a further s 25 notice by the competent landlord (Sched 6, para 6 of the 1954 Act). It is to be noted that there is no similar right to withdraw a counternotice given in response to a s 26 request.

4.3.2.2 Misdescription

If there is a misdescription in the landlord's name, the notice will not automatically be invalid. In *M & P Enterprises (London) Ltd v Norfolk Square Hotels Ltd,* the notice was not invalid for the reason that the landlord was described as 'Norfolk Square No 2 Ltd', instead of its correct name of 'Norfolk Square Hotels No 2 Ltd'.

4.3.2.3 Joint landlords

Where there is more than one landlord, all of them must join in the notice. In *Pearson v Alyo* the name of only one of two co-owners of the property was stated as the landlord in the s 25 notice. Following *Morrow v Nadeem* it was held that the notice was invalid. It made no difference that the co-owner, who was stated as the landlord in the s 25 notice, was solely and beneficially entitled to the property in equity, as s 44(1) of the 1954 Act is concerned only with legal owners. However, in *Leckhampton Dairies Ltd v Artus Whitfield Ltd* (1986) 130 Sol Jo 225, the notice was given by only one of the joint landlords but on the facts it was held to be valid. It is submitted that this case is confined to its own facts in the light of the decision in *Pearson v Alyo.*

4.3.2.4 The notice must be signed

The notice must be signed either by the landlord or its duly
authorised agent. If it is not signed but it is apparent from a
covering letter where it came from, then it will be valid (*Stidolph
v American School in London Educational Trust*). Lack of authority
to sign the notice will render it invalid (*London County Council v
Farren*).

4.3.2.5 Position where there is a mortgagee in possession or a receiver

The final point to note is that there is provision in s 67 of the
1954 Act dealing with the situation where the landlord has
taken out a mortgage and the mortgagee has taken possession
or appointed a receiver. In such a situation, the mortgagee in
possession or the receiver will be the landlord (see *Meah v
Mouskos* [1963] 3 All ER 908, CA).

4.3.3   The s 25 notice must be given to the tenant

The s 25 notice must be given to the tenant (s 25(1) of the 1954
Act). The methods of service are dealt with at 6.1. Whilst this
will not usually be a problem, the following points should be
noted.

4.3.3.1 Joint tenants

Where the tenancy is vested in more than one tenant, the notice
must be addressed to and served on all the joint tenants (*Booth
Investments Ltd v Reynolds* (1974) NLJ 119). A notice which is
addressed only to one of two or more joint tenants will be
defective; however, such a defect may be waived (*Norton v
Charles Deane Productions*).

4.3.3.2 Partnerships

Where the tenancy is held by a partnership, it is only necessary
to serve the tenants who are the current partners, provided that
none of the other tenants carries on business elsewhere at the
premises, in which case they must all be served (s 41A(4) of the
1954 Act). Thus, only the parties involved in running the
business need be served.

4.3.3.3 Limited companies

If the tenant is a limited company, it should be served at its registered office (s 725 of the Companies Act 1985).

4.3.3.4 Bankrupt tenant

If the tenant is bankrupt, the notice should be addressed to and served on the trustee in bankruptcy (*Gatwick Investments Ltd v Radivojevic* [1978] CLY 1768).

4.3.3.5 Deceased tenant

On the tenant's death the tenancy will pass to the tenant's personal representatives and the notice should be addressed to and served on them. Where the tenant has died intestate and letters of administration have not been taken out, the notice should be served on the Public Trustee.

4.3.3.6 Position where the premises have been sub-let

If the tenant has sub-let the whole of the premises and the sub-tenancy satisfies s 23 of the 1954 Act, the s 25 notice should be served on the sub-tenant. If, however, only part of the premises have been sub-let and the tenant is in business occupation of the unlet part, the s 25 notice should be served on the tenant. This will result in the renewal of the tenant's lease of the whole of the premises. Alternatively, the landlord may serve separate notices on the tenant and sub-tenant(s), which will result in separate leases being granted, one to the tenant for the part which it occupies, and one to the sub-tenant for the part which it occupies, with the effect that the sub-tenant will then become a tenant of the landlord. In theory, the landlord must first serve a s 25 notice on the tenant and then, as the landlord will, following this, be the competent landlord in respect of the sub-tenant(s), serve a s 25 notice(s) on the sub-tenant(s). In practice, if all the notices are served on the same day, it will be presumed that they are served in the correct order (*Keith Bayley Rogers and Co Ltd (A Firm) v Cubes Ltd*).

It is important for a landlord to know whether there has been a sub-letting, as even an unauthorised sub-letting may be protected by the 1954 Act (*D'Silva v Lister House Development Ltd*

[1971] Ch 17). Such information can be obtained under s 40 of the 1954 Act (see 6.2).

4.3.3.7 *Service on a trust*

Where the tenant is a trust, the s 25 notice should be addressed to 'the trustees for the time being', in order to cover any change in the trustees (*Hackney African Organisation v Hackney London Borough Council* [1998] EGCS 139, CA).

4.3.4   The s 25 notice must state the date on which the tenancy is to end

The s 25 notice must specify the date on which the current tenancy will come to an end. There are two requirements which must be satisfied in relation to this date:

(a) it must not be less than six months nor more than 12 months after the date of the giving of the notice (s 25(2) of the 1954 Act). It is not necessary to give a clear period of six or 12 months, and a notice which gives a date six months from the date of service of the notice will be valid (*Hogg Bullimore and Co v Co-operative Insurance Society* (1984) 50 P & CR 105). In calculating the period of notice required under the 1954 Act, the corresponding date rule is used (see 6.1.6);

(b) it must not be earlier than the date on which the tenancy could have been terminated at common law (s 25(3) of the 1954 Act). A notice which specifies a date earlier than the date on which the tenancy could have been terminated at common law will be void.

4.3.4.1 *Fixed term tenancies*

In the case of a fixed term tenancy, the relevant date will be the date on which, apart from the 1954 Act, the tenancy will expire by effluxion of time (s 25(4) of the 1954 Act). The notice must also comply with the requirement in s 25(2) of the 1954 Act that it give not less than six months' nor more than 12 months' notice. A notice specifying the last day of the contractual term will be valid (*Re Crowhurst Park* [1974] 1 WLR 583). Where the tenancy is being continued under s 24 of the 1954 Act, the notice need only comply with the maximum and minimum duration requirement of s 25(2) of the 1954 Act (*Lewis v MTC (Cars) Ltd* [1975] 1 All ER 874, CA).

Example: Suppose the tenancy is granted for a fixed term of 10 years, expiring on 31 December 2009. The landlord can serve a s 25 notice at any time between 1 January 2009 and 30 June 2009 to bring the tenancy to an end on 31 December 2009. If the notice is served after 30 June 2009, then the earliest it can bring the tenancy to an end is six months after it is served. Thus, if it is served on 30 July 2009, the earliest date that the tenancy can be brought to en end will be 30 January 2010.

4.3.4.2 Periodic tenancies

Where the tenancy is a periodic one, the date of termination must not be earlier than the date on which a notice to quit served by the landlord on the date on which the s 25 notice is served will expire (s 25(3)(a) of the 1954 Act). However, it does not literally have to be that date, so long as it is not earlier than that date. This can be illustrated by *Commercial Properties Ltd v Wood* [1968] 1 QB 15, CA. In this case, the tenancy was from month to month and started on the 18th of each month. On 4 October 1965, the landlord served a s 25 notice to expire on 11 April 1966. This notice was valid, as this date was 'not earlier' than the date on which the tenancy could be brought to an end by a notice to quit served on 4 October 1965, which would have been 1 December 1965. Thus, for example, suppose a tenancy was granted on 1 July 1996 from month to month. At common law, one month's notice to quit is required. However, under s 25 of the 1954 Act at least six months' notice must be given.

Where more than six months' notice to quit is required under the terms of the lease, the notice period must not exceed the length of notice required under the lease plus six months (s 25(3)(b) of the 1954 Act). Thus, by way of example, if the tenancy requires the landlord to give nine months' notice to quit, the landlord may serve a s 25 notice not more than 15 months before the date specified for termination.

4.3.4.3 Fixed term tenancies containing a break clause

Where a fixed term tenancy contains a provision allowing the landlord to serve a notice terminating the tenancy before the contractual term date, the date of termination will not be earlier than the date on which the landlord's notice will expire. Again, where more than six months' notice is required under the terms of the lease, the notice period must not exceed the length of notice required under the lease plus six months (s 25(3)(b) of the 1954 Act).

Does a landlord who wishes to exercise the break clause and terminate the tenancy have to serve two notices, one pursuant to s 25 of the 1954 Act and one pursuant to the break clause? Notice pursuant to the break provision will terminate the contractual term and the tenancy will then continue under s 24 of the 1954 Act until it is terminated in accordance with the 1954 Act. Therefore, it is clear that it will be insufficient if the landlord merely serves a notice under the terms of the break clause (*Morrison Holdings Ltd v Manders Property (Wolverhampton) Ltd* [1976] 1 WLR 533; *Weinbergs Weatherproofs Ltd v Radcliffe Paper Mill Co Ltd* [1958] Ch 437). However, in *Scholl Manufacturing Co Ltd v Clifton (Slim-Line) Ltd* [1967] Ch 41, CA, the service of just a s 25 notice was sufficient to terminate the lease, both under the 1954 Act and under the break clause, where the break notice was not required to be in any particular form and the notice period under the lease was consistent with the period under s 25 of the 1954 Act. When serving such a s 25 notice, it is good practice to state in a covering letter that the notice is being served under both s 25 of the 1954 Act and the break clause.

The s 25 notice must comply with the requirements of the break clause as well as those of s 25 of the 1954 Act. Thus, where there are preconditions to the landlord's right to terminate the lease, eg the break provision specifies that the landlord may only break where it wishes to raise the rent, it will be necessary to serve both a s 25 notice and a break notice. However, in *Aberdeen Steak Houses plc v Crown Estate Commissioners* (1997) 31 EG 101, the service of a s 25 notice, together with a covering letter which referred to the preconditions, was held to be valid as the two were read together; however, had the letter been silent as to these preconditions, then the s 25 notice would have been invalid. It is thus good practice in these circumstances to serve both notices.

4.3.5 Whether the landlord will oppose an application for a new tenancy

The notice must state whether the landlord is opposed to the grant of a new tenancy to the tenant (s 25(6) of the 1954 Act) and, if he is opposed, then the ground or grounds of opposition must be specified in the notice (s 25(7) of the 1954 Act). Two forms of s 25 notice are prescribed. Form 1 is used where the landlord is not opposed to the grant of a new tenancy; Form 2 is used where the landlord is opposed to the grant of a new tenancy (see Appendix 16).

It is not necessary for a landlord to set out the full wording of each ground of opposition in the notice. All that the landlord has to do is to insert into clause 4 of his notice the paragraph letter(s) of the grounds that he is relying on to oppose the grant of a new tenancy.

It is important that a landlord specifies in the notice all of the grounds on which he is going to rely on, as the notice cannot be amended once it has been served (*Nursey v P Currie (Dartford) Ltd* [1959] 1 All ER 497, CA; *Hutchinson v Lamberth* [1984] 1 EGLR 75, CA); nor can it be withdrawn (for an exception to this bar on withdrawal see 4.3.2.1). It is, however, still open for a landlord in these circumstances to bring the unspecified ground to the court's attention in order to influence the terms of the new tenancy (*Amika Motors Ltd v Colebrook Holdings Ltd* (1981) 259 EG 253).

A landlord may withdraw grounds of opposition on which he is no longer relying. In this respect, it is important to note that, if a ground has been included in the notice which the landlord knows is false, the notice will be void (*Earl of Stradbroke v Mitchell* [1991] 1 WLR 469, CA; *Viscount Chelsea v Morris* [1998] EGCS 156, CA). Where a landlord does withdraw a ground or, in fact, withdraws all the grounds, and such ground(s) would have entitled the tenant to claim compensation (see 10.1), the landlord will still have to pay compensation if the tenant vacates.

In *Barclays Bank plc v Bee*, the landlord served two s 25 notices together, one opposing renewal and the other not opposing renewal. The former was invalid, as it failed to specify a ground of opposition. The second notice was valid. However, both notices were held to be invalid as they were inconsistent with each other and a reasonable recipient could not conclude that the invalid notice should be ignored.

4.3.6   The landlord's proposals for a new tenancy

Where a landlord is not opposing the grant of a new tenancy he must set out in his s 25 notice his proposals for the new tenancy (s 25(8) of the 1954 Act). The prescribed form of notice (Form 1) specifically provides for this. The landlord's proposals must relate to:

(a) the property to be comprised in the new tenancy (being either the whole or part of the property comprised in the current tenancy);

(b) the rent to be payable under the new tenancy; and

(c) the other terms of the new tenancy.

These requirements mirror those placed on a tenant who requests a new tenancy under s 26 of the 1954 Act (see 5.1.2).

Form 1 contains a notice to the tenant explaining that the landlord's proposals are merely suggestions as a basis for negotiation and that the tenant is not bound to accept them. It also confirms that, in the event of a disagreement, the court will settle the terms of the new tenancy. The landlord's proposals are in effect an opening bid in the negotiations and the tenant can put forward his own proposals. There is no requirement that the landlord's proposals must be genuine (*Sun Life Assurance plc v Thales Tracs Ltd* [2001] EWCA Civ 704; [2002] 1 All ER 64). It would appear that the proposals have no legal consequences and do not commit the landlord or the tenant to anything, but are merely a prelude to a possible new tenancy on such terms as may be agreed by the parties or determined by the court.

4.3.7   The s 25 notice must relate to the whole of the premises comprised in the tenancy

The landlord's notice must relate to the whole of the premises which have been let to the tenant under the terms of the tenancy. This will still be the case, even where the tenant has sub-let part of the premises.

4.3.7.1 *The description of the premises*

The notice must accurately describe the premises. If they can be described by reference to a postal address, then this will suffice. The test which is applied when deciding whether a notice is void because of an inaccurate description is the same as the one discussed at 4.3.1.3. An example of the application of this test can be see in *M & P Enterprises (London) Ltd v Norfolk Square Hotels Ltd*, where the property '92 Sussex Gardens' was by typographical error referred to as a half bracket and 2 Sussex Gardens. This error did not invalidate the notice, as it in no way misled the recipients.

Difficulties arise where a notice only refers to part of the premises. In this situation, the validity of the notice depends on the extent of the premises in relation to those which have been omitted. If a significant part of the premises has been omitted, the notice will be invalid, as in *Kaiser Engineers and Contractors Incorporated v ER Squibb and Sons Ltd* (1971) 218 EG 1731, where the notice only referred to the fourth floor of a building where the premises consisted of both the fourth and ninth floors, and *Herongrove Ltd v Wates City of London Properties plc* [1988] 1 EGLR 82, where the notice referred to the ninth floor of a building and the premises consisted of the ninth floor, storage on two other floors and a car-parking space. By contrast, in *Safeway Food Stores Ltd v Morris*, the omission of a small piece of land at the rear of the premises did not render the notice invalid.

The notice will be invalid if the lease allows the landlord to terminate in relation to part of the premises only and the notice merely refers to part (*Southport Old Links Ltd v Naylor* [1985] 1 EGLR 66, CA). However, it is possible for a landlord to serve a valid notice as to part of the premises where the provisions of the lease allow it to be interpreted as creating two separate tenancies, as in *Moss v Mobil Oil Co* [1981] 1 EGLR 71, CA, where the lease of two physically separate properties provided that it should be construed as if separate and independent leases of each of the properties had been created. It will not be enough for the lease to contain a break clause allowing the landlord to terminate the lease in respect of part of the premises (*Southport Old Links Ltd v Naylor*).

4.3.7.2 Multiple tenancies

Where the tenant holds identical tenancies of several properties from the same landlord under separate leases, a single s 25 notice will be sufficient to terminate all the tenancies (*Tropis Shipping Ltd v Ibex Properties Ltd* [1967] EGD 433).

4.3.7.3 *Split reversions*

Where different landlords own parts of the reversion 'the landlord' for the purposes of the 1954 Act, will be all the landlords collectively (s 44(1A) of the 1954 Act). The landlords will need to take concerted action. This means that the landlords can get together and serve a single s 25 notice, or they could each serve separate notices relating to their individual parts of the premises to take effect simultaneously (*Nevill Long and Co (Boards) Ltd v Firmenich and Co* (1984) 47 P & CR 59, CA).

4.3.8   Restriction on serving a s 25 notice

A landlord cannot serve a s 25 notice where the tenant has already made a request for a new tenancy (s 26(4) of the 1954 Act) (see 5.1).

4.3.9   The effect of serving a s 25 notice

The effect of serving a s 25 notice is that the parties acquire the right to apply to the court, either for renewal or termination, depending on which s 25 notice the landlord has served. Where the landlord is not opposed to the grant of a new tenancy, the parties should try and agree the terms of the new tenancy. If these cannot be agreed, either the landlord or the tenant must apply to the court before the date specified in the s 25 notice for the end of the tenancy. The parties may extend the final deadline by written agreement, provided they do so before the deadline expires. If neither party applies to the court before the date specified in the s 25 notice or before the expiry of an agreed extension, the tenant will lose the right to renew.

Where the landlord is opposed to the grant of a new tenancy, and the tenant wants a new tenancy, the tenant must apply to the court for a new tenancy and successfully challenge the landlord's grounds of opposition. Such an application must be made before the date specified in the s 25 notice for the end of the tenancy; however, the parties may extend the final deadline by written agreement, provided they do so before the deadline expires. The tenant cannot apply if the landlord has already made an application for termination. If neither party applies to the court before the date specified in the s 25 notice or before the expiry of an agreed extension, the tenant will lose the right to renew.

In either of the two above situations, a party cannot apply to the court either for a new tenancy or, in the case of the landlord for termination, once the other party has applied for a new tenancy or, in the case of the landlord, for termination.

As previously mentioned, a landlord may not withdraw a s 25 notice except as mentioned at 4.3.2.1; nor may a notice be amended (*Hutchinson v Lamberth*).

What will be the position if, after the termination date or agreed extension has passed, the tenant refuses to leave, has failed to take the necessary procedural steps to protect its rights under the 1954 Act and the landlord requires vacant possession? It is submitted that, in this case, the tenant remaining in occupation will either be a tenant at will, where the landlord has consented in some way to the occupation, or a tenant at sufferance, where the landlord has not consented. As soon as the landlord brings the tenancy at will to an end or indicates that he no longer wishes the tenant at sufferance to occupy the premises, the tenant will become a trespasser. The landlord can then recover possession, either by peaceable re-entry or by obtaining a county court possession order.

4.3.10   Action following the service of a s 25 notice

Following the service of a s 25 notice, either the landlord or the tenant is entitled to apply to the court for a new tenancy (see 7.1). In effect, this puts both parties on an equal footing, and gives each of them the means to counter any delay by the other. Where the landlord is opposed to the grant of a new tenancy, the landlord can apply to the court for an order that the tenancy be terminated, provided no application has been made by the tenant to the court for a new tenancy (see 7.2).

A party does not have to wait before making an application to the court. Thus, a landlord can make an application immediately after he has served his s 25 notice for either the grant of a new tenancy or, if he is opposed to the grant of a new tenancy, for an order terminating the tenancy. There is no requirement that he has to wait for the tenant to make an application. Where either party has applied to the court for a new tenancy, or the landlord has applied for termination of the tenancy, the other party may not apply to the court for a new tenancy or, in the case of the landlord, for termination of the tenancy (s 24(2A) and s 24(2B) of the 1954 Act).

A landlord may not withdraw an application he has made to the court, whether for renewal or termination, unless the tenant agrees (s 24(2C) of the 1954 Act). This requirement acts as a safeguard for the tenant and protects his right to renew. It also avoids s 64(2) of the 1954 Act applying, which would mean that the tenancy would end three months after the withdrawal of the application.

The only time limit which applies to the making of an application to the court is the date stated in the landlord's s 25 notice for the end of the tenancy. An application to the court must be made before this date. However, this date can be extended by agreement between the parties, provided the agreement is made before the time limit it is to extend has expired (see 7.3).

4.4　　NOTICE UNDER SECTION 24(3) OF THE 1954 ACT

Where a tenancy is continuing under s 24 of the 1954 Act and ceases to be one to which the 1954 Act applies, usually because the tenant ceases to occupy the premises for business purposes, the continuation tenancy will not come to an end. However, where the continuation tenancy results from a fixed term tenancy, the landlord may terminate it by not less than three nor more than six months' notice in writing (s 24(3)(a) of the 1954 Act). This notice is without prejudice to the termination of the tenancy in accordance with its terms. This refers to a notice to quit given by the landlord, as well as the right of forfeiture. It may be possible for a tenant which receives a notice under s 24(3)(a) of the 1954 Act to shorten the notice period by serving a notice under s 27(2) of the 1954 Act (*Long Acre Securities Ltd v Electro Acoustic Industries Ltd* [1990] 1 EGLR 91, CA). If, following service of a notice under s 24(3)(a) of the 1954 Act, the tenancy becomes subject to the 1954 Act again, the notice remains valid (s 24(3)(b) of the 1954 Act).

Where the continuation tenancy results from a periodic tenancy, s 24(3)(a) of the 1954 Act does not apply and the continuation tenancy ends immediately the 1954 Act ceases to apply.

4.5   WHAT IF THE TENANT HAS CEASED OCCUPATION?

Where the tenant has ceased occupation before the end of the contractual tenancy, there will be no continuation tenancy. In the case of a periodic tenancy the landlord can therefore serve a notice to quit, and in the case of a fixed term tenancy the tenancy will end by effluxion of time. It is not necessary for the landlord to serve a s 25 notice in this situation. If a landlord is not sure about whether the 1954 Act has ceased to apply, it could still serve a s 25 notice, without prejudice to the fact that the 1954 Act does not apply.

Where a landlord gives a notice to quit at a time when the tenancy is not one to which the 1954 Act applies, the operation of the notice to quit is not affected just because the tenancy subsequently becomes one to which the 1954 Act applies (s 24(3)(b) of the 1954 Act). This covers the situation where, during the period of a notice to quit, the tenant might decide to start business occupation so as to gain the protection of the 1954 Act. Clearly, s 24(3)(b) of the 1954 Act applies to periodic tenancies and fixed term tenancies which include a break clause.

Difficulties could arise in the situation where a tenancy is not subject to the 1954 Act and, before the contractual term date, the tenant takes up business occupation. Such occupation could even take place on the last day of the term. The tenancy will then be continued under s 24 of the 1954 Act. The landlord would then have to serve a s 25 notice.

CHAPTER 5

TERMINATION AND RENEWAL BY A TENANT

Where a tenancy is protected by the 1954 Act, the tenant may be able to bring it to an end by:

(a) making a request for a new tenancy under s 26 (see 5.1);

(b) giving notice under s 27 (see 5.2);

(c) ceasing to occupy the premises for business purposes (see 5.3);

(d) notice to quit in the case of periodic tenancy (see 5.5);

(e) serving notice pursuant to a contractual break notice (see 5.6); or

(f) surrender (see 4.2).

5.1 THE TENANT'S REQUEST FOR A NEW TENANCY

Where a landlord has not taken any steps (see Chapter 4) to terminate the tenancy a tenant who wishes to renew the tenancy, may request a new tenancy from the landlord under s 26 of the 1954 Act.

5.1.1 When can a new tenancy be requested?

The tenant's request for a new tenancy is governed by s 26 of the 1954 Act. The right to request a new tenancy is given only to tenants who have been granted a tenancy for a term of years certain exceeding one year, or for a term of years certain and thereafter from year to year (s 26(1) of the 1954 Act). This means that periodic tenants and those with a fixed term tenancy of a year or less cannot avail themselves of s 26 of the 1954 Act. The important part of this rule is the word 'granted'. The tenancy when granted has to satisfy the test given in s 26(1) of the 1954 Act; it is not sufficient that it has started as a lesser tenancy and endured the necessary length of time. This means that a tenant who has been granted a tenancy for a year and which is continuing under s 24 of the 1954 Act has no right to claim a new tenancy.

A tenant granted a tenancy which is initially for at least two successive terms which together exceed a year seems to fall within s 26 of the 1954 Act. This is a potential trap for the draftsman. Thus, in *Doe d Chadborn v Green* (1839) 9 A & E 658, a tenancy of at least two years was created by a grant of 'one year from the date hereof, and so on from year to year'. The question is whether, on the correct interpretation of the grant, the minimum period is more than one year. The same effect as *Doe d Chadborn v Green* is achieved by a grant of 'three months from the date hereof and thereafter from year to year unless terminated by three months' notice'. The original tenancy is one year and three months in this case. In *Nicholls v Kinsey* [1994] 2 WLR 622, CA, it seems to have been accepted that the tenant could serve a valid s 26 request in a case where the wording was identical to *Doe d Chadborn v Green* but, curiously, the reasoning in the case (concerned with the interpretation of s 38(4)) suggests that this form of words cannot create a term certain. In practice, the lawyer cannot assume that a s 26 request can definitely be used in such cases and the prospect of litigation must be accepted.

In the following situations a tenant cannot make a s 26 request:

(a) where a s 25 notice has been served by the landlord (s 26(4) of the 1954 Act);

(b) where the tenant has given the landlord a notice to quit (s 26(4) of the 1954 Act). This will include a notice pursuant to a break clause (see 5.6);

(c) where the tenant has given notice under s 27 of the 1954 Act (see 5.2);

(d) where the tenant has previously made a s 26 request but has not applied to the court for a new tenancy (*Stile Hall Properties Ltd v Gooch* (1968) 207 EG 715, CA).

5.1.2   The contents of the tenant's request for a new tenancy

The tenant's request for a new tenancy must be in the prescribed form (s 26(3) of the 1954 Act). This is Form 3 of the Landlord and Tenant Act 1954, Part 2 (Notices) Regulations 2004 (SI 2004/1005) (see Appendix 16). As with the landlord's notice under s 25 of the 1954 Act, a notice in a form substantially to the like effect (cases on this point are found at

4.3.1) may be used instead of the prescribed form, although this is not recommended.

The request must specify the date on which the new tenancy is to commence (s 26(2) of the 1954 Act). This must not be more than 12 nor less than six months after the date of the request. In addition, it must not be earlier than either the date on which the current tenancy will end by effluxion of time or the date on which it could be ended by notice to quit given by the tenant. In *Garston v Scottish Widows Fund and Life Assurance Society* [1998] 3 All ER 596, CA, the s 26 request infringed s 26 of the 1954 Act, as the tenant had specified a date which was earlier than the date on which the current tenancy would come to an end by effluxion of time. The tenant had sought to break at the end of the 10th year, in accordance with the terms of the lease. It served both a s 26 request and a break notice at the same time. It was held that the tenant could not do this, as it infringed s 26(2) of the 1954 Act. In addition, the break notice was in effect a tenant's notice to quit and disqualified the tenant from using s 26 of the 1954 Act.

Where a tenant specifies an incorrect date, the notice will be invalid unless it can be saved by the principle in *Mannai Investment Co Ltd v Eagle Star Life Assurance Ltd* [1997] 3 All ER 352, HL (see 4.3.1.3), or it can be shown that the landlord has waived the defect or estoppel can be successfully argued.

The request must also contain the tenant's proposals as to:

(a) the property to be comprised in the tenancy (s 26(3) of the 1954 Act). This may either be the whole or part of the property comprised in the current tenancy. If the address clearly identifies the property, this will suffice; otherwise, a conveyancing description should be used;

(b) the rent to be payable under the new tenancy (s 26(3) of the 1954 Act);

(c) the other terms of the new tenancy (s 26(3) of the 1954 Act). These include the length of the new lease. In *Sidney Bolsom Investment Trust Ltd v E Karmlos and Co (London) Ltd* [1956] 1 All ER 536, CA, the tenant failed to specify a term but requested that the new tenancy be on the same terms as those of the current tenancy. It was held that it had impliedly requested a new term equivalent to that of its existing tenancy, which was seven years.

The inclusion of these proposals is a statutory formality and there is no requirement that they must be 'genuine proposals'.

In *Sun Life Assurance plc v Thales Tracs Ltd* [2001] EWCA Civ 704;
[2002] 1 All ER 64, CA, the Court of Appeal held that evidence
of a tenant's state of mind when he served a s 26 request was
inadmissible. This decision can be contrasted with *Cadogan v
Morris* [1999] 1 EGLR 59, CA, where a tenant's notice to acquire
a new lease under the Leasehold Reform Act 1993 was invalid,
as that Act required the notice to state the premium that the
tenant 'proposed' to pay. The tenant had inserted a nominal
figure instead of a genuine estimate of the sum it was asking
the landlord to accept.

It will not usually be in a tenant's interests to make a s 26
request, as it will probably be better off allowing the existing
tenancy, and thus the current rent, to continue for as long as
possible. However, in the following situations a tenant should
consider serving a s 26 request:

(a) where the tenant wishes to secure a new tenancy in order to
    sell the business, or to gain stability where, say, it wishes to
    expand its business; or

(b) where it thinks that the landlord is about to serve a s 25
    notice and it wishes to make a pre-emptive strike. As a
    result, the tenant will be able to obtain a rental advantage in
    that the s 26 request will extend the current tenancy at the
    existing rent for at least six months. However, there is
    nothing to prevent a landlord from applying for an interim
    rent (see 3.5).

The s 26 request must be served by or on behalf of the tenant on
the competent landlord or its agent (*Railtrack plc v Gojra* [1998] 1
EGLR 63, CA). If the s 26 request is served on the wrong person,
ie, someone who is not the competent landlord, it will be invalid
(*Railtrack plc v Gojra*). It must be given by all the tenants where
there is a joint tenancy (*Jacobs v Chaudhuri* [1968] 1 QB 470, CA),
unless s 41A of the 1954 Act applies where the joint tenancy is
held by a partnership, in which case only those tenants who are
partners carrying on the business need be party to the request.

5.1.3   The effect of making a s 26 request

Where a tenant has made a s 26 request, the current tenancy
will come to an end on the day immediately before the date
specified in the s 26 request for the start of the new tenancy if
the tenant does not apply to the court for a new tenancy (s 26(5)
of the 1954 Act). If either the tenant or the landlord makes a

valid application to the court, then the current tenancy is continued by s 64 of the 1954 Act (see 7.18).

5.1.4   Response by the landlord

A landlord who has received a request for a new tenancy and who does not wish to grant the tenant a new tenancy must, within two months of receipt of the request, give notice to the tenant, stating that the grant of a new tenancy is opposed and specifying the s 30 ground(s) on which it is intended to rely (s 26(6) of the 1954 Act). There is no prescribed form of notice; however, it should be in writing and be served on the tenant (see Appendix 20 for an example of a form of notice). In *M & P Enterprises (London) Ltd v Norfolk Square Hotels Ltd* [1994] 1 EGLR 129, the landlords served defective s 25 notices on the tenant after having received a s 26 request. The s 25 notices stated that the landlords would oppose the grant of a new tenancy. It was held that the landlords had complied with the requirement to give the tenant notice that they would oppose its application for a new tenancy.

If the landlord does not give notice to the tenant either at all or outside the two-month time limit, the right to oppose the tenant's application for a new tenancy is lost.

If the landlord changes within the two-month period for serving a counternotice, the incoming landlord is entitled to serve a counternotice if the outgoing landlord has not yet served one (*XL Fisheries v Leeds Corp* [1955] 2 QB 636, CA). Should there be a change of landlord after a counternotice has been given, the incoming landlord will take this over and can rely on any of the grounds of opposition which may have been included by the outgoing landlord in the counternotice (*Morris Marks v British Waterways Board* [1963] 1 WLR 1008).

5.1.5   Application to the court

If a tenant has made a s 26 request, either the tenant or the landlord may apply to the court for a new tenancy (s 24(1) of the 1954 Act). A landlord can apply to the court for an order for the termination of the tenancy without the grant of a new tenancy if he has, within two months of receipt of the s 26 request, given notice to the tenant stating that the grant of a new tenancy is opposed and specifying the s 30 ground(s) on which it is intended to rely.

An application to the court must be made before the date specified in the s 26 request. However, this can be extended by agreement.

5.1.6   Registration of the application for a new tenancy

See 7.12.

5.2   TERMINATION OF A FIXED TERM TENANCY BY TENANT'S NOTICE UNDER SECTION 27

5.2.1   At the end of the contractual term

Under s 27(1) of the 1954 Act, a tenant of business premises holding under a term of years certain to which the 1954 Act applies and who has been in occupation under the tenancy for at least one month, can serve a notice in writing on the immediate landlord (who may not be the competent landlord), stating that he does not wish the tenancy to be continued beyond the contractual term date under s 24 of the 1954 Act. Such a notice must be served not later than three months before the date on which, apart from the operation of the Act, the tenancy would come to an end by effluxion of time. The tenancy will then come to an end on that date, rather than being continued under s 24 of the 1954 Act. There is no prescribed form of notice.

The effect of a s 27(1) notice is that s 24 of the 1954 Act will not apply to the tenancy and so the tenancy will end on the expiry of the contractual term. A tenant who has given a s 27(1) notice is then prevented from serving a s 26 request (s 26(4) of the 1954 Act). A s 27(1) notice will not affect any sub-tenancy which is protected by the 1954 Act.

For s 27(1) of the 1954 Act to apply, the tenancy must be a 'term of years certain' and so the sub-section does not extend to include periodic tenancies. The phrase 'term of years certain' has been considered for the purposes of s 38(4) of the 1954 Act. In *Re Land and Premises at Liss, Hants* [1971] 3 All ER 380, it was held that it included a term for a period certain of less than one year, as well as a term of one year or more. In *Nicholls v Kinsey*, it was decided by the Court of Appeal that a tenancy for 12 months and thereafter from year to year determinable on the landlord giving 12 months' written notice was not a term of years certain.

5.2.2   After the contractual term has ended

Where the contractual term has ended and the tenancy is continuing under s 24 of the 1954 Act the tenant can, under s 27(2) of the 1954 Act, give the immediate landlord (who may not be the competent landlord) not less than three months' notice in writing to bring the tenancy to an end on any day. A s 27(2) notice cannot be given until the tenant has been in occupation for at least one month. There is no prescribed form of notice. A s 27(2) notice will not affect any sub-tenancy which is protected by the 1954 Act. Once a tenant has served a s 27(2) notice, it is not allowed to serve a s 26 request (s 26(4) of the 1954 Act).

Rent payable in advance for a period which begins before, and ends after, the tenancy is terminated is to be apportioned, and rent paid by the tenant in excess of the amount apportioned to the period before termination is recoverable by the tenant (s 27(3) of the 1954 Act).

5.3   CESSATION OF BUSINESS OCCUPATION BY THE TENANT

If, on or before the contractual term date, the tenant ceases to occupy the premises for the purposes of his business, the tenancy will not be continued under s 24 of the 1954 Act (s 27(1A) of the 1954 Act, which confirms the decision in *Esselte AB v Pearl Assurance* [1997] 2 All ER 41, CA).

Where the tenancy is continuing under s 24 of the 1954 Act and the tenant ceases business occupation after the contractual term date, then he must give the landlord not less than three months' notice in writing to bring the tenancy to an end on any day (s 27(2) of the 1954 Act).

5.4   EFFECT OF A PRIOR SECTION 25 NOTICE

Once a valid s 25 notice has been served by the landlord the tenant cannot serve a s 26 request (s 26(4) of the 1954 Act). A tenant can bring forward the termination date (clearly it cannot be brought forward so that it is earlier than the contractual term date) by serving:

(a) a notice under s 27(1) or s 27(2) of the 1954 Act (depending on when the notice is served) where the tenancy is for a fixed term; or

(b) a notice to quit where the tenancy is periodic.

5.5   TERMINATING A PERIODIC TENANCY

Section 26 of the 1954 Act does not apply to a periodic tenancy and so the tenant can only bring such a tenancy to an end by giving notice to quit in accordance with the terms of the lease (s 24(2) of the 1954 Act). The notice to quit must be given at least one month after the tenant has taken up occupation (s 24(2)(a) of the 1954 Act). 'Notice to quit' is defined in s 69(1) of the 1954 Act as being a notice to terminate the tenancy in accordance with its terms. It does not include a s 26 request. A notice to quit may not be served after the tenant has served a s 26 request (s 26(4) of the 1954 Act). At common law, a notice to quit will also bring to an end a sub-lease; however, a sub-lease which is itself protected by the 1954 Act will not be brought to an end in this way.

However, section 26 of the 1954 Act may apply to a tenancy which is continuing as a periodic tenancy. The requirement that there was a grant for a term certain exceeding one year must be satisfied. The tenancy may then be continuing in any way expressed in the grant, eg, from year to year or as a quarterly tenancy. In this case the date specified in the notice must be a date on which the tenancy could be terminated by a notice to quit.

5.6   TERMINATION DURING THE
           CONTRACTUAL TERM

A tenant can only end his tenancy during its contractual term if there is provision in the lease for this. Such a provision is commonly referred to as a 'break clause'. On the expiry of a notice served pursuant to a break clause, the tenancy will come to an end (s 24(2) of the 1954 Act). The reason for this is that such a notice comes within the definition of a 'notice to quit' in s 69(1) of the 1954 Act. The tenant will not be able to demand a new tenancy under s 26 of the 1954 Act at the same time as operating a break clause. It was held by the Court of Appeal in *Garston v Scottish Widows' Fund and Life Assurance Society* [1988] 3 All ER 596, CA that, in a fixed term tenancy, a s 26 request served with a break notice and which requested a new tenancy to run from the day after the break notice took effect infringed s 26(2) of the 1954 Act. The commencement date of the new tenancy could not be earlier than the date on which the tenancy would come to an end by effluxion of time; in other words, the contractual expiry date. Nourse LJ, in giving the court's judgment, agreed with the trial judge, Rattee J, who had said that *Garston v Scottish Widows' Fund and Life Assurance Society* [1996] 4 All ER 282 (at 287):

> ... in the case of a tenancy granted for a term of years exceeding one year, the date for the commencement of a new tenancy cannot be earlier than the date on which the current tenancy would, apart from the Act of 1954, come to an end by effluxion of time.

This effectively means that a tenant cannot operate a break clause and at the same time serve a s 26 request. The purpose of attempting this in *Garston v Scottish Widows' Fund and Life Assurance Society* was that the passing rent was far in excess of the market rent and the tenant hoped to obtain a new tenancy on more favourable terms. Where such circumstances reoccur, the tenant can only operate the break clause and obtain release from the onerous terms. According to Nourse LJ (at 602):

> One of the main purposes of Part II of the 1954 Act is to enable business tenants, where there is no good reason for their eviction, to continue in occupation after the expiration of their contractual tenancies. It is not a purpose of the Act to enable a business tenant who has chosen to determine his contractual tenancy to continue in occupation on terms different from those of that tenancy.

5.7   TERMINATION WHERE THERE IS NO PROTECTION BY THE ACT

5.7.1   Excluded tenancies

Where the tenancy has been excluded from the provisions of the 1954 Act by agreement between the parties pursuant to s 38(4) of the 1954 Act, then in the case of a fixed term tenancy it will terminate when the fixed term comes to an end. There is no need for the tenant to serve any notice on the landlord in this case and the tenant may simply vacate (for such tenancies, see further 2.2).

5.7.2   Licences and tenancies at will

Neither a licence nor a tenancy at will are subject to the 1954 Act (see 1.2.1 and 1.2.2). In the case of a tenancy at will, the tenant can quit the premises whenever he wants to. Where there is a licence, the licensee cannot leave until the end of the licence period, unless the licence provides otherwise. If he does, then he will be in breach of contract.

CHAPTER 6

SERVICE OF NOTICES AND OBTAINING INFORMATION

6.1 SERVICE OF NOTICES UNDER THE 1954 ACT

Notices under the 1954 Act should, by s 66(4) of the 1954 Act, be served pursuant to the provisions of s 23 of the Landlord and Tenant Act 1927 ('the 1927 Act'; see Appendix 2). The provisions of s 23 of the 1927 Act do not have to be used, but if they are not used, then difficulties may arise in proving service.

6.1.1 Statutory methods of service

Section 23(1) of the 1927 Act allows a notice to be served as follows:

(a) personally;
(b) by leaving it for the person on whom it is to be served 'at his last known place of abode in England and Wales';
(c) by sending it through the post in a registered letter addressed to the person on whom it is to be served 'at his last known place of abode in England and Wales'. A notice to be served in this way may also be sent by recorded delivery (s 1 of the Recorded Delivery Service Act 1962).

In the case of a local or public authority or a statutory or a public utility company, a notice may be served by sending it to the secretary or other proper officer at the principal office of the authority or company.

In addition, where the notice is to be served on the landlord, it may be served on any agent of the landlord who has been duly authorised to receive the notice (s 23(1) of the 1927 Act). Whilst s 23(1) of the 1927 Act does not specifically provide for service on the tenant's agent, such service is still permissible. However, the landlord may be faced with the difficulty of proving that the tenant has received a notice served on an agent, as in *Galinski v McHugh* (1988) 57 P & CR 359, CA, where Slade LJ said (at 365):

> ... section 23(1) is intended to assist the person who is obliged to serve the notice, by offering him choices of mode of service which will be deemed to be valid service, even if in the event the intended recipient does not in fact receive it.

6.1.2 Leaving a notice at the 'last known place of abode'

The term 'place of abode' includes both a recipient's business and personal addresses (*Price v West London Investment Building Society Ltd* [1964] 2 All ER 318, CA). In relation to a company, its place of abode will include its registered office (*National Westminster Bank v Betchworth Investments* [1975] 1 EGLR 57, CA). Where the person carrying on the business is resident abroad, the property contained in the tenancy may be the place of abode, if it is the only territorial link that the intended recipient has in England and Wales (*Italica Holdings SA v Bayadea* [1985] 1 EGLR 70).

In order to bring it to the notice of the intended recipient, a notice should be left at the relevant property in a way which would be used by a reasonable person. In *Newborough v Jones* [1975] Ch 90, CA, a notice was properly served by slipping it under the door and accidentally pushing it under the lino. In *Henry Smith's Charity Trustees v Kyriakou* [1989] 2 EGLR 110, CA, a notice put into the letterbox on the ground floor of a block of flats had been properly left for one of the tenants in the block.

6.1.3 Other methods of service

The methods of service contained in s 23(1) of the 1927 Act are not the only methods which can be used for service. It is possible for the giver of a notice to use a method not specified in s 23(1) of the 1927 Act; for example, ordinary post or, in the case of a notice to be served on a tenant, service on the tenant's agent. The difficulty in such cases will be proving service. Where a method not specified by s 23(1) of the 1927 Act is used, it will be the case that the giver of the notice will have to prove that it was received by the addressee; in other words, the risk of non-receipt is on the sender (*Chiswell v Griffon Land and Estates Ltd* [1975] 2 All ER 665, CA).

6.1.4 Proof of service

What is the position where a notice has been served but the recipient claims never to have received it? Where the notice has been served using one of the statutory methods of service in s 23(1) of the 1927 Act then, provided there is proof that one of these methods has been used, service is proved, even if the notice was not received by the intended recipient (*Chiswell v Griffon Land and Estates Ltd*; *Italica Holdings SA v Bayadea*; *Galinski v McHugh*; *Railtrack plc v Gojra* [1998] 1 EGLR 63, CA; *Commercial Union Life Assurance Co Ltd v Moustafa* [1999] 2 EGLR 44; *Blunden v Frogmore Investments Ltd* [2002] EWCA Civ 573; [2002] 2 EGLR 29, CA).

A notice served under s 23 of the 1927 Act will be validly served, even though it is returned to the sender undelivered (*Blunden v Frogmore Investments Ltd*).

The date of service for a notice served under s 23 of the 1927 Act is the date when the serving party entrusts the notice to the post (*Sun Alliance and London Assurance Co v Hayman* [1975] 1 All ER 248, CA; *Beanby Estates Ltd v Egg Stores (Stamford Hill) Ltd* [2003] EWHC 1252; [2003] 1 WLR 2064; *CA Webber (Transport) Ltd v Railtrack plc* [2003] EWCA Civ 1167; [2004] 1 WLR 320, CA). This provides certainty for the serving party.

It is generally accepted that s 7 of the Interpretation Act 1978 does not apply to s 23(1) of the 1927 Act (*CA Webber (Transport) Ltd v Railtrack plc*). If it did, then a rebuttable presumption would arise as to the time of delivery. The Court of Appeal, in *Lex Service v Johns* [1990] 1 EGLR 92, CA, proceeded on the basis that s 7 applied to s 23 of the 1927 Act. However, this case has subsequently been criticised (*Commercial Union Life Assurance Co Ltd v Moustafa*) and was treated as having been decided *per incuriam* in *CA Webber (Transport) Ltd v Railtrack plc*.

The position is therefore that, provided there is proof that one of the s 23(1) methods has been used, such as recorded delivery, service is proved, even if the notice was never received by the intended recipient.

However, what if the notice has been served by some method not laid down by s 23 of the 1927 Act? In this situation, it will be a matter of fact as to whether the notice was ever received by the intended recipient; the onus will be on the sender to prove receipt.

6.1.5   What if there is a change of landlord?

Until a tenant receives notice that the person entitled to the rents and profits, ie, the landlord, has ceased to be so entitled, together with notice of the name and address of the person who is now so entitled, the tenant can treat the original landlord as being the landlord for the purpose of serving notices (s 23(2) of

the 1927 Act). This means that whenever a landlord sells or
assigns its reversion or changes its identity in any way, notice
must be served on the tenant pursuant to s 23(2) of the 1927 Act.
In *Sector Properties Ltd v Meah* [1974] 229 EG 1097, CA, the
current landlord's managing agent wrote to the tenant advising
it that someone had agreed to purchase the freehold reversion
and giving the name and address of the new managing agents.
It was held that this was insufficient for the purposes of s 23(2)
of the 1927 Act.

Section 23(2) of the 1927 Act does not, in fact, fully protect a
tenant, as the immediate landlord may no longer be the
landlord for the purposes of s 44 of the 1954 Act yet still be
entitled to the rent and profits (see 4.3.2.1).

6.1.6   The corresponding date rule

The corresponding date rule applies to notices served under the
1954 Act. By virtue of ss 5 and 22(1) and Sched 2, para 4(1) of
the Interpretation Act 1975, 'month' means a calendar month.
The way in which the corresponding date rule applies was
considered in *Dodds v Walker* [1981] 1 WLR 1027, HL. Lord
Diplock explained it as follows (at 1029):

> ... when the relevant period is a month or specified number of
> months after the giving of the notice, the general rule is that
> the period ends upon the corresponding date in the
> appropriate subsequent month, ie the day of that month that
> bears the same number as the day of the earlier month on
> which the notice was given.

Thus, for example, a period of one month starting on 12 July
will end on 12 August. The only exceptions to the rule occur
where notices are given on the 31st day of a 31-day month and
which expire in a 30-day month, and notices expiring in
February and given on the 29th (except in a leap year), the 30th
or the 31st of any other month of the year. In these cases, the
rule is modified so that the notices expire on the last day of the
relevant month. Thus, for example, a period of one month from
31 October will expire on 30 November.

6.1.7   Serving notices on or by joint tenants

Where there are joint tenants, any notice under the 1954 Act
should be addressed to them all (*Booth Investments Ltd v
Reynolds* (1974) NLJ 119), and they should all join in the service

of such notices (*Harris v Black* (1983) 46 P & CR 366, CA). In the case of a partnership, there is a special provision in s 41A of the 1954 Act. This provides that where the premises are held by joint tenants, and only some of them occupy the premises for the partnership business, notice does not have to be served on all the joint tenants but only on those who are still part of the partnership. Similarly, only those who are still in the partnership have to join in the service of a notice.

6.1.8   Service where the intended recipient is dead

Where a notice under the 1954 Act is required to be served on a tenant who is dead, the personal representatives of the deceased are the tenants for the purposes of the 1954 Act (*Re Crowhurst Park* [1974] 1 All ER 991) and any notice should be addressed to them. Where the tenant has died intestate and letters of administration have not been taken out, the notice should be served on the Public Trustee (s 9(1) of the Administration of Estates Act 1925).

On the death of the landlord, the reversion will vest in the landlord's personal representatives. Where the landlord dies intestate and no letters of administration have been taken out, the reversion vests in the Public Trustee (s 9(1) of the Administration of Estates Act 1925).

6.1.9   Service on a company

Any notice under the 1954 Act which is to be served on a company should be served by leaving the notice at, or sending it by post to, the company's registered office (s 725 of the Companies Act 1985). The attitude of the courts where the company changes its registered office is illustrated by *Stylo Shoes Ltd v Prices Tailors Ltd* [1959] 3 All ER 901. In this case, the tenant told the landlord that its registered office had changed but the landlord sent its s 25 notice, by registered post, to the old registered office address. The notice was then redirected to the new registered office address where it was received by the tenant. It was held that the notice had been validly served, as it had been delivered to and received by the intended recipient.

6.1.10 Serving more than one notice

A party to a lease may be entitled to serve more than one notice at the same time. For example, a landlord who is entitled to bring the lease to an end prematurely by virtue of a break clause, can serve both a break notice and a s 25 notice together. In *Keith Bayley Rogers and Co Ltd (A Firm) v Cubes Ltd* (1975) 31 P & CR 412, it was held that the notices were delivered in the correct sequence, ie, the break notice first, then the s 25 notice, as the landlord had power to serve them in sequence.

6.1.11 Service by fax

Notices under the 1954 Act may be served by fax, provided that the copy of the notice which is received by the recipient is in a complete and legible state (*Hastie & Jenkerson v McMahon* [1991] 1 All ER 255, CA). The possible difficulties which could arise from serving a notice by fax include the recipient's fax machine not operating correctly or not using good quality fax paper, and so it is suggested that best practice would always be to serve 1954 Act notices by one of the methods prescribed by s 23(1) of the 1927 Act. Service of court papers by fax is dealt with under CPR Part 6 and PD 6.

6.2   OBTAINING INFORMATION

A tenant may need to make enquiries to ascertain the identity of the competent landlord so that a s 26 request can be properly served. A landlord may need to find out whether the demised premises has been sub-let and, if it has, the identity of the sub-tenants. The 1954 Act provides a procedure in s 40 whereby both the tenant and the landlord can obtain information from each other for the purposes of renewing or terminating the tenancy.

6.2.1 Obtaining information by the tenant

A tenant of business premises who is entitled to serve a s 26 request may serve on a reversioner, that is any person having an interest in the premises, being an interest in reversion expectant (whether immediately or not) on the tenant's, or on a reversioner's mortgagee in possession, a notice in the prescribed form requiring information (s 40(3) of the 1954 Act). If the tenant does not fall within the category of tenants which are entitled to serve a s 26 request, eg, a periodic tenant, then it has no right to serve a notice in the prescribed form requiring information.

No notice may be served earlier than two years before the date on which, apart from the 1954 Act, the tenancy would come to an end by effluxion of time or could be brought to an end by notice to quit given by the landlord (s 40(6) of the 1954 Act).

The prescribed form to be served on a reversioner or on a reversioner's mortgagee in possession is Form 5 of the Landlord and Tenant Act 1954, Part 2 (Notices) Regulations 2004 (SI 2004/1005) (see Appendix 16).

A reversioner or its mortgagee who receives a notice from the tenant is under a duty to notify the tenant in writing within one month after the service of the notice:

(a) whether he is the owner of the fee simple in respect of the premises or any part of them or the mortgagee in possession of such an owner;

(b) if he is not, then (to the best of his knowledge and belief) –

    (i)   the name and address of the person who is his or, as the case may be, his mortgagor's immediate landlord in respect of those premises or of the part in respect of which he or his mortgagor is not the owner in fee simple;

    (ii)   for what term his or his mortgagor's tenancy has effect and what is the earliest date (if any) at which that tenancy is terminable by notice to quit given by the landlord; and

    (iii) whether a notice has been given under s 25 or s 26(6) of the 1954 Act, or a request has been made under s 26 of the 1954 Act, in relation to the tenancy and, if so, details of the notice or request;

(c) (to the best of his knowledge and belief) the name and address of any other person who owns an interest in reversion in any part of the premises; and

(d) if he is a reversioner, whether there is a mortgagee in possession of his interest in the premises and, if so, (to the best of his knowledge and belief) what is the name and address of the mortgagee.

The usefulness to a tenant of all this information is that it allows the tenant to ascertain who is the competent landlord (see 4.3.2.1), as this will be the person to whom a s 26 request should be made. However, there is no provision for the tenant to be informed what notices, if any, have been served by or on the landlord or superior landlord and, of course, this is important in relation to who will fulfil the s 44 definition (but see *Shelley v United Artists Corp* [1989] EGCS 120, CA).

6.2.2   Obtaining information by the landlord

A landlord of business premises can, under s 40(1) of the 1954 Act, obtain information from the tenant by serving a notice in the prescribed form on the tenant (s 40(1) of the 1954 Act). The prescribed form to be served on a tenant is Form 4 of the Landlord and Tenant Act 1954, Part 2 (Notices) Regulations 2004 (SI 2004/1005) (see Appendix 16).

A tenant who receives a notice from its landlord is under a duty to notify the landlord in writing within one month after the service of the notice:

(a) whether the tenant occupies the premises or any part of them wholly or partly for the purposes of a business carried on by him;

(b) whether his tenancy has effect subject to any sub-tenancy on which his tenancy is immediately expectant and, if so –

  (i)   what premises are comprised in the sub-tenancy;

  (ii)   the term of the sub-tenancy (or, if it is terminable by notice, by what notice it can be terminated);

  (iii) what is the rent payable under it;

  (iv)   who is the sub-tenant;

  (v)   (to the best of his knowledge and belief) whether the sub-tenant is in occupation of the premises or of part of the premises comprised in the sub-tenancy and, if not, what is the sub-tenant's address;

  (vi)   whether an agreement is in force excluding in relation to the sub-tenancy the provisions of ss 24–28 of the 1954 Act; and

  (vii) whether a notice has been given under s 25 or s 26(6) of the 1954 Act, or a request has been made under s 26 of the 1954 Act, in relation to the sub-tenancy and, if so, details of the notice or request; and

(c) (to the best of his knowledge and belief) the name and address of any other person who owns an interest in reversion in any part of the premises.

No notice may be served earlier than two years before the date on which apart from the 1954 Act the tenancy would come to an end by effluxion of time or could be brought to an end by notice to quit given by the landlord (s 40(6) of the 1954 Act).

A tenant who receives a notice under s 40(1) is under a duty to notify the landlord about the matters within one month of service of the notice.

The advantages to a landlord of serving a request for information are as follows:

(a) the landlord will be able to discover whether or not the tenant has a tenancy to which the 1954 Act applies; and

(b) the landlord will be able to discover whether there are any sub-tenancies. If there are and the landlord serves a s 25 notice on the tenant, the landlord will also become the 'landlord' for the purposes of the 1954 Act in respect of any sub-tenant. A landlord may therefore decide to serve s 25 notices on any sub-tenants immediately after service of the s 25 notice on the tenant so as to avoid any sub-tenant being in a position to make a s 26 request.

6.2.3   Duty to respond to a request and to keep information up to date

The recipient of a s 40 request is under a duty to give the information requested within one month, beginning with the date of service of the notice (s 40(5)(a) of the 1954 Act). In addition, if within the period of six months beginning with the date of service of the notice, the recipient becomes aware that any information which has been given is not, or is no longer, correct, then the recipient is under a further duty to give the appropriate person correct information within the period of one month beginning with the date on which he becomes aware (s 40(5)(b) of the 1954 Act).

If the recipient of a s 40 notice breaks either of these duties, then the other party may sue for breach of statutory duty and the court may order that the recipient comply with its duty and that it pay damages (s 40B of the 1954 Act). It is also common to include in a lease covenants by both parties to comply with statutory requirements. Failure to comply with s 40 would then amount to breach of covenant.

6.2.4 Duties in transfer cases

It may be that, after receiving a s 40 notice, but within the six-month period within which he is required to update the original information, the recipient ceases to have an interest in the property, because, for example, he has sold his interest. Section 40A of the 1954 Act deals with this situation.

If the recipient of a s 40 notice has transferred his interest in the premises or any part of them to someone else and gives written notice of this transfer to the person who served the s 40 notice, together with the name and address of the transferee, then he ceases in relation to the premises or (as the case may be) to that part to be under any duty imposed by s 40 of the 1954 Act (s 40A(1) of the 1954 Act). In other words, he will no longer have to update information, provided he has given the appropriate notice to the person who served the s 40 notice.

Likewise, if the person who served the s 40 notice has transferred his interest in the premises to someone else, and either the transferor or the transferee has given the recipient of the s 40 notice written notice of the transfer, and of the transferee's name and address, then the updated information must be given to the transferee (s 40A(2) of the 1954 Act). If such a notice is not served, then the party under a duty to provide information can fulfil this obligation by providing it to either the transferor or the transferee (s 40A(3) of the 1954 Act).

There is no prescribed form for the notices referred to in s 40A of the 1954 Act. The only requirement is that they must be in writing and, thus, presumably a letter will suffice.

CHAPTER 7

THE APPLICATION TO THE COURT
FOR A NEW TENANCY

Either the landlord or the tenant may apply to the court for renewal of the tenancy following the service of a s 25 notice or a s 26 request. Additionally, a landlord may apply for termination without renewal. This chapter considers the application to the court.

7.1 WHEN IS A PARTY ENTITLED TO APPLY TO THE COURT FOR A NEW TENANCY?

Section 24(1) of the 1954 Act provides that either the tenant or the landlord can apply to the court for an order for the grant of a new tenancy if:

(a) the landlord has served a s 25 notice; or

(b) the tenant has made a s 26 request.

Duplicate applications to the court are not permitted. Neither party may make an application to the court under s 24(1) in the following circumstances:

(a) if the other party has already made an application and the application has been served (s 24(2A) of the 1954 Act); or

(b) if the landlord has made an application under s 29(2) of the 1954 Act for an order for the termination of the current tenancy and the application has been served (s 24(2B) of the 1954 Act).

Where the tenant has served a s 26 request for a new tenancy, he cannot apply to the court for an order for the grant of a new tenancy until either:

(a) the landlord has served a counternotice; or

(b) the two-month period for service of a counternotice has expired (s 29A(3) of the 1954 Act).

The landlord may not withdraw an application for renewal that he may have made, unless the tenant consents to the withdrawal (s 24(2C) of the 1954 Act). This protects the tenant, so that he does not have to make a separate application if he wishes to continue the renewal proceedings through the court.

7.2   APPLICATION BY A LANDLORD FOR AN ORDER FOR TERMINATION WITHOUT RENEWAL

A landlord is entitled under s 29(2) of the 1954 Act to apply to the court for an order for the termination of the current tenancy without the grant of a new tenancy if:

(a) he has served a s 25 notice stating that he is opposed to the grant of a new tenancy; or

(b) the tenant has made a s 26 request and the landlord has served a counternotice within two months of the s 26 request stating that he will oppose an application to the court for the grant of a new tenancy and specifying on which of the grounds in s 30 of the 1954 Act he will oppose the application.

A landlord may not apply for an order for termination without renewal if either party has made an application for the grant of a new tenancy under s 24(1) of the 1954 Act (s 29(3) of the 1954 Act). There is no need for the application to have been served in order to preclude the landlord from making an application.

The landlord may not withdraw an application for an order for the termination of the current tenancy without the grant of a new tenancy that he may have made, unless the tenant consents to the withdrawal (s 29(6) of the 1954 Act). This protects the tenant so that he does not have to make a separate application if he wishes to continue the renewal proceedings through the court.

7.3   WHEN MUST THE APPLICATION BE MADE?

The application to the court by either party must be made before the end of the 'statutory period' (s 29A(1) of the 1954 Act).

The 'statutory period' is defined in s 29A(2) of the 1954 Act as a period ending:

(a) where the landlord served a s 25 notice, on the date specified in the s 25 notice; and

(b) where the tenant made a s 26 request, immediately before the date specified in the s 26 request.

The effect of this is that there will be at least six months and possibly as much as 12 months in which the application may be made.

Where the landlord has served a s 25 notice, an application to the court can be made at any time after the s 25 notice has been served. This means that a landlord could apply to the court the day after he has served a s 25 notice.

It was held in *Hodgson v Armstrong* [1967] 1 All ER 307, CA that where the last day on which the application can be made is one on which the court office is closed, eg, a Sunday or a bank holiday, and the application cannot be made because of this, it will be in order to make the application on the next day on which the court office is open. Procedures governed by the Civil Procedure Rules are also subject to this rule (CPR 2.8(5)).

The 'statutory period' may be extended by agreement between the landlord and the tenant (s 29B of the 1954 Act). Such an agreement should be in writing. After the landlord has served a s 25 notice or the tenant has made a s 26 request, but before the end of the 'statutory period', the landlord and the tenant may agree that an application to the court by either party for an order for the grant of a new tenancy, or an application by the landlord for an order for termination without renewal, may be made before the end of a period specified in the agreement which will expire after the end of the 'statutory period' (s 29B(1) of the 1954 Act). Once such an agreement has been made the parties may, before the end of the period specified in the agreement, agree further to extend the period for making an application (s 29B(2) of the 1954 Act).

Where the parties have made an agreement to extend the 'statutory period', the relevant court application should be made before the extended 'statutory period' has ended (s 29B(3) of the 1954 Act).

The effect of an agreement to extend the 'statutory period' is that the s 25 notice or s 26 request is treated as terminating the tenancy at the end of the period specified in the final agreement (s 29B(4) of the 1954 Act).

In most cases, the parties will use the facility to agree to extend the 'statutory period' to allow negotiations for a new tenancy to take place and, thus, there will be no need for an application to the court once agreement has been reached within the 'statutory period'. Thus, an application to the court will only be necessary where:

(a) the 'statutory period' is about to expire without being extended;

(b) the parties have been unable to reach agreement on the terms of the new tenancy; or

(c) one party wishes to expedite matters.

7.4   FAILURE TO APPLY TO THE COURT

If no application for a new tenancy is made to the court before the expiry of the statutory period or any agreed extension, the tenancy will end either on the date for termination specified in the s 25 notice, or on the date for the commencement of the new tenancy specified in the s 26 request.

7.5   WHICH COURT?

Since 1 July 1991, the county court has had unlimited jurisdiction in 1954 Act matters (s 63(2) of the 1954 Act, as amended by the High Court and County Courts Jurisdiction Order 1991 (SI 1991/724)). The claim must be started in the county court, save in exceptional circumstances (CPR 56.2; PD 56.2 para 2.2). If the claim is started in the High Court, the claimant must file with the claim a certificate stating the reasons why the claim has been brought in the High Court (CPR 56.2(2)). Proceedings should only be issued in the High Court if there are complicated disputes of fact or there are points of law of general importance (PD 56.2, para 2.4). The value of the property and the amount of any financial claim may be relevant as to whether or not a claim should be started in the High Court, but they are not conclusive and will not alone normally justify starting the claim in the High Court (PD 56.2, para 2.5).

In practice, the majority of claims will be issued in the county court. The claim must be issued in the county court for the district in which the land is situated (CPR 56.2(1)).

Proceedings may be transferred between the High Court and the county court and vice versa (see 7.6).

Where there is both a claim for a new tenancy under the 1954 Act and a claim for compensation for improvements under the Landlord and Tenant Act 1927 before the courts, either party may apply to the court for the proceedings to be transferred to the court where the other proceedings are if it appears desirable that both sets of proceedings should be in the same court (s 63(4)(b) of the 1954 Act).

7.6   TRANSFER BETWEEN COURTS

7.6.1   Transfer from the High Court to the county court

The High Court can order proceedings to be transferred to the county court (s 40 of the County Courts Act 1984). Consideration by the Master of the Chancery Division must be given on the first hearing as to whether the matter is suitable for transfer to the county court. The criteria which should be taken into account when considering a transfer are those in CPR 30.3(2) (see 7.6.2). If the proceedings are transferred, then they will be transferred to the Central London County Court (Chancery List), unless the parties ask for them to be transferred to a local county court (Chancery Guide, para 13.6).

If proceedings have been started in the High Court, when they should have been started in the county court, the High Court will either strike out the claim or transfer it to the county court on its own initiative, and the costs of starting the claim in the High Court and of any transfer will normally be disallowed (PD 56.2, para 2.3).

The High Court may, on the application of any interested person, order that the proceedings be transferred to the county court, if it appears that they and any other proceedings before the county court should be heard by the county court (s 63(4)(b) of the 1954 Act).

7.6.2   Transfer from the county court to the High Court

The High Court can order proceedings to be transferred from the county court (s 41, County Courts Act 1984). Under CPR 30.3, the matters which the High Court must have regard to include:

(a) the financial value of the claim and the amount in dispute, if different;

(b) whether it would be more convenient or fair for hearings (including the trial) to be held in some other court;

(c) the availability of a judge specialising in the type of claim in question;

(d) whether the facts, legal issues, remedies or procedures involved are simple or complex;

(e) the importance of the outcome of the claim to the public in general;

(f) the facilities available at the court where the claim is being dealt with and whether they may be inadequate because of any disabilities of a party or potential witness; and

(g) whether the making of a declaration of incompatibility under section 4 of the Human Rights Act 1998 has arisen or may arise.

There is a right of appeal against an order for transfer (see PD 30.5 for the procedure). An application to set aside an order for transfer can be made to the court which made the order and the application should be made in accordance with CPR 23 and its Practice Direction (PD 30.6).

In addition, the county court can also order proceedings to be transferred to the High Court (s 42 of the County Courts Act 1984). This will usually occur where the court considers that some important question of law or fact is likely to arise (PD 56.2, para 4).

7.6.3   Transfer from one county court to another county court

Where the application is started in the wrong county court, the court may transfer the proceedings to the correct court, order that they continue in the county court in which they were started or strike them out (CPR 30.2(2)). An application for such an order must be made to the county court where the claim is proceeding (CPR 30.2(3)).

An application which is made in time to the wrong county court and which is subsequently sent to the right court but arrives out of time will be treated as being made within time (*Sharma v Knight* [1986] 1 WLR 757, CA).

7.6.4   Transfer in the High Court

The High Court may transfer the proceedings from the Royal Courts of Justice to a district registry (CPR 30.2(4)). Proceedings may also be transferred from a district registry to another district registry, or to the Royal Courts of Justice. The court must have regard in all these cases to the criteria in CPR 30.3.

7.7   ACTION BEFORE ISSUING PROCEEDINGS

There is no pre-action protocol in respect of 1954 Act proceedings. However, the parties are still expected, in accordance with the overriding objective and the matters referred to in CPR 1.1(2)(a), (b) and (c), to act reasonably in exchanging information and documents relevant to the claim and generally in trying to avoid the necessity for the start of proceedings (PD Protocols, para 4.1). Proceedings are usually always required in 1954 Act matters because of the requirements of the statute. However, the parties should ensure that, before proceedings are issued, they comply with the requirement to exchange relevant information and documents. This means that where, for example, the landlord is relying on a ground of opposition, information and documents concerning that ground, eg, planning permission, should be given to the tenant if available. In addition, where the rent is in dispute, it may be wise for the parties to try to agree on an expert so that there is an agreement at the case management conference.

The Property Litigation Association has drafted an informal protocol setting out directions in 1954 Act renewal cases. This is available at www.pla.org.uk.

7.8   CLAIMS FOR A NEW TENANCY

The procedure for a claim depends on whether the claim is unopposed or opposed, or is an application for the termination of a tenancy under s 29(2) of the 1954 Act.

7.8.1   Precedence of claim forms where there is more than one application

Where more than one application is made to the court, either for a new tenancy or for termination without renewal, then under PD 56, para 3.2:

(a) once an application for a new tenancy has been served on a defendant, no further application to the court in respect of the same tenancy for either a new tenancy or termination without renewal may be served by that defendant without the permission of the court;

(b) if more than one application to the court for a new tenancy in respect of the same tenancy is served on the same day, the

application by the landlord shall be stayed until further
order of the court;

(c) if applications to the court for either a new tenancy or
termination without renewal in respect of the same tenancy
are served on the same day, the application by the tenant
shall be stayed until further order of the court; and

(d) if a defendant is served with an application for termination
without renewal which was issued at a time when an
application to the court for a new tenancy had already been
made by that defendant, the service of the application for
termination without renewal shall be deemed to be a notice
under CPR 7.7 requiring service or discontinuance of the
application for a new tenancy within 14 days after the
service of the application for termination without renewal.

7.8.2   Form of application

The claim form to be used depends on whether the claim is
unopposed, opposed or is a claim by a landlord for termination
without renewal. Where the claim is unopposed, ie the landlord
is not opposing the grant of a new tenancy, the claim form is the
Part 8 claim form with the incorporation of certain additional
prescribed information. The Part 8 claim form is Form N208.
Where the claim is opposed, or it is a claim for the termination
of a tenancy under s 29(2) of the 1954 Act, the claim form is the
Part 7 claim form with the incorporation of certain additional
prescribed information. The Part 7 claim form is Form N1.

7.8.3   Contents of the claim form in all cases

By PD 56, para 3.4, the claim form must include details of:

(a) the property to which the claim relates;

(b) the particulars of the current tenancy (including date,
parties and duration), the current rent (if not the original
rent) and the date and method of termination;

(c) every s 25 notice or s 26 request given or made; and

(d) the expiry date of either the statutory period under s 29A(2)
of the 1954 Act or any agreed extension period made under
s 29B(1) or 29B(2) of the 1954 Act.

The claim form must also contain additional information,
depending on the identity of the party making the application.

Where the Part 8 claim form is being used, it must contain the information required by both Part 8 and PD 56. CPR 8.2 provides that it must state:

(a) that Part 8 applies to the claim;

(b) either the question which the claimant wants the court to decide, or the remedy which the claimant is seeking and the legal basis for the claim to that remedy;

(c) if the claim is being made under an enactment, what that enactment is;

(d) if the claimant is claiming in a representative capacity, what that capacity is; and

(e) if the defendant is sued in a representative capacity, what that capacity is.

The claim form must be verified by a statement of truth (CPR 22.1). This will then allow the claimant to rely on the matters contained in the claim form as evidence in support of the application (CPR 8.5(7)). Any additional written evidence which the claimant intends to rely on must accompany the claim form (CPR 8.5(1)).

The claim will be allocated to the multitrack (CPR 8.9(c)).

A failure by a claimant to set out in his claim form his proposals as to the duration, rent and other terms of the new tenancy is unlikely to render the application null and void. CPR 3.10 provides that, where there has been an error of procedure, such as a failure to comply with a rule or practice direction, the error does not invalidate any step taken in the proceedings unless the court so orders, and the court may make an order to remedy the error.

Care should, however, be taken by the claimant when setting out its proposals, as it was argued in *Lovely and Orchard Services Ltd v Daejan Investments (Grove Hall) Ltd* [1978] 1 EGLR 44 that such proposals could constitute an offer by the claimant which the defendant could then accept. Although the court did not rule on this point, it is thought that it would be unlikely to be found to be an offer as it would fall foul of s 2 of the Law of Property (Miscellaneous Provisions) Act 1989. In any event, the claimant should set out realistic proposals for the new tenancy, rather than merely stating that it wishes the old terms, including the rent, to continue. As the claimant must verify its claim by way of the statement of truth, it could be argued that, by putting forward the old terms as the terms for the new tenancy, it is claiming a new tenancy at a rent which it knows is below the market rent. This could possibly amount to a contempt of court, as CPR 32.14(1) provides that proceedings for contempt of court 'may be brought against a person if he makes, or causes to be made, a false statement in a document verified by a statement of truth without an honest belief in its truth'. A claimant should therefore take steps before it issues its claim to ascertain the market rent, or at least to obtain an idea of the likely market rent.

7.8.3.1 Claim form where the claimant is the tenant making a claim for a new tenancy

Where it is the tenant who is making a claim for a new tenancy, then PD 56, para 3.5 provides that, in addition to the details specified in PD 56, para 3.4, the claim form must also contain details of:

(a) the nature of the business carried on at the property;

(b) whether the claimant relies on s 23(1A) of the 1954 Act, s 41 of the 1954 Act, or s 42 of the 1954 Act and, if so, the basis on which he does so;

(c) whether the claimant relies on s 31A of the 1954 Act and, if so, the basis on which he does so;

(d) whether any, and if so what, part of the property comprised in the tenancy is occupied neither by the claimant nor by a person employed by the claimant for the purposes of his business;

(e) the claimant's proposed terms of the new tenancy; and

(f) the name and address of anyone known to the claimant who has an interest in the reversion in the property (whether immediate or in not more than 15 years) on the termination of the claimant's current tenancy and who is likely to be affected by the grant of a new tenancy, or if the claimant does not know of any such person, anyone who has a freehold interest in the property.

7.8.3.2 Claim form where the claimant is the landlord making a claim for a new tenancy

Where the claimant is the landlord making a claim for a new tenancy, then PD 56, para 3.7 provides that, in addition to the details specified in PD 56, para 3.4, the claim form must also contain details of:

(a) the claimant's proposed terms of the new tenancy;

(b) whether the claimant is aware that the defendant's tenancy is one to which s 32(2) of the 1954 Act applies and, if so, whether the claimant requires that any new tenancy shall be a tenancy of the whole of the property comprised in the defendant's current tenancy or just of the holding as defined by s 23(3) of the 1954 Act; and

(c) the name and address of anyone known to the claimant who has an interest in the reversion in the property (whether immediate or in not more than 15 years) on the termination of the claimant's current tenancy and who is likely to be affected by the grant of a new tenancy; or if the claimant does not know of any such person, anyone who has a freehold interest in the property.

7.8.3.3 Claim form where the claimant is the landlord making an application for the termination of the tenancy

Where the claimant is the landlord making an application for the termination of the tenancy, then PD 56, para 3.9 provides that, in addition to the details specified in PD 56, para 3.4, the claim form must also contain details of:

(a) the claimant's grounds of opposition;

(b) full details of those grounds of opposition; and

(c) the terms of the new tenancy that the claimant proposes in the event that his claim fails.

7.8.4 The parties to the claim

The claimant must be the person who is the tenant at the date of the issue of the claim.

Where the tenancy is held by joint tenants, all of them must make the application (*Jacobs v Chaudhuri* [1968] 2 All ER 124, CA; *Harris v Black* (1983) 46 P & CR 366, CA). Section 41A provides an exception to this rule in the case of a partnership. It applies where:

(a) the tenancy is held jointly by two or more persons;

(b) the property comprised in the tenancy is or includes premises occupied for the purposes of a business;

(c) the business (or some other business) was at some time during the existence of the tenancy carried on in partnership by all the persons who were then the joint tenants or by those and other persons and the joint tenants' interest in the premises was then partnership property; and

(d) the business is carried on (whether alone or in partnership with other persons) by one or some only of the joint tenants and no part of the property is occupied in right of the tenancy for the purposes of a business by the other joint tenant(s).

Where these conditions are satisfied, the application may be made by the joint tenants who are carrying on the business at the time of the application.

It may be that, following the issue of the claim, the tenant assigns its tenancy to a third party; for example, on the sale of the business. In such circumstances, the assignee will have to apply to the court under CPR 19.1(4) to be substituted as the applicant.

The defendant to the application must be the person who, at the date of the application, is the landlord, as defined by s 44 of the 1954 Act (PD 56.2, para 3.3; see 4.3.2.1 as to the definition of 'landlord'). If during the proceedings the defendant should cease to be the competent landlord, for example because of an assignment of the reversion to a third party, the new competent landlord must be added or substituted as defendant. The application to substitute the defendant by the new landlord may be made either by the applicant or by the new landlord, and may be made without notice (CPR 19.3). The application must be supported by evidence showing the stage the proceedings have reached and the changes which have occurred to cause the transfer of interest (PD 19, para 5.2). If the court makes an order for substitution it may direct:

(a) the claimant to file with the court within 14 days (or as ordered) an amended claim form and particulars of claim for the court file;

(b) a copy of the order to be served on all parties to the proceedings and any other person affected by it;

(c) the amended claim form and particulars of claim, forms for admitting, defending and acknowledging the claim and copies of the statements of case and any other documents referred to in any statement of case to be served on the new defendant; and

(d) unless the court orders otherwise, the amended claim form and particulars of claim to be served on any other defendants (PD 19, para 3.2).

Where a claimant intended to sue his competent landlord but, by mistake, named the wrong person, the claimant can apply to substitute the correct person under CPR 19.5(3)(a) (*Parsons v George* [2004] EWCA Civ 912; [2004] 3 All ER 633, CA).

A new defendant does not become a party to the proceedings until he has been served with the amended claim form (PD 19, para 3.3).

7.8.5   Service of the claim form

The claim form must be served within two months after the date of issue (CPR 56.3(3)(b) and 57.3(4)(b)).

In addition to being served on the defendant, where the claim is for a new tenancy, the claim form must also be served on the following:

(a) where the claimant is the tenant – on anyone known to the claimant who has an interest in the reversion in the property (whether immediate or in not more than 15 years) on the termination of the claimant's current tenancy and who is likely to be affected by the grant of a new tenancy, or if the claimant does not know of any such person, on anyone who has a freehold interest in the property;

(b) where the claimant is the landlord – on anyone known to the claimant who has an interest in the reversion in the property (whether immediate or in not more than 15 years) on the termination of the claimant's current tenancy and who is likely to be affected by the grant of a new tenancy, or if the claimant does not know of any such person, on anyone who has a freehold interest in the property.

The claimant may apply to extend the time for service (CPR 7.6(1)). Such an application must be made within the period for serving the claim (ie, the two-month period specified by CPR 56.3(3)(b)), or where an order has already been made to extend the time for service within the period specified in the order (CPR 7.6(2)). Detailed provisions concerning the methods of service can be found in CPR Part 6.

A court may only extend the time for service if under CPR 7.6(3):

(a) the court has been unable to serve the claim form; or

(b) the claimant has taken all reasonable steps to serve the claim form but has been unable to do so; and

(c) in either case, the claimant has acted promptly in making the application to extend.

The claimant must support the application to extend with evidence, and it may be made without notice (CPR 7.6(4)). It should also be borne in mind that under CPR 3.1(2) the court may extend or shorten the time for compliance with any rule or practice direction.

It is of the greatest importance that the defendant should be informed promptly of the issue of the claim form and it is not to be assumed that the time for service will necessarily be extended if it is not served strictly within the two-month time limit (Chancery Division Practice Direction 4(ii)).

Where a claim form has been issued but has not been served, the defendant can serve a notice on the claimant requiring the claim form to be served, or for the claim to be discontinued within the period stated for this in the defendant's notice, which must not be less than 14 days (CPR 7.7(1), (2)). If the notice is not complied with, the court may dismiss the claim, or make such order as it thinks just (CPR 7.7(3)). Alternatively, the defendant can waive service and be heard on the claim (*Pike v Nairn and Co* [1960] Ch 553).

7.8.6   Acknowledgment of service

The defendant must file an acknowledgment of service not more than 14 days after the claim form has been served and serve the acknowledgment of service on the claimant and any other party.

7.8.6.1 *Acknowledgment of service where the claim is unopposed and the claimant is the tenant*

Where the claim is unopposed and the claimant is the tenant, PD 56, para 3.10 provides that the acknowledgment of service must be in Form N210 and state with particulars:

(a) whether, if a new tenancy is granted, the defendant objects to any of the terms proposed by the claimant and if so the terms to which he objects; and the terms that he proposes in so far as they differ from those proposed by the claimant;

(b) whether the defendant is a tenant under a lease having less than 15 years unexpired at the date of the termination of the claimant's current tenancy and, if so, the name and address of any person who, to the knowledge of the defendant, has an interest in the reversion in the property expectant (whether immediate or in not more than 15 years from that date) on the termination of the defendant's tenancy;

(c) the name and address of any person having an interest in the property who is likely to be affected by the grant of a new tenancy; and

(d) if the claimant's current tenancy is one to which s 32(2) of the 1954 Act applies, whether the defendant requires that any new tenancy shall be a tenancy of the whole of the property comprised in the claimant's current tenancy.

There is no requirement that the defendant file a defence (CPR 8.9).

If the defendant fails to respond to the claim form by filing an acknowledgment of service within the time period for doing so, he may still attend any hearing but cannot take part in it unless the court grants permission for him to do so (CPR 8.4).

7.8.6.2 Acknowledgment of service where the claim is unopposed and the claimant is the landlord

Where the claim is unopposed and the claimant is the landlord, PD 56, para 3.11 provides that the acknowledgment of service must be in Form N210 and state with particulars:

(a) the nature of the business carried on at the property;

(b) if the defendant relies on s 23(1A) of the 1954 Act, s 41 of the 1954 Act or s 42 of the 1954 Act, the basis on which he does so;

(c) whether any, and if so what part, of the property comprised in the tenancy is occupied neither by the defendant nor by a person employed by the defendant for the purpose of the defendant's business;

(d) the name and address of anyone known to the defendant who has an interest in the reversion in the property (whether immediate or in not more than 15 years) on the termination of the defendant's current tenancy and who is likely to be affected by the grant of a new tenancy; or if the defendant does not know of such person, anyone who has a freehold interest in the property; and

(e) whether, if a new tenancy is granted, the defendant objects to any of the terms proposed by the claimant and, if so the terms to which he objects; and the terms that he proposes in so far as they differ from those proposed by the claimant.

There is no requirement that the defendant file a defence (CPR 8.9).

If the defendant fails to respond to the claim form by filing an acknowledgment of service within the time period for doing so, he may still attend any hearing but cannot take part in it unless the court grants permission for him to do so (CPR 8.4).

7.8.6.3 *Acknowledgment of service where the claim is opposed and the claimant is the tenant*

Where the claim is opposed and the claimant is the tenant PD 56, para 3.12 provides that the acknowledgment of service must be in form N9 and in his defence the defendant must state with particulars:

(a) his grounds of opposition;

(b) full details of those grounds of opposition;

(c) whether, if a new tenancy is granted, the defendant objects to any of the terms proposed by the claimant and if so the terms to which eh objects and the terms he proposes in so far as they differ from those proposed by the claimant;

(d) whether the defendant is a tenant under a lease having less than 15 years unexpired at the date of the termination of the claimant's current tenancy and, if so, the name and address of any person who, to the knowledge of the defendant, has an interest in the reversion in the property expectant (whether immediately or in not more than 15 years from that date) on the termination of the defendant's tenancy;

(e) the name and address of any person having an interest in the property who is likely to be affected by the grant of a new tenancy; and

(f) if the claimant's current tenancy is one to which s 32(2) of the 1954 Act applies, whether the defendant requires that any new tenancy shall be a tenancy of the whole of the property comprised in the claimant's current tenancy.

7.8.6.4 *Acknowledgment of service and defence where the claimant is the landlord making an application for the termination of a tenancy under s 29(2) of the 1954 Act*

Where the claim is an opposed claim and the claimant is the landlord, PD 56, para 3.13 provides that the acknowledgment of service must be in Form N9, and in his defence the defendant must state with particulars:

(a) whether the defendant relies on s 23(1A), 41 or 42 of the 1954 Act and, if so, the basis on which he does so;

(b) whether the defendant relies on s 31A of the 1954 Act and, if so, the basis on which he does so; and

(c) the terms of the new tenancy that the defendant would propose in the event that the claimant's claim to terminate the current tenancy fails.

7.8.7 Action following receipt of an acknowledgement of service where the claim is unopposed

Following receipt of an acknowledgment of service the court will give directions about the future management of the claim (CPR 56.3(3)(c)).

7.8.8 Evidence in an unopposed claim

Where the claim is unopposed, no evidence need be filed unless and until the court directs it to be filed (PD 56, para 3.13).

7.8.9 Evidence in an opposed claim

Where the claim is opposed, evidence, including expert evidence, must be filed by the parties as the court directs and the landlord shall be required to file his evidence first (PD 56, para 3.15).

7.8.10 Grounds of opposition to be tried as a preliminary issue

Any grounds of opposition must be tired as a preliminary issue, unless in the circumstances of the case it is unreasonable to do this (PD 56, para 3.16).

7.8.11   Discontinuing the application

The claimant may discontinue the claim by notice without leave (CPR 38.2). However, the defendant can apply to set aside the notice of discontinuance (CPR 38.4).

7.9   SUMMARY JUDGMENT

CPR Part 24 sets out a procedure by which the court may decide a claim or a particular issue by summary judgment without a trial (CPR 24.1). The court may give summary judgment against a claimant or a defendant in 1954 Act proceedings (CPR 24.3(1)). This would allow an issue in a 1954 Act renewal to be decided without the need for a trial, thus reducing the time and cost involved. The procedure should only be used where the issue to be determined is clear and no witnesses are required to give oral evidence. It could be suitable for determining whether a tenant's breaches are substantial under ground (c) of s 30(1) of the 1954 Act, and could also be used where the landlord can show compliance with grounds (f) and (g). A tenant could also use the procedure to try to force the landlord's hand under grounds (f) and (g), or to determine whether the accommodation offered under ground (d) is suitable.

Useful guidance on the use of applications for summary judgment was given in *Swain v Hillman* [2001] 1 All ER 91, CA, where Lord Woolf MR said:

> It is important that judges should, in appropriate cases, use the powers contained in CPR Part 24, since they give effect to the overriding objectives in CPR Part 1 by saving expense, by achieving expedition, by avoiding the courts' resources being used up in cases where no purpose would be served, and generally in the interests of justice. If the claimant has a case which is either bound to fail or bound to succeed, it is in his interest to know as soon as possible.

7.9.1   Grounds for summary judgment

CPR 24.2 states that:

> The court may give summary judgment against a claimant or defendant on the whole of a claim or on a particular issue if:

(a) it considers that –

  (i) that claimant has no real prospect of succeeding on the claim or issue; or

  (ii) that defendant has no real prospect of successfully defending the claim or issue; and

(b) there is no other reason why the case or issue should be disposed of at a trial.

The ability to seek judgment on part only of a claim will, in practice, be very useful in narrowing down the issues in dispute.

7.9.2   Procedure

An application for summary judgment may be made by either the landlord or the tenant. A claimant may not apply for summary judgment until the defendant has filed an acknowledgment of service or a defence (CPR 24.4(1)). Where a summary judgment hearing is fixed, the respondent to the application for summary judgment (or the parties where the hearing is fixed of the court's own initiative) must be given at least 14 days' notice of the date fixed for the hearing; and the issues which it is proposed that the court will decide at the hearing (CPR 24.4(3)).

The application notice must include a statement that it is an application for summary judgment made under Part 24 (PD 24, para 2). The application notice or the evidence contained or referred to in it or served with it must:

(a) identify concisely any point of law or provision in a document on which the applicant relies; and/or

(b) state that it is made because the applicant believes that on the evidence the respondent has no real prospect of succeeding on the claim or issue or (as the case may be) of successfully defending the claim or issue to which the application relates,

and, in either case, state that the applicant knows of no other reason why the disposal of the claim or issue should await trial (PD 24, para 3).

7.9.3   Evidence

The application is supported with written evidence. There is no requirement that this must be affidavit evidence, as evidence at hearings other than the trial is to be by witness statement (CPR 32.6). If the respondent to an application for summary judgment wishes to rely on written evidence at the hearing, he must file the written evidence and serve copies on every other party to the application, at least seven days before the summary judgment hearing (CPR 24.5(1)). If the applicant wishes to rely on written evidence in reply, he must file the written evidence and serve a copy on the respondent, at least three days before the summary judgment hearing (CPR 24.5(2)). Where a summary judgment hearing is fixed by the court of its own initiative, any party who wishes to rely on written evidence at the hearing must file the written evidence and, unless the court orders otherwise, serve copies on every other party to the proceedings, at least seven days before the date of the hearing; any party who wishes to rely on written evidence at the hearing in reply to any other party's written evidence must file the written evidence in reply and, unless the court orders otherwise, serve copies on every other party to the proceedings, at least three days before the date of the hearing (CPR 24.5(3)). There is no requirement for written evidence to be filed if it has already been filed, or for it to be served on a party on whom it has already been served (CPR 24.5(4)).

7.9.4   The court's powers when it determines a
summary judgment application

The application will usually be determined by a master or a district judge; the master or district judge may direct that the application be heard by a High Court judge (if the case is in the High Court) or a circuit judge (if the case is in a county court) (PD 24, para 3). The court may give judgment on the claim, strike out or dismiss the claim, dismiss the application or make a conditional order which requires a party to pay a sum of money into court, or to take a specified step in relation to his claim or defence, as the case may be, and provides that that party's claim will be dismissed or his statement of case will be struck out if he does not comply (PD 24, para 5.1). This means that, in practice, if the court gives summary judgment, it can strike out the tenant's application for a new tenancy, or strike out the landlord's ground or grounds of opposition, as appropriate. There must be no other reason why the case or issue should be disposed of at a trial. If the application for summary judgment is unsuccessful, the court may give directions as to the filing and service of a defence, or give further directions about the management of the case (CPR 24.6).

7.9.5   Costs of summary judgment applications

The costs of hearings lasting no more than a day are assessed summarily at the end of the hearing and are normally payable by the unsuccessful party within 14 days of the hearing.

7.10   ASSESSORS

A judge can appoint an assessor (or assessors) to assist the court, although this is rare in practice. In the High Court, an assessor may be appointed where the court regards it as expedient (s 70 of the Supreme Court Act 1981), and in the county court one may be appointed where the court thinks fit (s 63 of the County Courts Act 1984). In the county court, s 63(1) of the County Courts Act 1984 provides that a party may apply for an assessor to be appointed. Section 63(5) of the 1954 Act gives the court the power to appoint one of its own accord. An assessor is merely an adviser to the judge and may be useful where the court has to decide the amount of the rent payable, or whether a landlord's proposed works are realistic. An assessor may be directed to inspect the land and to report to the judge in writing (s 63(5) of the 1954 Act). The court will then consider the report and any observations of the parties before giving judgment (s 63(6) of the 1954 Act).

Not less than 21 days before appointing an assessor, the court will notify each party in writing of the name of the proposed assessor, of the matter in respect of which the assistance of the assessor will be sought and of the qualifications of the assessor to give that assistance (PD 35, para 7.1). Within seven days following receipt of this notice, a party may object to the proposed appointment (PD 35, paras 7.2 and 7.3). The court must then have regard to such objections when deciding whether to make the appointment (PD 35, para 7.3).

The court will determine the part which the assessor will play in the proceedings and this may include preparing a report and attending the whole or any part of the trial in order to give advice (CPR 35.15(3)). Copies of any report prepared by the assessor will be sent to each of the parties and they may then use it at the trial (CPR 35.15(4)); however, the assessor will not give oral evidence or be open to cross-examination or questioning if he attends the trial (PD 35, para 7.4).

The costs of the assessor are payable out of funds provided by Parliament at a rate fixed by the Lord Chancellor with Treasury approval (s 63(6)(c) of the 1954 Act).

7.11   DISCLOSURE

Under the CPR, disclosure of documents is not automatic, and will only take place where the court orders it to take place. The provisions as to disclosure and inspection of documents can be found in CPR Part 31. An order to give disclosure is an order to give standard disclosure, unless the court directs otherwise (CPR 31.5(1)). The court may dispense with or limit standard disclosure (CPR 31.5(2)). Alternatively, the parties may agree in writing to dispense with or limit standard disclosure (CPR 31.5(3)).

Under CPR 31.6, standard disclosure only requires a party to disclose:

(a) the documents on which he relies; and

(b) the documents which –

   (i)   adversely affect his own case;

   (ii) adversely affect another party's case; or

   (iii) support another party's case; and

(c) the documents which he is required to disclose by a relevant practice direction.

7.12   PROTECTING THE APPLICATION FOR A NEW TENANCY

Where the title is unregistered, the tenant's solicitor should consider protecting the tenant's application for a new tenancy by registering it as a pending land action. It will then be binding on a purchaser of the reversion. In the case of a registered title, there is no need to register if the tenant is in actual occupation as it will be an overriding interest under the Land Registration Act 2002. If the tenant is not in actual occupation, then the tenancy will not be one to which the 1954 Act applies.

7.13 EXPERT EVIDENCE

It is usual for the parties to call expert evidence in the following situations:

(a) where the amount of the rent payable under the new tenancy is in dispute;

(b) to decide whether the landlord has the requisite intention under s 30(1)(f) of the 1954 Act, eg, what impact will the landlord's proposed works have on the tenant's business, how long will the works take to be completed, etc.

Expert evidence is only admissible with the permission of the court (CPR 35.4(1)) and will be restricted to that which is reasonably required to resolve the proceedings (CPR 35.1). A party cannot call an expert or adduce an expert's report without the permission of the court (CPR 35.4(1)). When seeking permission, the party must identify the field in which he wishes to rely on expert evidence and, where practicable, the expert on whose evidence he wishes to rely (CPR 35.4(2)). If the court grants permission, it will be confined to the field and expert so identified (CPR 35.4(3)). The court may limit the amount of the expert's fee and expenses that the party who wishes to rely on the expert may recover from the other party (CPR 35.4(4)). Generally, expert evidence must be given in a written report, unless the court directs otherwise (CPR 35.5(1)).

7.13.1 Single joint experts

The court can limit the number of experts by requiring the parties to agree on a single expert (CPR 35.4(3), (4)). This single joint expert is instructed by all of the parties and each party must send a copy of its instructions to the other parties (CPR 35.8(1), (2)). If the parties cannot agree on an expert, the court can either select one from a list provided by the parties or direct some other way of selecting an expert (CPR 35.7(3)). The court can also give directions regarding the payment of a single joint expert (CPR 35.8(3)(a)) and of any inspections, examinations or experiments carried out by the expert (CPR 35.8(3)(b)). The parties are jointly and severally liable for these payments, unless the court directs otherwise (CPR 35.8(5)). It is also possible for the court to set a limit on the amount which the expert can be paid and order that this sum be paid into court (CPR 35.8(4)).

The use of a single joint expert may in fact be counterproductive in trying to limit the number of experts involved in a case. This is because either or both parties may wish to have their own expert to vet the single expert's report and to instruct their legal representative in court as to questions to put to the single expert. In any event, a party may wish to instruct an expert at a very early stage in order to decide whether the case is worth arguing. However, the possibility of a single joint expert may encourage the parties to avail themselves of the Professional Arbitration on Court Terms (PACT) scheme (see 7.15).

7.13.2 The expert's duty to the court

The expert's paramount duty is to assist the court and this duty takes precedence over the expert's duty to any of the parties (CPR 35.3). In his report, the expert should state that he understands this duty and has complied with it (CPR 35.10(2); PD 35, para 1.2(7)).

The duties and responsibilities of expert witnesses were set out by Cresswell J in *National Justice Compania Naviera SA v Prudential Assurance Co Ltd (The Ikarian Reefer)* [1993] 2 EGLR 183 as follows:

> The duties and responsibilities of expert witnesses in civil cases include the following:
>
> (a) Expert evidence presented to the court should be, and should be seen to be, the independent product of the expert uninfluenced as to formal content by the exigencies of litigation (*Whitehouse v Jordan* [1981] 1 WLR 246 at 256 *per* Lord Wilberforce).
>
> (b) An expert witness should provide independent assistance to the Court by way of objective unbiased opinion in relation to matters within his expertise (see *Polivitte Ltd v Commercial Union Assurance Co plc* [1987] 1 Lloyd's Rep 379 at 386 *per* Mr Justice Garland and *Re J* [1990] FCR 193 *per* Mr Justice Cazalet). An expert witness in the High Court should never assume the role of an Advocate.

(c) An expert witness should state the facts or assumptions upon which his opinion is based. He should not omit to consider material facts which could detract from his concluded opinion (*Re J*).

(d) An expert witness should make it clear when a particular question or issue falls outside his expertise.

(e) If an expert's opinion is not properly researched because he considers that insufficient data is available, then this must be stated with an indication that his opinion is no more than a provisional one (*Re J*). In cases where an expert witness who has prepared a report could not assert that the report contained the truth, the whole truth and nothing but the truth, without some qualification, the qualification should be stated within the report (*Derby and Co Ltd and Others v Weldon and Others* (2000) *The Times*, 9 November *per* Lord Justice Staughton).

(f) If, after exchange of reports an expert witness changes his view on a material matter having read the other side's expert's report or for any other reason, such change of view should be communicated (through legal representatives), to the other side without delay and, when appropriate, to the court.

(g) Where expert evidence refers to photographs, plans, calculations, analysis, measurements, survey reports or other similar documents, these must be provided to the opposite party at the same time as the exchange of reports (see 15.5 of the *Guide to Commercial Court Practice*).

The CPR reflects and reinforces the statements of an expert's duties set out in *The Ikarian Reefer*. The requirements of the CPR have been considered by the Court of Appeal in *Stevens v Gullis* [2000] 1 All ER 527, CA, where the expert failed to include in his report a statement confirming that he understood his duty to the court and that he had complied with his duty. He also failed to include his instructions and he failed to co-operate with the other experts in preparing a memorandum of agreement and disagreement following a meeting of the experts. The party who had instructed him did not provide any evidence to explain these failures and so the expert was debarred by the court from acting as a witness in the proceedings. Despite the fact that the parties agreed that this decision would be set aside, the Court of Appeal refused to interfere and the judge's decision debarring the expert was upheld. The court confirmed that the new Civil Procedure Rules underlined the existing duty which an expert owed to the court as well as to the party he represents. Lord Woolf MR said (at 533): 'It is now clear from the rules that, in addition to the duty that an expert owes to a party, he is also under a duty to the court.'

In *Anglo Group plc v Winther Brown and Co Ltd* [2000] All ER (D) 294, Judge Toulmin QC said that the analysis of the role of the expert witness in *The Ikarian Reefer* now needed to be extended in accordance with the CPR, as follows:

(a) An expert witness should at all stages in the procedure, on the basis of the evidence as he understands it, provide independent assistance to the court and the parties by way of objective unbiased opinion in relation to matters within his expertise. This applies as much to the initial meetings of experts as to evidence at trial. An expert witness should never assume the role of an advocate.

(b) The expert's evidence should normally be confined to technical matters on which the court will be assisted by receiving an explanation, or to evidence of common professional practice. The expert witness should not give evidence or opinions as to what the expert himself would have done in similar circumstances or otherwise seek to usurp the role of the judge.

(c) He should co-operate with the expert of the other party or parties in attempting to narrow the technical issues in dispute at the earliest possible stage of the procedure and to eliminate or place in context any peripheral issues. He should co-operate with the other expert(s) in attending without prejudice meetings as necessary and in seeking to find areas of agreement and to define precisely areas of disagreement to be set out in the joint statement of experts ordered by the court.

(d) The expert evidence presented to the court should be, and be seen to be, the independent product of the expert uninfluenced as to form or content by the exigencies of the litigation.

(e) An expert witness should state the facts or assumptions upon which his opinion is based. He should not omit to consider material facts which could detract from his concluded opinion.

(f) An expert witness should make it clear when a particular question or issue falls outside his expertise.

(g) Where an expert is of the opinion that his conclusions are based on inadequate factual information he should say so explicitly.

(h) An expert should be ready to reconsider his opinion, and if appropriate, to change his mind when he has received new information or has considered the opinion of the other expert. He should do so at the earliest opportunity.

A failure by an expert to take an independent approach will not be in the interest of the clients who retain the expert, since an expert taking a partisan approach, resulting in a failure to resolve before trial or at trial issues on which experts should agree, will inflate the costs of resolving the dispute and may prevent the parties from resolving their disputes long before trial.

It appears that an expert employed by one of the parties may be used by that party as an expert witness (*Field v Leeds City Council* [2000] 1 EGLR 54, CA). It was stressed that such a witness must be fully familiar with the need for objectivity, and be aware of the difficult nature of the role of an expert.

7.13.3 Surveyors acting as expert witnesses

The Royal Institution of Chartered Surveyors has issued a Practice Statement and Guidance Notes for surveyors acting as expert witnesses. Both of these apply, with effect from 1 March 1997, where any chartered surveyor agrees or is required to provide expert evidence, whether oral or in writing, which may be relied on by any judicial or quasi-judicial body in the United Kingdom.

The principal message of the Practice Statement is that 'expert evidence provided by chartered surveyors must be, and must be seen to be, the independent product of the surveyor'.

The Practice Statement provides that a surveyor's primary duty when providing evidence is to the judicial body to whom his evidence is given. The duty is to be truthful as to fact, honest as to opinion and complete as to coverage of relevant matters. The duty is the same if the surveyor is giving evidence to a judicial body, whether or not on oath. The surveyor's evidence must be independent, objective and unbiased. In particular, it must not be biased towards the party who is responsible for paying him. The evidence should be the same whoever is paying for it. The duty applies as much to the preparation of a statement of opinion intended to be used as part of written representations in an arbitration or elsewhere, where oral evidence is not given, as to a statement intended to be used at a hearing before a judicial body.

7.13.4 Expert's report

An expert's report should be addressed to the court and not to the party from whom the expert has received his instructions (PD 35, para 2.1). It must also, under PD 35, para 2.2:

(1) give details of the expert's qualifications;

(2) give details of any literature or other material which the expert has relied on in making the report;

(3) contain a statement setting out the substance of all facts and instructions given to the expert which are material to the opinions expressed in the report or upon which those opinions are based;

(4) make clear which of the facts stated in the report are within the expert's own knowledge;

(5) say who carried out any examination, measurement, test or experiment which the expert has used for the report, give the qualifications of that person, and say whether or not the test or experiment has been carried out under the expert's supervision;

(6) where there is a range of opinion on the matters dealt with in the report – summarise the range of opinion, and give reasons for his own opinion;

(7) contain a summary of the conclusions reached;

(8) if the expert is not able to give his opinion without qualification, state the qualification; and

(9) contain a statement that the expert understands his duty to the court, and has complied and will continue to comply with that duty.

An expert's report must be verified by a statement of truth as well as containing the statements required in (8) and (9) above (PD 35, para 2.3). The form of the statement of truth is: 'I confirm that insofar as the facts stated in my report are within my own knowledge I have made clear which they are and I believe them to be true, and that the opinions I have expressed represent my true and complete professional opinion' (PD 35, para 2.4).

7.13.5 Providing information to other parties

Under CPR 35.9, the court may direct a party with access to information which is not reasonably available to another party to serve on that other party a document which records the information. The document served must include sufficient details of all the facts, tests, experiments and assumptions which underlie any part of the information to enable the party on whom it is served to make, or to obtain, a proper interpretation of the information and an assessment of its significance (PD 35, para 3).

7.13.6   Questions to experts

Once a party has been served with an expert's report, CPR 35.6 provides that that party has one opportunity to put written questions to the expert about the report. These questions must be asked solely for the purpose of clarifying the expert's report, unless the court permits otherwise or the party instructing the expert agrees and should be put, in writing, to the expert not later than 28 days after receipt of the expert's report. Where a party sends a written question or questions direct to an expert and the other party is represented by solicitors, a copy of the questions should, at the same time, be sent to those solicitors (PD 35, para 5.2). The party or parties instructing the expert must pay any fees charged by that expert for answering questions put under CPR 35.6 (PD 35, para 5.3). However, this does not affect any decision of the court as to the party who is ultimately to bear the expert's costs. An expert's answers become part of the original report (CPR 35.6(3)).

If the expert does not reply to the questions, the court may direct that the party which instructed the expert cannot rely on the expert's evidence and, or alternatively, that the party cannot recover the expert's fees and expenses from the other party (CPR 35.6(4)).

7.13.7   Disclosure and use of an expert's report

Where a party has disclosed an expert's report, any party may then at the trial put the report in evidence (CPR 35.11). If, however, a party fails to disclose an expert's report, then that party cannot use the report nor call the expert at the trial, unless the court gives permission (CPR 35.13).

7.13.8 Discussions amongst the experts

The court has power under CPR 35.12(1) to order that the experts instructed by the parties meet and discuss their evidence in order to identify the issues in the proceedings and, where possible, reach agreement on an issue. In addition, the court may specify the issues which the experts must discuss (CPR 35.12(2)). The court can also direct that, following a discussion between the experts, they must prepare a statement for the court showing both the issues which they agree on and the issues which they disagree on, together with a summary of their reasons for disagreeing (CPR 35.12(3)). Where the experts reach agreement on an issue, that agreement is not binding on the parties, unless the parties expressly agree to be bound by it (CPR 35.12(5)). The contents of the discussion between the experts cannot be referred to at the trial unless the parties agree (CPR 35.12(4)).

The combined effect of CPR 35.12(1) and CPR 35.12(2) seems to be that the court can order a meeting in order to identify the issues in the proceedings and at the same time tell the experts what the issues are which they should be discussing! In practice, what will usually happen is that an agenda for the experts' meeting will be agreed between the parties and this is then followed by the experts.

The usual form of order by the court in respect of a meeting of experts will order the experts to meet by a specific date, prepare a joint memorandum as a result of the meeting by a later specific date, and exchange reports by a later specific date.

The CPR do not lay down any guidance on the conduct of expert meetings. A *Draft Code of Guidance* for experts published in 1999 provides that the meeting will take place, preferably face to face, and that the parties' lawyers will not usually be present.

7.13.9 Valuation evidence

Where there is a dispute as to the amount of the rent payable under the new tenancy, the parties will invariably each want to call a surveyor to give valuation evidence which will include details of comparables. The principles governing the admissibility of comparables were said by Megarry J in *English Exporters (London) v Eldonwall* [1973] Ch 415 to be as follows:

Putting matters shortly, and leaving on one side the matters that I have mentioned, such as the Civil Evidence Act 1968 and anything made admissible by questions in cross-examination, in my judgment a valuer giving expert evidence in chief (or in re-examination):

(a) may express the opinions that he has formed as to values even though substantial contributions to the formation of those opinions have been made by matters of which he has no first-hand knowledge;

(b) may give evidence as to the details of any transactions within his personal knowledge, in order to establish them as matters of fact; and

(c) may express his opinion as to the significance of any transactions which are or will be proved by admissible evidence (whether or not given by him) in relation to the valuation with which he is concerned; but

(d) may not give hearsay evidence stating the details of any transactions not within his personal knowledge in order to establish them as matters of fact.

To those propositions I would add that for counsel to put in a list of comparables ought to amount to a warranty by him of his intention to tender admissible evidence of all that is shown on the list.

An expert can use professional literature within his field of expertise, such as textbooks, journals, reports of auctions and other dealings, and information obtained from professional colleagues (*English Exporters (London) v Eldonwall*). The expert need not have first-hand knowledge of the facts which were used in compiling the material used (*R v Abadom* [1983] 1 WLR 126, CA).

It will often be the case that the expert will be using comparables of which he does not have first-hand knowledge, in other words hearsay, thus strictly inadmissible. However, the Civil Evidence Act 1995 has abolished the rule against hearsay in civil proceedings and such evidence will now be admissible, provided that the requirements of the Civil Evidence Act 1995 and the CPR are complied with.

A party intending to adduce hearsay evidence should notify the other parties of his intention to rely on hearsay evidence and, on request, give to the other parties such particulars of or relating to the hearsay evidence as is reasonable and practicable in order to enable them to deal with matters arising from its hearsay nature (s 2(1) of the Civil Evidence Act 1995). The parties may agree to exclude the operation of s 2(1) and a party entitled to receive notice under the section may waive that entitlement (s 2(3) of the Civil Evidence Act 1995). Failure to comply with the requirements of s 2(1) does not affect the admissibility of the hearsay evidence, but may be relevant when the court is exercising its powers concerning the course of proceedings and costs and may adversely affect the weight of the hearsay evidence (s 2(4) of the Civil Evidence Act 1995).

Where hearsay evidence is either to be proved by the oral testimony of a witness or is contained in the witness statement of a person who is not to be called, service of a witness statement on the other parties in compliance with the order of the court satisfies the notice requirement imposed by s 2(1)(a) of the Civil Evidence Act 1995 (CPR 33.2(1)). In the latter case, however, the party intending to rely upon the hearsay evidence must, at the time when the witness statement is served, both inform the other parties that the witness is not to be called and state why the witness is not to be called (CPR 33.2(2)).

Where hearsay evidence is neither to be proved by the oral testimony of a witness nor is contained in the witness statement of a person who is not to be called, a party who intends to rely upon such evidence satisfies the requirements of s 2(1)(a) of the Civil Evidence Act 1995 by serving a notice, within the time limits for service of witness statements, on the other parties (CPR 33.2(3), (4)). The notice must:

(a) identify the hearsay evidence;

(b) state that the party serving it intends to rely on the evidence; and

(c) state why the witness will not be called.

If the hearsay statement is in a document, any party who so requests must be provided with a copy.

The notice requirements imposed by s 2(1) of the Civil Evidence Act 1995 do not apply:

(a) where the hearsay evidence is to be given at a hearing other than a trial;

(b) in relation to affidavits or witness statements not containing hearsay evidence which are to be used at the trial;

(c) where the hearsay statement was allegedly made by the person whose estate forms the subject of a probate action and a party to the action wishes to put it in evidence;

(d) where a practice direction excludes the requirements of s 2(1).

A party who seeks permission to call the maker of the original statement for cross-examination on his hearsay statement must apply to the court for permission within 14 days of receiving notice from the party intending to rely on the hearsay statement of his intention to rely on it (CPR 33.4).

Where the maker of a hearsay statement or the maker of a statement tendered to prove another statement is not called, evidence may be adduced to discredit him or to support his credibility to the extent to which such evidence could have been adduced had he been called (s 5(2)(a) of the Civil Evidence Act 1995). Additionally, s 5(2)(b) provides that, in order to prove that the maker of either type of statement contradicted himself, evidence of inconsistent statements made by him is admissible. Evidence will not be admissible in relation to collateral matters if the evidence would have been inadmissible had the maker of the relevant statement testified and denied the matter during cross-examination. A party who wishes to attack the credibility of the maker of the original statement must notify the party tendering the hearsay statement of his intent within 14 days of service of a hearsay notice upon him (CPR 33.5).

7.14 STRIKING OUT THE APPLICATION

An application may be struck out under CPR 3.4 if it appears to the court that:

(a) the statement of case discloses no reasonable grounds for bringing or defending the claim;

(b) the statement of case is an abuse of the court's process or is otherwise likely to obstruct the just disposal of the proceedings; or

(c) there has been a failure to comply with a rule, practice direction or court order.

CPR 3.4(5) preserves any other pre-existing power to strike out. Thus, the application will be struck out where the tenancy is no longer one to which the 1954 Act applies (*I & H Caplan Ltd v Caplan (No 2)* [1963] 2 All ER 930), and where the landlord has forfeited the tenancy and the tenant is not seeking relief or relief would not be granted (*Meadows v Clerical Medical and General Life Assurance Society* [1981] Ch 70).

7.15   PROFESSIONAL ARBITRATION ON COURT TERMS (PACT)

The Professional Arbitration on Court Terms scheme is offered by the Law Society and the Royal Institution of Chartered Surveyors as an alternative to the parties having to ask the court to determine disputes in unopposed lease renewals. It provides the parties with a means of having disputes over the terms and rent decided by a surveyor or a solicitor, acting as either an arbitrator or an independent expert. Its use is purely voluntary and neither party can force the other to agree to it being used.

7.15.1   Matters covered by PACT

PACT can be used to resolve disputes over the following matters:

(a) the interim rent;

(b) the rent payable under the new tenancy;

(c) other terms of the new tenancy;

(d) detailed drafting of the provisions to be included in the new tenancy; and

(e) a combination of the above.

7.15.2   Using PACT

The procedure involved in using PACT is as follows:

(a) Either party makes an application to the court for a new tenancy in the usual manner.

(b) The parties then resolve any argument over grounds of opposition.

(c) The parties then agree whether it would be best to refer any unresolved matters to a surveyor or a solicitor acting as either an arbitrator or an independent expert, and they must also make sure that all other issues have been resolved.

(d) The parties then decide which matters are to be determined by a solicitor and which by a surveyor and in what order.

(e) The capacity of the third party, ie arbitrator or expert, is then decided.

(f) A consent order is then drawn up setting out the terms which have been agreed and referring those outstanding to an arbitrator or an independent expert.

(g) Application is made to the court for consent using one of the Model Consent Orders (see 7.15.3). Once the order has been made, the court proceedings are suspended whilst the matters in dispute are resolved by the third party. If either party fails to comply with the order, the other party can ask the court to enforce it.

(h) Application is made to the RICS or the Law Society for the appointment of a third party, unless this can be agreed. Both bodies have a panel of trained arbitrators and independent experts for PACT matters. There is a standard form of application to be used. The third party will be appointed by the President of the RICS or the President of the Law Society.

(i) The third party is appointed and proceeds to determine the matters. At any time the tenant may discontinue its application for a new tenancy and the landlord may discontinue its application for an interim rent.

(j) The award is received subject to cooling-off rights and, in arbitration, any right of appeal.

(k) Once the terms have been finally determined either party can, under the terms of the consent order, apply to the court for the grant of a new tenancy under s 29 of the 1954 Act.

7.15.3 Model Consent Orders

Four forms of Model Consent Orders have been produced, together with a form of joint application to the court (see Appendices 21–25) and are used as follows:

Model Order 1
This is used in cases where all outstanding issues are to be referred to arbitration (see Appendix 22).

Model Order 2
This is used in cases where the initial rent is to be referred to an independent expert and the interim rent is to be referred to arbitration (see Appendix 23).

Model Order 3
This is used in cases where issues other than rent are to be referred to arbitration before the rent is agreed and then, failing agreement, referring the initial rent to an independent expert and the interim rent to arbitration (see Appendix 24).

Model Order 4
This is used in cases where the text, or any part of the text, of the lease is to be drafted by an expert (see Appendix 25).

Each of the forms consists of an order with a schedule which records the terms which have already been agreed by the parties or determined by the court. The order then makes it clear which other terms are in dispute and are to be determined by the third party.

The arbitrator or independent expert has to follow any requirements contained in the 1954 Act. This means that the following criteria must be used:

(a) s 33 when determining the duration of the tenancy (see 9.3);

(b) s 34 when determining the rent (see 9.4);

(c) s 35 when determining the other terms of the tenancy (see 9.5);

(d) s 24A when determining the interim rent; and

(e) s 32 when determining the premises to be comprised in the new tenancy (see 9.2). It should be noted that the Model Consent Orders do not envisage that this will need to be determined and, thus, if it has to be, an amendment must be made to the appropriate form.

7.15.4　Discontinuance

The tenant can bring its application for a new tenancy to an end at any time during the PACT procedure by filing notice of discontinuance with the court, the landlord and the third party (CPR 38.2). This will then bring the third party proceedings to an end, except any reference to the third party of the interim rent, which will continue. A landlord may also discontinue its interim rent application.

The Model Consent Orders provide that the discontinuing party is responsible for the abortive costs, in the case of arbitration, of the arbitrator and the other party, and, in the case of an expert determination, of the expert, with the option of also being responsible for the other party's costs.

7.15.5 Disputing the third party's award

Once the third party has made an award, the tenant can still exercise its right under s 36(2) of the 1954 Act to elect not to take up a new tenancy (see 9.7). In order to make such an election, it will first have to apply to the court for an order for the grant of a new tenancy on the terms agreed between the parties and those determined by the third party and then, within 14 days of the order being made, apply under s 36(2) for it to be revoked.

Where the matter has been determined by an arbitrator, either party may challenge the award within 28 days of it being made. The court can be asked to extend this time limit. There are three grounds on which such an award may be challenged:

(a) substantive jurisdiction (s 67 of the Arbitration Act 1996);

(b) serious irregularity (s 68 of the Arbitration Act 1996); and

(c) a point of law (s 69 of the Arbitration Act 1996).

7.16   COSTS

The court has discretion as to whether costs are payable by one party to another, the amount of those costs and when they are to be paid (CPR 44.3(1)). In 1954 Act renewals, this had been the practice since *The Decca Navigator Co Ltd v Greater London Council* [1974] 1 All ER 1178, CA, where Lord Denning MR said (at 1181) that costs 'should be in the discretion of the county court judge to do as he thinks just'. Detailed provisions governing costs and their assessment can be found in CPR 44 and its practice direction. The following is a summary of the main provisions.

If the court decides to make an order about costs, the general rule is that the unsuccessful party will be ordered to pay the costs of the successful party; however, the court may make a different order (CPR 44.3(2)). In 1954 Act cases, it may be difficult to decide which party has been successful. Where the landlord has opposed the grant of a new tenancy under s 30(1) of the 1954 Act, it will be clear which party has been successful. However, where the parties cannot agree on the rent, it may be that the rent set by the court is some way off the figures put forward by both the parties and, in such a situation, it may not therefore be obvious which party has been successful.

In deciding what order (if any) to make about costs, the court must have regard to all the circumstances, including:

(a) the conduct of all the parties;

(b) whether a party has succeeded on part of his case, even if he has not been wholly successful; and

(c) any payment into court or admissible offer to settle made by a party which is drawn to the court's attention (whether or not made in accordance with CPR Part 36: CPR 44.3(4)). A party can, in order to protect its position on costs, make an offer to settle under CPR Part 36.

The conduct of the parties includes:

(a) conduct before, as well as during, the proceedings;

(b) whether it was reasonable for a party to raise, pursue or contest a particular allegation or issue;

(c) the manner in which a party has pursued or defended his case or a particular allegation or issue; and

(d) whether a claimant who has succeeded in his claim, in whole or in part, exaggerated his claim (CPR 44.3(5)).

The orders which the court may make include an order that a party must pay:

(a) a proportion of another party's costs;

(b) a stated amount in respect of another party's costs;

(c) costs from or until a certain date only;

(d) costs incurred before proceedings have begun;

(e) costs relating to particular steps taken in the proceedings;

(f) costs relating only to a distinct part of the proceedings; and

(g) interest on costs from or until a certain date, including a date before judgment (CPR 44.3(6)).

Where the court would otherwise consider making an order under CPR 44.3(6)(f), it must instead, if practicable, make an order under CPR 44.3(6)(a) or (c) (CPR 44.3(7)).

Where the court has ordered a party to pay costs, it may order an amount to be paid on account before the costs are assessed (CPR 44.3(8)). Where a party entitled to costs is also liable to pay costs, the court may assess the costs which that party is liable to pay and either:

(a) set off the amount assessed against the amount the party is entitled to be paid and direct him to pay any balance; or

(b) delay the issue of a certificate for the costs to which the party is entitled until he has paid the amount which he is liable to pay (CPR 44.3(9)).

The general rule is that the court should make a summary assessment of the costs:

(a) at the conclusion of the trial of a case which has been dealt with on the fast track, in which case the order will deal with the costs of the whole claim; and

(b) at the conclusion of any other hearing, which has lasted not more than one day, in which case the order will deal with the costs of the application or matter to which the hearing related. If this hearing disposes of the claim, the order may deal with the costs of the whole claim,

unless there is good reason not to do so, eg, where the paying party shows substantial grounds for disputing the sum claimed for costs that cannot be dealt with summarily or there is insufficient time to carry out a summary assessment (PD 43–48, para 13.2).

7.16.1 Consent orders

Where an application has been made and the parties to the application agree an order by consent without any party attending, the parties should agree a figure for costs to be inserted in the consent order or agree that there should be no order for costs. If the parties cannot agree the costs position, attendance will be necessary. However, unless good reason can be shown for the failure to deal with costs as set out above, no costs will be allowed for that attendance (CPR, PD 43–48, para 13.4).

7.16.2 Costs on revocation

Where an order made under the 1954 Act is revoked on the application of the tenant under s 36(2) of the 1954 Act (see 9.7) the court may, if it thinks fit, revoke or vary any provision in the order for costs or, where no costs have been awarded in the proceedings for the revoked order, award such costs (s 36(3) of the 1954 Act).

7.17   SETTLEMENT BY AGREEMENT

If, after the tenant has applied to the court for a new tenancy, the parties reach agreement on the terms of the new tenancy, the parties have two alternatives: they could have their agreement embodied in a court order; or, alternatively, the tenant could agree to withdraw its application for a new tenancy on a new tenancy being granted. The parties' agreement should be in writing, otherwise it will not be binding on either party (s 69(2) of the 1954 Act). It should also satisfy the requirements of s 2 of the Law of Property (Miscellaneous Provisions) Act 1989, ie, it should be in writing, incorporate all the agreed terms and be signed. Once a binding agreement has been made, the 1954 Act will no longer apply to the current tenancy (s 28 of the 1954 Act). The agreement should also deal with the matter of costs.

If the parties agree that the tenant is not to have a new tenancy, ie, because the tenant accepts that the landlord has a valid ground of opposition, then again there are two alternatives. The parties can either have their agreement embodied in a court order, or the tenant could withdraw its application. If the parties decide to deal with the matter by way of a court order, the order should specify that the tenant accepts that the landlord has established a ground of opposition and that its application for a new tenancy is dismissed. The terms of the agreement should also deal with costs.

If the matter is dealt with by way of withdrawal of the tenant's application for a new tenancy, there is no right of appeal and the current tenancy will come to an end under s 64 of the 1954 Act (see 7.18). However, if the matter is dealt with by way of a court order, then it is technically possible for there to be an appeal against it with leave of the court (s 18(1)(f) of the Supreme Court Act 1981). The s 64 period will not therefore start to run until the period in which an appeal can be made has expired (see 7.18).

7.18   INTERIM CONTINUATION OF TENANCIES PENDING DETERMINATION BY THE COURT

Section 64(1) of the 1954 Act provides that:

In any case where:

(a) a s 25 notice has been given or a s 26 request has been made, and

(b) an application for either a new tenancy or for termination without renewal has been made to the court, and

(c) the effect of the s 25 notice or s 26 request would otherwise be to terminate the tenancy before the expiration of the period of three months beginning with the date on which the application is finally disposed of,

the effect of the s 25 notice or s 26 request shall be to terminate the tenancy at the expiration of the three month period and not at any other time.

The effect of this provision is to continue the tenancy automatically for three months after the application has been finally disposed of. This will be the case even if the application for a new tenancy has been made outside the time limits laid down by the 1954 Act, as these time limits are procedural and can be waived (*Zenith Investments (Torquay) Ltd v Kammins Ballrooms Co Ltd (No 2)* [1971] 3 All ER 1281, CA). Where an application is made by someone who is no longer the tenant, s 64 of the 1954 Act will not continue the tenancy (*Meah v Sector Properties Ltd* [1974] 1 All ER 1074, CA).

An application is finally disposed of on the earliest date by which the proceedings, including any appeal, have been determined and any time for appealing or further appealing has expired, except that, if the application is withdrawn or any appeal is abandoned, the date of final disposal will be the date of the withdrawal or abandonment (s 64(2) of the 1954 Act). Where the application has been resolved by a consent order, the time limit in which an appeal may be made must be taken into account, as it is possible for an appeal to be made against a consent order (s 18(1)(f) of the Supreme Court Act 1981).

If the Court of Appeal refuses to grant a new tenancy and refuses leave to appeal to the House of Lords, the three-month period under s 64 of the 1954 Act will not start until the end of the month which is allowed for lodging a petition to the House of Lords for leave to appeal (*Re 20 Exchange Street, Manchester*

Austin Reed Ltd v Royal Insurance Co Ltd (No 2) [1956] 3 All ER 490).

Where the tenant applies for an extension of time in which to appeal where it is out of time, the proceedings are not 'proceedings on or in consequence of an appeal' within s 64(2) of the 1954 Act. The application is no more than an attempt to commence an appeal. If an extension is granted, the appeal is then in being and the tenancy will determine on the final disposal of that appeal (*Shotley Point Marina (1986) v Spalding* [1997] 1 EGLR 233, CA).

CHAPTER 8

THE GROUNDS OF OPPOSITION

A landlord can only oppose the tenant's application for a new tenancy on one or more of the grounds of opposition contained in s 30(1) of the 1954 Act. In order to be able to rely on any of these grounds the landlord must state the relevant ground or grounds in either a s 25 notice or a s 26(6) counternotice. It is open to a successor in title to rely on a ground put forward in the appropriate notice by a predecessor in title (*Wimbush (AD) and Son v Franmills Properties* [1961] Ch 419; *Morris Marks v British Waterways Board* [1963] 3 All ER 28, CA).

8.1 GROUND (A) – FAILURE TO REPAIR

8.1.1 Section 30(1)(a)

... where under the current tenancy the tenant has any obligations as respects the repair and maintenance of the holding, that the tenant ought not to be granted a new tenancy in view of the state of repair of the holding, being a state resulting from the tenant's failure to comply with the said obligations.

8.1.2 The requirements of s 30(1)(a)

There are three requirements which a landlord must satisfy in order to be able to rely on this ground:

(a) the tenant must have an obligation to repair and maintain the holding. Such an obligation will usually be expressly set out in the lease; however, it may arise impliedly, or under a statutory obligation. Repair is defined in s 69(1) of the 1954 Act as including 'any work of maintenance, decoration or restoration, and references to repairing, to keeping or yielding up in repair and to state of repair shall be construed accordingly';

(b) the failure to repair must relate to the holding (see 9.2);

(c) the holding must be in disrepair at the date of the hearing. In practice, the holding must also be in disrepair at the date of the service of the landlord's notice. The tenant's neglect to

repair should be substantial (*per* Ormerod LJ (at 774) in
Lyons v Central Commercial Properties Ltd [1958] 2 All ER 767,
CA).

8.1.3   The court's discretion

The use of the words 'ought not to be granted a new tenancy' in
s 30(1)(a) of the 1954 Act gives the court a discretion as to
whether or not to refuse to grant a new tenancy. This was
accepted in *Lyons v Central Commercial Properties Ltd*, where the
court considered how the discretion should be exercised. The
majority of the court (Morris and Ormerod LJJ) felt that the
discretion was wide and that the court could take into account
all the relevant circumstances, including the tenant's conduct in
relation to his obligations under the tenancy and the reasons for
the breach of the repairing covenant. Morris LJ said (at 773):

> I do not think that it is desirable to say more than that once a
> court has found the facts as regards the tenant's past
> performances and behaviour and any special circumstances
> which exist, then, while remembering that it is the future that
> is being considered, in that the issue is whether the tenant
> should be refused a new tenancy for the future, the court has to
> ask itself whether it would be unfair to the landlord, having
> regard to the tenant's past performances and behaviour, if the
> tenant were to enjoy the advantage which the Act gives to him.

And Ormerod LJ said (at 774):

> Without attempting to define the precise limits of that
> discretion, the judge, as I see it, may have regard to the conduct
> of the tenant in relation to his obligations, and the reasons for
> any breach of the covenant to repair which has arisen.

The view of Ormerod LJ was subsequently applied in *Eichner v
Midland Bank Executor & Trustee Co Ltd* [1970] 2 All ER 597, CA.

8.1.4   Forfeiture

As an alternative to relying on ground (a), a landlord may
consider the use of forfeiture proceedings. However, if
forfeiture proceedings are used, the tenant will usually be
granted relief on condition that the repairs be carried out,
whereas under ground (a) in such a situation, the court's
discretion will not be exercised as automatically in favour of the
tenant.

8.1.5 Practical issues – acting for the landlord

The landlord should serve a schedule of dilapidations on the tenant, together with a request that the repairs be carried out. In practice, this will be prepared by the landlord's surveyor. Evidence that the landlord has brought forfeiture proceedings will also be of value. The landlord's surveyor will be able to give evidence as to the estimated cost of the repairs and the likely time for carrying them out, together with whether they have caused any loss in value to the landlord's reversion.

8.1.6 Practical issues – acting for the tenant

The tenant should consider offering the landlord an undertaking to carry out the repairs within a specified time. This can then be taken into account by the court, which will also want to have details of the tenant's financial status to satisfy itself that the tenant has funds to complete the works.

8.1.7 Compensation

If the landlord establishes ground (a), the tenant will not be entitled to compensation (see Chapter 10).

8.2 GROUND (B) – PERSISTENT DELAY IN PAYING RENT

8.2.1 Section 30(1)(b)

> … that the tenant ought not to be granted a new tenancy in view of his persistent delay in paying rent which has become due.

8.2.2 'Persistent delay'

The words 'persistent delay' in the wording of this ground imply that there must be a series of arrears of rent on more than one occasion. It may be that there is a long history of arrears or that just a couple of payments have been in arrears for some time. It is clear from *Horowitz v Ferrand* [1956] CLY 4843 that the rent need not be substantially in arrears nor need the arrears last a long time.

8.2.3   What payments are included in 'rent'?

The ground refers to 'rent' and it will be a matter of construction of the lease as to what is included in this term. Certainly, all items which have been reserved in the lease as rent will be included.

8.2.4   The court's discretion

The words 'ought not' give the court a discretion as to whether or not to grant a new tenancy. The court will consider whether it is likely that there will be delays in paying the rent should a new tenancy be granted. The tenant's conduct generally may be taken into account as well (*Eichner v Midland Bank Executor and Trustee Co Ltd*), and the court will also consider other complaints against the tenant when exercising its discretion (*Hutchinson v Lamberth* [1984] 1 EGLR 75, CA).

It is for the landlord to prove that a new tenancy should not be granted. However, the tenant must explain why there has been a persistent delay and satisfy the court that there will be no recurrence of the delay if a new tenancy is granted (*Hurstfell Ltd v Leicester Square Property Co Ltd* [1988] 2 EGLR 189, CA).

Examples of the exercise of the court's discretion in relation to this ground include:

(a) *Freeman v Barclays Bank Ltd* [1958] EGD 93, CA, where the landlord was not prevented from relying on this ground even although a draft lease had been served on the tenant just before the landlord's s 25 notice was served indicating opposition to a new tenancy under ground (b). The court would take this into account when considering whether to exercise its discretion;

(b) *Hopcutt v Carver* (1969) 209 EG 1069, CA, where a new tenancy was refused as the tenant had been late in paying the rent over the preceding two years;

(c) *Hutchinson v Lamberth*, where it was held that where no rent was paid for four years, the tenant only putting matters right after legal proceedings had been commenced, ground (b) had been made out;

(d) *Hurstfell Ltd v Leicester Square Property Co Ltd*, where a new tenancy was granted. All payments of rent between 1984 and the end of 1986 had been between four and nineteen weeks late. However, once a s 25 notice had been served in

1987 stating opposition on ground (b), the rent had been paid on time;

(e) *Rawashdeh v Lane* [1988] 2 EGLR 109, CA, where a new tenancy was refused where all but the first and last payments of rent under a 21-year lease had been made late, four cheques had not initially been honoured and possession proceedings had been brought twice. The tenant also offered security for future payments. The Court of Appeal said that it would only interfere with the exercise of the judge's discretion 'if it is apparent that the judge made an error of principle; if he exercised his discretion in a way which was patently perverse or if he took into account an irrelevant factor or failed to take into account a relevant factor'; and

(f) *Hazel v Akhtar* [2001] EWCA Civ 1883; (2002) 2 P & CR 17, CA, where the landlord's acquiescence to the tenant's persistent failure to pay the rent on time prevented both the landlord and his successor in title from being able to rely on ground (b) until reasonable notice was given to the tenant that he should start complying once again with the lease.

8.2.5   The relevant date

In *Betty's Cafés Ltd v Phillips Furnishing Stores* [1958] 1 All ER 607, HL, it was said that the court will necessarily take into consideration the tenant's persistent delay in paying rent which has become due not only at the date of the notice but also at the date of the hearing (*per* Viscount Simonds (at 613)). This does not mean that there must be arrears of rent at the date of the hearing for the landlord to succeed under this ground, as what the court is looking at is the whole history of payment by the tenant.

8.2.6   Practical issues – acting for the landlord

In order to establish this ground, a landlord will need to prepare a schedule of arrears. This should set out the dates when the rent became due, the dates the rent was received, the amount of arrears and details of dishonoured cheques, proceedings to recover the rent and costs incurred. The schedule can then be agreed with the tenant. If this is not possible, the landlord can serve the schedule on the tenant with a 'Notice to Admit Facts' under CPR 32.18.

8.2.7   Practical issues – acting for the tenant

A tenant must show the court that, if a new tenancy is granted, there will be no delay in paying the rent. Evidence of the tenant's finances should be given to the court. It may be wise for the tenant to offer some form of security, such as a guarantor, the advance payment of rent, or the deposit of a lump sum, although where this was done in *Rawashdeh v Lane*, a new tenancy was not granted. A tenant who receives a notice specifying opposition under ground (b) should therefore start paying the rent on time and put forward proposals guaranteeing future payments.

8.2.8   Compensation

If the landlord establishes ground (b), the tenant will not be entitled to compensation (see Chapter 10).

8.3   GROUND (C) – SUBSTANTIAL BREACHES OF OTHER OBLIGATIONS

8.3.1   Section 30(1)(c)

... that the tenant ought not to be granted a new tenancy in view of other substantial breaches by him of his obligations under the current tenancy, or for any other reason connected with the tenant's use or management of the holding.

There are two limbs to this ground. The first covers 'other substantial breaches', whilst the second covers 'any other reason'.

8.3.2   Other substantial breaches

Under the first limb, a landlord can oppose the grant of a new tenancy on the ground that the tenant has committed 'other substantial breaches' of the lease. The use of the word 'other' excludes from this ground breaches of a repairing covenant and persistent arrears of rent (grounds (a) and (b)). A landlord who therefore relies on ground (c) where there are breaches of the lease which would come within grounds (a) and (b) cannot complain of those breaches as proof of ground (c), although he could use either or both of grounds (a) or (b) as well in his notice. However, where a landlord relies on either or both of grounds (a) and (b), evidence of matters which would be covered by ground (c) can be relied on in support of these grounds (*Hutchinson v Lamberth*). If ground (c) is used, the landlord must be able to prove the breaches are supported on the evidence put forward (*Jones v Jenkins* [1986] 1 EGLR 113, CA).

The breach must be 'substantial'. In *Palser v Grinling* [1948] 1 All ER 1, HL Viscount Simon said (at 11):

> One of the primary meanings of the word is equivalent to considerable, solid or big. It is in this sense that we speak of a substantial fortune, a substantial meal, a substantial man, a substantial argument or ground of defence. Applying the word in this sense, it must be left to the discretion of the judge of fact to decide as best he can according to the circumstances in each case, the onus being on the landlord.

Therefore, it will always be a question of fact as to whether or not the breaches put forward are substantial.

The reference in ground (c) to 'breaches' would not seem to preclude a landlord from using the ground where there is only one substantial breach. This is substantiated by s 6 of the Interpretation Act 1978, which confirms that in an Act of Parliament, unless the contrary intention appears, words in the singular include the plural and words in the plural include the singular.

The breach need not be subsisting and, indeed, could be one which occurred some time ago and for which the landlord has waived his right to forfeit.

There is no requirement that the breaches must relate to the 'holding'. Thus, the landlord may use this ground where the breaches relate to other parts of the property comprised in the tenancy, ie, parts which are occupied by, say, a residential sub-tenant.

8.3.3   Other reasons

Ground (c) also refers to 'any other reason connected with the tenant's use or management of the holding'. This refers to a reason which does not fall within either of grounds (a) or (b), or within the first part of ground (c). There is no requirement that the reason must be confined to matters which are directly connected with the relationship of the parties *qua* landlord and tenant, and so the court can look at everything which it thinks is relevant in connection with the tenant's use or management of the holding, past, present or future, which may enable the court fairly to exercise its discretion (*Turner & Bell v Searles (Stanford-Le-Hope) Ltd* [1977] 2 EGLR 58, CA). In *Beard v Williams* [1986] 1 EGLR 148, CA, the court considered that the tenant's living arrangements were within 'any other reason connected with the tenant's use or management of the holding', as they were relevant to whether the tenant could continue his business on the premises.

Unlike 'other substantial breaches', provided they have something to do with the use and management of the holding, the 'other reasons' do not have to occur on the holding (*Beard v Williams*).

8.3.4   The court's discretion

The words 'ought not' give the court a discretion as to whether or not to grant a new tenancy. In considering whether to exercise this discretion or not, the court should consider whether the landlord's interest is likely to have been prejudiced by the occurrence of the matters relied upon as constituting reasons within ground (c) (*Beard* v *Williams*). The tenant's conduct generally may be taken into account as well (*Eichner v Midland Bank Executor and Trustee Co Ltd*).

8.3.5   The relevant date

The landlord must establish matters constituting reasons within ground (c) at both the date of the notice and the date of the hearing (*Betty's Cafés Ltd v Phillips Furnishing Stores*).

8.3.6   Practical issues – acting for the landlord

A landlord will need to adduce evidence to prove that, either there are breaches of the terms of the tenancy, or that the tenant's use or management of the holding is illegal or immoral or contrary to public policy.

8.3.7   Practical issues – acting for the tenant

The tenant will need to put forward reasons for its behaviour, together with its proposals for the future.

8.3.8   Compensation

If the landlord establishes ground (c), the tenant will not be entitled to compensation (see Chapter 10).

8.4   GROUND (D) – SUITABLE ALTERNATIVE ACCOMMODATION

8.4.1   Section 30(1)(d)

> … that the landlord has offered and is willing to provide or secure the provision of alternative accommodation for the tenant, that the terms on which the alternative accommodation is available are reasonable having regard to the terms of the current tenancy and to all other relevant circumstances, and that the accommodation and the time at which it will be available are suitable for the tenant's requirements, (including the requirement to preserve goodwill) having regard to the nature and class of his business and to the situation and extent of, and facilities afforded by, the holding.

8.4.2   The requirements of ground (d)

A landlord seeking to rely on ground (d) must establish that:

(a) alternative accommodation has been offered to the tenant and he is willing to provide or secure the provision of that alternative accommodation (see 8.4.3);

(b) the terms on which the alternative accommodation is available are reasonable, having regard to the terms of the current tenancy and to all other relevant circumstances (see 8.4.4); and

(c) the accommodation and the time at which it will be available are suitable for the tenant's requirements (including the requirement to preserve goodwill), having regard to the nature and class of his business and to the situation and extent of, and facilities afforded by, the holding (see 8.4.5).

If the landlord establishes these four requirements, the court must refuse to grant a new tenancy.

8.4.3 The offer of alternative accommodation

The landlord must have offered either to provide the tenant with, or to secure the provision of, alternative accommodation. There does appear to be some uncertainty about the timing of the landlord's offer, ie, does it have to have been made before the landlord serves notice on the tenant stating opposition under ground (d), or can the offer be made at the same time as the notice is served? In *M Chaplin Ltd v Regent Capital Holdings Ltd* [1994] 1 EGLR 249, it was held in the county court that the requirement that the landlord has offered alternative accommodation is satisfied if the offer is made before the issue is joined in the pleadings, namely, before the landlord files its answer. Consequently, the offer did not have to have been made before the landlord served its s 25 notice and an offer made in a covering letter which accompanied the landlord's s 25 notice was sufficient. This decision, however, conflicts with the view of Lord Denning in *Betty's Cafés Ltd v Phillips Furnishing Stores* where he said (at 622) that:

> If a landlord opposes on the ground that: 'I have offered you alternative accommodation and am willing to provide it,' he clearly means that, *in the past*, at some time before the notice, *he has* offered alternative accommodation, and that, *in the present*, at the time of giving the notice, he *is willing* to provide it.

However, the county court judge agreed with Viscount Simonds in *Betty's Cafés Ltd v Phillips Furnishing Stores*, who thought it would not 'be reasonable to reduce the time within which the landlord should have the opportunity of finding and offering alternative accommodation'. He also noted that the House of Lords was considering proceedings following a s 26 request rather than a s 25 notice and that a landlord may experience problems if he has to prove that he has offered alternative accommodation before the two-month period for the service of the counternotice has expired.

It is therefore suggested that it will be sufficient if the landlord's offer is made before the issue is joined in the pleadings, ie it does not necessarily have to be made before the landlord serves either a s 25 notice or a counternotice to a s 26 request made by the tenant.

There is nothing in ground (d) requiring the landlord not to withdraw the offer of alternative accommodation. Consequently, a landlord is free at any time to withdraw an offer. Obviously, if this is done, the landlord will no longer be able to proceed to oppose the grant of a new tenancy under this ground. If the landlord therefore wishes to rely on ground (d) at the hearing, the offer should not be withdrawn (*M Chaplin Ltd v Regent Capital Holdings Ltd*). However, it is suggested that this would not in fact prevent a landlord from making an offer and then later making a fresh offer, for example, where more suitable alternative accommodation becomes available, or where the accommodation originally offered is no longer available.

8.4.4   The terms on which the accommodation is offered

The alternative accommodation must be offered on terms which are reasonable, having regard to the terms of the current tenancy and to all relevant circumstances. This invariably means that the terms of the current tenancy and those offered must be compared.

8.4.5   Suitability of the alternative accommodation

Ground (d) provides that the alternative accommodation offered by the landlord and the time at which it will be available must be suitable for the tenant's requirements. In determining the suitability of the alternative accommodation, the court must have regard to:

(a) the requirement to preserve goodwill;
(b) the nature and class of the tenant's business – ie, whether the alternative accommodation is suitable for the tenant's business;
(b) the situation and extent of the holding. In *M Chaplin Ltd v Regent Capital Holdings Ltd*, the judge accepted that alternative accommodation did not have to mirror exactly the tenant's existing accommodation;
(d) the facilities afforded by the holding.

8.4.6   The relevant date

The relevant date for the purposes of ground (d) is the date of the hearing. This is when the reasonableness of the terms on which the alternative accommodation is offered, together with the suitability of the alternative accommodation, will be considered. It follows that the terms do not have to be reasonable when the offer is made; only at the time of the hearing. The willingness to provide or secure the provision of the alternative accommodation must also be established at the hearing.

8.4.7   Compensation

If the landlord succeeds under this ground, the tenant will not be entitled to compensation (see Chapter 10).

8.4.8   What happens if the landlord succeeds under ground (d)?

If the landlord successfully opposes the grant of a new tenancy under ground (d), the tenant should accept the landlord's offer of alternative accommodation without delay. There is no requirement in the wording of the ground that the offer must remain open forever after the hearing; thus, it is possible that a landlord could withdraw an offer if the tenant delays. Alternatively, it is open to a tenant to decide not to accept an offer and to move out into accommodation which it has itself found.

8.4.9   Practical issues – acting for the landlord

A landlord will need to prove that an offer of alternative accommodation has been made to the tenant. Such an offer should therefore always be made in writing, setting out the terms of the offer. Details of the alternative accommodation must be provided to the court. A plan showing the location both of the tenant's current premises and the alternative accommodation should be supplied, together with details such as their respective dimensions and layout. It may well be that expert evidence on the suitability of the alternative accommodation will be required to be given by a surveyor. In addition, the landlord will have to prove that it is willing to provide, or secure the provision of, the alternative accommodation. This will usually be proved by oral evidence from the landlord, or a board resolution where the landlord is a corporation. If the landlord does not own the alternative accommodation, the owner will need to be called to confirm that it is willing to let it to the tenant, or alternatively sell or lease it to the landlord. Finally, the landlord must prove that the alternative accommodation is suitable for the requirements of the tenant.

8.4.10   Practical issues – acting for the tenant

The tenant must consider whether the alternative accommodation is suitable for its requirements. The tenant may therefore need to prove that its business has special requirements which mean that the alternative accommodation is not suitable. Evidence may also need to be called to show that the goodwill will be affected, if this is the case.

8.5   GROUND (E) – POSSESSION IS REQUIRED FOR LETTING OR DISPOSING OF THE PROPERTY AS A WHOLE

8.5.1   Section 30(1)(e)

> … where the current tenancy was created by the sub-letting of part only of the property comprised in a superior tenancy and the landlord is the owner of an interest in reversion expectant on the termination of that superior tenancy, that the aggregate of the rents reasonably obtainable on separate lettings of the holding and the remainder of that property would be substantially less than the rent reasonably obtainable on a letting of that property as a whole, that on the termination of the current tenancy the landlord requires possession of the holding for the purpose of letting or otherwise disposing of the said property as a whole, and that in view thereof the tenant ought not to be granted a new tenancy.

It should be said at the outset that this ground is rarely encountered in practice as it is only available as between a superior landlord and a sub-tenant. In *Betty's Cafés Ltd v Phillips Furnishing Stores*, Viscount Simonds said (at 611) that neither side in the case found it 'helpful or wholly intelligible'.

8.5.2   Conditions to be satisfied

The conditions which must be satisfied for this ground are as follows:

(a) The current tenancy must be a sub-tenancy of part of the premises comprised in the superior tenancy.

(b) The landlord must own an interest expectant on the termination of the superior tenancy. In *Greaves v Stanhope* (1973) 228 EG 725, the landlord could not rely on ground (e) as the superior tenancy had been surrendered before the s 25 notice had been served.

(c) The aggregate of the rents reasonably obtainable on separate lettings of the holding and the remainder of that property must be substantially less than the rent reasonably obtainable on a letting of that property as a whole. This is a question of fact and is one on which valuation evidence will be required. In *Greaves v Stanhope* the landlord was unable to show that the aggregate of the rents obtainable would be 'substantially less' and so the ground failed.

(d) On the termination of the current tenancy the landlord must require possession of the holding for the purpose of letting or otherwise disposing of it as a whole.

8.5.3   The court's discretion

If the conditions set out in 8.5.2 are satisfied the court then has a discretion as to whether or not to grant a new tenancy to the tenant. There are no reported cases on how the discretion under this ground is to be exercised. Unlike the other discretionary grounds, ground (e) requires no fault on the tenant's part and it is suggested that the court should therefore balance the relative hardship to each party.

8.5.4   The relevant date

No opinion was expressed in *Betty's Cafés Ltd v Phillips Furnishing Stores* about the time when ground (e) must be proved. It is suggested that the requirement of possession and proof of the substantial difference in rent must be proved at the date of the hearing, whereas the ownership of the relevant interest must exist at the date of the service of the relevant notice by the landlord.

8.5.5   Compensation

If the landlord establishes this ground of opposition, the tenant will be entitled to compensation (see Chapter 10).

8.5.6   Practical issues – acting for the landlord

In order to rely successfully on ground (e), a landlord will need to prove its title to the premises, together with the creation of the superior tenancy and the sub-tenancy. Expert evidence will then be required to prove the rental issues mentioned in 8.5.2, and also to prove the landlord's intention to let or dispose of the property as a whole.

8.5.7   Practical issues – acting for the tenant

The tenant will need to consider whether it can put forward expert evidence to challenge the evidence put forward by the landlord regarding the rental issues.

8.6   GROUND (F) – DEMOLITION AND RECONSTRUCTION

8.6.1   Section 30(1)(f)

> ... that on the termination of the current tenancy the landlord intends to demolish or reconstruct the premises comprised in the holding or a substantial part of those premises or to carry out substantial work of construction on the holding or part thereof and that he could not reasonably do so without obtaining possession of the holding.

Along with ground (g) this is probably the most frequently used ground. In practice, a landlord seeking to rely on this ground will also consider using ground (g) as well, as there is an overlap in the circumstances in which they are usually used. In order to succeed under ground (f) a landlord must prove that:

(a) he has the necessary intention to carry out the works;

(b) the works which he intends to carry out are within the wording of the ground; and

(c) possession of the holding is needed in order to carry out those works.

8.6.2   Intention

The biggest hurdle that a landlord must overcome in order to succeed under ground (f) is to establish that he has the necessary intention to carry out the works. It will not do for the landlord merely to declare that he intends to carry out the works, as this would allow him to change his mind after possession has been obtained (*Roehorn v Barry Corp* [1956] 2 All ER 742, CA). What is required is something more than this; in other words, a fixed and settled intention on the part of the landlord to carry out the works. The test which is to be applied in determining whether the landlord has the necessary intention was laid down by Asquith LJ in *Cunliffe v Goodman* [1950] 1 All ER 720, CA, where he said (at 724):

> An 'intention', to my mind, connotes a state of affairs which the party 'intending' ... does more than merely contemplate. It connotes a state of affairs which, on the contrary, he decides, so far as in him lies, to bring about, and which, in point of possibility, he has a reasonable prospect of being able to bring about by his own act of volition.

And:

> Not merely is the term 'intention' unsatisfied if the person professing it has too many hurdles to overcome or too little control of events; it is equally inappropriate if at the material date that person is in effect not deciding to proceed but feeling his way and reserving his decision until he shall be in possession of financial data sufficient to enable him to determine whether the project will be commercially worth while. A purpose so qualified and suspended does not, in my view, amount to an 'intention' or 'decision' within the principle. It is mere contemplation until the materials necessary to a decision on the commercial merits are available and have resulted in such a decision.

In concluding, he laid down that the test to apply is whether the landlord's project has 'moved out of the zone of contemplation – out of the sphere of the tentative, the provisional and the exploratory – into the valley of decision' (at 725). If it has, then intention is established. This test was subsequently approved by Viscount Simonds in *Betty's Cafés Ltd v Phillips Furnishing Stores Ltd* [1957] 1 All ER 1, who did not dissent from the following observations of Lord Evershed MR, when that case was in the Court of Appeal (at 17):

> In my judgment, the adoption of the language of Asquith LJ by this court in the later cases cannot be treated as having, in effect, substituted for the word 'intends' in s 30(1)(f) (as in s 30(1)(g)) the words 'is ready and able', so as to impose on the landlord the onus of proving that, at whatever be the proper

date, he has not only finally determined on the course proposed, but has also taken all necessary steps for the satisfaction of any requisite conditions to which the course proposed is subject. The relevant word is 'intends', a simple English word of well-understood meaning. The question whether the intention is at the relevant date proved has, in my judgment, to be answered by the ordinary standards of common sense. If there are conditions to which the course proposed is subject, and if the landlord has no reason to suppose that there will be difficulty in their fulfilment, then *prima facie*, in my view, the landlord would not fail to prove intention within the meaning of s 30(1)(f) merely because he could not prove at the date in question that all steps had been taken to satisfy the conditions. It might well be otherwise, however, if the course proposed were conditional on other things being done which were by no means matters of course, for example, the successful raising of large sums of money not presently available to him. In such a case the proposed course, although it might well have been adopted as one to be aimed at and, if possible, attained, could not, or could not easily, be said to be 'intended' in the sense of having been finally resolved on.

It is now well established (*Gregson v Cyril Lord Ltd* [1962] 3 All ER 907, CA; *Dolgellau Golf Club v Hett* [1998] 2 EGLR 75, CA; *Coppin v Bruce-Smith* [1998] EGCS 55, CA) that in order to satisfy the test of intention, which is both subjective and objective, a landlord must prove both a genuine and definite intention to carry out the works within a short or reasonable time after the termination of the tenancy, and a reasonable prospect of achieving it. A landlord does not, however, have to prove that the project will be a commercial success. All that must be proved is an intention to carry it out (*Dolgellau Golf Club v Hett*).

8.6.2.1 When must the intention exist?

The landlord's intention must exist at the date of the hearing (*Betty's Cafes Ltd v Phillips Furnishing Stores Ltd*). This means that, when the landlord notifies the tenant in either the s 25 notice or the counternotice to a s 26 request that renewal will be opposed under this ground, there is no need for there to be definite plans for demolition or reconstruction in existence at that stage.

8.6.2.2 What if the landlord changes before the hearing?

A change in the identity of the landlord after it has notified the tenant of its intention to oppose but before the hearing does not matter, as it is the intention of the competent landlord (see 4.3.2.1) at the date of the hearing which is relevant (*XL Fisheries Ltd v Leeds Corp* [1955] 2 All ER 875, CA; *Morris Marks v British Waterways Board*). Thus if, for example, the landlord sells the reversion, the purchaser, provided it intends to redevelop, will be able to rely on ground (f).

8.6.2.3 How can intention be proved?

In order to prove that the landlord has a genuine and definite intention to redevelop, ie, in order to move out of the 'zone of contemplation' into the 'valley of decision', there must be definite plans on the landlord's part to carry out the works. It is suggested that a landlord should consider the following matters:

(a) obtaining planning permission (see 8.6.2.4);

(b) instructing professional advisers;

(c) preparing drawings, plans, contracts, timetable for the works, etc;

(d) obtaining finance (see 8.6.2.5);

(e) ensuring that there are no remaining obstacles to be overcome, eg, easements enjoyed by adjoining owners, restrictive covenants and consents from superior landlords and any mortgagee.

Where there are obstacles which need to be overcome, a landlord must show that it is likely that they will be overcome, if they have not been overcome at the date of the hearing.

A landlord who is an individual will prove its intention by giving oral evidence. In the case of a company landlord a resolution to proceed with the works will be the best evidence of its intention. In *Betty's Cafés Ltd v Phillips Furnishing Stores Ltd*, the landlord company made a resolution during the course of the hearing and this was held to be sufficient evidence. However, a resolution may not be necessary where the company directors give evidence, provided it can be said that they represent the company's mind and will and control what it does (*Bolton Engineering Co Ltd v TJ Graham and Sons Ltd* [1956] 3

All ER 624, CA). In *Europarks (Midland) Ltd v Town Centre Securities plc* [1985] 1 EGLR 88, it was accepted that minutes of board meetings, evidence of quotations from suppliers and an affidavit from the landlords' property director as to the landlords' intention was sufficient to show the necessary intention on the part of the landlords.

In the case of a local authority landlord, a resolution of the council or its relevant sub-committee will be the best evidence of intention, although in *Poppett's (Caterers) Ltd v Maidenhead Borough Council* [1970] 3 All ER 289, CA, minutes of the council's committees which had been approved by the council were accepted in the absence of any formal resolutions.

8.6.2.4 Planning permission

One of the deciding factors in establishing a firm and settled intention is whether or not the landlord has obtained or has applied for planning permission. In practice, a landlord should ensure that planning permission is applied for and obtained as early as is practicably possible. The test to be used where planning permission has been applied for but has not been obtained by the time of the hearing is whether there is a reasonable prospect that planning permission will be granted (*Westminster City Council v British Waterways Board* [1984] 3 WLR 1047, HL). This was explained by Saville LJ in *Cadogan v McCarthy & Stone Developments Ltd* [1996] EGCS 94, CA as follows:

> The reason why it must be established that there is a reasonable prospect of obtaining permission is that otherwise the landlords could only be said to be contemplating, rather than genuinely intending, the desired course of action. A reasonable prospect in this context accordingly means a real chance, a prospect that is strong enough to be acted on by a reasonable landlord minded to go ahead with plans which require permission, as opposed to a prospect that should be treated as merely fanciful or as one that should sensibly be ignored by a reasonable landlord. A reasonable prospect does not entail that it is more likely than not that permission will be obtained.

In practice, this means that a landlord has to show that there is a more than even chance that planning permission will be granted, as opposed to a fanciful prospect of it being granted.

This reasonable prospect test has subsequently been applied in *Aberdeen Steak Houses Group Ltd v Crown Estates Commissioners* (1997) 31 EG 101; *Coppin v Bruce-Smith* and *Gatwick Parking Service Ltd v Sargent* [2000] 2 EGLR 45. In *Coppin v Bruce-Smith*, concerning Thames Ditton Lawn Tennis Club, the landlord decided to demolish the tennis courts and pavilion so that it would be easier to obtain planning permission in the future for redevelopment. Planning permission for redevelopment had already been refused on the ground of the loss of a recreational open space. The Court of Appeal decided that the landlord would need planning permission for the demolition works and would encounter the same objection again. Consequently, the landlord did not have a reasonable prospect of being able to carry out the proposed works and so could not show a firm and settled intention to demolish. The tenant was therefore entitled to a new lease.

Even where planning permission has been granted, it is still possible for the landlord to fail to prove intention. This occurred in *Edwards v Thompson* (1990) 29 EG 41, CA, where it could not be shown that a developer would be prepared to proceed on the basis of the planning permission which the landlord had obtained.

8.6.2.5 Finance

The availability of finance will assist a landlord in proving intention and a letter from a bank manager promising finance can suffice (*DAF Motoring Centre (Gosport) Ltd v Hutfield & Wheeler Ltd* (1982) 263 EG 976, CA). A landlord will usually put forward a detailed financial plan; however, the absence of such a plan may not be fatal (*A Levy and Son Ltd v Martin Brent Developments Ltd*).

8.6.2.6 Who must carry out the works?

A landlord must intend to carry out the works either itself, or by its agents or employees. A landlord will not succeed where it intends to sell the premises once it has obtained possession and let the buyer carry out the works. However, it will succeed if it intends that the works are to be carried out by a tenant under a building lease which is to be granted once it has obtained possession. In *Gilmour Caterers Ltd v St Bartholomew's Hospital Governors* [1956] 1 All ER 314, CA, the landlord succeeded under this ground where it had entered into an agreement to grant a building lease once it obtained possession. However, such a formal agreement to grant a building lease may be unnecessary and in *PF Ahern and Sons Ltd v Hunt* (1988) 21 EG 69, CA, the landlord succeeded where there was no formal agreement. This case can be compared with *Roehorn v Barry Corp*, where the landlord was unsuccessful as its plans to redevelop through a building lease were so insufficiently advanced that it had not proved intention. In this particular case, the landlord provided no evidence of financial arrangements, no detailed plans of the proposed development had been agreed, nor had the amount of rent nor the terms of the building lease been agreed.

It is irrelevant that the building lease is only to be granted for a fairly short term. In *Spook Erection Ltd v British Railways Board* [1988] EGLR 76, CA, the term was for 99 years, but in *Turner v Wandsworth London Borough Council* (1994) 25 EG 148, CA it was only four years. In both cases intention had been proved. The essence of these cases is that the landlord retains some control via the building lease over the development. Consequently, it will not be sufficient for a landlord to show that it intends to sell the property to a developer once planning permission had been obtained as the landlord would not then have control over the future development (*Edwards v Thompson*).

8.6.2.7 When must the works be carried out?

The wording of ground (f) provides that the works must be carried out 'on the termination of the current tenancy'. In *London Hilton Jewellers Ltd v Hilton International Hotels Ltd* [1990] 1 EGLR 112, CA, it was held that this must mean within a reasonable time from the date of the termination of the tenancy. What is a reasonable time after termination will be a question of fact in each case. In this particular case a 'month or so' was not felt to be unreasonably long. In *Livestock Underwriting Agency Ltd v Corbett and Newson Ltd* (1955) 165 EG 469, it was held that it would be sufficient if the works were started within three months of the termination of the current tenancy as the court felt that a reasonable view should be taken, rather than requiring the landlord to start the works 'the moment other people walk out'.

In practice, the reference to 'termination of the current tenancy' will include any continuation tenancy under s 64 of the

1954 Act, as the landlord must be entitled to possession before the works can be carried out. If either party lodges an appeal, the date of termination may not be ascertainable until the appeal has been resolved. The Court of Appeal has criticised the use of the right to appeal where it is clearly a delaying tactic (*AJA Smith Transport Ltd v British Railways Board* (1980) 257 EG 1257, CA).

8.6.2.8 The use of undertakings

A landlord may give an undertaking to the court to carry out the proposed works once possession has been obtained, as in *Betty's Cafés Ltd v Phillips Furnishing Stores Ltd* (see also *Espresso Coffee Machine Co Ltd v Guardian Assurance Co Ltd* [1959] 1 All ER 458, CA). Such an undertaking will not, in itself, be sufficient to prove the necessary intention but will go some way towards this and, coupled with other evidence, can amount to proof, as with for example a board resolution as in *Betty's Cafés Ltd v Phillips Furnishing Stores Ltd*. In *London Hilton Jewellers Ltd v Hilton International Hotels Ltd,* an undertaking was the decisive factor in the landlord's case. In all these cases the courts agreed that the undertakings 'compelled fixity of intention'.

8.6.2.9 Motive

If the landlord's intention to carry out ground (f) works is genuine, his motive is irrelevant. Thus, in *Fisher v Taylors Furnishing Stores Ltd* [1956] 2 All ER 78, CA, where the landlords intended to demolish the premises, rebuild on the site and occupy the new buildings for their business, a new lease was refused as the landlords had satisfied ground (f) by showing a genuine intention to demolish the premises, notwithstanding that they also intended to occupy the newly constructed premises for their business. Parker LJ said (at 84):

> Thus, if the ground specified in para (f) is proved to the satisfaction of the court, it matters not to what use the landlord ultimately intends to put the holding. He may intend to let it when the work is done to a third party; he may intend ultimately to occupy it himself for his own business; or he may not have made up his mind at all. To suggest that, if his intention is ultimately to occupy it himself and he cannot by reason of s 30(2) rely on para (g), he is thereby debarred from relying on para (f), is to apply a proviso to the operation of para (f) which is not there and for which there is no warrant.

Another example of this principle is *Turner v Wandsworth London Borough Council* (1994) 25 EG 148, CA, where the landlord agreed with an adjoining owner that that owner would carry out the ground (f) works and, once completed, would be granted a four-year lease of the property. The landlord in fact wanted eventually to sell the property. The landlord's motive in ultimately wishing to sell was irrelevant as it had a genuine intention to carry out ground (f) works.

It therefore follows that, if the landlord obtains possession using ground (f) and then has a change of mind and decides not to carry out the works, the tenant has no recourse, provided that the landlord's change of mind is an honest one (*Fisher v Taylors Furnishing Stores Ltd*).

8.6.3   The types of works within ground (f)

The second hurdle which a landlord must overcome in order to succeed under this ground is to prove that the works which are intended to be carried out fall within those prescribed by the ground. The works which fall within ground (f) may be categorised as follows:

(a) demolition of the whole of the premises comprised in the holding;

(b) reconstruction of the whole of the premises comprised in the holding;

(c) demolition of a substantial part of the premises comprised in the holding;

(d) reconstruction of a substantial part of the premises comprised in the holding;

(e) substantial work of construction on the holding;

(f) substantial work of construction on part of the holding.

In order to succeed, a landlord merely has to establish that the works fall within one of the categories in this list (*Turner v Wandsworth London Borough Council*).

8.6.3.1 *Demolition of the whole of the premises comprised in the holding*

In this case the landlord must intend to demolish the whole of the premises comprised in the holding. This necessarily means that there must be some property on the holding which is capable of being demolished, eg, a building or a wall. In *Houseleys Ltd v Bloomer-Holt Ltd* [1966] 2 All ER 966, CA, the demolition of a wall and a garage, being the only objects on the premises, was sufficient (see also *Turner v Wandsworth London Borough Council*). However, a landlord will not succeed where the land is bare with no buildings on it (*Coppin v Bruce-Smith*). Premises comprising an 'eggshell', ie, premises which consist only of the internal skin of the part of the building occupied by the tenant and none of the structural parts of the building, are capable of being demolished (*Pumperninks of Piccadilly Ltd v Land Securities plc* [2002] EWCA Civ 621; [2002] 3 All ER 609, CA).

A tenant may pre-empt a landlord from using this ground by carrying out, before the hearing, the works which the landlord is proposing to carry out. Obviously this tactic will only be available to the tenant where it has a right to carry out the works under the terms of its current tenancy. If the works are carried out there will then be nothing for the landlord to demolish at the date of the hearing. Consequently, the landlord will then not succeed under this ground and the tenant will be entitled to a new tenancy.

8.6.3.2 Reconstruction of the whole of the premises comprised in the holding

'Reconstruct' means that the landlord must intend a substantial interference with the structure of the premises, followed by the rebuilding of the parts which have been interfered with (*Percy E Cadle and Co Ltd v Jacmarch Properties Ltd* [1957] 1 All ER 148, CA; *Romulus Trading Co Ltd v Henry Smith's Charity Trustees* [1990] 2 EGLR 75, CA). This goes further than merely changing the identity of the premises, as in *Percy E Cadle and Co Ltd v Jacmarch Properties Ltd*, where the landlord proposed to convert a two-storey property into one self-contained unit, install new staircases, a new floor and new lavatories, but was said in *Cook v Mott* (1961) 178 EG 637, CA, to involve demolition followed by rebuilding. The interference need not be limited to exterior or load-bearing walls (*Graysim Holdings v P & O Property Holdings* [1993] 1 EGLR 96).

8.6.3.3 Demolition of a substantial part of the premises comprised in the holding

Where the landlord does not intend to demolish the whole of the premises, but rather only a part of them, it must be proved that the part to be demolished is 'substantial'. This will ultimately be a question of fact for the court to decide.

In *Atkinson v Bettison* [1953] 3 All ER 340, CA, the removal and replacement of the shop front and the removal of a rear wall did not fall within this ground.

In *Marazzi v Global Grange Ltd* [2002] EWHC 3010 (Ch); [2003] 2 EGLR 42 works to upgrade a two-star hotel into a four-star hotel included removal of a basement wall, installation of a new lift, removal of part of the roof, restoration of the staircase and opening up an access in a party wall. The total cost of the works was approximately £2 million and they would take 12 months to complete. The landlord was unsuccessful in relying on ground (f) as, whilst the works amounted to 'demolition and reconstruction', they would not affect a 'substantial part of the premises'. However, in *Ivorygrove Ltd v Global Grange Ltd* [2003] EWHC 1409 (Ch); [2003] 1 WLR 2090, where the facts were very similar to *Marazzi*, the court held that the landlord came within the ground.

8.6.3.4 Reconstruction of a substantial part of the premises comprised in the holding

The same considerations as to whether the part of the premises in question is substantial apply as discussed in 8.6.3.3.

8.6.3.5 Substantial work of construction on the holding

Two questions arise here. First, is the work one of construction and, secondly, is the work substantial?

In answering the first question it must be noted that there is no definition in the 1954 Act of 'construction'. In *Barth v Pritchard* [1990] 1 EGLR 109, CA, the Court of Appeal said that whether or not works fall within 'construction' will depend on the facts of each case and that what is required is some form of building on the premises which involves the structure. In that case, the installation of wooden partitions did not fall within the definition. The following guidance from Stocker LJ (at 111) is useful:

One of the difficulties ... is that there is no statutory definition of the word 'construction' and dictionary definitions such as 'to build up', 'compile', 'put together the parts of' (*Chambers*) or 'to make or form by fitting the parts together', 'to frame, build, erect' (*Shorter Oxford*) beg rather than resolve the problem. A bookcase, purpose built *in situ*, would fall within these definitions, but it is not contended that to erect such a bookcase would constitute construction for the purpose of section 30(1)(f) ... I must consider that whether or not the works fall within the definition of 'construction' must depend upon the facts in each case in which the problem falls to be considered ... If it is necessary to decide whether or not in any given case it is necessary for works to involve directly the structure of the building in some way, my own view would be that this is implicit in the generality of section 30(1)(f). In other words, that some form of building upon the premises which involves the structure is required. I would not consider wooden partitions, however extensive, as falling within the definition of 'construction', but the situation would have to be reviewed in accordance with the facts of any given case.

It has been suggested that putting down a sufficient area of concrete may be a substantial work of construction (*Houseleys Ltd v Bloomer-Holt Ltd*). Landscaping works will not be a substantial work of construction; in *Botterill v Bedfordshire County Council* [1985] EGLR 82, CA, infilling a former brick pit and putting top soil on as a cover was not a work of construction.

It is clear that the Court of Appeal will not interfere with the trial judge's decision as to what constitutes 'construction', unless he is clearly wrong (*Romulus Trading Co Ltd v Henry Smith's Charity Trustees*).

The second question to be resolved is whether the works of construction amount to substantial works of construction. The answer to this question will be a matter of fact and degree for the court to decide (*Atkinson v Bettison*). In considering the meaning of 'substantial' it has been said that, 'One of the primary meanings of the word is equivalent to considerable, solid or big. It is in this sense that we speak of a substantial fortune, a substantial meal, a substantial man, a substantial argument or ground of defence. Applying the word in this sense, it must be left to the discretion of the judge of fact to decide as best he can according to the circumstances in each case, the onus being on the landlord' (*per* Viscount Simon (at 11) in *Palser v Grinling*, and used by Hodson LJ in *Atkinson v*

Bettison). It will therefore always be a question of fact and degree as to whether or not the works of construction amount to substantial works of construction. In considering this, the court must not take into account any works which the landlord may be entitled to carry out under the terms of the lease (*Romulus Trading Co Ltd v Henry Smith's Charity Trustees*). Additionally, if none of the individual works comprising the works proposed by the landlord amount in themselves to a works of construction, the proposed works cannot amount to substantial works of construction (*Barth v Pritchard*).

By way of illustrating the way in which the court has applied this test of fact and degree, the following examples are useful:

(a) *Percy E Cadle and Co Ltd v Jacmarch Properties Ltd*: installing a wooden staircase so that three floors of a building would be made into a self-contained unit, installing a better floor in the basement, eliminating the sources of damp in the basement and constructing new toilets on a floor of the building which was not within the lease. It was held that these works did not amount to substantial works of construction.

(b) *Joel v Swaddle* [1957] 3 All ER 325, CA: the landlord intended to convert the whole of the ground floor and a yard into one enclosed area by taking away partition walls and the back wall, putting in steel girders and pillars to support the upstairs, lowering the floor by eight inches and putting in a new front. It was held that these works amounted to substantial works of construction.

(c) *Bewlay (Tobacconists) Ltd v British Bata Shoe Co Ltd* [1958] 3 All ER 652, CA: amalgamating two shops into one by removing three-quarters of the dividing wall, putting in a new shop front, and carrying out a small amount of demolition and reconstruction of the lavatory accommodation. It was held that these works amounted to substantial works of construction.

(d) *Morar v Chauhan* [1985] 3 All ER 493, CA: the building of an extension at a cost of £7,500/£8,000 which would take three and a half to four months was held to amount to substantial works of construction.

(e) *Blackburn v Hussain* [1988] 1 EGLR 77, CA: it was held that the following works amounted to substantial works of construction, namely demolishing the walls bounding two premises in order to convert them into one, demolishing and replacing the shop fronts, removing the lavatories and installing a staircase, as well as generally refurbishing the premises.

(f) *Barth v Prichard*: works comprising blocking up the access from an adjoining building, rewiring, resiting of toilets to another floor, constructing new toilet cubicles, providing a new gas boiler and constructing a boiler room did not amount to substantial works of construction.

8.6.3.6 *Substantial work of construction on part of the holding*

There is no requirement for the part of the holding in question to amount to a substantial part. It is only the work of construction which must be substantial. The same test for deciding whether the work is substantial applies as discussed in 8.6.3.5.

8.6.4   Entitlement to carry out the works

A landlord must show that it cannot reasonably carry out the works without obtaining possession of the holding. In this context 'possession' means legal possession rather than physical possession (*Heath v Drown* [1972] 2 All ER 561, HL). This means that if the lease includes a reservation of sufficient rights in favour of the landlord to allow him to carry out the works, eg, a right to enter to carry out improvements and alterations, the landlord will not succeed under ground (f). In *Heath v Drown*, the lease reserved a right for the landlord to enter to repair and it was held that as this right would be included in any new tenancy it was not reasonably necessary for the landlord to obtain possession of the holding (see also *Price v Esso Petroleum Co* [1980] 2 EGLR 58, CA). This principle will not, however, apply where the landlord intends to carry out works on completion of which the tenant would not be able to carry on its business in the reconstructed premises and the lease contains sufficient rights to allow the landlord to carry out the works; in such a case the landlord will need to obtain legal possession in order to carry out the works (*Leathwoods v Total Oil (Great Britain) Ltd* [1985] 2 EGLR 237, CA).

8.6.5   Section 31A of the 1954 Act

To prevent the landlord from gaining possession where he only intends to carry out work on part of the premises, or where the work will be carried out relatively quickly, the tenant has a defence under s 31A(1) of the 1954 Act. This provides that the court cannot hold that the landlord could not reasonably carry out the demolition or other work without obtaining possession if:

(a) the tenant agrees to the inclusion in the terms of the new tenancy of terms giving the landlord access and other facilities for carrying out the work intended and, given that access and those facilities, the landlord could reasonably carry out the work without obtaining possession of the holding and without interfering to a substantial extent or for a substantial time with the use of the holding for the purposes of the business carried on by the tenant; or

(b) the tenant is willing to accept a tenancy of an economically separable part of the holding and either para (a) of this section is satisfied with respect to that part or possession of the remainder of the holding would be reasonably sufficient to enable the landlord to carry out the intended work.

There are thus two limbs, each of which can amount to a defence (*Romulus Trading Co Ltd v Henry Smith's Charity Trustees (No 2)* (1991) 11 EG 112).

8.6.5.1 Grant of facilities

To succeed under this ground, the court cannot hold that the landlord could not reasonably carry out the demolition or other work without obtaining possession if:

> ... the tenant agrees to the inclusion in the terms of the new tenancy of terms giving the landlord access and other facilities for carrying out the work intended and, given that access to those facilities, the landlord could reasonably carry out the work without obtaining possession of the holding and without interfering to a substantial extent or for a substantial time with the use of the holding for the purposes of the business carried on by the tenant (s 31A(1)(a) of the 1954 Act).

A tenant will only need to rely on this limb if the lease does not include a reservation of sufficient rights in favour of the landlord to allow him to carry out the works. In *Heath v Drown*, the lease reserved a right for the landlord to enter to repair and it was held that, as this right would be included in any new tenancy, s 31A of the 1954 Act had no relevance as the landlord could carry out the works under this right (see also *Price v Esso Petroleum Co*).

Where a tenant seeks to rely on s 31A of the 1954 Act, the court must start by considering the works which the landlord intends to carry out. There is no power for the court to consider whether the landlord should be carrying out different works. In *The Decca Navigator Co Ltd v Greater London Council* [1974] 1 All ER 1178, CA Lord Denning MR said (at 1180):

> The county court judge put it well when he said: '... the words "the intended work" in s 31A mean the work which the landlord in fact intends to do, and leave no room for a tenant to argue, or the court to decide, that it would be in his interests, or the interests of the tenant, or the interests of the public generally, or that it would be sensible for him to achieve his purpose by doing some different work.'

The court is entitled to look beyond the landlord's intended works and if, after the works have been completed, the premises would not exist precisely as they had before, then that would be relevant in considering whether the works could be carried out without obtaining possession. Thus, where eggshell premises were to be demolished, the tenant could not rely on s 31A(1)(a) of the 1954 Act as, once demolished, the premises would be unusable for the purpose of the tenant's business (*Pumperninks of Piccadilly Ltd v Land Securities plc*).

The court must then decide whether any of the works can be carried out under any rights reserved to the landlord in the lease and, if any of the works can be carried out, then these must be eliminated from its considerations. The next question for the court is whether the remaining works can reasonably be carried out without interfering to a substantial extent or for a substantial time with the use of the holding. This is a question of fact and degree (*Price v Esso Petroleum Co; Cerex Jewels Ltd v Peachey Property Corp plc* [1986] 2 EGLR 65, CA). The word 'or' is construed in this context as 'and' (*Cerex Jewels Ltd v Peachey Property Corp plc*).

The interference which must be considered is the interference with the tenant's use of the holding for its business purposes, rather than any potential interference with the business itself or the goodwill, and so a tenant cannot rely on s 31A of the 1954 Act if it intends to leave whilst the works are carried out and then return with goodwill intact (*Redfern v Reeves* [1978] 2 EGLR 52, CA).

Examples of the courts' interpretation of 'substantial interference' include:

(a) *Redfern v Reeves* [1978] 2 EGLR 52, CA: it was 'substantial interference' where the works would have excluded the tenant for between two and four months;

(b) *Price v Esso Petroleum Co*: it was 'substantial interference' where the works would have excluded the tenant for 16 weeks;

(c) *Cerex Jewels Ltd v Peachey Property Corporation plc*: it was not 'substantial interference' where the works would have excluded the tenant for two weeks;

(d) *Blackburn v Hussain*: it was 'substantial interference' where the works would have interfered with the tenant's business (which was a café) for 12 weeks;

(e) *Graysim Holdings v P & O Property Holdings*: it was 'substantial interference' where the works would have excluded the tenant for eight weeks (this point was not appealed).

8.6.5.2 New tenancy of part of the holding

The court cannot hold that the landlord could not reasonably carry out the demolition or other work without obtaining possession if:

> ... the tenant is willing to accept a tenancy of an economically separable part of the holding and either [s 31A(1)(a) of the 1954 Act] is satisfied with respect to that part or possession of the remainder of the holding would be reasonably sufficient to enable the landlord to carry out the intended work (s 31A(1)(b) of the 1954 Act).

The tenant must be willing to accept a tenancy of an economically separable part of the holding. A part of the holding will be an economically separable part if, and only if, the aggregate of the rents which, after the completion of the intended work, would be reasonably obtainable on separate lettings of that part and the remainder of the premises affected by or resulting from the work would not be substantially less than the rent which would then be reasonably obtainable on a letting of those premises as a whole (s 31A(2) of the 1954 Act).

If the part of the holding is held to be economically separable, then the tenant must show that it is willing to accept a tenancy of an economically separable part of the holding and either:

(a) it agrees to the inclusion in the terms of the new tenancy of the economically separable part of terms giving the landlord access and other facilities for carrying out the work intended and, given that access and those facilities, the landlord could reasonably carry out the work without obtaining possession of the economically separable part and without interfering to a substantial extent or for a substantial time with the use of the economically separable part for the purposes of the business carried on by the tenant; or

(b) the landlord is able reasonably to carry out the works without being granted facilities or access over the economically separable part.

If the tenant succeeds under s 31A(1)(b) of the 1954 Act, the order for the new tenancy will be only of the economically separable part (s 32(1A) of the 1954 Act).

8.6.6   Compensation

If the landlord succeeds under this ground, the tenant will be entitled to compensation (see Chapter 10).

8.6.7   Practical issues – acting for the landlord

A landlord relying on ground (f) will need to prove, first, that it has the necessary intention (see 8.6.2) and, secondly, that the proposed works fall within those included in ground (f) (see 8.6.3).

Intention will be proved by oral evidence from the landlord or, in the case of a corporation, by a board resolution. In addition, the landlord should adduce evidence of:

(a) the history of the proposed development and its financial viability;

(b) the grant of planning permission, or the application for planning permission and the progress which has been made, or the fact that planning permission is not required;

(c) any other permissions or consents which may be required, eg consent under restrictive covenants, rights of access, consents of any superior landlord;

(d) the financial arrangements; and

(e) building contracts, building leases, etc.

Where the tenant is relying on a defence under s 31A of the 1954 Act, a landlord will need to put forward evidence rebutting the tenant's argument that s 31A of the 1954 Act should apply, eg, the tenant's proposals will make the works more expensive, or will mean that they will take longer to complete.

8.6.8   Practical issues – acting for the tenant

A tenant will need to decide whether or not to rely on s 31A of the 1954 Act. If it does so rely then, if it is relying on s 31A(1)(a), evidence must be put forward to show that the access and facilities offered to the landlord will allow it to carry out the work reasonably without obtaining possession of the holding and without interfering to a substantial extent or for a substantial time with the use of the holding for the purposes of the business carried on by the tenant. If the tenant is relying on s 31A(1)(b), the tenant will need to show by way of expert evidence that it is willing to accept a tenancy of an economically separable part of the holding and either:

(a) it agrees to the inclusion in the terms of the new tenancy of the economically separable part of terms giving the landlord access and other facilities for carrying out the work intended and, given that access and those facilities, the landlord could reasonably carry out the work without obtaining possession of the economically separable part and without interfering to a substantial extent or for a substantial time with the use of the economically separable part for the purposes of the business carried on by the tenant; or

(b) the landlord is able reasonably to carry out the works without being granted facilities or access over the economically separable part.

8.7   GROUND (G) – OCCUPATION BY THE LANDLORD

8.7.1   Section 30(1)(g)

Subject as hereinafter provided, that on the termination of the current tenancy the landlord intends to occupy the holding for the purposes, or partly for the purposes, of a business to be carried on by him therein, or as his residence.

There is no discretion under this ground so, once the landlord has established that it applies, the court must refuse the grant of a new tenancy.

8.7.2   Intention to occupy

The landlord must intend to occupy the premises either for business purposes, or as his residence. The meaning of the word 'intends' for the purposes of this ground is the same as that required under ground (f) (see 8.6.2). The landlord must therefore prove that it has a firm and settled intention to occupy and that there is a reasonable prospect of being able to implement this (see 8.6.2.3). Practically speaking this means that a court may have to decide whether a business, which may not yet exist, is genuinely intended. This will ultimately be a question of fact for the court and regard will be taken of whether matters such as any relevant planning permission, any necessary consents and finance have been obtained.

Where the landlord requires planning permission, eg, for change of use, before it can take up occupation, it is not necessary for such permission to have been granted by the time of the hearing. The test is an objective one of whether or not the landlord has a reasonable prospect of obtaining planning permission. This test was laid down by the Court of Appeal in *Gregson v Cyril Lord* [1962] 3 All ER 907 and was set out by Upjohn LJ (at 911) as follows:

> The question whether the landlords intend to occupy the premises is primarily one of fact, but the authorities establish that to prove such intention, the landlords must prove two things. First, a genuine *bona fide* intention on the part of the landlords that they intend to occupy the premises for their own purposes ... Secondly, the landlords must prove that in point of possibility they have a reasonable prospect of being able to bring about this occupation by their own act of volition.

This was approved by the House of Lords in *City of Westminster v British Waterways Board* [1984] 3 All ER 737, HL where the landlord sought possession of premises let to the tenant council. The tenant indicated that it would refuse any planning permission applied for by the landlord for its intended use. The House of Lords decided that the landlord had at least a reasonable prospect of success if planning permission was applied for and refused the grant of a new tenancy.

In *Gatwick Parking Service Ltd v Sargent* it was held that it was enough for a landlord to show a real, as opposed to a fanciful, prospect of obtaining the necessary planning permission.

A landlord is merely required to satisfy the court of its intention; it is not necessary for it to prove that either its plans are desirable or that they are the foundation of long-term business success. In *Dolgellau Golf Club v Hett*, the tenant sought a new lease of a nine-hole golf course. The landlord had obtained planning permission for adjoining land to build his own nine-hole golf course, and he intended to amalgamate the two to create an 18-hole golf course. The landlord succeeded, even though the tenant produced evidence that such a course could not be profitable, and the landlord was unable to produce details of his proposals. All that the landlord was required to demonstrate was an intention to start the business. Its potential profitability or success was irrelevant. Auld LJ said (at 79):

> ... the issue as to a landlord's entitlement to rely, under section 30(1)(g), on his intention to occupy demised land on the termination of a tenancy for the purpose of establishing a business is one of intention, and its reasonable practicability, to start such a business, not of the probability of achieving its start or its likely success once established. It is not an incident of the statutory formula nor of the present judicial gloss on it that a landlord, in seeking to satisfy the court of the reality of his intention, should be subjected to minute examination of his finances with a view to determining the financial viability and durability of the business he intends to establish. The court is not there to police a landlord's entitlement to recover possession of his own property by examining the financial wisdom of his genuinely held plans for it.

There is no requirement that the court consider the two limbs of the test laid down by *Gregson v Cyril Lord* in the order they were laid down, and it is open to the court to consider the second limb first. In *Zarvos v Pradhan* [2003] EWCA Civ 208; [2003] 2 P

& CR 9, CA, the trial judge's decision that the landlord did not have a reasonable prospect of realising his intention to run a business from the premises was upheld despite the judge not considering the genuineness of the landlord's intention under the first limb of the test.

In *Cox v Binfield* [1989] 1 EGLR 97, CA, the landlady succeeded under ground (g) as her plans were not so unrealistic as not to be genuine, even though they were said to be ill-thought out and likely to fail. The case concerned an elderly lady and her husband, who lived over a ground-floor café let by the landlady on a seven-year lease. The landlady sought to occupy it under ground (g), partly as additional living accommodation and partly to run a small café. Both the couple were pensioners, the husband was infirm and they had little experience of catering. Evidence was put forward to show that they might have difficulties in financing the equipment and the running of the café and that the financial advantages of the venture were doubtful. Despite this, the landlady succeeded as her intention was genuine.

The landlord's intention may be proved by the landlord giving an undertaking to the court to occupy the holding 'for the purposes, or partly for the purposes of a business to be carried on by him therein, or as his residence'. Such an undertaking was accepted by the court in *Espresso Coffee Machine Co Ltd v Guardian Assurance Co Ltd* and *Chez Gérard Ltd v Greene Ltd* (1983) 268 EG 575, CA. In *London Hilton Jewellers Ltd v Hilton International Hotels Ltd*, such an undertaking was held to be decisive. However, such an undertaking will not be acceptable to the court where the landlord's intention is not firm and settled (see *Lightcliffe and District Cricket and Lawn Tennis Club v Walton* [1978] 1 EGLR 35, CA). Following the House of Lords decision in *Co-operative Insurance Society Ltd v Argyll Stores (Holdings) Ltd* [1997] 3 All ER 297, CA the question must now arise as to whether such an undertaking, which is in effect an undertaking to carry on business, will be accepted by the court as, in this case, the House of Lords refused to grant specific performance of a positive obligation in a lease to use the premises as a supermarket and to keep them open during business hours. The reason for the refusal was that it was settled practice not to make such an order based on sound sense, as such an order required constant supervision, was only enforceable by the quasi-criminal procedure of punishment for contempt and might cause injustice by allowing the landlord to enrich itself at the tenant's expense if the tenant was forced to run a business at a loss. Notwithstanding this, it is suggested that if an undertaking to occupy is given by the landlord it may still be acceptable to the court as it goes to intention rather than enforceability.

The landlord must intend to occupy the holding within a reasonable time after the termination of the current tenancy (*Method Developments Ltd v Jones* [1971] 1 All ER 1027, CA). Consequently, if the landlord intends to carry out alterations to the holding before it goes into occupation, can it rely on ground (g)? In *Nursey v P Currie (Dartford) Ltd* [1959] 1 All ER 497, CA the landlord did not succeed under ground (g) where it intended to demolish the buildings on the holding, build new ones and then occupy these. It was held that an intention to occupy the holding meant an intention to occupy the property as described in the parcels clause of the lease (*per* Willmer LJ). This decision has subsequently been distinguished in every case on this point, and so should not be relied upon now. In the following cases the landlord succeeded under ground (g):

(a) *Method Developments Ltd v Jones*: the landlord intended to occupy most of the holding, but with a different partitioning layout;

(b) *Cam Gears Ltd v Cunningham* [1981] 2 All ER 560, CA: the landlord intended to incorporate the land into its business and to build on it a workshop, offices and inspection pits;

(c) *Leathwoods v Total Oil Great Britain*: the landlord intended to demolish the premises, which was a petrol filling station, and build a new petrol filling station which it intended to occupy;

(d) *JW Thornton Ltd v Blacks Leisure Group plc* [1986] 2 EGLR 61, CA: the landlord, which occupied the adjoining shop to the tenant's, intended to remove the dividing walls and turn both shops into one which it then intended to occupy.

In any event, it may well be the case that *Nursey v P Currie (Dartford) Ltd* was decided *per incuriam*, as the court did not consider the decision in *McKenna v Porter Motors* [1956] AC 688, PC, where, in considering a similar provision, the Privy Council agreed that a landlord could take occupation, demolish the buildings and build others which would then be occupied, as the landlord would be occupying the premises if he occupied the land and such buildings as from time to time are situated on that land.

There is no requirement for the landlord to show that he intends to occupy the holding for any length of time and it may even be that, shortly after taking occupation, the landlord sells the holding. In *Willis v Association of Universities of the British Commonwealth* [1964] 2 All ER 39, CA, Lord Denning MR said (at 43):

> Section 30(1)(g) of the Landlord and Tenant Act, 1954, does not say for how long the landlord must intend to occupy himself, and the court must fill the gap. It seems to me that, in some cases, even a short time may suffice. Take the case where the landlord intends to occupy the premises and to carry on business himself there for six months, and then transfer the business to his son as a family arrangement. I should have thought that the father would have sufficient intention to satisfy s 30(1)(g). However, suppose the intention was after six months to transfer to a purchaser for cash, I should not expect that intention to suffice. Just as a purchaser within the previous five years cannot defeat the tenant (see s 30(2) of the Act of 1954) so, also, a purchaser shortly afterwards should not be able to defeat him. The matters that influence me are these: It is open to the landlord to complete the transfer before the day of hearing, in which case it is the successor's intention which counts – see s 30(1)(g) – save only that, if that successor falls foul of s 30(2), his intention does not count. Hence I would say that, if the landlord intends to occupy the premises and carry on business himself there for a time, and then to transfer to a successor, his intention is sufficient to satisfy s (1)(g), unless the intended transfer is one which, if it had been made before the hearing, would have fallen within s 30(2) so as to render s 30(1)(g) unavailable.

8.7.3   Occupation of the holding

The landlord must intend to occupy the holding 'for the purposes, or partly for the purposes of a business to be carried on by him therein, or as his residence'.

The occupation for business purposes need not be by the landlord personally. It will be sufficient if the occupation is to be by a partnership of which the landlord is a partner (*Re Crowhurst Park* [1974] 1 All ER 991; *Skeet v Powell-Sheddon* [1988] 40 EG 116, CA) or through a management company (*Teesside Indoor Bowls Ltd v Stockton-on-Tees Borough Council* [1990] 2 EGLR 87, CA).

The landlord does not have to show that it intends to make physical use of the entire premises. In *Method Developments Ltd v Jones*, it was held to be sufficient for the landlord to prove it intended to occupy part of the holding for business purposes.

It is suggested that where there are two or more joint landlords, and not all of them intend to occupy, ground (g) will not be satisfied. This is based on the decision in *Wetherall & Co Ltd v Stone* [1950] 2 All ER 1209, CA, which related to similar wording contained in s 5(3)(b) of the Landlord and Tenant Act 1927.

8.7.3.1 Occupation by beneficiaries

Where the landlord's interest is held on trust, the intention of any beneficiary to occupy will be sufficient (s 41(2) of the 1954 Act). The occupation must be as beneficiary and so, in *Meyer v Riddick* [1990] 1 EGLR 107, CA, it was not sufficient where the trustees proposed to enter into a lease to two of themselves plus someone who had nothing to do with the trust.

It will be sufficient if the trustees intend to occupy themselves (*Morar v Chauhan* [1983] 3 All ER 493, CA).

8.7.3.2 Occupation by group companies

Where the landlord is a member of a group of companies, ground (g) will be satisfied where any member of the group intends to occupy for the purposes of a business to be carried on by that member of the group (s 42(3) of the 1954 Act).

8.7.3.3 Occupation by the landlord's company or a person controlling the landlord company

Where a landlord has a controlling interest in a company, the reference in ground (g) to the landlord is construed as a reference to the landlord or that company (s 30(1A) of the 1954 Act). The test for 'control' is contained in the definitions of 'company' and 'subsidiary' in ss 735 and s 736 of the Companies Act 1985.

Where the landlord is a company and a person has a controlling interest in the company, the reference in ground (g) to the landlord is construed as a reference to the landlord or that person (s 30(1B) of the 1954 Act). However, this will not apply if the controlling interest was acquired after the beginning of the period of five years which ends with the termination of the current tenancy, and at all times since the acquisition of the controlling interest the holding has been comprised in a tenancy or successive tenancies protected by the 1954 Act (s 30(2A) of the 1954 Act).

8.7.4   The five-year rule

A landlord may not use ground (g) where his interest, or an interest which has merged in that interest and, but for the merger, would be the interest of the landlord, was purchased or created after the beginning of the period of five years which ends with the termination of the current tenancy, and at all times since the purchase or creation of that interest the holding has been comprised in a tenancy or successive tenancies of the description specified in s 23(1) of the 1954 Act (s 30(2) of the 1954 Act). The effect of this provision is to prevent a person from purchasing the reversion and then recovering possession under ground (g) within the following five years, as Danckwerts LJ said in *Artemiou v Procopiou* [1965] 3 All ER 539, CA (at 543):

> The object of the subsection is clearly to prevent exploitation of tenants by landlords who acquire the reversion with the object of forthwith evicting the tenant on the expiration of his tenancy.

In order to discover whether the landlord is subject to the five-year rule, first 'the interest of the landlord' must be identified and then, using the date for the termination of the tenancy specified in either the s 25 notice or s 26 request, a period of five years must be counted back in order to see whether the landlord's interest was purchased or created before or after this date.

8.7.4.1   'Purchased'

The word 'purchased' means 'bought for money' (*HL Bolton (Engineering) Co Ltd v TJ Graham and Sons Ltd* [1956] 3 All ER 624, CA) and does not include:

(a) a transfer in consideration of an indemnity covenant (*HL Bolton (Engineering) Co Ltd v TJ Graham and Sons Ltd*); nor

(b) a lease surrendered by operation of law for no valuable consideration (*Frederick Lawrence Ltd v Freeman, Hardy & Willis* [1959] 3 All ER 77, CA).

The time at which the purchase takes place is the date of the exchange of the contracts (*HL Bolton (Engineering) Co Ltd v TJ Graham and Sons Ltd*).

8.7.4.2 'Created'

The word 'created' refers to the creation of the landlord's interest not his title, so where the landlord is a trustee it may rely on ground (g) where the trust is created or where the trustee or the beneficiaries have changed identity during the five-year period (*Morar v Chauhan*). If, however, it was the beneficiaries who wished to rely on ground (g), then the five-year period would run from the date of the creation of the trust. Where the landlord's interest is leasehold, it is created when the lease is executed, and not when the term begins (*Northcote Laundry Ltd v Frederick Donnelly Ltd* [1968] 1 WLR 562, CA), nor, if it is registrable at HM Land Registry, when it is so registered.

8.7.4.3 'The interest of the landlord'

The interest of the landlord is the interest of the landlord in the holding from the time when it originally arose by purchase or creation (*per* Danckwerts LJ in *Artemiou v Procopiou* at 544–45), and will usually be either a fee simple or an interest under a long lease. It can, however, be a series of successive leases (*Artemiou v Procopiou*), or an interest held first as a freehold and then subsequently as a lease or successive leases (*VCS Car Park Management Ltd v Regional Railways North East Ltd* [2000] 1 All ER 403, CA).

The landlord's interest is determined as at the date of the service of the s 25 notice. In case of the service of a s 26 request it is not clear whether the relevant date for determining the landlord's interest would be the date of the s 26 request or the date of the landlord's counternotice. In *Diploma Laundry Ltd v Surrey Timber Ltd* [1955] 2 All ER 922, CA, the court confirmed that it would be one of these dates, but it was unnecessary for the purposes of the case to decide which it would be.

8.7.5   The overlap of grounds (f) and (g)

Where the landlord intends to demolish the premises on the holding and then occupy the holding, can either or both of these grounds be relied upon?

In *Nursey v Currie* ground (g) was not established where the landlord intended to demolish the building on the holding and build a new one to occupy. This was because the landlord did not intend to occupy the 'holding' but new premises substituted in its place. This decision was distinguished in *Cam Gears Ltd v Cunningham*, where the landlord intended to build on part of the holding which comprised a vacant piece of land. The reasoning in this case was that the landlord was going to occupy the whole of the 'holding' and it was irrelevant that premises were to be built and occupied. Doubts about the correctness of the decision in *Nursey v Currie* were expressed by Salmon LJ in *Method Developments Ltd v Jones*. The matter was resolved by the Court of Appeal in *JW Thornton Ltd v Blacks Leisure Group plc*. Here, it was unreasonable to apply the decision in *Nursey v Currie* to the situation where the landlord only intended to remove two non-load-bearing partition walls. It did intend to occupy the holding.

8.7.6   Compensation

If the landlord succeeds under ground (g), the tenant will be entitled to compensation (see Chapter 10).

8.7.7   Practical issues – acting for the landlord

A landlord relying on ground (g) will need to prove that it intends to occupy the holding for the purposes, or partly for the purposes, of a business to be carried on by him therein, or as his residence. This will be done in a similar manner to that discussed in connection with ground (f) (see 8.6.2). Evidence should be adduced to show that the landlord can actually carry out its intention, eg, what business is going to be run from the premises, what steps have been taken or will be taken in order to reach that goal, details of finances, etc.

A landlord must also prove that s 30(2) of the 1954 Act (see 8.7.4) does not apply. This can be done by putting forward evidence of the landlord's title to the property.

8.7.8 Practical issues – acting for the tenant

A tenant should consider whether there is any evidence it can put forward to dispute the landlord's intention.

8.8 DISPOSAL OF THE APPLICATION

8.8.1 Dismissal of the tenant's application

Where the landlord establishes a ground of opposition, the court cannot make an order for a new tenancy and must dismiss the tenant's application (s 31(1) of the 1954 Act). If the tenant lodges an appeal against the court's decision which is unsuccessful, the tenancy will come to an end three months later, beginning on the date on which the appeal is finally disposed of (s 64 of the 1954 Act). An appeal should not be used merely as a delaying tactic (*AJA Smith Transport Ltd v British Railways Board*). In *Shotley Point Marina (1986) Ltd v Spalding* [1997] 1 EGLR 233, CA, the appeal had not been properly lodged and so a subsequent application for leave to extend time was in fact an attempt to start an appeal. However, that application failed. If an extension had been granted, the appeal would have then existed and the tenancy would have ended on the final disposal of that appeal.

The tenant's application will also be dismissed where the tenancy ceases to be one to which the 1954 Act applies or where the application is dismissed for want of prosecution.

If the tenant is refused a new tenancy because the landlord establishes any of grounds (e), (f) or (g) of s 30(1) of the 1954 Act, the court order should state the grounds on which the court has refused the new tenancy, as this will be required for the tenant's compensation claim; otherwise, an application will have to be made to the court for a certificate to that effect.

8.8.2 Near miss cases

If the landlord opposes the grant of a new tenancy or applies for an order for the termination of the tenancy without the grant of a new tenancy and is relying on grounds (d), (e) and/or (f) of s 30(1) of the 1954 Act, but is unable to prove any of those ground(s) at the time of the hearing but can show that he would have been able to if the date specified in the s 25 notice or s 26 request had been not more than one year later than the date which was actually specified, then the court must refuse the tenant's application for a new tenancy and must make a declaration specifying the later date and the ground(s) of opposition which would have been satisfied on that later date (s 31(2) of the 1954 Act).

The effect of such a declaration is that the tenancy will then come to an end under s 64 of the 1954 Act. The tenant does, however, have the right within 14 days of the making of the declaration to ask the court to substitute the later date for the date specified in the notice. The tenancy will then continue until that later date.

Section 31(2) was applied in *Accountancy Personnel Ltd v Salters' Company* (1972) 222 EG 1589, CA, where the court granted a six-month tenancy to allow the landlord to demolish and reconstruct the premises once planning permission had been obtained. This was subsequently extended for a further three months by the Court of Appeal in the light of new information concerning the landlord's application for planning permission.

8.8.3   Where a new tenancy is granted

If the landlord is not successful in opposing the tenant's application for a new tenancy, the court must make an order for a new tenancy, the terms of which are discussed in Chapter 9.

8.8.4   Agreement between the parties

The landlord and the tenant may agree that the application for a new tenancy should be dismissed, struck out or granted.

8.9   COMPENSATION FOR MISREPRESENTATION

Where the court makes an order for the termination of the tenancy but does not make an order for the grant of a new tenancy, or the court refuses an order for the grant of a new tenancy, and it is subsequently made to appear to the court that the order was obtained, or the court induced to refuse the grant, by misrepresentation or the concealment of material facts, the court may order the landlord to pay to the tenant such sum as appears sufficient as compensation for damage or loss sustained by the tenant as the result of the order or refusal (s 37A(1) of the 1954 Act).

Compensation is also payable where the tenant is induced not to apply to the court for a new tenancy or to withdraw his application by reason of misrepresentation or the concealment of material facts (s 37A(2) of the 1954 Act).

It may be the case that, after the court hearing but before it obtains possession, the landlord changes its mind. Provided that this is a genuine change, there will be no entitlement to compensation as no misrepresentation to the court will have been made.

CHAPTER 9

THE TERMS OF THE NEW TENANCY

9.1   INTRODUCTION

Where an application has been made to the court for a new
tenancy, the court can either dismiss the application or grant the
tenant a new tenancy. Where an application for termination
without renewal has been made, the court can either grant the
application or order a new tenancy. A new tenancy will be
refused or a termination order granted where either:

(a) the landlord has successfully established one or more of the
grounds of opposition specified in the s 25 notice or in the
counternotice to the s 26 request (s 31(1) of the 1954 Act); or

(b) the court is precluded by s 31(2) of the 1954 Act from
ordering a new tenancy (see 8.8.2).

If neither of these two reasons for dismissal exists, then the
court must order the grant of a new tenancy 'comprising such
property, at such rent and on such other terms as are hereinafter
provided' (s 29(1) of the 1954 Act). The parties will normally
reach agreement on the terms of the new tenancy but, in the
absence of such agreement, there are provisions in ss 33–35
(inclusive) of the 1954 Act which set out the property, the
duration, the rent and the other terms of the new tenancy. The
following points should be noted in relation to any agreement
between the parties:

(a) such agreement must be in writing and be legally binding
(s 60(5) of the 1954 Act). An agreement made 'subject to
contract' will not be sufficient (*Derby v ITC* [1977] 2 All ER
890). The question of whether the agreement must comply
with s 2 of the Law of Property (Miscellaneous Provisions)
Act 1989 is not clear. It could be argued that s 2 does not
apply as the agreement is being made for the purposes of
the 1954 Act. However, the prudent course to adopt will be
to ensure that the agreement does comply with s 2. This will
then avoid any argument that the agreement is ineffective;

(b) it need not relate to all the terms of the tenancy. The parties
may only reach agreement on certain terms, those not
agreed will then be determined by the court.

Thus, the court may be called upon to determine all or just some of the provisions of the new tenancy. The relevant provisions to be considered are as follows:

(a) the property to be comprised in the new tenancy (s 32 of the 1954 Act);

(b) the duration of the new tenancy (s 33 of the 1954 Act);

(c) the rent to be paid under the new tenancy (s 34 of the 1954 Act);

(d) other terms, such as alienation, user, repairs, service charge, guarantors, costs (s 35 of the 1954 Act).

9.2   THE PROPERTY TO BE COMPRISED IN THE NEW TENANCY

In the absence of agreement between the parties, s 32 of the 1954 Act provides that the property to be comprised in the new tenancy will be 'the holding', ie, the parts of the property comprised in the original tenancy which the tenant is occupying or which are occupied by an employee of the tenant for the business which brings the tenancy within the 1954 Act. This means that the new tenancy will not include any parts of the property comprised in the original tenancy which have been sub-let or which are not used for the purposes of the tenant's business. In order to discover the extent of the holding it will be necessary to check the terms of the current tenancy; it may also be necessary to serve a notice requesting information under s 40 of the 1954 Act, as well as carrying out an inspection of the premises.

The tenant need not be occupying the whole of the premises for business purposes. It is sufficient that the tenant occupies part of the premises for business purposes and the remainder for some other purpose, eg residential use. The holding will then be made up of both parts which the tenant occupies. For this principle, the tenant can rely on the occupation of its employee unless the residential occupation is by an employee who is employed by the tenant in a different business from the one which brings the tenancy within the 1954 Act.

In deciding what comprises the holding, the court must have 'reference to the circumstances existing at the date of the order' (s 32(1) of the 1954 Act). In this context, 'the date of the order' means the date of the order for the new tenancy and not, for example, the date of the hearing of an appeal to the Court of Appeal on a preliminary matter (*I & H Caplan Ltd v Caplan (No 1)* [1961] 3 All ER 1174, HL).

9.2.1   Appurtenant rights

Where the current tenancy includes 'rights enjoyed by the tenant in connection with the holding', those rights are to be included in the new tenancy (s 32(3) of the 1954 Act). This will clearly include easements (eg, a right of access as in *Nevill Long and Co (Boards) Ltd v Firmenich and Co* (1984) 47 P & CR 59, CA). Section 32(3) of the 1954 Act cannot be used to enlarge the tenant's holding and so it will not include personal rights, such as a licence. Thus, a right to display advertisements on the side of a building is not a 'right' under s 32(3) of the 1954 Act (*Re No 1 Albemarle Street* [1959] 1 All ER 250); nor is a licence to park cars on adjacent land owned by the landlord (*G Orlick (Meat Products) Ltd v Hastings and Thanet Building Society* (1974) 29 P & CR 126, CA). However, it may be possible to include such terms under s 35 of the 1954 Act (see 9.5.1). The right must be being enjoyed by the tenant at the time of the hearing. Thus, in *Kirkwood v Johnson* (1979) 38 P & CR 392, CA, an unexercised option which had lapsed could not fall within the category of 'rights' for s 32(3) of the 1954 Act.

In *J Murphy and Sons Ltd v Railtrack plc* [2002] EWCA Civ 679; (2002) 1 P & CR 7, CA, it was held that the holding cannot be enlarged by implying new rights of access which the tenant had not previously enjoyed.

Section 32(3) of the 1954 Act also provides that the parties may agree, or the court may determine if agreement cannot be reached, that some of the rights which the tenant has been enjoying should not be part of the new tenancy.

9.2.2   Tenancies comprising property other than the holding

Where the tenancy is made up of other property as well as property occupied by the tenant, ie where part is sub-let, the landlord has the right to insist that any new tenancy granted must be a new tenancy of the whole of the premises comprised in the tenancy (s 32(2) of the 1954 Act). This right allows the landlord to continue to deal only with the tenant, rather than having to deal with different tenants, which may cause administrative headaches for the landlord. A landlord who wishes to take advantage of this right must say so in the answer (PD 56, para 3.12(2)(f)).

9.2.3   Economically separable part

The court has power under s 32(1A) of the 1954 Act to order a new tenancy in respect of that part of the premises of which the tenant has indicated that he was willing to accept a tenancy under s 31A(1)(b) of the 1954 Act (see 8.6.5.2).

9.3   DURATION OF THE NEW TENANCY

9.3.1   The length and commencement of the new tenancy

Section 33 of the 1954 Act provides that, in the absence of agreement between the parties, the length of the new tenancy will be such as the court considers is 'reasonable in all the circumstances'. The court can grant either a periodic tenancy, which in practice is not common, or a fixed term tenancy, in which case the length of the tenancy is subject to a maximum length of 15 years. The parties can, however, agree that the tenancy is to be longer than 15 years and this can be incorporated into the court order (*Janes (Gowns) Ltd v Harlow Development Corp* (1979) 253 EG 799). However, only a maximum of 15 years can be awarded by the court where there is no agreement.

The new tenancy will commence on the coming to an end of the current tenancy under s 64 of the 1954 Act (see 7.18) and not the date on which the contractual term ends, nor the date for termination specified in either the s 25 notice or s 26 request. It is, however, open for the parties to agree an earlier commencement date than the date provided for by s 64 of the 1954 Act. When making an order in respect of the length of the new tenancy, the court should provide that the term is to start on the final disposal of the application and finish on a specified date. This will then provide certainty for both parties as to when the new tenancy is to start and end.

9.3.2   The court's discretion

The court has a discretion under s 33 of the 1954 Act to order a new tenancy for any duration which it thinks is reasonable in all the circumstances, subject to a maximum term of 14 years. In exercising its discretion, the court will usually look first at the length of the current lease as in *Betty's Cafés Ltd v Phillips Furnishings Stores Ltd* [1957] 1 All ER 1, CA where a 14-year term was reduced to five years having regard to the duration of the tenant's previous leases, none of which had ever exceeded a term of eight years.

Other factors which the courts will have regard to when determining the length of the new tenancy include:

(a) the difficulty which a landlord may encounter in reletting the premises if a short term were to be granted. In *Re Sunlight House, Quay Street, Manchester* (1959) 173 EG 311, the tenant had occupied large office premises under a number of leases, the last of which had been for 10 years. The tenant proposed to relocate and so sought a six-month lease. The landlord proposed a three-year lease so as to give it time to relet the premises. The court decided to grant a term of a little over 10 months expiring on a quarter day in order to give the landlord sufficient time to relet the premises. The period which the landlord would have to relet the premises was also one of the factors considered by the court in *CBS (United Kingdom) Ltd v London Scottish Properties Ltd* [1985] 2 EGLR 125;

(b) the length of the continuation tenancy. In *London & Provincial Millinery Stores Ltd v Barclays Bank Ltd* [1962] 2 All ER 163, CA a 12-month term was granted following a four-year continuation tenancy in order to allow the tenant to find suitable alternative accommodation as the landlord had, just before the original hearing, contracted to sell the premises to a property developer and they were now ripe for redevelopment;

(c) the approaching retirement of the tenant. In *Becker v Hill Street Properties Ltd* [1990] 2 EGLR 78, CA, the tenant intended to retire in December 1993, and so the court granted him a new tenancy for a term to expire in December 1993. It was also relevant in this case that the tenant would have difficulty finding alternative accommodation, and that the landlord would need at least a year before it would be ready to redevelop;

(d) possible hardship to the landlord if a long term is granted. In *Upsons Ltd v E Robins Ltd* [1955] 3 All ER 348, CA, the tenant had a chain of approximately 250 shops throughout the country, whereas the landlord had only one other property which it occupied and of which the lease was due to come to an end. The landlord therefore wanted the tenant to be granted a short term lease so that it could then occupy the premises when it had to vacate its existing shop. The court was entitled to take into account the personal circumstances of the parties and to reach a decision to avoid excessive hardship to the landlord. A new tenancy for 12 months was granted;

(e) possible hardship to the tenant if a short term lease is granted. In *Amika Motors Ltd v Colebrook Holdings Ltd* [1981] 2 EGLR 62, CA, the tenant of premises which it used as a car showroom wanted a reasonably long lease as its franchise to sell motor cars required that it retained showrooms near to premises which it had bought and equipped as a repairs workshop. The landlord wished to redevelop the premises. The court decided that the best solution was to grant the tenant a five-year lease with an option for the landlord to break after three years;

(f) where the landlord wishes to occupy the premises under s 30(1)(g) of the 1954 Act but is prevented from doing so by the five-year rule in s 30(2) of the 1954 Act. In *Upsons Ltd v E Robins Ltd*, the landlord had purchased the reversion some four years and ten months before the hearing. The tenant was therefore granted a one-year tenancy. In this case, the fact that the landlord was a small company and the tenant a large retailer which would find alternative premises more easily than the landlord, was also relevant. In *Wig Creations Ltd v Colour Film Services Ltd* [1969] 20 P & CR 870, CA, the landlord had only owned the reversion for three years, and a new tenancy was granted for three years, the court taking into account that the tenant would have to find alternative premises. In this case, Lord Denning MR said (at 874) that the policy of the 1954 Act 'is to give a landlord (who has purchased more than five years ago) an absolute right to get possession for his own business: leaving it to the court to do what is reasonable if he has purchased *less* than five years ago. In doing what is reasonable, the five-year period is a factor which is permissible for the judge to take into account. The weight of it is for him';

(g) that the new tenancy will be subject to the 1954 Act. In *National Car Parks Ltd v The Paternoster Consortium Ltd* [1990] 1 EGLR 99, the landlord wished to redevelop the premises in the future along with other property and so a break clause was to be included in the new tenancy. The court bore in mind that the tenant would be protected by the 1954 Act and that if the landlord served a notice under the break clause it would need to establish ground (f) of s 30(1) of the 1954 Act before it would be entitled to possession and this was likely to take a considerable amount of time after the break notice had expired. The tenant would therefore be adequately protected by the 1954 Act if the landlord were given a general right to break on giving six months' notice of its intention to redevelop;

(h) the business needs of the tenant. In *CBS (United Kingdom) Ltd v London Scottish Properties Ltd*, the tenant was granted a 12-month term instead of the 14-year term which the landlord desired. One of the factors leading to this decision was the fact that the tenant was relocating its business and that it would have had difficulty in disposing of what would have been a 13-year lease. However, in *Charles Follett Ltd v Cabtell Investments Co Ltd* (1988) 55 P & CR 36, the court preferred to give more weight to the landlord's need for certainty, rather than give the tenant the flexibility to keep its future options open, and so a 10-year lease with a tenant's break clause was granted rather than the one-year term requested by the tenant. This decision was subsequently applied in *Ganton House Investments v Crossman Investments* [1995] 1 EGLR 239, where the court took the view that it was desirable to have stability in the market and that this would be best served by granting a long lease, in this case for 14 years, with a tenant's break clause;

(i) the possible future redevelopment of the property. In *Roehorn v Barry Corp* [1956] 2 All ER 742, CA, it was held that, as the land was ripe for development, the new tenancy should not impede this. A new tenancy was granted which included provision for it to be ended by six months' notice by either party. This was also a factor in *London & Provincial Millinery Stores Ltd v Barclays Bank Ltd, Amika Motors Ltd v Colebrook Holdings Ltd* and *National Car Parks Ltd v The Paternoster Consortium Ltd*;

(j) the fact that the tenant is applying for a new tenancy purely for the benefit of a buyer of the tenancy. In *Lyons v Central Commercial Properties Ltd* [1958] 2 All ER 767, CA, a new tenancy was refused, as the application was really that of the buyer and not of an occupying tenant for whom the 1954 Act was intended to provide.

Since the coming into force of the Landlord and Tenant (Covenants) Act 1995, the fact that the tenant will be subject to original tenant liability will no longer be relevant as this has been abolished by this Act. Whilst the 1954 Act has been amended so that the effect of the 1995 Act must be taken into account when determining the rent and other terms of the new tenancy, there is no such requirement in respect of the duration of the new tenancy. It is possible that the courts may, however, take the effect into account when exercising the discretion under s 33 of the 1954 Act.

The court will not usually order that the new tenancy is to be for longer than the tenant has asked for (*CBS (United Kingdom) v London Scottish Properties*). However, this may not always be the case and so in *Re Sunlight House, Quay Street, Manchester* the tenancy asked for would not have given the landlord a chance to relet the premises before the tenant quit; the court therefore ordered that a longer term be granted.

9.3.3   Future development or occupation of the premises

Where the landlord wishes to redevelop or occupy the premises in the future but is unable, at the date of the hearing, to prove the necessary intention or falls foul of the five-year rule, the court may decide to grant a short term tenancy or include a break clause in the new tenancy if in either case the landlord looks likely in the near future to satisfy either ground (f) or (g) of s 30(1) of the 1954 Act.

9.3.3.1 Short term tenancy – redevelopment

The court may decide to grant a short-term tenancy where the landlord intends to redevelop or occupy in the future. In these situations, the court must not stop the landlord from being able to redevelop when the intention to do so has been established, but this must be balanced against the fact that the tenant will need some degree of security. The court must therefore exercise its discretion in such a way as to balance the needs of both parties. Thus, in *Roehorn v Barry Corp*, where the landlord did not yet have firm plans for redevelopment, the court granted a short term tenancy and thereafter determinable on six months' notice so as not to impede the redevelopment of the property once the landlord had the necessary intention. In *London & Provincial Millinery Stores Ltd v Barclays Bank Ltd*, a 12-month term was granted in respect of premises said to be 'ripe for redevelopment'.

9.3.3.2 Short term tenancy – occupation

The position is similar where the landlord wishes to occupy under s 30(1)(g) of the 1954 Act. In *Wig Creations Ltd v Colour Film Services Ltd*, the landlord wished to occupy the premises, but fell foul of the five-year rule. A tenancy was granted which expired one year after the five-year rule would be satisfied.

9.3.3.3 Break clause – redevelopment

As an alternative solution to a short-term tenancy the court may decide to grant a long-term tenancy which includes a break clause, allowing the landlord to bring the lease to an end prematurely should its plans for redevelopment come to fruition. It was confirmed in *McCombie v Grand Junction Co Ltd* [1962] 2 All ER 65 that the court could include such a provision in the new tenancy. An example of such a provision being incorporated into the new tenancy is *Amika Motors Ltd v Colebrook Holdings Ltd*. In this case, the new tenancy was granted for five years with a break clause exercisable so as to take effect three years after the commencement of the new term. The court recognised that the tenant would suffer hardship, having recently expanded its business, but followed the view that where there is a *bona fide* intention on the part of the landlord to redevelop in the future, that redevelopment should not be prohibited by the terms of the new lease.

It is clear from case law that at the hearing the landlord does not have to prove that it will probably redevelop. All that is required is a possibility that there may be redevelopment (*JH Edwards and Sons Ltd v Central London Commercial Estates Ltd* [1984] 2 EGLR 103, CA; *Adams v Green* (1978) 247 EG 49; *National Car Parks Ltd v The Paternoster Consortium Ltd*).

If the landlord is intending to redevelop a site comprising other property as well as that comprised in the current tenancy, it is not necessary for the landlord to have possession of the other property. Evidence that the other property will be purchased will be sufficient (*National Car Parks Ltd v The Paternoster Consortium Ltd*). Neither does the landlord have to have obtained planning permission for the proposed redevelopment (*Adams v Green; Becker v Hill Street Properties Ltd*).

Fresh evidence adduced before the trial judge's decision on a redevelopment break clause can be taken into consideration in deciding what the correct period of the break clause should be (*Davy's of London (Wine Merchants) Ltd v City of London Corp* [2004] EWHC 2224; [2004] 49 EG 136)

9.3.3.4 Break clause – occupation

A break clause can also assist in cases where the landlord may wish to occupy the premises in the future. In *Peter Millett and Son Ltd v Salisbury Handbags Ltd* [1987] 2 EGLR 104, a break clause was included in the renewal lease, which allowed the landlord to break on six months' notice should it decide to occupy the premises for its own business.

9.4   RENT

9.4.1   When should the rent for the new tenancy be determined?

It is well established that the court must first consider all the other terms of the new lease before determining the new rent (*Cardshops Ltd v Davies* [1971] 2 All ER 721, CA).

9.4.2   Determining the rent

Under s 34 of the 1954 Act, the rent payable under the new tenancy is to be determined by the court only if the parties themselves cannot reach agreement. It should be noted that the parties will usually have regard to the terms of s 34 in their negotiations, although they are not confined to these terms.

In order to determine the rent, s 34 of the 1954 Act provides that the court must have regard to the terms of the tenancy (other than those relating to rent) and then decide the rent for which the holding might reasonably be expected to be let in the open market by a willing lessor disregarding:

(a) any effect on rent of the fact that the tenant has or his predecessors in title have been in occupation of the holding;

(b) any goodwill attached to the holding by reason of the carrying on thereat of the business of the tenant (whether by him or by a predecessor of his in that business);

(c) any effect on rent of an improvement; and

(d) in the case of a holding comprising licensed premises, any addition to its value attributable to the licence, if it appears to the court that, having regard to the terms of the current tenancy and any other relevant circumstances, the benefit of the licence belongs to the tenant.

These matters are exhaustive and no others can be disregarded (*J Murphy and Sons Ltd v Railtrack plc*).

In order to decide the new rent, the holding is valued. However, in the two following situations it will not be the holding which is valued:

(a) Where the landlord has exercised the right to require the tenant to take a new tenancy of the whole of the property comprised in the present tenancy under s 32(2) of the 1954 Act then the whole of the premises will be valued.

(b) Where the tenant has successfully obtained a new tenancy of an economically separable part of the holding under s 31A(1)(b) of the 1954 Act, then only that part will be valued.

The new rent will in practice be determined as at the hearing date, although strictly it should be determined as at the date on which the new tenancy is to commence (*Lovely and Orchard Services v Daejan Investments (Grove Hall)* [1978] 1 EGLR 44). Consequently, the court should take into account any matters which may be reasonably expected to occur between the hearing and the start of the new tenancy.

9.4.3   Open market rent

The new rent must be an open market rent. There is no definition of 'open market rent' in the 1954 Act and so it will usually be established by expert evidence from a surveyor, together with evidence of lettings of comparable properties. In practice, it may be quite difficult to find a comparable on similar terms to those proposed in the new letting and so particular regard must be had, when considering the terms, to ensure that differences in terms are taken into account. It was said in *GREA Real Property Investments Ltd v Williams* [1979] 1 EGLR 121 by Forbes J (at 122) that:

> It is a fundamental aspect of valuation that it proceeds by analogy. The valuer isolates those characteristics of the object to be valued which in his view affect value and then seeks another object of known or ascertainable value possessing some or all of those characteristics with which he may compare the object he is valuing. Where no direct comparable object exists the valuer must make allowances of one kind or another, interpolating or extrapolating from his given data. The less closely analogous the object chosen for comparison is the greater the allowances which have to be made and the greater the opportunity for error.

In *Baptist v Masters of the Bench and Trustees of the Honourable Society of Gray's Inn* (1993) 42 EG 287, the fact that the landlord owned all the property in the locality, Gray's Inn, did not prevent the comparable from being one in the open market; nor did the fact that most of the occupiers belonged to the same profession. In this case, the county court judge decided that for s 34 of the 1954 Act an 'open market rent' includes:

(a) a situation to create a market, ie, a sufficient number of lessors and lessees;

(b) a willing lessor and a willing lessee;

(c) a reasonable period to negotiate;

(d) arm's length negotiations;

(e) the property freely exposed to the market; and

(f) no account being taken of any higher rent which might be paid by a potential lessee with a special interest in the premises.

The parties will usually each put forward their own comparables. In practice, these should be agreed, if possible. The court must then decide which of these are relevant. It may be that adjustments must be made to the comparables in order to bring them into line with the property in question. The court will usually want to consider the terms of the leases for the comparables. Useful examples of the way in which the courts treat comparables can be found in *Newey & Eyre Ltd v J Curtis and Son Ltd* [1984] 2 EGLR 105 and *French v Commercial Union Life Assurance Co plc* [1993] 1 EGLR 113, CA. In *Newey & Eyre Ltd v J Curtis and Son Ltd* the court, when considering the rent of a warehouse, eliminated all the comparables put forward bar one, the adjoining property, and then (at 105–06) considered, first, the similarities which allowed the court to use the comparable property and, secondly, the differences between the two properties which the court had to take into account when applying the rent of the comparable to the property in question. The similarities were:

(a) the comparable was on the same estate and was next door;

(b) the comparable had exactly similar problems and advantages of access;

(c) the comparable had the same floor area;

(d) the comparable had the same rent review period; and

(e) the rent of the comparable had recently been reviewed.

The differences were:

(a) the comparable was a new building, some five years old, whereas the property in question was built in the late 1950s;

(b) the comparable had a modern clearspan layout;

(c) the lease of the property in question contained a full repairing covenant;

(d) the comparable had a very much more liberal user clause;

(e) the comparable had lavatories and ablution facilities included in its lease which the property in question did not have. These had been demolished and a joint lavatory block built between the two properties for their joint use; and

(f) the rent for the comparable was a reviewed rent agreed between a landlord and a sitting tenant, whereas the rent for the property in question was to be a rent obtainable in the open market.

The court must also decide the extent of the area from which the comparables it takes into account should come. Thus, in *Baptist v Masters of the Bench and Trustees of the Honourable Society of Gray's Inn* the comparables came from within Gray's Inn. In *French v Commercial Union Life Assurance Co plc*, they came from the shopping centre in which the property was situated, whereas in *Ganton House Investments v Crossman Investments*, the comparables came from the surrounding area.

In the absence of suitable comparables, or where the comparables cannot be adjusted to make them suitable, the court may instead have regard to general increase in rents in the area (*National Car Parks Ltd v Colebrook Estates Ltd*).

In determining the new rent the court cannot have regard to the existing rent; nor are the values for rating shown in the valuation list reliable.

9.4.4   A willing lessor and a willing lessee

Section 34 of the 1954 Act refers to a 'willing lessor', but not to a 'willing lessee'. Nonetheless, a willing lessee must be assumed to exist for the 'open market' concept to work (*Dennis & Robinson Ltd v Kiossos Establishment* [1987] 1 EGLR 133, CA).

The personal circumstances of the tenant are irrelevant and a rent cannot be set below the market level merely because the tenant cannot afford to pay (*Giannoukakis Ltd v Saltfleet Ltd* [1988] 1 EGLR 73, CA).

In *Northern Electric plc v Addison* [1997] 2 EGLR 111, CA, where the premises comprised an electricity substation, it was held that the combination of considerations to which the court has to have regard when assessing the rent under s 34 preclude a notional lessor unwilling to let the premises for such a restricted use, unless a premium was paid to take into account other potential uses. This means that the rent should not reflect a ransom element.

9.4.5   The effect of the terms of the tenancy on the rent

In determining the rent, the court must have 'regard to the terms of the tenancy (other than those relating to rent)'. In practice, this confirms that the court must first settle all the other terms of the new tenancy before deciding the rent. In addition, s 34(4) of the 1954 Act (as amended) provides that any effect on rent due to the operation of the Landlord and Tenant (Covenants) Act 1995 is to be taken into account. In practice, the most important effect of this Act will be the automatic release of a tenant on the assignment of the lease.

The terms to be taken into account are those contained in the new tenancy. It is for this reason that the terms must be agreed or determined before the rent. This allows the court to take into account covenants relating to insurance, repair, alienation, user and service charge when determining the new rent. One of the most common clauses which is taken into account is that restricting the use of the premises. In *Plinth Property Investments Ltd v Mott, Hay and Anderson* [1979] 1 EGLR 17, CA (a rent review case), the lease provided that the premises could only be used as offices for the tenant's business of consulting engineers. The rent was determined by the court at over 30% below the market rent because of this restricted user clause. This decision can be contrasted with that in *Law Land Co Ltd v The Consumers' Association Ltd* [1980] 2 EGLR 109, CA, where the use was restricted to that of the Consumers' Association and associated organisations. It was held that the premises were to be valued on the basis that they could be used as offices by a willing lessee and not just by the Consumers' Association.

Where the premises may be used for some other use than the present use, in other words, under the terms of the current lease the landlord cannot reasonably refuse a change of use, and that use will attract a higher rent, then it is to be taken into account (*Aldwych Club v Copthall Property Co* (1962) 185 EG 219).

In *Amarjee v Barrowfen Properties Ltd* (1993) 30 EG 98, the use of the premises was restricted in the lease to a retail furniture and carpet warehouse and as a result the rent was reduced by 12.5 per cent.

The length of the new tenancy may also affect the rent, and the effect will be a matter of valuation.

9.4.6   Vacant possession

There is no requirement in s 34 of the 1954 Act for the court to assume that the premises are being let with vacant possession. It is, however, to be assumed that the tenant is not in possession. Where part of the premises has been sub-let, the presence of a rent-controlled, residential sub-tenant of part should be taken into account (*Oscroft v Benabo* [1967] 1 WLR 1087). The position should be the same where there is a business sub-tenant, although there is no direct authority on this particular point.

9.4.7   Repair

The court does not have to make any assumptions as to the repair of the holding. Where the tenant is responsible for the repairs and the property is in disrepair, the court may disregard the disrepair when setting the new rent (*Family Management v Gray* [1980] 1 EGLR 46, CA). Where the property is in disrepair and the landlord is responsible for the repairs, the holding will be valued in its actual condition, so that the tenant is not penalised for the landlord's default.

9.4.8   Disregards

When determining the new rent, the court is expressly required by s 34(1) of the 1954 Act to disregard the following four matters:

(a) any effect on the rent due to the tenant or its predecessors having been in occupation of the premises;

(b) any goodwill attached to the tenant's business;

(c) improvements; and

(d) in the case of licensed premises, any addition to its value attributable to the licence, provided that the benefit of the licence belongs to the tenant.

Where the premises are landlocked, the lack of access is not a matter to be disregarded (*J Murphy and Sons Ltd v Railtrack plc*).

9.4.9   Disregard of occupation and goodwill

Under s 34(1)(a) and (b) of the 1954 Act, any effect on the rent due to the fact the tenant has, or his predecessors in title have, been in occupation of the holding, and any goodwill attached to the holding by reason of their carrying on their business there, are to be disregarded when determining the rent.

In *Harewood v Harris* [1958] 1 All ER 104, CA, it was held that evidence of the tenant's trading at the premises, which comprised a hotel, could be used to show what sort of profit such a hotel might make and what rent a potential lessee might pay. However, in *WJ Barton Ltd v Long Acre Securities Ltd* [1982] 1 WLR 398, CA, it was held that the decision in *Harewood v Harris* had a limited application and would only apply to premises such as hotels, petrol filling stations, theatres and racecourses. In *WJ Barton Ltd v Long Acre Securities Ltd*, the premises comprised a shop and, as there was plenty of comparable evidence available, the open market rent could be determined without taking into account the trading performance of the tenant. It was said that, in general, evidence of the tenant's trading would only indicate whether his business had been successful or not and so would be an indication of how much rent a tenant might be prepared to pay, but would have no direct effect on the open market rent.

9.4.10   Disregard of improvements

Paragraph (c) of s 34(1) of the 1954 Act requires that any effect on the rent of an improvement must be disregarded. Requirements which must be satisfied for an improvement to be disregarded are to be found in s 34(2) of the 1954 Act. The rationale behind this disregard is to avoid the unfairness of rentalising improvements carried out at the tenant's expense (*per* Dillon LJ in *Historic House Hotels Ltd v Cadogan Estates Ltd* [1995] 1 EGLR 117, CA).

Section 34(2) of the 1954 Act provides that for an improvement to be disregarded:

(a) it must have been carried out by a person who at the time was the tenant;

(b) it must not have been carried out under an obligation to the immediate landlord; and

(c) it must have been carried out either:

   (i)   during the current tenancy; or

   (ii) not more than 21 years before the application for a new tenancy was made and, since it was completed, the 1954 Act has applied to the holding and on the termination of a tenancy the tenant did not quit.

Each of these is now considered in turn:

9.4.10.1 *The improvement must have been carried out by a person who at the time was the tenant*

The effect of this is that any improvements made by the tenant before becoming the tenant will not be disregarded. In *Euston Centre Securities v H & J Wilson* [1982] 1 EGLR 57, the tenant was allowed access as a licensee before the lease was granted and improvements which it carried out before the tenancy was granted were not disregarded. The works do not have to be physically carried out by the tenant and it will be sufficient if they are carried out by a third party, such as a contractor (*Durley House Ltd v Earl Cadogan* [2000] 1 EGLR 60). However, a tenant may not satisfy the statutory requirement where a third party has carried out the improvements, unless the tenant can establish some involvement in identifying, supervising and/or financing them (*Durley House Ltd v Earl Cadogan*).

There is no requirement that the tenant must have paid for the improvement. In *Durley House Ltd v Earl Cadogan*, Neuberger J said (at 62) that:

> In my judgment, the requirement that the tenant arranges for the works to be effected not only satisfies the actual words that the legislature has used. It will normally carry with it the consequence that he will have contributed in some way and to some extent to the cost of the works, either by forgoing some benefit or by incurring some other liability.

Where a tenant has done no more than to have required a subtenant or licensee to carry out the work, it is doubtful whether the tenant could claim a disregard (*Durley House Ltd v Earl Cadogan*).

9.4.10.2 The improvement must not have been carried out under an obligation to the immediate landlord

Such an obligation will usually be found in the lease and may take the form of a covenant by the tenant to:

(a) carry out specific works;

(b) carry out works pursuant to a covenant to repair; or

(c) carry out works to comply with statutory requirements. In *Forte v General Accident Fire & Life Assurance plc* [1986] 2 EGLR 115, the works were taken into account as they had been carried out under the Fire Precautions Act 1971 pursuant to the tenant's covenant to comply with statutory requirements.

An obligation may also be found in a supplemental document, such as a licence to alter or carry out works. The wording of such documents must be carefully considered. In *Godbold v Martin the Newsagent* [1983] 2 EGLR 128, it was held that the wording of the licence merely permitted the tenant to carry out the improvements, rather than imposing an obligation to carry them out.

9.4.10.3 *When the improvement must have been carried out*

The improvement must have been carried out either during the current tenancy, or not more than 21 years before the application for a new tenancy was made. In addition, since it was completed, the 1954 Act must have applied to the holding and on the termination of a tenancy the tenant must not have quit.

If the improvement was carried out during the current tenancy, then it will be disregarded, providing it satisfies the other requirements mentioned above. However, if it was not carried out during the current tenancy, then to be disregarded it must have been carried out not more than 21 years before the application for the new tenancy and there must have been continuity of protected tenancies since the improvement was completed.

9.4.11   How is an improvement to be disregarded?

Where an improvement falls to be disregarded, what actually has to be disregarded is the effect of the improvement on the rent. This can only be established by valuation evidence. Guidance on this point was given in the case of rent review by Forbes J in *GREA Real Property Investments Ltd v Williams* and *Estates Projects Ltd v Greenwich London Borough* [1979] 2 EGLR 85.

9.4.12   The disregard in licensed premises

Where the premises in question are licensed premises, s 34(1)(d) of the 1954 Act requires that any addition to the value of the holding as a result of the licence must be disregarded if it appears to the court that, having regard to the terms of the current tenancy and any other relevant circumstances, the benefit of the licence belongs to the tenant.

Licensed premises not only include premises with the benefit of a justices' licence permitting the sale of intoxicating liquor, but also include betting shops licensed under the Betting, Gaming and Lotteries Act 1963 (*Ganton House Investments v Crossman Investments*).

9.4.13 Rent review provisions in the new tenancy

The court can, if it thinks fit, include a rent review clause in the new tenancy (s 34(4) of the 1954 Act). The questions which arise if the court decides to include a rent review in the new tenancy are, first, what the period of review should be and, secondly, whether the review should be upwards only or both upwards and downwards and, finally, what the terms of the rent review clause should be.

Where the current tenancy includes rent review provisions, then these will be included in the new tenancy. However, if no such provisions are included in the current tenancy and one of the parties wishes the new tenancy to include provisions for rent review, that party will have to persuade the court by expert evidence that rent review provisions should be included. In any event, where a new tenancy is granted for more than five years, the court will usually include rent review provisions.

9.4.13.1 Period of review

Whilst the period of review is a matter for the court's discretion, it does seem that the courts tend to favour a five-year review pattern. The following are the decided cases on this point:

(a) *Janes (Gowns) Ltd v Harlow Development Corp*: the renewal lease was granted for a term of 20 years with rent reviews every five years;

(b) *Charles Follett Ltd v Cabtell Investments Ltd*: the renewal lease was granted for a term of 10 years with a rent review at the end of the fifth year;

(c) *Boots the Chemists Ltd v Pinkland Ltd* [1992] 2 EGLR 98: the renewal lease was granted for a term of 14 years from 25 March 1992 with rent reviews in 1997 and 2002;

(d) *Amarjee v Barrowfen Properties Ltd*: the renewal lease was granted for a term of 14 years with rent reviews every five years;

(e) *Forbuoys plc v Newport Borough Council* [1994] 1 EGLR 138: the renewal lease was granted for a term of nine years with rent reviews every three years.

9.4.13.2 Upwards or downwards?

Whilst it is usual for the parties to a new lease to agree on an upwards only rent review in the new lease, the courts, in the absence of a rent review provision in the existing lease, will invariably decide that the rent review provisions in the renewal lease will be both upwards and downwards (see *Stylo Shoes Ltd v Manchester Royal Exchange* [1967] EGD 743; *Janes (Gowns) Ltd v Harlow Development Corp; Boots the Chemists Ltd v Pinkland Ltd; Amarjee v Barrowfen Properties Ltd; Forbuoys plc v Newport Borough Council*). This approach was not taken in *Blythewood Plant Hire Ltd v Spiers Ltd (In Receivership)* [1992] 2 EGLR 103, where the court ordered an upwards only clause as the receiver of the landlord company was hoping to grant a new lease and then sell the reversion, and the court felt that an upwards or downwards clause would affect the receiver's ability to do this. In *Northern Electric plc v Addison*, CA, the court refused to include a rent review clause in a 14-year renewal lease of an electricity substation as, in view of the low rent of £40 per annum, the cost of the review would be greater than the reviewed rent.

Where the current lease includes provision for rent review, the courts are reluctant to interfere with the existing arrangements. Thus, in *Charles Follett Ltd v Cabtell Investments Ltd*, where the current lease included an upwards only rent review, a similar provision was included in the renewal lease.

9.4.13.3 The terms of the rent review machinery

The detailed terms of the machinery for the rent review will usually be agreed between the parties once the court has decided that there should be a rent review in the renewal lease. Should they not be able to agree on the terms, then the court will have to set the terms based on s 34 of the 1954 Act. The practice will normally be that the hypothetical term will be valued on the unexpired residue of the existing term and the court may even give guidance on how the terms of the rent review provisions should be interpreted in the future (*Boots the Chemists Ltd v Pinkland Ltd*).

9.4.14   Variable rent

The court can decide on a rent which increases by fixed amounts over time. Thus, in *Fawke v Viscount Chelsea* [1980] QB 441, the premises needed repairing which was the landlord's responsibility and the rent was fixed so that once the repairs had been carried out the rent would increase.

9.5   THE OTHER TERMS OF THE NEW TENANCY

9.5.1   Section 35

The other terms of the new tenancy (ie, terms other than as to property, duration and rent) are to be decided under s 35(1) of the 1954 Act which provides that, in the absence of agreement between the landlord and the tenant, they are to be determined by the court, having 'regard to the terms of the current tenancy and to all relevant circumstances'. The reference to 'all relevant circumstances' includes a reference to the operation of the provisions of the Landlord and Tenant (Covenants) Act 1995 (s 35(2) of the 1954 Act); the effect of this will be to allow the landlord an opportunity to include controls on assignment and to require an outgoing tenant to enter into an authorised guarantee agreement. In *Wallis Fashion Group Ltd v CGU Life Assurance Ltd* [2000] 27 EG 145, Neuberger J allowed the inclusion into the new tenancy of a requirement that any licence to assign would be subject to a condition that the tenant would enter into an authorised guarantee agreement where reasonable. It was felt that this wording struck a fair balance between the interests of the parties.

Section 35 of the 1954 Act gives the court a discretion in setting the terms. Guidance on how this should be exercised was given by Lord Hailsham of St Marylebone LC in *O'May v City of London Real Property Co Ltd* [1982] 1 All ER 660, HL (at 665):

> ... the court must begin by considering the terms of the current tenancy, that the burden of persuading the court to impose a change in those terms against the will of either party must rest on the party proposing the change and the change proposed must in the circumstances of the case be fair and reasonable and should take into account, amongst other things, the comparatively weak negotiating position of a sitting tenant requiring renewal, particularly in conditions of scarcity, and

the general purpose of the Act which is to protect the business interests of the tenant so far as they are affected by the approaching termination of the current lease, in particular as regards his security of tenure.

This means, therefore, that either party can argue for a change to the terms of the current tenancy. That party must then prove that the proposed change is fair and reasonable and takes into account those matters referred to by Lord Hailsham.

Often, in practice, the lease which is being renewed is out of date and does not reflect current practice. The landlord will frequently seek to have it 'modernised'. Usually, the parties will be able to agree on how it should be brought up to date. However, where they cannot agree, the landlord will have to satisfy the court that the proposed changes satisfy the test laid down in *O'May v City of London Real Property Co Ltd*.

9.5.2   User

One of the parties may wish to vary the provisions in the lease dealing with the use of the premises; for example, the landlord may wish to widen the use so as to obtain more rent, or the tenant may wish to make the use wider so as to be able to assign the lease more freely. It is clear that the court will only permit a change to the user clause where there is a good reason for the change. Thus, an attempt by a landlord to make the use wider so as to obtain more rent and which is of no benefit to the tenant is unlikely to be successful (*Charles Clements (London) Ltd v Rank City Wall Ltd* [1978] 1 EGLR 47).

The landlord may wish the use to be more restrictive so that it covers only the use by the current tenant. In *Gold v Brighton Corp* [1956] 3 All ER 442, CA, the user clause in the existing lease allowed the tenant to use the premises as a shop. The tenant in fact sold new and second-hand furs and new and second-hand ladies' wear, the sale of second-hand clothing being the main part of her business. The landlord sought to restrict the use so as to prohibit the sale of second-hand clothing other than furs, on the basis that it wished to maintain the tone of the street. The landlord called no substantial evidence that the tone would be affected by the sale of second-hand clothing. In addition, the lease of the landlord's adjoining property had been renewed permitting the sale of second-hand clothing. It was held that a restriction preventing the tenant from being able to carry on an important part of her business, ie, the sale of

second-hand clothing, should not be imposed as there was not
sufficient evidence to justify its imposition. Denning LJ said (at
443):

> In as much as the tenant is to be protected in respect of his
> business, the terms of the new tenancy should be such as to
> enable him to carry on his business as it is. They should not
> prevent him from carrying on an important part of it. At any
> rate, if he is to be prevented from using the premises in the
> future in the way in which he has used them in the past, it is
> for the landlord to justify the restriction: and there ought to be
> strong and cogent evidence for the purpose. I find no such
> evidence here. The mere suggestion or hint that the tone of the
> street would be lowered is not enough.

The new tenancy therefore permitted the tenant to carry on her
existing business of a furrier and seller of new and second-hand
ladies' wear, as well as the additional business of selling new
and second-hand children's wear.

Where the current user clause prevents the landlord from
unreasonably withholding consent to a change of use, the
tenant cannot ask for a more restrictive clause in the new lease
so as to gain a rental advantage (*Aldwych Club v Copthall
Property Co*).

An example of a tenant obtaining a restrictive user clause is
Amarjee v Barrowfen Properties Ltd. The current tenancy had no
terms in writing and the tenant argued for a user clause in the
new tenancy which was restricted to his business. The county
court judge accepted this as the current tenancy had no terms in
it dealing with user, but he did say that if the tenancy had
contained a general user clause then he would not have
considered changing it to a restricted user provision.

In *Boots the Chemists Ltd v Pinkland Ltd*, the tenant sought
unsuccessfully to remove a positive covenant which required it
to keep the premises open for business as such covenants were
said to be of value not only to the landlord but also to the tenant
and the other tenants of the shopping centre where the
premises were situated. The tenant argued that, if it were to
breach the covenant, it could be liable to pay substantial
damages for breach of covenant. As a breach of covenant has
always given rise to a claim for damages, the court found it
surprising and somewhat difficult to believe that multiple
retailers had only recently become aware of the fact that they
would be liable to pay damages if they did not perform such
covenants.

The tenant may wish the user clause in the new lease to be wider so as to make the lease more marketable. It is unlikely that such an application will be successful. As Denning LJ in *Gold v Brighton Corp* said (at 443), the object of the 1954 Act was to protect the tenant and his business and not to give him a saleable asset. Alternatively, the tenant may wish to widen the use clause so that his current use is brought within it. Again, this is unlikely to be successful and the correct course of action is for the tenant to seek consent from the landlord for a change of use (*Davis v Brighton Corp* (1956) 106 LJ 556).

It may be that the user clause refers to a use under an old Use Classes Order, eg, the Town and Country Planning (Use Classes) Order 1972. If both parties agree, this reference may be brought up to date by referring to the current use classes order; however, if the tenant refuses and the landlord wishes to make the change, it will have to justify it under the test in *O'May v City of London Real Property Co Ltd*.

9.5.3   Alienation

A landlord may try to tighten up an existing alienation clause. For this to be successful, he will have to show very good reasons for the change. In *Cardshops Ltd v Davies*, CA, the landlord was unsuccessful in having a surrender-back clause included in an alienation covenant, which provided that the tenant could not assign without the landlord's consent, such consent not to be unreasonably withheld. It is also clear that where there is no restriction on assignment in the current tenancy, the landlord cannot seek to introduce one (*Fitzpatrick Bros v Bradford Corp* (1960) 110 LJ 208). A landlord will now be able to have included in a renewal lease a provision that any licence to assign is subject to a condition that the tenant will, where it is reasonable, enter into an authorised guarantee agreement complying with s 16 of the Landlord and Tenant (Covenants) Act 1995 (*Wallis Fashion Group Ltd v CGU Life Assurance Ltd*). It was felt by the court that this would strike a fair balance between the interests of the parties as, in the event of an alleged unreasonable refusal of consent, the burden would lie on the tenant to show that no reasonable landlord would insist on an authorised guarantee agreement.

9.5.4   Service charge

The court has power under s 35 of the 1954 Act to include service charge provisions in the new lease. The tenant cannot, however, be required to pay towards the costs of structural repairs or to the repair of capital equipment if such liability was not included in the current tenancy (*O'May v City of London Real Property Co Ltd*). The usual service costs such as cleaning, heating and decorating should be paid for by way of a fluctuating service charge (*Hyams v Titan Properties* (1972) 24 P & CR 358, CA).

9.5.5   Repairs

A landlord who is responsible for the repair of the premises cannot ask the court to pass this on to the tenant, either by means of a tenant's repairing covenant or by seeking to recover the costs through a service charge (*O'May v City of London Real Property Co Ltd*). The position is similar for a landlord, as in *Bullen v Goodland* (1961) 105 SJ 231, where the landlord under a seven-year lease was not required to take responsibility for structural repairs.

9.5.6   Guarantors

The court has power to require the tenant to provide guarantors for the new tenancy (*Cairnplace Ltd v CBL (Property Investment) Co Ltd* [1984] 1 All ER 315). In practice, the provisions will require the tenant to obtain a satisfactory guarantor within a specified period of time. If the tenant fails to do so, the landlord can then forfeit the lease, and it is suggested that relief would not be granted to the tenant unless a satisfactory guarantor is produced. This requirement is likely to be included in the following situations:

(a) where the tenant is a recently incorporated company;

(b) where the tenant has taken an assignment just before the term of the current tenancy has expired;

(c) where the tenant has a bad record of rent payment or performance of other covenants.

There is no limit on the number of guarantors which the court can require the tenant to provide. In addition, the court can lay down requirements as to the status of the guarantors. Thus, for example, in *Cairnplace Ltd v CBL (Property Investment) Co Ltd* the guarantors had to be directors of the tenant company.

9.5.7   Costs of the new lease

The tenant should not, in the absence of an agreement to pay, be made to pay the landlord's costs incurred in connection with the new lease (*Cairnplace Ltd v CBL (Property Investment) Co Ltd*). This reflects the position under s 1 of the Costs of Leases Act 1958 which provides that:

> 1 – Notwithstanding any custom to the contrary, a party to a lease shall, unless the parties thereto agree otherwise in writing, be under no obligation to pay the whole or any part of any other party's solicitor's costs of the lease.

9.6   THE EFFECT OF AN ORDER FOR A NEW TENANCY

Where the court makes an order for the grant of a new tenancy, then, unless the order is revoked (see 9.7), or the landlord and the tenant agree not to act upon the order, the landlord shall be bound to execute or make in favour of the tenant, and the tenant shall be bound to accept, a lease or agreement for a tenancy of the holding embodying the terms agreed between the landlord and the tenant or determined by the court in accordance with the 1954 Act. Where the landlord executes or makes such a lease or agreement the tenant shall be bound, if so required by the landlord, to execute a counterpart or duplicate thereof (s 36(1) of the 1954 Act).

There is nothing in the 1954 Act specifying when the parties must execute and accept a lease. It is suggested that, as the new tenancy will not come into effect until the termination of the existing tenancy under ss 24 and 64 of the 1954 Act, the new lease does not have to be executed and accepted straight away and the parties can wait until nearer the date for the commencement of the new tenancy.

There is also nothing in the 1954 Act dealing with the enforcement of an order for a new tenancy. It is suggested that if one of the parties refuses to carry out the order, it will amount to a contempt of court and, in addition, an order for specific performance may be used to force compliance. The doctrine in

Walsh v Lonsdale (1882) 21 Ch D 9 will apply so that equity will treat the parties as if the order had been carried out.

The parties may agree not to act on the order. Such an agreement must be in writing (s 69(2) of the 1954 Act) and must also be binding under ordinary principles of contract law.

9.7 REVOKING THE ORDER FOR A NEW LEASE

Section 36(2) of the 1954 Act gives a tenant the right to apply to the court within 14 days of the order for it to be revoked. This protects a tenant which is not satisfied with the new terms granted by the court. If applied for, revocation must be ordered. Once an order has been revoked, the existing tenancy will continue at least until the date on which it ends, under ss 24 and 64 of the 1954 Act. The parties can, however, agree that it should continue for longer and, in the absence of agreement, the court can order that it continues for as long as is determined to be necessary to afford to the landlord a reasonable opportunity for reletting or otherwise disposing of the premises (s 36(2) of the 1954 Act). Whilst tenancy continues by virtue of s 36(2) of the 1954 Act, it will not be a tenancy to which the 1954 Act applies.

Where an order for a new tenancy is revoked, any provision as to payment of costs will still apply. However, the court may, if it thinks fit, revoke or vary any such provision or, where no costs have been awarded in the proceedings for the revoked order, award such costs (s 36(3) of the 1954 Act).

9.8 PROVISIONS AS TO REVERSIONS

As the 1954 Act applies to a sub-tenancy (see 1.2.3), it is possible that a sub-tenancy can be continued under the 1954 Act beyond the end of the head-tenancy, or the sub-tenant may be granted a reversionary lease which extends beyond the end of the head-tenancy. These situations could, in practice, cause problems for the parties involved and so s 65 of the 1954 Act provides as follows:

(a) Where by virtue of any provision of the 1954 Act a tenancy is continued for a period which extends it to or beyond the end of the term of a superior tenancy, the superior tenancy shall be deemed so long as it subsists to be an interest in reversion expectant upon the termination of the inferior tenancy and, if there is no intermediate tenancy, to be the interest in reversion immediately expectant upon the termination of the inferior tenancy (s 65(1) of the 1954 Act).

(b) Where a tenancy is continuing under the 1954 Act after the coming to an end of the interest in reversion immediately expectant upon the termination of the tenancy, s 139(1) of the Law of Property Act 1925 (which only applies where a reversion is surrendered or merged) applies as if references in it to the surrender or merger of the reversion include references to the coming to an end of the reversion for any reason other than surrender or merger (s 65(2) of the 1954 Act). The effect of this is that the estate or interest which as against the continuing tenant confers the next vested right to the land is to be deemed to be the reversion, and the incidents and obligations of the inferior tenancy continue to have effect and govern the relationship between the continuing tenant and the person who becomes the immediate landlord.

(c) Where a tenancy is continued beyond the beginning of a reversionary tenancy which was granted so as to begin on or after the date on which apart from the 1954 Act the continuing tenancy would have come to an end, the reversionary tenancy shall have effect as if it had been granted subject to the continuing tenancy (s 65(3) of the 1954 Act). The effect of this provision is that if a continuation tenancy extends beyond the date on which the reversionary lease is to start, the reversionary lease takes effect subject to the continuation tenancy. This will include the rights which the continuing tenant has to renew its lease under the 1954 Act.

(d) Where a tenancy is granted under the 1954 Act for a period beginning on the same date as a reversionary tenancy or for a period such as to extend beyond the beginning of the term of a reversionary tenancy, the reversionary tenancy shall have effect as if it had been granted subject to the new tenancy (s 65(4) of the 1954 Act). The effect of this provision is to deal with the situation where a tenancy is to be renewed after the reversionary lease has been granted. The reversionary lease will then take effect subject to the new tenancy.

The court has the power to grant a new tenancy beyond the date on which the immediate landlord's lease will come to an end (Sched 6, para 2 of the 1954 Act). This is done by creating such reversionary tenancies as may be necessary to secure the grant of the new tenancy.

9.9   AGREEMENTS MADE BY THE COMPETENT LANDLORD

An agreement made by the competent landlord with the tenant in respect of the grant, duration or terms of a future tenancy will bind any mesne landlord (Sched 6, para 3(1) of the 1954 Act). The competent landlord also has the power to give effect to any agreement with the tenant for the grant of a new tenancy beginning with the coming to an end of the relevant tenancy, notwithstanding that the competent landlord will not be the immediate landlord at the commencement of the new tenancy, and any instrument made in the exercise of this will have effect as if the mesne landlord had been a party to it (Sched 6, para 3(2) of the 1954 Act).

If, however, the competent landlord, not being the immediate landlord, makes any such agreement without the consent of every mesne landlord, any mesne landlord whose consent has not been given is entitled to compensation from the competent landlord for any loss arising in consequence of the making of the agreement (Sched 6, para 4 of the 1954 Act).

The consent of the mesne landlord must not be unreasonably withheld, although reasonable conditions may be attached to the consent (Sched 6, para 4 of the 1954 Act). Any question as to whether consent has been unreasonably withheld or whether any conditions imposed on the giving of consent are unreasonable shall be determined by the court (Sched 6, para 4 of the 1954 Act).

Any agreement between the competent landlord and the tenant where:

(a) the competent landlord is himself a tenant; and

(b) the agreement would operate as respects any period after the coming to an end of the interest of the competent landlord, shall not have effect, unless every superior landlord who will be the immediate landlord of the tenant during any part of that period is a party to the agreement (Sched 6, para 5 of the 1954 Act).

CHAPTER 10

COMPENSATION FOR DISTURBANCE

A tenant may, in certain circumstances, be entitled to be compensated by the landlord when a new tenancy is not granted, so as to compensate for the disturbance which may be caused in having to relocate the business to new premises.

10.1   QUALIFYING CONDITIONS

Under s 37 of the 1954 Act, a tenant is entitled to be paid compensation by the landlord on quitting the holding in the following three situations.

10.1.1   Where the tenant's application for a new tenancy is dismissed by the court

Where the landlord has opposed the grant of a new tenancy under grounds (e), (f) and/or (g) of s 30(1) of the 1954 Act (together with other ground(s), if appropriate), the tenant will be entitled to compensation if the landlord successfully opposes only on grounds (e), (f) and/or (g) (s 37(1A) of the 1954 Act). Where the landlord has opposed on one or more of the non-fault grounds, eg, grounds (a), (b), (c), and (d), as well as grounds (e), (f) and/or (g), and has been successful under one of the non-fault grounds, the tenant must apply to the court for a certificate confirming that the landlord successfully opposed only on grounds (e), (f) and/or (g) and no other ground (s 37(4) of the 1954 Act). The tenant will then be entitled to compensation. This means that, where a landlord specifies a non-fault ground of opposition as well as a fault ground, the tenant will only be entitled to compensation if an application for a new tenancy is made and then followed through to judgment. A landlord may therefore decide to include one or more of the non-fault grounds in its grounds of opposition. Care must be taken to ensure that only those grounds are specified on which the landlord has a *bona fide* intention to rely; otherwise, the notice containing them will be invalid and unenforceable if they are false and made fraudulently by the landlord by reason of knowing them to be untrue or being reckless whether they are true or false (*Rous v Mitchell* [1991] 1 All ER 676, CA).

10.1.2 Where the landlord successfully applies for an order for termination without renewal

Where the landlord has obtained an order for the termination of the tenancy without the grant of a new tenancy under s 29(2) of the 1954 Act by reason of grounds (e), (f) and/or (g) and not any of the other grounds in s 30(1) of the 1954 Act, the tenant will be entitled to compensation (s 37(1B) of the 1954 Act).

10.1.3 The tenant does not apply to the court for a new tenancy or withdraws its application

If the tenant receives a s 25 notice or a counternotice to a s 26 request in which the landlord opposes the grant of a new tenancy on one or more of grounds (e), (f) and/or (g), then the tenant is entitled to compensation if either (i) the tenant does not apply for a new tenancy or the landlord does not apply for an order for the termination of the tenancy without the grant of a new tenancy, or (ii) such an application is made but is subsequently withdrawn (s 37(1C) of the 1954 Act). This entitlement arises automatically and a landlord who serves a notice stating opposition on one or more of grounds (e), (f) and/or (g) and who later changes its mind and decides not to oppose will still be liable to pay compensation to the tenant.

10.1.4 Application for a certificate under s 37(4)

There are no provisions in CPR 56 or its PD dealing with how an application should be made under s 37(4) of the 1954 Act. It is submitted that an application should be made under CPR 23 or orally at the hearing.

10.2 AMOUNT OF COMPENSATION

The amount of compensation payable to the tenant will be the rateable value of the holding multiplied by the 'appropriate multiplier' (s 37(2) of the 1954 Act). Where there are different landlords for different parts of the holding, compensation is determined separately and is payable by each landlord for its part (s 37(3B) of the 1954 Act).

10.2.1   The 'appropriate multiplier'

The 'appropriate multiplier' is such multiplier as the Secretary of State may prescribe by statutory instrument (s 37(8) of the 1954 Act). This is currently the Landlord and Tenant Act 1954 (Appropriate Multiplier) Order 1990 (SI 1990/363), which provides that the appropriate multiplier is one (unless the date of service of the landlord's s 25 notice or s 26(6) counternotice was on or before 31 March 1990, in which case the appropriate multiplier is three).

The situation may arise where the appropriate multiplier changes between the date of service of the landlord's s 25 notice or s 26(6) counternotice and the date on which the tenant quits the premises. Compensation is only payable on the tenant quitting the premises (see 10.4). It has in the past been held in relation to such a situation, where the change had the effect of increasing the appropriate multiplier, that the new appropriate multiplier applied where the tenant quit after the new appropriate multiplier had come into force (*International Military Services Ltd v Capital and Counties plc* [1982] 2 All ER 20; *Cardshops Ltd v John Lewis Properties Ltd* [1982] 3 All ER 746, CA). It is submitted that the position would be the same where the appropriate multiplier decreases.

10.2.2   Entitlement to double compensation

If the following conditions are satisfied in relation to the whole of the holding, the appropriate multiplier is doubled and so the tenant will receive double compensation:

(a) that, during the whole of the 14 years immediately preceding the termination of the current tenancy, premises being or comprised in the holding have been occupied for the purpose of a business carried on by the occupier or for those and other purposes;

(b) that, if during those 14 years there was a change in the occupier of the premises, the person who was the occupier immediately after the change was the successor to the business carried on by the person who was the occupier immediately before the change (s 37(3) of the 1954 Act).

The 14-year period of occupation must be for the whole of the
14 years immediately preceding the termination of the current
tenancy. What has to be done to discover whether there has
been the correct length of occupation is to take the date of
termination of the tenancy and then work backwards from it.
For these purposes, the date of termination is the date of
termination specified in either the landlord's s 25 notice, or the
date specified in the s 26 request as the date from which the
new tenancy is to start (s 37(7) of the 1954 Act). The effect of
sub-sections (3) and (7) is that the 14-year period must be
satisfied up to the appropriate date of termination.

A tenant who vacates the property before the date of
termination may therefore lose its entitlement to double
compensation. However, where the tenant vacates a few days
early the entitlement may not be lost. A court will be unlikely to
find that business occupancy has ceased (or not started) where
the premises are empty for only a short period, whether mid-
term or before or after trading at the end of the lease, provided
that always during that period there was no rival for the role of
business occupier and that the premises were not being used for
some other non-business purpose. In *Bacchiocchi v Academic
Agency Ltd* [1998] 2 All ER 241, CA (a case on similar wording in
s 38(2) of the 1954 Act), the tenant vacated 12 days early as he
had run down and closed his business. He was held to have
been in occupation for the relevant period immediately
preceding the date of termination. The Court of Appeal
overruled the decision in *Department of the Environment v Royal
Insurance plc* (1987) 282 EG 208 where the tenant had not been
entitled to double compensation as it had been in occupation
for one day less than 14 years, having entered into occupation
one day after the term had started.

Where there is a more significant gap between the tenant
vacating and the date of termination, the position will be
different. In *Sight & Sound Education Ltd v Books etc Ltd* [1999] 3
EGLR 45, the tenant occupied premises under a lease that was
due to expire on 28 September 1997. At the end of February
1997, the landlord served a s 25 notice, specifying a termination
date of 25 February 1998 and indicating its opposition to the
grant of a new tenancy under paras (f) and (g) of s 30(1) of the
1954 Act. The tenant served a counternotice, expressing its
unwillingness to give up possession, and then applied to the
court for a new lease. However, the tenant changed its mind,
discontinued its application and vacated the property shortly

before the contractual term date and some five months before the date of termination in accordance with s 37(7) of the 1954 Act (and considerably longer than the 12 days in *Bacchiocchi v Academic Agency Ltd*). The tenant's claim to double compensation failed as it had not been in occupation for 14 years 'immediately preceding' the termination date. As the tenant had vacated shortly before the contractual term date, following *Esselte AB v Pearl Assurance* (1995) 37 EG 173 (see 5.3) the tenancy had therefore been brought to an end on the contractual term date and was not therefore continued pursuant to s 24 of the 1954 Act and so the tenant did not qualify for double compensation. Judge Robert Pryor QC, sitting as a judge of the High Court, explained the decision in *Bacchiocchi v Academic Agency Ltd* (at 47) as follows:

> ... what [the Court of Appeal] really said was that where you have a relatively short period – in that case something like 12 days – [before] the end of the period in question – and the tenant is in a position where he has got to make up his mind whether to stay or go, and he makes his arrangements and leaves a few days before the end of the term that he could have enjoyed, it really flies in the face of common sense to say that by so doing he has ceased to occupy for business purposes. The process of moving out and timing your move out is part of the general process of occupation and a few days either at the beginning or the end – at the beginning when you take up occupation or at the end when you go out of occupation – cannot destroy the general continuity of occupation for business purposes.

Had the tenant waited until the s 25 notice had expired and then vacated, it would have satisfied the 14-year rule and have been entitled to compensation. The difference between this decision and that in *Bacchiocchi v Academic Agency Ltd* is that in the latter the tenancy was continuing and the tenant vacated after the expiry of the s 25 notice but before the continuation tenancy came to an end under s 64 of the 1954 Act. The case can also be distinguished on the fact that the period was too long and the tenant had actually moved out and would have been a trespasser if he had tried to move back in again or hang on to the premises until the date of termination specified in the s 25 notice. The warning for a tenant is clear – the s 25 notice or s 26 request sets the date for termination for the purposes of s 37(3) and if the tenant vacates before that date, it will lose the right to double compensation. When acting for a tenant in such situations, the implications of the time of vacating the premises must be carefully considered if the tenant is to be entitled to double compensation.

If the tenant has not occupied the whole of the premises comprised in the holding for the 14-year period, then compensation must be calculated for each part of the premises and the total amount of compensation payable to the tenant will be the aggregate of such sums (s 37(3A) of the 1954 Act).

The tactics available to a landlord who wishes to avoid paying double compensation are discussed at 10.8.

10.2.2.1 Occupation by group companies

Where s 42 of the 1954 Act applies (see 1.4.5), an assignment from one member of the group to another is not a change of tenant so as to fall foul of the 14-year rule (s 42(2)(c) of the 1954 Act).

10.2.2.2 Trustees

Where s 41 of the 1954 Act applies (see 1.4.3), a change in the trustees is not a change of tenant (s 41(1)(c) of the 1954 Act).

10.2.3   Rateable value

In order to calculate the amount of compensation payable, the rateable value to be used is taken from the valuation list in force at the date of service of the landlord's s 25 notice or s 26(6) counternotice (s 37(5)(a) of the 1954 Act). In *Plessey and Co Ltd v Eagle Pension Funds Ltd* [1989] EGCS 149, the Lands Tribunal held that, where the valuation list is subject to a proposal that it be altered and the list is then altered, the rateable value for compensation purposes is the one showing on the list on the date of service of the relevant notice. Where there is no rateable value shown in relation to the holding but there is a rateable value shown in relation to premises of which the holding forms part, then an apportionment must be made. Similarly, where the holding comprises a number of premises, each of which have their own rateable value, these rateable values must be aggregated (s 37(5)(b) of the 1954 Act).

In the event of any dispute as to the rateable value, it will be determined by a valuation officer appointed by the Commissioners of the Inland Revenue under the Landlord and

Tenant (Determination of Rateable Value Procedure) Rules 1954 (SI 1954/1255) (see Appendix 14) (s 37(5)(c) of the 1954 Act). There is a right of appeal against the decision of the valuation officer to the Lands Tribunal; otherwise, the decision of the valuation officer is final.

The procedure prescribed under the Landlord and Tenant (Determination of Rateable Value Procedure) Rules 1954 is as follows. An application for a determination may be made either by one of the parties or jointly by two or more of them on the prescribed form (Form A). Unless the application is made by all of the parties jointly, the party or parties making the application must, on the same day the application is made, send a copy of it to all the other parties to the dispute. Once the valuation officer receives a copy of the application from the Commissioners of the Inland Revenue, he must inform all the parties that the dispute has been referred to him for determination and that they may make representations on the matter to him in writing within 28 days (or such longer time as he may allow). The valuation officer may require the parties to furnish him with such information as he may reasonably require for the proper determination of the rateable value of the holding. The valuation officer does not decide the application as an arbitrator, but acts as an expert public official, deciding the matter on such information as he considers relevant. The valuation officer also has the power, before making his determination, to invite all the parties to a meeting at his office or at such other place as he may think convenient. Whilst he must invite all the parties, he can proceed even though they may all not accept. When he has determined the rateable value of the holding he sends a notification, using Form B, of his decision to the Commissioners and to each of the parties, together with a statement of their right of appeal to the Lands Tribunal.

10.2.4 Domestic property

Where part of the holding comprises 'domestic property' (defined in s 66 of the Local Government Finance Act 1988), then such property is disregarded when determining the rateable value (Sched 7, para 2(3)(a) of the Local Government and Housing Act 1988). In addition, if the tenant occupied the domestic property (either the whole or any part of it) at the date of the landlord's s 25 notice or s 26 counternotice, the compensation payable is increased by the addition of a sum equal to the tenant's reasonable expenses in removing from the domestic property (s 37(5A)(b) of the 1954 Act). The amount of the removal expenses is to be determined in default of agreement by the court (s 37(5B) of the 1954 Act).

Where the whole holding comprises domestic property, eg, where the tenant's business is the provision of residential accommodation (see 1.4.2), the rateable value of the holding is an amount equal to the rent at which it is estimated the holding might reasonably be expected to be let from year to year if the tenant undertook to pay all the usual tenant's rates and taxes and to bear the cost of the repairs and insurance and the other expenses (if any) necessary to maintain the holding in a state to command that rent (s 37(5C) of the 1954 Act). The date on which the valuation is to be made is the date of the landlord's s 25 notice or s 26 counternotice (s 37(5D)(a) of the 1954 Act). In the event of a dispute, application for a decision by a valuation officer may be made to the Commissioners of Inland Revenue (s 37(5D)(b) of the 1954 Act) and an appeal lies to the Lands Tribunal but, subject to this, the valuation officer's decision is final (s 37(5D)(c) of the 1954 Act).

10.2.5   The extent of the holding

The extent of the holding which is to be taken into account is that which is occupied by the tenant at the date of the landlord's s 25 notice or s 26 counternotice (*Edicron Ltd v William Whiteley Ltd* (1983) 46 P & CR 388; this point was not appealed). The effect of this is that where the tenant sub-lets part of the property comprised in its tenancy, the holding will comprise the part which the tenant occupies on the date of service of the relevant notice.

10.3   TRANSITIONAL PROVISIONS

A transitional basis of compensation may be available to a tenant under Sched 7, para 4 of the Local Government and Housing Act 1989. This basis will be available where the following conditions are met:

(a) the tenancy was entered into before 1 April 1990 or was entered into on or after that date in pursuance of a contract made before that date;

(b) the s 25 notice or s 26(6) counternotice is given before 1 April 2000; and

(c) the tenant elects to take this basis of compensation by giving notice to the landlord between two and four months of the giving of the s 25 notice or s 26 request.

In addition, there must be a rateable value shown on the valuation list as at 31 March 1990. If there is not, then it would appear that no notice may be given.

There is no prescribed form of notice for a tenant to use to elect to take the transitional basis of compensation. In *Busby v Co-operative Insurance Society Ltd* [1994] 1 EGLR 136, the notice set out the compensation payable both under the normal rule and under the transitional rule and then stated that it would be in the tenant's interests to adopt the latter. This was held to be a sufficient notice.

Where the transitional rules apply, the appropriate multiplier will be either eight times the rateable value on 31 March 1990, or in the case where s 37(3) of the 1954 Act applies, it will be 16 times that rateable value.

It was unclear until *Busby v Co-operative Insurance Society Ltd* whether these transitional provisions applied at all to a holding consisting entirely of business property, or whether they were confined to a holding comprising both business property and domestic property. In this case, the county court judge held that the transitional provisions only apply to a holding which consists of or includes domestic property.

10.4   WHEN IS COMPENSATION PAYABLE?

The tenant is entitled to be paid compensation 'on quitting the holding' (s 37(1) of the 1954 Act). This means that the tenant must give up vacant possession of the holding before compensation is paid. The question of whether the tenant had 'quit' within the meaning of s 37(1) of the 1954 Act was considered in *Webb v Sandown Sports Club Ltd* [2000] EGCS 13. Following service of a s 25 notice in which the landlord stated it would oppose a new tenancy under s 30(1)(g) of the 1954 Act and a subsequent threat by the landlord to withdraw car-parking, toilet and other facilities it provided to the tenant and his customers by virtue of a licence agreement, without which the tenant would presumably find it difficult to operate the business, the tenant advertised his intention to relocate the business. Once alternative premises had been found, the tenant ceased trading and removed nearly all the stock from the premises. Several days later the tenant returned to collect the remaining stock, and subsequently withdrew his application for a new tenancy. The landlord argued that the tenant was not entitled to compensation as it had not quit the holding at any material time. It was held that, whilst it was clear that a tenant who absented himself from a holding for reasons outside his control remained in occupation for the purposes of the 1954 Act, so long as he continued to assert his right to occupy (*Morrison Holdings Ltd v Manders Property (Wolverhampton) Ltd* [1976] 1 EGLR 70), in the present case the natural inference to be drawn from the tenant's final visits to the premises was that he intended to quit.

10.5   CONTRACTING OUT

Section 38(2) of the 1954 Act provides that any agreement (whether contained in the instrument creating the tenancy or not and whether made before or after the termination of that tenancy) which purports to exclude or reduce compensation is void. Where s 38(2) of the 1954 Act does not apply, the parties are free to agree to exclude or modify the right to compensation (s 38(3) of the 1954 Act). Section 38(2) of the 1954 Act does, however, contain the following two exceptions.

10.5.1 Five-year proviso

Any agreement made between the landlord and the tenant which excludes or restricts the tenant's right of compensation will only be effective where:

(a) during the whole of the five years immediately preceding the date on which the tenant quits the holding, premises being or comprised in the holding have been occupied for the purposes of a business carried on by the occupier or for those and other purposes; and

(b) if during those five years there was a change in the occupier of the premises, the person who was the occupier immediately after the change was the successor to the business carried on by the person who was the occupier immediately before the change.

The words 'during the whole of the five years immediately preceding' were considered in *Bacchiocchi v Academic Agency Ltd*, where the tenancy ended 12 days after the tenant had run down and closed his business and vacated the premises. It was held that the tenant had been in occupation for the five years immediately preceding the date the tenancy ended.

10.5.2   Agreements as to the amount of compensation

Any agreement as to the amount of compensation which is made after the right to compensation has accrued is valid. The right to compensation does not accrue until the tenant has quit the holding and so any agreement should not be entered into until after then.

10.6   TENANCIES WHICH EXISTED ON 1 OCTOBER 1954

Where a tenant holds under a tenancy which subsisted on 1 October 1954 and qualifies for compensation under both s 37 of the 1954 Act and compensation under the terms of the tenancy, the tenant must choose one or the other, but not both (Sched 9, para 5 of the Landlord and Tenant Act 1954). In addition, such a tenancy only qualifies for compensation if the holding (or relevant part) has at the date for quitting been continuously occupied for the purposes of the tenant's business for at least five years. Such occupation may have been by the tenant or any other person.

10.7   COMPENSATION IN SPECIAL CASES

Compensation for disturbance on the failure to be granted a new tenancy of the holding may arise on the grounds of public interest or national security. Where the interest of the landlord or any superior landlord in the property comprised in the tenancy belongs to or is held for the purposes of a government department or is held by a local authority, statutory undertaker or a development corporation, the minister may certify that it is requisite for the purposes of the department etc that the use or occupation of the whole or part of the property shall be changed (s 57(1) of the 1954 Act). There is a similar provision on

the ground of national security (s 58(1) of the 1954 Act). In both
these circumstances, compensation for disturbance is available
to the tenant (s 59(1) of the 1954 Act).

The 1954 Act also provides for compensation for
disturbance where:

(a) the property comprised in a tenancy consists of premises,
    situated in a development area or an intermediate area, of
    which the Secretary of State or an English Industrial Estates
    Corporation is the landlord and the Secretary of State
    certifies that it is necessary or expedient for achieving the
    purpose of s 2(1) of the Local Employment Act 1972 that the
    use or occupation of the property should be changed (s 60 of
    the 1954 Act); or

(b) the property comprised in the tenancy consists of premises
    of which the Welsh Development Agency is the landlord
    and the Secretary of State certifies that it is necessary or
    expedient for the purpose of providing employment
    appropriate to the needs of the area in which the premises
    are situated that the use or occupation of the property
    should be changed (s 60A of the 1954 Act).

10.8   TACTICAL CONSIDERATIONS FOR THE LANDLORD

A landlord may be able to prevent a tenant from becoming
entitled to compensation by including a s 30 fault ground in the
s 25 notice or s 26(6) counternotice. If this ground is then
successfully proved the tenant will not be entitled to
compensation. In any event, compensation would only be
payable in these circumstances where the tenant pursues the
application for a new tenancy and is refused a new tenancy by
the court on a non-fault ground. It may be that, rather than
pursuing such an application, the tenant merely quits; in such a
case no compensation is payable. It must be remembered,
however, that a ground of opposition must be included for
genuine reasons (see 4.3.6).

The timing of a s 25 notice may also be important. A tenant
who may be entitled to double compensation could be
prevented from being so entitled by a carefully timed s 25
notice, as the 14-year period is calculated from the date
specified in the s 25 notice.

10.9   TACTICAL CONSIDERATIONS FOR THE TENANT

As with a s 25 notice, the timing of a s 26 request may be important where the tenant may become eligible to double compensation.

CHAPTER 11

COMPENSATION FOR IMPROVEMENTS

A tenant of business premises who has made improvements to the premises or whose predecessor in title to the tenancy has made improvements may be entitled to compensation from the landlord for those improvements when quitting the premises at the end of the tenancy. This right arises under the provisions of Part 1 of the Landlord and Tenant Act 1927 (the 1927 Act) and applies notwithstanding any contract to the contrary made after 8 February 1927. The 1927 Act used to allow contracting out for adequate consideration, but this was abolished by s 49 of the 1954 Act. It also allows a tenant who complies with it to carry out improvements notwithstanding an absolute covenant in the lease prohibiting this.

The 1927 Act lays down procedures and requirements which must be followed and satisfied before compensation will be available. These procedures and requirements are as follows:

(a) Are the premises ones to which the 1927 Act applies?

(b) Is the improvement one to which the 1927 Act applies?

(c) Has the correct procedure been followed before the improvement was carried out?

(d) Has the correct procedure been followed in relation to the application for compensation?

(e) What amount of compensation is payable?

11.1 ARE THE PREMISES ONES TO WHICH THE 1927 ACT APPLIES?

11.1.1 The holding

The compensation provisions in the 1927 Act apply to a 'holding', which is defined in s 17(1) of the 1927 Act as:

> ... any premises held under a lease, other than a mining lease, made whether before or after the commencement of this Act, and used wholly or partly for the carrying on thereat any trade or business, and not being –

(a) agricultural holdings within the meaning of the Agricultural Holdings Act 1986 held under leases in relation to which that Act applies, or

(b) holdings held under farm business tenancies within the meaning of the Agricultural Tenancies Act 1995.

A lease is defined in s 25(1) of the 1927 Act as being a lease, underlease or other tenancy, an assignment operating as a lease or underlease, or an agreement for such a lease, underlease, tenancy or assignment.

The use of the word 'partly' means that a tenancy of mixed use premises will qualify so far as improvements relate to the trade or business and provided also that either the Leasehold Reform Act 1967 or the Leasehold Reform, Housing and Urban Development Act 1993 do not apply to the tenancy.

It should also be noted that a tenancy which is excluded from the protection of the 1954 Act because either it has been contracted out or it was granted for less than six months will qualify.

The following leases and arrangements are thus excluded from the provisions:

(a) a mining lease. This is defined in s 25(1) of the 1927 Act to mean a lease for any mining purposes or purposes connected therewith. Section 25(1) of the 1927 Act also contains a definition of 'mining purposes';

(b) an agricultural holding;

(c) holdings held under a farm business tenancy;

(d) a holding let to a tenant as the holder of any office, appointment or employment, provided that where such a tenancy is created after the commencement of the 1927 Act, it must be in writing and express the purpose for which the tenancy is created (s 17(2) of the 1927 Act);

(e) a licence;

(f) long mixed business and residential leases to which either the Leasehold Reform Act 1967 or the Leasehold Reform, Housing and Urban Development Act 1993 apply.

It is not clear whether the 1927 Act applies to a tenancy at will.

The 1927 Act applies to land belonging to Her Majesty in right of the Crown or the Duchy of Lancaster, to land belonging to the Duchy of Cornwall and to land belonging to any government department (s 24(1) of the 1927 Act).

11.1.2   Trade or business use

There is no definition of 'trade or business' in the 1927 Act; nor can any assistance be found in the definition of 'business' contained in the 1954 Act. Some assistance is found in s 17 of the 1927 Act, so that premises which are regularly used for carrying on a profession are deemed, for improvement purposes, to be premises used for carrying on a trade or business (s 17(3) of the 1927 Act). In addition, the business of sub-letting residential flats is expressly excluded (s 17(3)(b) of the 1927 Act). Some assistance is also found from case law. Thus, it has been said that a person carries on a trade or business when he 'habitually does and contracts to do a thing capable of producing profit' (*Erichsen v Last* (1881) 8 QBD 414, CA, *per* Cotton LJ). It has, however, also been said that someone carrying on a trade need not make or desire to make a profit (*Re Duty on Estate of Incorporated Council of Law Reporting for England and Wales, Re* (1888) 22 QBD 279, *per* Coleridge CJ). In *Town Investments Ltd v Department of the Environment* [1978] 1 All ER 813, Lord Kilbrandon said (at 835) that 'business' denoted the carrying on of a serious occupation, not necessarily confirmed to commercial or profit-making undertakings, and included government administrative functions.

11.2   IS THE IMPROVEMENT ONE TO WHICH THE 1927 ACT APPLIES?

There is no definition of 'improvement' in the 1927 Act; however, it does include the erection of any building (s 1(1) of the 1927 Act). The demolition of a building and its rebuilding may amount to an improvement notwithstanding that, following the rebuilding, the premises may be used for a different purpose from the original use (*National Electric Theatres Ltd v Hudgell* [1939] 1 All ER 567). It will not cover a trade or other fixture which a tenant is by law entitled to remove (s 1(1) of the 1927 Act).

The improvement must have been carried out by the tenant or a predecessor in title to the tenancy (*Pelosi v Newcastle Arms Brewery Ltd* [1981] 2 EGLR 36, CA). An improvement which has been carried out by a predecessor to the tenant's business and who is not also a predecessor to the tenancy will not come within the 1927 Act (*Williams v Portman* [1951] 2 All ER 539, CA; *Pasmore v Whitbread and Co Ltd* [1953] 1 All ER 361, CA; *Corsini v Montague Burton Ltd* [1953] 2 All ER 8, CA).

Neither the 1927 Act nor case law make it clear whether an improvement must have been made during the current tenancy during which the claim for compensation is made, or whether it can have been made during a previous tenancy which has been renewed. It is submitted that the first of these is the correct position.

11.3   HAS THE CORRECT PROCEDURE BEEN FOLLOWED BEFORE THE IMPROVEMENT WAS CARRIED OUT?

A tenant cannot claim compensation unless the statutory procedural requirements have been complied with before the improvement has been carried out, and the claim is made within the statutory time limits.

The procedural requirements can be illustrated as follows:

Diagram 11.1 Procedural requirements

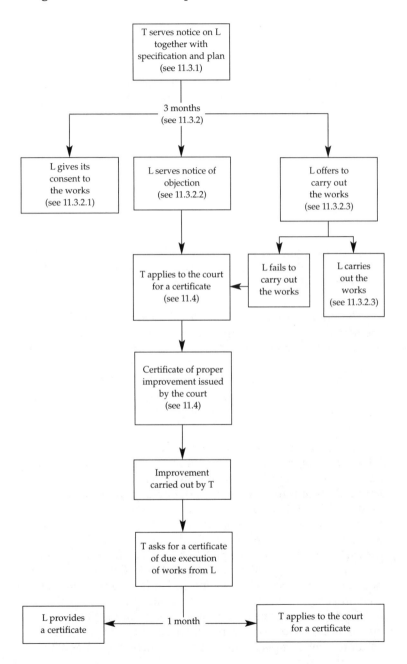

11.3.1 Notice of improvements

Before carrying out improvements a tenant must serve notice of
its intention to do so on the landlord, accompanied by a
specification and plan showing the proposed improvement and
the part of the existing premises affected by it (s 3(1) of the 1927
Act). There is no prescribed form for this notice; however, it
must be in writing and a letter will suffice (*Deerfield Travel
Services Ltd v Wardens and Society of the Mistery or Art of the
Leathersellers of the City of London* (1982) 46 P & CR 132, CA). An
example of a notice of intention to make an improvement can
be found in Appendix 26. The notice need not actually refer to
the 1927 Act, but it should make it clear to a reasonable
landlord that the tenant is intending to exercise its rights under
the 1927 Act, rather than just asking for consent to carry out
alterations under a lease covenant. The notice will not be
invalid where some of the work mentioned is not improvement
but rather repair work. The specification must contain all the
information which the landlord will need so that the landlord
can consider during the three-month time period what action it
will take.

The notice, specification and plan need not all be served at
the same time but they must all be connected either by their
wording or by the circumstances. If they are served separately,
then the three-month period which the landlord has to consider
what action to take starts when the last document is served.

Where a tenant is required by a statutory obligation to carry
out an improvement, notice must still be given to the landlord
(s 48(1) of the 1954 Act).

Where a tenant has served notice on a landlord which is itself
a tenant (a 'mesne' landlord), the mesne landlord will in turn
need to serve copies of all the documents on its immediate
landlord 'within the time and in the manner prescribed' (s 8(1)
of the 1927 Act). However, there is nothing in CPR Part 56
dealing with this. Prior to CPR Part 56 coming into force, CPR
Sched 1, RSC Ord 97, r 4(2) and CPR Sched 2, CCR Ord 43, r 3(2)
provided that these copies had to be served 'forthwith' and be
accompanied by a notice in writing stating the date when the
document was received by the mesne landlord. These provisions
were revoked when CPR Part 56 came into force. A mesne
landlord does not have to serve copies on its immediate landlord
but, if it does not, it will not then be able to claim from its
landlord any compensation which the mesne landlord has to
pay to the tenant.

Once a tenant has served a notice of intention to carry out improvements, he must wait until either the three-month time period for the landlord to object has passed or any objection raised by the landlord has been dealt with, before carrying out the improvements.

11.3.2   What can the landlord do following receipt of a notice of intention?

A landlord who receives from a tenant a notice of intention to carry out improvements has the following options open to it:

(a) it may within three months of service either consent to the work or serve a notice of objection;

(b) it may offer to carry out the work itself; or

(c) it may do nothing at all.

11.3.2.1 Consent to the work

A landlord may give its consent to the proposed improvements. For the avoidance of doubt, such consent should be given in writing. An example of a notice of consent to an improvement can be found in Form 3 in Appendix 26. Once the tenant receives consent, the works can be carried out at any time thereafter.

11.3.2.2 Objection by the landlord

If a landlord wishes to object to the proposed improvement, then notice of objection must be served on the tenant within three months after the service of the tenant's notice. A superior landlord who has been served with copies of the documents may also object. The only improvement which a landlord cannot object to is one which must be carried out by the tenant under a statutory obligation (s 48(1) of the 1954 Act). There is no prescribed form for an objection. It is suggested that it should be in writing and amount to an objection to the tenant making the proposed improvement. An example of a notice of objection to a proposed improvement can be found in Form 2 in Appendix 26. If a landlord serves a notice of objection the tenant may then apply to the court for a certificate that the improvement is a proper one (see 11.4).

11.3.2.3 Landlord offers to carry out the improvements itself

A landlord may decide to carry out the improvements itself. Where the landlord offers to carry out an improvement, a tenant cannot be made to accept the improvement (*Norfolk Capital Group Ltd v Cadogan Estates Ltd* [2004] EWHC 384; [2004] 3 All ER 889). The landlord should offer to carry out the improvements in consideration of a reasonable increase in the rent, or of such increase of rent as the court may determine (s 3(1) of the 1927 Act). An example of a notice of willingness to carry out an improvement can be found in Form 5 in Appendix 26.

Where a lease does not provide for any improvements carried out by the tenant to be rentalised the landlord should make an offer. There is no time limit by which a landlord has to make an offer. In practice, a landlord contemplating making an offer should, in any event, serve a notice of objection within the three-month time limit, in order to prevent the tenant from ignoring the landlord's offer and carrying out the improvements itself. If a landlord fails to carry out its offer, the tenant may then apply to the court for a certificate that the improvement is a proper one. The court may not give a certificate unless it is subsequently shown to the court's satisfaction that the landlord has failed to carry out its undertaking (s 3(1) of the 1927 Act).

If a landlord decides to offer to carry out the improvements in return for a specified increase in rent, the tenant may challenge this by seeking a certificate of proper improvement. This will be granted where the court decides that the rent specified by the landlord is not reasonable. There is unfortunately no definition in the 1927 Act of what will amount to a reasonable increase of rent, nor are there any decided authorities on this point. Should the landlord not specify a rental figure but instead offer to carry out the improvements in return for such increase as the court may determine, then the court has to decide what would be the correct increase and refuse to issue a certificate of proper improvement. The 1927 Act is silent as to the date after which the increased rent is payable, but it is generally thought that it will be payable from the date of completion of the improvements.

If a tenant decides that it does not want to pay the increased rent it can refuse the landlord's offer to carry out the improvements, but the tenant will not then be able to carry out the improvements itself.

A landlord or any person authorised by it may at all reasonable times enter on to the holding or any part of it in order to execute any improvement which the landlord has undertaken to execute and to make any inspection of the premises which may reasonably be required for the purposes of Part 1 of the 1927 Act (s 10 of the 1927 Act).

11.3.2.4 What if the landlord does nothing?

If the landlord does not do anything within the three-month time period, the tenant can go ahead and carry out the improvements in accordance with the plan and specification, notwithstanding anything to the contrary in the lease (s 3(4) of the 1927 Act). However, this does not permit a tenant to carry out an improvement in contravention of any restriction created or imposed for naval, military or air-force purposes or for civil aviation purposes under the powers of the Civil Aviation Act 1982, or for securing any rights of the public over the foreshore or seabed (s 3(4) of the 1927 Act).

11.4   APPLICATION TO THE COURT FOR A CERTIFICATE OF PROPER IMPROVEMENT

A tenant which receives a notice of objection within the three-month time period may 'in the prescribed manner' apply to the court for a certificate that the improvement is a proper one (s 3(1) of the 1927 Act). The court to which application is made is the court exercising jurisdiction in accordance with s 63 of the 1954 Act (s 21 of the 1927 Act). This will be either the High Court or the county court. The claim should normally be started in the county court for the district in which the land is situated (CPR 56.2 and PD 56, para 2.2). No application is necessary where the improvement is one being carried out under a statutory obligation (s 48(1) of the 1954 Act).

11.4.1 The claim form

An application for a certificate is made by a Part 8 claim form (PD 56, para 2.1). The claim form must include the matters required by Part 8, and the following additional matters set out in PD 56, para 5.2:

(a) the nature of the claim or the matter to be determined;

(b) the property to which the claim relates;

(c) the nature of the business carried on at the property;

(d) particulars of the lease or agreement for the tenancy including:

    (i)   the names and addresses of the parties to the lease or agreement;

    (ii)   its duration;

    (iii)   the rent payable;

    (iv)   details of any assignment or other devolution of the lease or agreement;

    (v)   the date and mode of termination of the tenancy;

    (vi)   if the claimant has left the property, the date on which he did so;

    (vii) particulars of the improvement or proposed improvement to which the claim relates; and

    (viii) if the claim is for payment of compensation, the amount claimed.

11.4.2   The parties

The party who is seeking to carry out the improvement will be the claimant. The claimant's immediate landlord must be a defendant to the claim (PD 56, para 5.4).

11.4.3   Service

The claim form must be served within four months of issue (CPR 7.5(2)). According to PD 56, para 5.5, the defendant must immediately serve a copy of the claim form and any document served with it and of his acknowledgment of service on his immediate landlord.

11.4.4   Acknowledgment of service

The defendant must serve an acknowledgment of service not more than 14 days after service of the claim form (CPR 8.3(1)). The acknowledgment of service must state whether the defendant contests the claim and if he seeks a different remedy to the one claimed and, if he does, what it is (CPR 8.3(2)).

11.4.5   Evidence and directions

Evidence need not be filed either with the claim form or with the acknowledgment of service (PD 56, para 5.6). The claim is automatically allocated to the multitrack and the court will fix a date for a hearing when it issues the claim form (PD 56, para 5.3). The first hearing will normally be a directions hearing. If the court intends to certify that an improvement is a proper improvement or has been duly executed, it shall do so by way of an order (PD 56, para 5.7).

11.4.6   Conditions for the grant of a certificate

Before a court can certify that an improvement is a proper improvement the tenant must, under s 3(1) of the 1927 Act, satisfy the court that the improvement:

(a) is of such a nature as to be calculated to add to the letting value of the holding at the termination of the tenancy;

(b) is reasonable and suitable to the character thereof; and

(c) will not diminish the value of any other property belonging to the same landlord, or to any superior landlord from whom the immediate landlord of the tenant directly or indirectly holds.

In considering whether the improvement is reasonable and suitable to the character of holding, the court shall have regard to any evidence brought before it by the landlord or any superior landlord (but not any other person) that the improvement is calculated to injure the amenity or convenience of the neighbourhood (s 3(2) of the 1927 Act). The effect of this provision is that only the landlord and any superior landlord can object to the proposed improvement.

Once the tenant has satisfied the court on these three matters, the court may grant a certificate after making any modifications in the specification or plan as the court thinks fit, or imposing such other conditions as the court may think reasonable. If the landlord had offered to carry out the works and fails to do so, the court can grant a certificate once it is satisfied that the landlord has failed to carry out his undertaking.

A court cannot grant a certificate in relation to works which have already been carried out, or which have already been started and are as yet unfinished (*Hogarth Health Club Ltd v Westbourne Investments Ltd* [1990] 1 EGLR 89, CA).

11.4.7 Effect of a certificate

The effects of a certificate of proper improvement being granted by the court are as follows:

(a) it entitles the tenant to carry out the works certified. However, it should be noted that the tenant does not have to carry out the works if it decides that it no longer wishes to go ahead with them;

(b) it establishes in part the tenant's right to compensation at the end of the lease. In order to claim compensation a tenant must carry out the works specified in the certificate, comply with any conditions laid down by the court and complete the work within any time limit imposed by the court or agreed between the landlord and the tenant (s 3(5) of the 1927 Act). Failure to abide by any of these requirements will not render the improvements unlawful, but will prevent the tenant from being able to claim compensation at the end of the tenancy;

(c) it may make an improvement lawful which would otherwise have been in breach of the terms of the lease.

11.5 CERTIFICATE OF EXECUTION

Once the tenant has carried out an improvement in respect of which notice was given under s 3 and either no notice of objection has been served by the landlord or a certificate of proper improvement has been obtained from the court, the tenant should ask the landlord for a certificate confirming that the improvement has been duly executed (s 3(6) of the 1927 Act). An example of a certificate of execution of an improvement can be found in Form 6 in Appendix 26. If the landlord refuses to give such a certificate or does not give one within one month of the tenant's request, the tenant can apply to the court which, if satisfied that the improvement has been duly executed, must give a certificate to that effect. The tenant is liable to pay any reasonable expenses incurred by the landlord where the landlord furnishes a certificate, and any question as to the reasonableness of such expenses must be determined by the court.

The certificate of execution confirms that the improvements have been carried out and that the 1927 Act has been complied with. If there are a number of years left to run on the lease, it may otherwise be difficult to prove such matters without such a certificate.

11.6 LANDLORD'S RIGHT TO REIMBURSEMENT OF INCREASED RATES AND INSURANCE PREMIUMS

Where an improvement carried out by the tenant increases the rateable value of the holding and/or the fire insurance premiums and the landlord is liable to pay these, the rent is to be increased to cover these additional payments (s 16 of the 1927 Act).

11.7 RIGHT TO COMPENSATION

The 1927 Act gives a tenant the right to compensation for improvements, provided that certain conditions are satisfied (see Diagram 11.2). The tenant is defined as meaning any person entitled in possession to the holding under any contract of tenancy, whether the interest of such tenant was acquired by original contract, assignment, operation of law or otherwise (s 25(1) of the 1927 Act).

Diagram 11.2 Eligibility for compensation

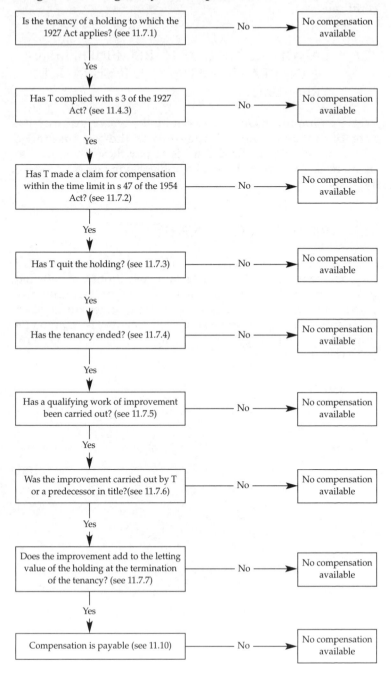

11.7.1   Is the tenancy of a holding to which the 1927 Act applies?

The conditions which must be satisfied for the 1927 Act to apply are considered at 11.1. It is generally accepted that these conditions must be satisfied, both at the time when the tenant gives notice of the claim for compensation and when the tenant quits the holding at the end of the tenancy.

11.7.2   Has the tenant made a claim for compensation within the prescribed time limit?

The tenant must make a claim for compensation in writing within the time limits set out in s 47 of the 1954 Act. These time limits are as follows:

(a) within three months of the service of a notice to quit by either the landlord or the tenant, or the receipt of a notice opposing the tenant's request for a new tenancy under s 26 of the 1954 Act. Where the landlord does not serve a counternotice to the tenant's request for a new tenancy under s 26 of the 1954 Act, the claim must be made within three months of the latest date on which the landlord could have served such a counternotice;

(b) where the tenancy comes to an end by effluxion of time, not earlier than six months nor later than three months before the expiry of the tenancy;

(c) within three months of the effective date of a court order for the forfeiture of the lease or within three months of re-entry.

The effective date of an order is the date on which the order is to take effect according to the terms thereof or the date on which it ceases to be subject to appeal, whichever is the later (s 47(4) of the 1954 Act).

The claim must be made in the prescribed manner which is laid down in PD 56, para 5.8. This provides that the claim is to be in writing, signed by the claimant, his solicitor or agent and shall include details of:

(a) the name and address of the claimant and of the landlord against whom the claim is made;

(b) the property to which the claim relates;

(c) the nature of the business carried on there;

(d) a concise statement of the nature of the claim;

(e) particulars of the improvement, including the date when it
    was completed and costs; and

(f) the amount claimed.

An example of a notice of claim for compensation for an
improvement can be found in Form 7 in Appendix 26. If any of
the prescribed information is not included in the notice of
claim, the notice will be invalid and leave will not be given to
amend it out of time (*British and Colonial Furniture Co Ltd v
William McIlroy Ltd* [1952] 1 All ER 12).

The claim should be served pursuant to s 23 of the 1927 Act,
and where received by a mesne landlord a copy should be
served on the superior landlord, and so on up the chain (PD 56,
para 5.9). An example of a notice to a superior landlord of a
claim for compensation for an improvement by a sub-tenant can
be found in Form 8 in Appendix 26.

11.7.3   Has the tenant quit the holding?

The tenant must have quit the holding in order to be entitled to
compensation. This means that if the tenant holds over, the
claim to compensation will not arise until the tenant has
actually left the premises. However, what is the position of a
tenant who renews the tenancy? In such a situation, it is
generally accepted that the tenant loses the right to
compensation and cannot make a later claim when eventually
quitting the holding.

11.7.4   When can the compensation be determined?

Compensation can be determined either after the tenancy has
come to an end and the tenant has quit, or it can be determined
before the tenant has quit, although it will not be payable until
the tenant has in fact quit (*Pelosi v Newcastle Arms Brewery Ltd*).

11.7.5   Has a qualifying work of improvement been
          carried out?

The improvement must be a qualifying improvement. There are
particular improvements which are excluded from being
eligible for compensation and these are:

(a) trade or other fixtures which the tenant is by law entitled to remove (s 1(1) of the 1927 Act). These will be determined at the date of termination of the tenancy;

(b) any improvement which the tenant or his predecessors in title were under an obligation to make in pursuance of a contract entered into for valuable consideration, including a building lease (s 2(1)(b) of the 1927 Act). There is no requirement in this provision that the contract must be between the landlord and the tenant; thus, works carried out under a contract between a tenant and a sub-tenant will not be eligible for compensation (*Owen Owen Estate Ltd v Livett* [1955] 2 All ER 513). Where there is no contract but a tenant or his predecessors in title have received some benefit in consideration of the improvement from the landlord or his predecessors in title, any compensation shall be reduced to take into account such benefit (s 2(3) of the 1927 Act).

11.7.6   Was the improvement carried out by the tenant or a predecessor in title?

The improvement must have been carried out by the tenant or his predecessor in title (s 1(1) of the 1927 Act).

11.7.7   Does the improvement add to the letting value of the holding at the termination of the tenancy?

The improvement must, at the termination of the tenancy, add to the letting value of the holding (s 1(1) of the 1927 Act). This will be determined at the date of termination of the tenancy and will require a valuation.

11.8   APPLICATION FOR COMPENSATION

The landlord and the tenant may agree between themselves that the tenant is entitled to compensation and the amount of compensation payable. In the absence of agreement on either or both of these, the right to compensation and/or the amount payable must be determined by the court (s 1(3) of the 1927 Act).

Diagram 11.3 Application for compensation

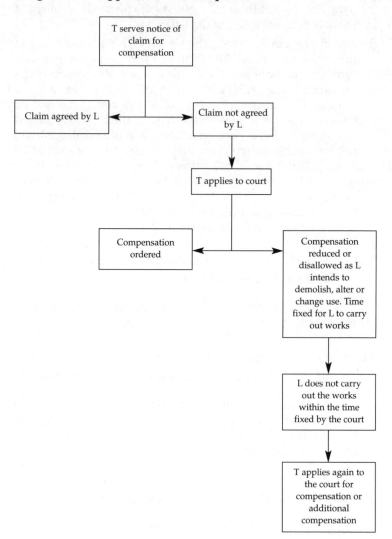

11.8.1 Which court?

The court to which application is made is the court exercising jurisdiction in accordance with s 63 of the 1954 Act (s 21 of the 1927 Act). This will be either the High Court or the county court. The claim should normally be started in the county court for the district in which the land is situated (CPR 56.2 and PD 56, para 2.2).

11.8.2   The claim form

An application for a certificate is made by a Part 8 claim form (PD 56, para 2.1). The claim form must include the matters required by Part 8, and the following additional matters set out in PD 56, para 5.2:

(a) the nature of the claim or the matter to be determined;

(b) the property to which the claim relates;

(c) the nature of the business carried on at the property;

(d) particulars of the lease or agreement for the tenancy including:

  (i)   the names and addresses of the parties to the lease or agreement;

  (ii)   its duration;

  (iii) the rent payable;

  (iv)   details of any assignment or other devolution of the lease or agreement;

  (v)   the date and mode of termination of the tenancy;

  (vi)   if the claimant has left the property, the date on which he did so;

  (vii) particulars of the improvement or proposed improvement to which the claim relates; and

  (viii) if the claim is for payment of compensation, the amount claimed.

11.8.3   The parties

The party who is seeking to carry out the improvement will be the claimant. The claimant's immediate landlord must be a defendant to the claim (PD 56, para 5.4).

11.8.4   Service

The claim form must be served within four months of issue (CPR 7.5(2)). According to PD 56, para 5.5, the defendant must immediately serve a copy of the claim form and any document served with it and of his acknowledgment of service on his immediate landlord.

11.8.5 Acknowledgment of service

The defendant must serve an acknowledgment of service not more than 14 days after service of the claim form (CPR 8.3(1)). The acknowledgment of service must state whether the defendant contests the claim and if he seeks a different remedy to the one claimed and, if he does, what it is (CPR 8.3(2)).

11.8.6 Evidence and directions

Evidence need not be filed either with the claim form or with the acknowledgment of service (PD 56, para 5.6). The claim is automatically allocated to the multitrack and the court will fix a date for a hearing when it issues the claim form (PD 56, para 5.3). The first hearing will normally be a directions hearing.

11.9   THE AMOUNT OF COMPENSATION

Section 1(1) of the 1927 Act specifies that the sum to be paid as compensation for any improvement shall not exceed:

(a) the net addition to the value of the holding as a whole which may be determined to be the direct result of the improvement; nor

(b) the reasonable cost of carrying out the improvement at the termination of the tenancy, subject to a deduction of an amount equal to the cost, if any, of putting the works constituting the improvement into a reasonable state of repair, except so far as such cost is covered by the liability of the tenant under any covenant or agreement as to the repair of the premises.

In determining the amount of the net addition, regard shall be had to the purposes for which it is intended that the premises shall be used after the termination of the tenancy (s 1(2) of the 1927 Act). If it is intended to demolish or to make structural alterations in the premises or any part thereof or to use the premises for a different purpose, regard shall be had to the effect of such demolition, alteration or change of user on the additional value attributable to the improvement, and to the length of time likely to elapse between the termination of the tenancy and the demolition, alteration or change of user (s 1(2) of the 1927 Act). The result of this is that if the landlord only intends to use the premises for, say, two years before demolishing them, the tenant will be entitled to two years' value rather than the to value of the improvements as if they would be there for ever.

Section 2(3) of the 1927 Act provides that the court is to take into account any benefits which the tenant or his predecessors in title may have received from the landlord or his predecessors in title in consideration expressly or impliedly of the improvement. An example of such a benefit would be a rent-free period.

11.10   THE PAYMENT OF THE COMPENSATION

Compensation is only payable once the tenancy has come to an end and the tenant has quit the holding. Where the compensation is not payable for some time later, say because there is some dispute, the landlord must pay as soon as the dispute has been resolved. There is no provision in the 1927 Act for the payment of interest on unpaid compensation.

11.10.1 Who pays the compensation?

Compensation is paid to the tenant by his landlord (s 1(1) of the 1927 Act). 'Landlord' is defined in s 25(1) of the 1927 Act to mean 'any person who under a lease is, as between himself and the tenant or other lessee, for the time being entitled to the rents and profits of the demised premises payable under the lease'. Exactly who fulfils this definition for the purposes of paying compensation will be determined at the date of termination of the tenancy.

11.10.2 Rights of mesne landlords

Where there is a chain of reversionary interests, s 8 of the 1927 Act is applicable. This allows a mesne landlord who has paid or is liable to pay compensation to be entitled, at the end of his term, to compensation from his immediate landlord in like manner and on the same conditions as if he had himself made the improvement. Such a claim by a mesne landlord must be

made at least two months before the expiration of his term. A
mesne landlord is not entitled to claim compensation under s 8
of the 1927 Act unless he has served on his immediate superior
landlord copies of all documents relating to the improvement
and claim for compensation. Where this is done, the superior
landlord then has all the powers conferred by the 1927 Act and
so may appear before the court and is bound by the
proceedings.

11.10.3 Right to make deductions

A landlord has a right to deduct out of the compensation any
sum due to him from the tenant under or in respect of the
tenancy (s 11(1) of the 1927 Act). Similarly, a tenant has the right
to deduct out of any sum due from him to the landlord under
or in respect of the tenancy any sum payable to him by the
landlord by way of compensation (s 11(1) of the 1927 Act).

11.10.4 Charging order

A landlord who has paid compensation, or who has himself
carried out an improvement, has a right under Sched 1 to the
1927 Act to obtain an order from the Minister of Agriculture,
Fisheries and Food charging the holding with repayment of the
expenditure and so he will be able to recover such sums from
his superior landlord. Such a charge is registrable as a Class A
Land Charge, where appropriate. There are special provisions
relating to the charging of ecclesiastical and charity land (s 24
and Sched 2, Part 2 of the 1927 Act).

11.10.5 Settled land

There are provisions in s 13 of the 1927 Act which allow capital
money to be used in payment for improvements carried out by
a landlord under the 1927 Act, payment of compensation
awarded and any incidental costs, charges and expenses, and
the payment of the costs, charges and expenses of opposing any
proposal by a tenant to make an improvement.

CHAPTER 12

CROWN TENANCIES

Section 56 of the 1954 Act deals with the application of the 1954 Act to the Crown. Where the Crown is the landlord, the 1954 Act rights granted to the tenant may be modified under s 57 of the 1954 Act, and there are special rights to terminate such tenancies in s 58 of the 1954 Act. There are also special provisions dealing with property in development and intermediate areas (s 60 of the 1954 Act), and premises leased by the Welsh Development Agency (s 60A of the 1954 Act).

12.1   THE 1954 ACT WHERE THE CROWN IS THE TENANT

The 1954 Act will apply to a tenancy where the Crown is the tenant (s 56(1) of the 1954 Act). The premises under the tenancy must be occupied for the purposes of a business. The exception to this is where a tenancy is held by or on behalf of a government department. In this case, where the premises are occupied for any purposes of a government department, the tenancy will be subject to the 1954 Act, ie, the premises are deemed to be occupied for the purposes of a business (s 56(3) of the 1954 Act). In *Town Investments Ltd v Department of the Environment* [1978] AC 359, HL, it was decided that a tenancy granted to a government department was in effect granted to the Crown. It was said in *Linden v Department of Health and Social Security* [1986] 1 All ER 691 by Scott J (at 697):

> In my judgment section 56(3) brings within Part II of the 1954 Act any tenancy held by a government department if the premises are being occupied for any purpose of any government department.

Where the premises are not occupied for the purposes of a government department, the government department is deemed in this situation still to occupy for its own purposes provided that no rent is payable by any other occupier (s 56(4) of the 1954 Act).

Where, for the purposes of any provision of the 1954 Act, it is a condition that, on any change of occupier of the premises, the new occupier must have succeeded to the business of the former occupier, that condition is deemed to be satisfied if immediately before and immediately after the change the premises were occupied for the purposes of a government department (s 56(3) of the 1954 Act).

12.2 THE 1954 ACT WHERE THE CROWN IS THE LANDLORD

The 1954 Act applies to any interest belonging to Her Majesty in right of the Crown or the Duchy of Lancaster or belonging to the Duchy of Cornwall, or belonging to a government department or held on behalf of Her Majesty for the purposes of a government department (s 56(1) of the 1954 Act).

Where an interest in any property comprised in a tenancy belongs to Her Majesty in right of the Duchy of Lancaster, the Chancellor of the Duchy represents Her Majesty and is deemed to be the owner of the interest (Sched 8, para 1 of the 1954 Act). Where an interest in property belongs to the Duchy of Cornwall, the Duchy is represented by such person as the Duke of Cornwall may appoint and the appointed person is deemed to be the owner of that interest (Sched 8, para 2 of the 1954 Act).

12.2.1 Public interest

Under s 57(1) of the 1954 Act, the rights of a tenant under the 1954 Act may be modified where the interest of the landlord or any superior landlord:

(a) belongs to or is held for the purposes of a government department; or

(b) is held by a local authority, statutory undertakers, or a development corporation.

In these situations, the minister in charge of any government department may certify that it is requisite for the purposes of the department or for the purposes of the local authority, statutory undertakers or development corporation that the use or occupation of the property or a part of it should be changed by a specified date (s 57(1) of the 1954 Act).

12.2.2 The procedure for a s 57 certificate

Under s 57(2) of the 1954 Act, before a certificate can be issued the tenant must be given a notice stating:

(a) that the question of the giving of the certificate is under consideration by the minister specified in the notice; and

(b) that if within 21 days of the giving of the notice the tenant makes representations to that minister, the representations will be considered before the question is determined.

No certificate may be given unless such a notice has been given. If representations are made within the time the minister must consider them before determining whether to give the certificate. There is no appeal against the issue of a certificate, but the decision to issue may be subjected to judicial review.

12.2.3 Effect of a s 57 certificate

A certificate when granted has no effect straight away on the rights of a contractual tenant of business premises. However, if the tenancy is terminated, the effect of the certificate is to prevent any new tenancy from being granted beyond the certified date.

Where:

(a) the tenancy is terminated by a s 25 notice; and

(b) the date of termination is not earlier than the date specified in the certificate; and

(c) the s 25 notice contains a copy of the certificate,

then the s 25 notice need not require the tenant to serve a counternotice, and it need not specify any grounds of opposition (s 57(3) of the 1954 Act). In addition, the tenant is not entitled to apply to the court for the grant of a new tenancy.

However, if the s 25 notice specifies as the termination date a date earlier than the date specified in the certificate, and the notice contains a copy of the certificate, then the court can make an order for the grant of a new tenancy but the new tenancy must not expire later than the date specified in the certificate, and the new tenancy will not be one to which the 1954 Act applies (s 57(3) of the 1954 Act).

Where a tenant makes a s. 26 request for a new tenancy, its effect depends on whether a certificate has already been given.

If one has, and within two months after the making of the s 26 request the landlord gives the tenant notice that the certificate has been given and the notice contains a copy of the certificate, then:

(a) if the date specified in the certificate is not later than that specified in the s 26 request, the tenant cannot apply to the court for the grant of a new tenancy;

(b) if, in any other case, the court makes an order for the grant of a new tenancy, the new tenancy must not expire later than the certified date; and the new tenancy will not be one to which the 1954 Act applies (s 57(4)(a) of the 1954 Act).

If a certificate has not been issued, but the tenant has had notice either before the s 26 request or within two months after the giving of the s 26 request that the issuing of a certificate is being considered, the s 26 request is ineffective (s 57(4)(b) of the 1954 Act). This will not, however, prevent the tenant from making a fresh s 26 request when the minister has determined whether or not to give a certificate (s 57(4)(b) of the 1954 Act).

12.2.4 National security

Where the landlord's interest in the property belongs to or is held for the purposes of a government department, and the minister in charge of any government department certifies that for reasons of national security it is necessary that the use or occupation of the property should be discontinued or changed, then under s 58 of the 1954 Act:

(a) where the landlord gives a s 25 notice containing a copy of the certificate the tenant cannot serve a counternotice and cannot apply to the court for the grant of a new tenancy;

(b) if the tenant makes a s 26 request, and within two months the landlord notifies the tenant that a certificate has been given and the notice contains a copy of the certificate, then the tenant cannot apply to the court for the grant of a new tenancy. If the landlord's notification specifies a date earlier than that specified in the s 26 request, but which is at least six months after the notification, and no earlier than the date on which the tenancy could have been terminated at common law, the tenancy will terminate on the date specified in the landlords notification.

12.3   CONTRACTING OUT OF THE 1954 ACT

Where the landlord's interest belongs to or is held for the purposes of a government department the landlord can validly agree with the tenant that if the minister or board in charge of the department issues a certificate that for reasons of national security it is necessary that the use or occupation of the property should be discontinued or changed, the tenancy may be terminated by notice to quit given by the landlord of such length as may be specified in the agreement, provided the notice contains a copy of the certificate (s 58(2) of the 1954 Act). It may also be agreed that, after the giving of such a notice containing the copy certificate, the tenancy shall not be one to which the 1954 Act applies (s 58(2) of the 1954 Act).

Where the landlord's interest is held by statutory undertakers, the landlord can agree with the tenant that upon the minister or board in charge of a government department certifying that possession of the property, or part, is urgently required for carrying out repairs (whether on that property or elsewhere) which are needed for the proper operation of the landlord's undertaking, the tenancy may be terminated by notice to quit given by the landlord of such length as may be specified in the agreement, provided the notice contains a copy of the certificate (s 58(3) of the 1954 Act). It may also be agreed that, after the giving of such a notice containing the copy certificate, the tenancy shall not be one to which the 1954 Act applies (s 58(3) of the 1954 Act).

If the court makes an order under the 1954 Act for the grant of a new tenancy where the landlord's interest belongs to or is held for the purposes of a government department, then, if the minister or board in charge of any government department certifies that the public interest so requires, the court must make it a term of the new tenancy that a contracting out agreement shall be embodied in the new tenancy (s 58(4) of the 1954 Act). There is a similar rule for statutory undertakers (s 58(4) of the 1954 Act).

12.4   OTHER OFFICIAL ORGANISATIONS

Where either the Secretary of State for Trade and Industry or the Urban Regeneration Agency is the landlord, and the premises are situated in either a development area or an intermediate area, and the Secretary of State certifies that it is necessary or expedient for achieving the purpose mentioned in s 2(1) of the Local Employment Act 1972 that the use or occupation of the property should be changed, s 58(1)(a) and (b) of the 1954 Act apply in just the same way as where a certificate is given under s 58(1)(a) and (b) of the 1954 Act in respect of premises where the landlord's interest belongs to or is held for the purposes of a government department (s 60 of the 1954 Act).

Where the premises are owned by the Welsh Development Agency, the National Assembly for Wales has powers corresponding to those given to the Secretary of State for Trade and Industry (s 60A of the 1954 Act). Similar rules used to apply where the premises were leased by the Development Board for Rural Wales, but these have been repealed by the Government of Wales Act 1998.

APPENDIX 1

LAW OF PROPERTY ACT 1925

196 Regulations respecting notices

(1) Any notice required or authorised to be served or given by this Act shall be in writing.

(2) Any notice required or authorised by this Act to be served on a lessee or mortgagor shall be sufficient, although only addressed to the lessee or mortgagor by that designation, without his name, or generally to the persons interested, without any name, and notwithstanding that any person to be affected by the notice is absent, under disability, unborn, or unascertained.

(3) Any notice required or authorised by this Act to be served shall be sufficiently served if it is left at the last-known place of abode or business in the United Kingdom of the lessee, lessor, mortgagee, mortgagor, or other person to be served, or, in case of a notice required or authorised to be served on a lessee or mortgagor, is affixed or left for him on the land or any house or building comprised in the lease or mortgage, or, in case of a mining lease, is left for the lessee at the office or counting-house of the mine.

(4) Any notice required or authorised by this Act to be served shall also be sufficiently served, if it is sent by post in a registered letter addressed to the lessee, lessor, mortgagee, mortgagor, or other person to be served, by name, at the aforesaid place of abode or business, office, or counting-house, and if that letter is not returned through the post-office undelivered; and that service shall be deemed to be made at the time at which the registered letter would in the ordinary course be delivered.

(5) The provisions of this section shall extend to notices required to be served by any instrument affecting property executed or coming into operation after the commencement of this Act unless a contrary intention appears.

(6) This section does not apply to notices served in proceedings in the court.

APPENDIX 2

LANDLORD AND TENANT ACT 1927

PART I

Compensation for Improvements and Goodwill on the termination of Tenancies of Business Premises

1 Tenant's right to compensation for improvements

(1) Subject to the provisions of this Part of this Act, a tenant of a holding to which this Part of this Act applies shall, if a claim for the purpose is made in the prescribed manner [and within the time limited by section forty-seven of the Landlord and Tenant Act 1954], be entitled, at the termination of the tenancy, on quitting his holding, to be paid by his landlord compensation in respect of any improvement (including the erection of any building) on his holding made by him or his predecessors in title, not being a trade or other fixture which the tenant is by law entitled to remove, which at the termination of the tenancy adds to the letting value of the holding:

> Provided that the sum to be paid as compensation for any improvement shall not exceed—

> (a) the net addition to the value of the holding as a whole which may be determined to be the direct result of the improvement; or

> (b) the reasonable cost of carrying out the improvement of the termination of the tenancy, subject to a deduction of an amount equal to the cost (if any) of putting the works constituting the improvement into a reasonable state of repair, except so far as such cost is covered by the liability of the tenant under any covenant or agreement as to the repair of the premises.

(2) In determining the amount of such net addition as aforesaid, regard shall be had to the purposes for which it is intended that the premises shall be used after the termination of the tenancy, and if it is shown that it is intended to demolish or to make structural alterations in the premises or any part thereof or to use the premises for a different purpose, regard shall be had to the effect of such demolition, alteration or change of user on the additional value attributable to the improvement, and to the length of time likely to elapse between the termination of the tenancy and the demolition, alteration or change of user.

(3) In the absence of agreement between the parties, all questions as to the right to compensation under this section, or as to the amount thereof, shall be determined by the tribunal hereinafter mentioned, and

if the tribunal determines that, on account of the intention to demolish or alter or to change the user of the premises, no compensation or a reduced amount of compensation shall be paid, the tribunal may authorise a further application for compensation to be made by the tenant if effect is not given to the intention within such time as may be fixed by the tribunal.

2 Limitation on tenant's right to compensation in certain cases

(1) A tenant shall not be entitled to compensation under this Part of this Act—

(a) in respect of any improvement made before the commencement of this Act; or

(b) in respect of any improvement made in pursuance of a statutory obligation, or of any improvement which the tenant or his predecessors in title were under an obligation to make in pursuance of a contract entered into, whether before or after the passing of this Act, for valuable consideration, including a building lease; or

(c) in respect of any improvement made less than three years before the termination of the tenancy; or

(d) if within two months after the making of the claim under section one, subsection (1), of this Act the landlord serves on the tenant notice that he is willing and able to grant to the tenant, or obtain the grant to him of, a renewal of the tenancy at such rent and for such term as, failing agreement, the tribunal may consider reasonable; and, where such a notice is so served and the tenant does not within one month from the service of the notice send to the landlord an acceptance in writing of the offer, the tenant shall be deemed to have declined the offer.

(2) Where an offer of the renewal of a tenancy by the landlord under this section is accepted by the tenant, the rent fixed by the tribunal shall be the rent which in the opinion of the tribunal a willing lessee other than the tenant would agree to give and a willing lessor would agree to accept for the premises, having regard to the terms of the lease, but irrespective of the value attributable to the improvement in respect of which compensation would have been payable.

(3) The tribunal in determining the compensation for an improvement shall in reduction of the tenant's claim take into consideration any benefits which the tenant or his predecessors in title may have received from the landlord or his predecessors in title in consideration expressly or impliedly of the improvement.

3 Landlord's right to object

(1) Where a tenant of a holding to which this Part of this Act applies proposes to make an improvement on his holding, he shall serve on his landlord notice of his intention to make such improvement, together with a specification and plan showing the proposed improvement and the part of the existing premises affected thereby, and if the landlord, within three months after the service of the notice, serves on the tenant notice of objection, the tenant may, in the prescribed manner, apply to the tribunal, and the tribunal may, after ascertaining that notice of such intention has been served upon any superior landlords interested and after giving such persons an opportunity of being heard, if satisfied that the improvement—

(a) is of such a nature as to be calculated to add to the letting value of the holding at the termination of the tenancy; and

(b) is reasonable and suitable to the character thereof; and

(c) will not diminish the value of any other property belonging to the same landlord, or to any superior landlord from whom the immediate landlord of the tenant directly or indirectly holds;

and after making such modifications (if any) in the specification or plan as the tribunal thinks fit, or imposing such other conditions as the tribunal may think reasonable, certify in the prescribed manner that the improvement is a proper improvement:

> Provided that, if the landlord proves that he has offered to execute the improvement himself in consideration of a reasonable increase of rent, or of such increase of rent as the tribunal may determine, the tribunal shall not give a certificate under this section unless it is subsequently shown to the satisfaction of the tribunal that the landlord has failed to carry out his undertaking.

(2) In considering whether the improvement is reasonable and suitable to the character of the holding, the tribunal shall have regard to any evidence brought before it by the landlord or any superior landlord (but not any other person) that the improvement is calculated to injure the amenity or convenience of the neighbourhood.

(3) The tenant shall, at the request of any superior landlord or at the request of the tribunal, supply such copies of the plans and specifications of the proposed improvement as may be required.

(4) Where no such notice of objection as aforesaid to a proposed improvement has been served within the time allowed by this section, or where the tribunal has certified an improvement to be a proper improvement, it shall be lawful for the tenant as against the immediate and any superior landlord to execute the improvement according to the plan and specification served on the landlord, or according to such plan and specification as modified by the tribunal or by agreement

between the tenant and the landlord or landlords affected, anything in any lease of the premises to the contrary notwithstanding:

Provided that nothing in this subsection shall authorise a tenant to execute an improvement in contravention of any restriction created or imposed—

(a) for naval, military or air force purposes;

(b) for civil aviation purposes under the powers of the Air Navigation Act 1920;

(c) for securing any rights of the public over the foreshore or bed of the sea.

(5) A tenant shall not be entitled to claim compensation under this Part of this Act in respect of any improvement unless he has, or his predecessors in title have, served notice of the proposal to make the improvement under this section, and (in case the landlord has served notice of objection thereto) the improvement has been certified by the tribunal to be a proper improvement and the tenant has complied with the conditions, if any, imposed by the tribunal, nor unless the improvement is completed within such time after the service on the landlord of the notice of the proposed improvement as may be agreed between the tenant and the landlord or may be fixed by the tribunal, and where proceedings have been taken before the tribunal, the tribunal may defer making any order as to costs until the expiration of the time so fixed for the completion of the improvement.

(6) Where a tenant has executed an improvement of which he has served notice in accordance with this section and with respect to which either no notice of objection has been served by the landlord or a certificate that it is a proper improvement has been obtained from the tribunal, the tenant may require the landlord to furnish to him a certificate that the improvement has been duly executed; and if the landlord refuses or fails within one month after the service of the requisition to do so, the tenant may apply to the tribunal who, if satisfied that the improvement has been duly executed, shall give a certificate to that effect.

Where the landlord furnishes such a certificate, the tenant shall be liable to pay any reasonable expenses incurred for the purpose by the landlord, and if any question arises as to the reasonableness of such expenses, it shall be determined by the tribunal.

8 Rights of mesne landlords

(1) Where, in the case of any holding, there are several persons standing in the relation to each other of lessor and lessee, the following provisions shall apply—

Any mesne landlord who has paid or is liable to pay compensation under this Part of this Act shall, at the end of his term, be entitled to compensation from his immediate landlord in like manner and on the same conditions as if he had himself made the improvement … in question, except that it shall be sufficient if the claim for compensation is made at least two months before the expiration of his term:

A mesne landlord shall not be entitled to make a claim under this section unless he has, within the time and in the manner prescribed, served on his immediate superior landlord copies of all documents relating to proposed improvements and claims which have been sent to him in pursuance of this Part of this Act:

Where such copies are so served, the said superior landlord shall have, in addition to the mesne landlord, the powers conferred by or in pursuance of this Part of this Act in like manner as if he were the immediate landlord of the occupying tenant, and shall, in the manner and to the extent prescribed, be at liberty to appear before the tribunal and shall be bound by the proceedings:

(2) In this section, references to a landlord shall include references to his predecessors in title.

9 Restriction on contracting out

This Part of this Act shall apply notwithstanding any contract to the contrary, being a contract made at any time after the eighth day of February, nineteen hundred and twenty-seven.

10 Right of entry

The landlord of a holding to which this Part of this Act applies, or any person authorised by him may at all reasonable times enter on the holding or any part of it, for the purpose of executing any improvement he has undertaken to execute and of making any inspection of the premises which may reasonably be required for the purposes of this Part of this Act.

11 Right to make deductions

(1) Out of any money payable to a tenant by way of compensation under this Part of this Act, the landlord shall be entitled to deduct any sum due to him from the tenant under or in respect of the tenancy.

(2) Out of any money due to the landlord from the tenant under or in respect of the tenancy, the tenant shall be entitled to deduct any sum payable to him by the landlord by way of compensation under this Part of this Act.

12 Application of 13 and 14 Geo 5 c 9, s 20

Section twenty of the Agricultural Holdings Act 1923 (which relates to charges in respect of money paid for compensation), as set out and modified in the First Schedule to this Act, shall apply to the case of money paid for compensation under this Part of this Act, including any proper costs, charges, or expenses incurred by a landlord in opposing any proposal by a tenant to execute an improvement, or in contesting a claim for compensation, and to money expended by a landlord in executing an improvement the notice of a proposal to execute which has been served on him by a tenant under this Part of this Act.

13 Power to apply and raise capital money

(1) Capital money arising under the Settled Land Act 1925 ... or under the University and College Estates Act 1925, may be applied—

(a) in payment as for an improvement authorised by the Act of any money expended and costs incurred by a landlord under or in pursuance of this Part of this Act in or about the execution of any improvement;

(b) in payment of any sum due to a tenant under this Part of this Act in respect of compensation for an improvement ... and any costs, charges, and expenses incidental thereto;

(c) in payment of the costs, charges, and expenses of opposing any proposal by a tenant to execute an improvement.

(2) The satisfaction of a claim for such compensation as aforesaid shall be included amongst the purposes for which a tenant for life, statutory owner ... may raise money under section seventy-one of the Settled Land Act 1925.

(3) Where the landlord liable to pay compensation for an improvement ... is a tenant for life or in a fiduciary position, he may require the sum payable as compensation and any costs, charges, and expenses incidental thereto, to be paid out of any capital money held on the same trusts as the settled land.

In this subsection 'capital money' includes any personal estate held on the same trusts as the land ...

14 Power to sell or grant leases notwithstanding restrictions

Where the powers of a landlord to sell or grant leases are subject to any statutory or other restrictions, he shall, notwithstanding any such restrictions or any rule of law to the contrary, be entitled to offer to sell or grant any such reversion or lease as would under this Part of this Act relieve him from liability to pay compensation thereunder, and to convey and grant the same, and to execute any lease which he may be ordered to grant under this Part of this Act.

15 Provisions as to reversionary leases

(1) Where the amount which a landlord is liable to pay as compensation for an improvement under this Part of this Act has been determined by agreement or by an award of the tribunal, and the landlord had before the passing of this Act granted or agreed to grant a reversionary lease commencing on or after the termination of the then existing tenancy, the rent payable under the reversionary lease shall, if the tribunal so directs, be increased by such amount as, failing agreement, may be determined by the tribunal having regard to the addition to the letting value of the holding attributable to the improvement:

> Provided that no such increase shall be permissible unless the landlord has served or caused to be served on the reversionary lessee copies of all documents relating to the improvement when proposed which were sent to the landlord in pursuance of this Part of this Act.

(2) The reversionary lessee shall have the same right of objection to the proposed improvement and of appearing and being heard at any proceedings before the tribunal relative to the proposed improvement as if he were a superior landlord, and if the amount of compensation for the improvement is determined by the tribunal, any question as to the increase of rent under the reversionary lease shall, where practicable, be settled in the course of the same proceedings.

16 Landlord's right to reimbursement of increased taxes, rates or insurance premiums

Where the landlord is liable to pay any ... rates (including water rate) in respect of any premises comprised in a holding, or has undertaken to pay the premiums on any fire insurance policy on any such premises, and in consequence of any improvement executed by the tenant on the premises under this Act the assessment of the premises or the rate of premium on the policy is increased, the tenant shall be liable to pay to the landlord sums equal to the amount by which—

(a) the ... rates payable by the landlord are increased by reason of the increase of such assessment;

(b) the fire premium payable by the landlord is increased by reason of the increase in the rate of premium;

and the sums so payable by the tenant shall be deemed to be in the nature of rent and shall be recoverable as such from the tenant ...

17 Holdings to which Part I applies

(1) The holdings to which this Part of this Act applies are any premises held under a lease, other than a mining lease, made whether before or after the commencement of this Act, and used wholly or partly for carrying on thereat any trade or business, and [not being—

(a) agricultural holdings within the meaning of the Agricultural Holdings Act 1986 held under leases in relation to which that Act applies, or

(b) holdings held under farm business tenancies within the meaning of the Agricultural Tenancies Act 1995.]

(2) This Part of this Act shall not apply to any holding let to a tenant as the holder of any office, appointment or employment, from the landlord, and continuing so long as the tenant holds such office, appointment or employment, but in the case of a tenancy created after the commencement of this Act, only if the contract is in writing and expresses the purpose for which the tenancy is created.

(3) For the purposes of this section, premises shall not be deemed to be premises used for carrying on thereat a trade or business—

(a) by reason of their being used for the purpose of carrying on thereat any profession;

(b) by reason that the tenant thereof carries on the business of subletting the premises as residential flats, whether or not the provision of meals or any other service for the occupants of the flats is undertaken by the tenant:

Provided that, so far as this Part of this Act relates to improvements, premises regularly used for carrying on a profession shall be deemed to be premises used for carrying on a trade or business.

(4) In the case of premises used partly for purposes of a trade or business and partly for other purposes, this Part of this Act shall apply to improvements only if and so far as they are improvements in relation to the trade or business.

PART III

General

21 The tribunal

The tribunal for the purposes of Part I of this Act shall be the court exercising jurisdiction in accordance with the provisions of section sixty-three of the Landlord and Tenant Act 1954.

23 Service of notices

(1) Any notice, request, demand or other instrument under this Act shall be in writing and may be served on the person on whom it is to be served either personally, or by leaving it for him at his last known place of abode in England or Wales, or by sending it through the post in a registered letter addressed to him there, or, in the case of a local or public authority or a statutory or a public utility company, to the secretary or other proper officer at the principal office of such authority or company, and in the case of a notice to a landlord, the person on whom it is to be served shall include any agent of the landlord duly authorised in that behalf.

(2) Unless or until a tenant of a holding shall have received notice that the person theretofore entitled to the rents and profits of the holding (hereinafter referred to as 'the original landlord') has ceased to be so entitled, and also notice of the name and address of the person who has become entitled to such rents and profits, any claim, notice, request, demand, or other instrument, which the tenant shall serve upon or deliver to the original landlord shall be deemed to have been served upon or delivered to the landlord of such holding.

24 Application to Crown, Duchy, ecclesiastical and charity lands

(1) This Act shall apply to land belonging to His Majesty in right of the Crown or the Duchy of Lancaster and to land belonging to the Duchy of Cornwall, and to land belonging to any Government department, and for that purpose the provisions of the Agricultural Holdings Act 1923, relating to Crown and Duchy Lands, as set out and adapted in Part I of the Second Schedule to this Act, shall have effect.

(2) The provisions of the Agricultural Holdings Act 1923, with respect to the application of that Act to ecclesiastical and charity lands, as set out and adapted in Part II of the Second Schedule to this Act, shall apply for the purposes of this Act.

(4) Where any land is vested in the [official custodian for charities] in trust for any charity, the trustees of the charity and not the [custodian] shall be deemed to be the landlord for the purposes of this Act.

25 Interpretation

(1) For the purposes of this Act, unless the context otherwise requires—

The expression 'tenant' means any person entitled in possession to the holding under any contract of tenancy, whether the interest of such tenant was acquired by original contract, assignment, operation of law or otherwise;

The expression 'landlord' means any person who under a lease is, as between himself and the tenant or other lessee, for the time being entitled to the rents and profits of the demised premises payable under the lease;

The expression 'predecessor in title' in relation to a tenant or landlord means any person through whom the tenant or landlord has derived title, whether by assignment, by will, by intestacy, or by operation of law;

The expression 'lease' means a lease, under-lease or other tenancy, assignment operating as a lease or under-lease, or an agreement for such lease, under-lease tenancy, or assignment;

The expression 'mining lease' means a lease for any mining purpose or purposes connected therewith, and 'mining purposes' include the sinking and searching for, winning, working, getting, making merchantable, smelting or otherwise converting or working for the purposes of any manufacture, carrying away, and disposing of mines and minerals, in or under land, and the erection of buildings, and the execution of engineering and other works suitable for those purposes;

The expression 'term of years absolute' has the same meaning as in the Law of Property Act 1925;

The expression 'statutory company' means any company constituted by or under an Act of Parliament to construct, work or carry on any … tramway, hydraulic power, dock, canal or railway undertaking; and the expression 'public utility company' means any company within the meaning of the Companies (Consolidation) Act 1908, or a society registered under the Industrial and Provident Societies Acts, 1893 to 1913, carrying on any such undertaking;

The expression 'prescribed' means prescribed by County Court Rules, except that in relation to proceedings before the High Court, it means prescribed by rules of the Supreme Court.

(2) The designation of landlord and tenant shall continue to apply to the parties until the conclusion of any proceedings taken under or in pursuance of this Act in respect of compensation.

26 Short title, commencement and extent

(1) This Act may be cited as the Landlord and Tenant Act 1927.

(3) This Act shall extend to England and Wales only.

SCHEDULE 1

PROVISIONS AS TO CHARGES

Section 12

(1) A landlord, on paying to the tenant the amount due to him under Part I of this Act, in respect of compensation for an improvement …

under that Part, or on expending after notice given in accordance with that Part such amount as may be necessary to execute an improvement, shall be entitled to obtain from the Minister of Agriculture, Fisheries and Food (hereinafter referred to as the Minister) an order in favour of himself and the persons deriving title under him charging the holding, or any part thereof, with repayment of the amount paid or expended, including any proper costs, charges or expenses incurred by a landlord in opposing any proposal by a tenant to execute an improvement or in contesting a claim for compensation, and of all costs properly incurred by him in obtaining the charge, with such interest, and by such instalments, and with such directions for giving effect to the charge, as the Minister thinks fit.

(2) Where the landlord obtaining the charge is not an absolute owner of the holding for his own benefit, no instalment or interest shall be made payable after the time when the improvement ... in respect whereof compensation is paid will, in the opinion of the Minister, have become exhausted.

(3) Where the estate or interest of a landlord is determinable or liable to forfeiture by reason of his creating or suffering any charge thereon, that estate or interest shall not be determined or forfeited by reason of his obtaining such a charge, anything in any deed, will or other instrument to the contrary thereof notwithstanding.

(4) The sum charged shall be a charge on the holding, or the part thereof charged, for the landlord's interest therein and for interests in the reversion immediately expectant on the termination of the lease; but so that, in any case where the landlord's interest is an interest in a leasehold, the charge shall not extend beyond that leasehold interest.

(5) Any company now or hereafter incorporated by Parliament, and having power to advance money for the improvement of land, may take an assignment of any charge made under this Schedule, upon such terms and conditions as may be agreed upon between the company and the person entitled to the charge, and may assign any charge so acquired by them.

(6) Where a charge may be made under this Schedule for compensation due under an award, the tribunal making the award shall, at the request and cost of the person entitled to obtain the charge, certify the amount to be charged and the term for which the charge may properly be made, having regard to the time at which each improvement ... in respect of which compensation is awarded is to be deemed to be exhausted.

(7) A charge under this Schedule may be registered under section ten of the Land Charges Act 1925, as a land charge of Class A.

SCHEDULE 2

Section 24

PART I

Application to Crown and Duchy Land

1 (a) With respect to any land belonging to His Majesty in right of the Crown, or to a Government department, for the purposes of this Act, the Commissioners of Crown Lands, or other the proper officer or body having charge of the land for the time being, or, in case there is no such officer or body, then such person as His Majesty may appoint in writing under the Royal Sign Manual, shall represent His Majesty, and shall be deemed to be the landlord.

2 (a) With respect to land belonging to His Majesty in right of the Duchy of Lancaster, for the purposes of this Act, the Chancellor of the Duchy shall represent His Majesty, and shall be deemed to be the landlord.

(b) The amount of any compensation under Part I of this Act payable by the Chancellor of the Duchy shall be raised and paid as an expense incurred in improvement of land belonging to His Majesty in right of the Duchy within section twenty-five of the Act of the fifty-seventh year of King George the Third, chapter ninety-seven.

(3) (a) With respect to land belonging to the Duchy of Cornwall, for the purposes of this Act, such person as the Duke of Cornwall, or the possessor for the time being of the Duchy of Cornwall appoints, shall represent the Duke of Cornwall or other the possessor aforesaid, and be deemed to be the landlord, and may do any act or thing under this Act which a landlord is authorised or required to do thereunder.

(b) Any compensation under Part I of this Act payable by the Duke of Cornwall, or other the possessor aforesaid, shall be paid, and advances therefor made, in the manner and subject to the provisions of section eight of the Duchy of Cornwall Management Act 1863, with respect to improvements of land mentioned in that section.

PART II

Application to Ecclesiastical and Charity Land

1 (a) Where lands are assigned or secured as the endowment of a see, the powers by this Act conferred on a landlord in respect of charging land shall not be exercised by the bishop in respect of those lands,

except with the previous approval in writing of the Estates Committee of the Ecclesiastical Commissioners.

(c) The Ecclesiastical Commissioners may, if they think fit, on behalf of an ecclesiastical corporation, out of any money in their hands, pay to the tenant the amount of compensation due to him under Part I of this Act, and thereupon they may, instead of the corporation obtain from the minister a charge on the holding in respect thereof in favour of themselves ...

2 The powers by this Act conferred on a landlord in respect of charging land shall not be exercised by trustees for ecclesiastical or charitable purposes, except with the approval in writing of the Charity Commissioners or the Board of Education, as the case may require.

APPENDIX 3

LANDLORD AND TENANT ACT 1954

PART I

SECURITY OF TENURE FOR RESIDENTIAL TENANTS

Provisions as to possession on termination of a long tenancy

Compensation for possession obtained by misrepresentation

14A Where an order is made for possession of the property comprised in a tenancy to which section 1 of this Act applies and it is subsequently made to appear to the court that the order was obtained by misrepresentation or the concealment of material facts, the court may order the landlord to pay to the tenant such a sum as appears sufficient as compensation for damage or loss sustained by the tenant as the result of the order.

PART II

SECURITY OF TENURE FOR BUSINESS, PROFESSIONAL AND OTHER TENANTS

Tenancies to which Part II applies

Tenancies to which Part II applies

23-(1) Subject to the provisions of this Act, this Part of this Act applies to any tenancy where the property comprised in the tenancy is or includes premises which are occupied by the tenant and are so occupied for the purposes of a business carried on by him or for those and other purposes.

(1A) Occupation or the carrying on of a business-

by a company in which the tenant has a controlling interest; or

   (b) where the tenant is a company, by a person with a controlling interest in the company,

shall be treated for the purposes of this section as equivalent to occupation or, as the case may be, the carrying on of a business by the tenant.

(1B) Accordingly references (however expressed) in this Part of this Act to the business of, or to use, occupation or enjoyment by, the tenant shall be construed as including references to the business of, or to use, occupation or enjoyment by, a company falling within subsection (1A)(a) above or a person falling within subsection (1A)(b) above.

(2) In this Part of this Act the expression 'business' includes a trade, profession or employment and includes any activity carried on by a body of persons, whether corporate or unincorporate.

(3) In the following provisions of this Part of this Act the expression 'the holding,' in relation to a tenancy to which this Part of this Act applies, means the property comprised in the tenancy, there being excluded any part thereof which is occupied neither by the tenant nor by a person employed by the tenant and so employed for the purposes of a business by reason of which the tenancy is one to which this Part of this Act applies.

(4) Where the tenant is carrying on a business, in all or any part of the property comprised in a tenancy, in breach of a prohibition (however expressed) of use for business purposes which subsists under the terms of the tenancy and extends to the whole of that property, this Part of this Act shall not apply to the tenancy unless the immediate landlord or his predecessor in title has consented to the breach or the immediate landlord has acquiesced therein.

In this subsection the reference to a prohibition of use for business purposes does not include a prohibition of use for the purposes of a specified business, or of use for purposes of any but a specified business, but save as aforesaid includes a prohibition of use for the purposes of some one or more only of the classes of business specified in the definition of that expression in subsection (2) of this section.

Continuation and renewal of tenancies

Continuation of tenancies to which Part II applies and grant of new tenancies

24-(1) A tenancy to which this Part of this Act applies shall not come to an end unless terminated in accordance with the provisions of this Part of this Act; and, subject to the following provisions of this Act either the tenant or the landlord under such a tenancy may apply to the court for an order for the grant of a new tenancy-

(a) if the landlord has given notice under section 25 of this Act to terminate the tenancy, or

(b) if the tenant has made a request for a new tenancy in accordance with section 26 of this Act.

(2) The last foregoing subsection shall not prevent the coming to an end of a tenancy by notice to quit given by the tenant, by surrender or forfeiture, or by the forfeiture of a superior tenancy unless-

(a) in the case of a notice to quit, the notice was given before the tenant had been in occupation in right of the tenancy for one month;

(2A) Neither the tenant nor the landlord may make an application under subsection (1) above if the other has made such an application and the application has been served.

(2B) Neither the tenant nor the landlord may make such an application if the landlord has made an application under section 29(2) of this Act and the application has been served.

(2C) The landlord may not withdraw an application under subsection (1) above unless the tenant consents to its withdrawal.

(3) Notwithstanding anything in subsection (1) of this section-

(a) where a tenancy to which this Part of this Act applies ceases to be such a tenancy, it shall not come to an end by reason only of the cesser, but if it was granted for a term of years certain and has been continued by subsection (1) of this section then (without prejudice to the termination thereof in accordance with any terms of the tenancy) it may be terminated by not less than three nor more than six months' notice in writing given by the landlord to the tenant;

(b) where, at a time when a tenancy is not one to which this Part of this Act applies, the landlord gives notice to quit, the operation of the notice shall not be affected by reason that the tenancy becomes one to which this Part of this Act applies after the giving of the notice.

Applications for determination of interim rent while tenancy continues

24A-(1) Subject to subsection (2) below, if-

(a) the landlord of a tenancy to which this Part of this Act applies has given notice under section 25 of this Act to terminate the tenancy; or

(b) the tenant of such a tenancy has made a request for a new tenancy in accordance with section 26 of this Act,

either of them may make an application to the court to determine a rent (an 'interim rent') which the tenant is to pay while the tenancy ('the relevant tenancy') continues by virtue of section 24 of this Act and the court may order payment of an interim rent in accordance with section 24C or 24D of this Act.

(2) Neither the tenant nor the landlord may make an application under subsection (1) above if the other has made such an application and has not withdrawn it.

(3) No application shall be entertained under subsection (1) above if it is made more than six months after the termination of the relevant tenancy.

Date from which interim rent is payable

24B-(1) The interim rent determined on an application under section 24A(1) of this Act shall be payable from the appropriate date.

(2) If an application under section 24A(1) of this Act is made in a case where the landlord has given a notice under section 25 of this Act, the appropriate date is the earliest date of termination that could have been specified in the landlord's notice.

(3) If an application under section 24A(1) of this Act is made in a case where the tenant has made a request for a new tenancy under section 26 of this Act, the appropriate date is the earliest date that could have been specified in the tenant's request as the date from which the new tenancy is to begin.

Amount of interim rent where new tenancy of whole premises granted and landlord not opposed

24C-(1) This section applies where-

(a) the landlord gave a notice under section 25 of this Act at a time when the tenant was in occupation of the whole of the property comprised in the relevant tenancy for purposes such as are mentioned in section 23(1) of this Act and stated in the notice that he was not opposed to the grant of a new tenancy; or

(b) the tenant made a request for a new tenancy under section 26 of this Act at a time when he was in occupation of the whole of that property for such purposes and the landlord did not give notice under subsection (6) of that section,

and the landlord grants a new tenancy of the whole of the property comprised in the relevant tenancy to the tenant (whether as a result of an order for the grant of a new tenancy or otherwise).

Subject to the following provisions of this section, the rent payable under and at the commencement of the new tenancy shall also be the interim rent.

Subsection (2) above does not apply where-

(a) the landlord or the tenant shows to the satisfaction of the court that the interim rent under that subsection differs substantially from the relevant rent; or

(b) the landlord or the tenant shows to the satisfaction of the court that the terms of the new tenancy differ from the terms of the relevant tenancy to such an extent that the interim rent under that subsection is substantially different from the rent which (in default of such agreement) the court would have determined under section 34 of this Act to be payable under a tenancy which commenced on the same day as the new tenancy and whose other terms were the same as the relevant tenancy.

In this section 'the relevant rent' means the rent which (in default of agreement between the landlord and the tenant) the court would have determined under section 34 of this Act to be payable under the new tenancy if the new tenancy had commenced on the appropriate date (within the meaning of section 24B of this Act).

The interim rent in a case where subsection (2) above does not apply by virtue only of subsection (3)(a) above is the relevant rent.

The interim rent in a case where subsection (2) above does not apply by virtue only of subsection (3)(b) above, or by virtue of subsection (3)(a) and (b) above, is the rent which it is reasonable for the tenant to pay while the relevant tenancy continues by virtue of section 24 of this Act.

In determining the interim rent under subsection (6) above the court shall have regard-

(a) to the rent payable under the terms of the relevant tenancy; and

(b) to the rent payable under any sub-tenancy of part of the property comprised in the relevant tenancy,

but otherwise subsections (1) and (2) of section 34 of this Act shall apply to the determination as they would apply to the determination of a rent under that section if a new tenancy of the whole of the property comprised in the relevant tenancy were granted to the tenant by order of the court and the duration of that new tenancy were the same as the duration of the new tenancy which is actually granted to the tenant.

(8) In this section and section 24D of this Act 'the relevant tenancy' has the same meaning as in section 24A of this Act.

Amount of interim rent in any other case

24D-(1) The interim rent in a case where section 24C of this Act does not apply is the rent which it is reasonable for the tenant to pay while the relevant tenancy continues by virtue of section 24 of this Act.

(2) In determining the interim rent under subsection (1) above the court shall have regard-

(a) to the rent payable under the terms of the relevant tenancy; and

(b) to the rent payable under any sub-tenancy of part of the property comprised in the relevant tenancy,

but otherwise subsections (1) and (2) of section 34 of this Act shall apply to the determination as they would apply to the determination of a rent under that section if a new tenancy from year to year of the whole of the property comprised in the relevant tenancy were granted to the tenant by order of the court.

(3) If the court-

(a) has made an order for the grant of a new tenancy and has ordered payment of interim rent in accordance with section 24C of this Act, but

(b) either-

    (i) it subsequently revokes under section 36(2) of this Act the order for the grant of a new tenancy; or

    (ii) the landlord and tenant agree not to act on the order,

the court on the application of the landlord or the tenant shall determine a new interim rent in accordance with subsections (1) and (2) above without a further application under section 24A(1) of this Act.

Termination of tenancy by the landlord

25-(1) The landlord may terminate a tenancy to which this Part of this Act applies by a notice given to the tenant in the prescribed form specifying the date at which the tenancy is to come to an end (hereinafter referred to as "the date of termination"):

> Provided that this subsection has effect subject to the provisions of section 29B(4) of this Act and Part IV of this Act as to the interim continuation of tenancies pending the disposal of applications to the court.

(2) Subject to the provisions of the next following subsection, a notice under this section shall not have effect unless it is given not more than twelve nor less than six months before the date of termination specified therein.

(3) In the case of a tenancy which apart from this Act could have been brought to an end by notice to quit given by the landlord-

(a) the date of termination specified in a notice under this section shall not be earlier than the earliest date on which apart from this Part of this Act the tenancy could have been brought to an end by notice to quit given by the landlord on the date of the giving of the notice under this section; and

(b) where apart from this Part of this Act more than six months' notice to quit would have been required to bring the tenancy to an end, the last foregoing subsection shall have effect with the substitution for twelve months of a period six months longer than the length of notice to quit which would have been required as aforesaid.

(4) In the case of any other tenancy, a notice under this section shall not specify a date of termination earlier than the date on which apart

from this Part of this Act the tenancy would have come to an end by effluxion of time.

(5) ...

(6) A notice under this section shall not have effect unless it states whether the landlord is opposed to the grant of a new tenancy to the tenant.

(7) A notice under this section which states that the landlord is opposed to the grant of a new tenancy to the tenant shall not have effect unless it also specifies one or more of the grounds specified in section 30(1) of this Act as the ground or grounds for his opposition.

(8) A notice under this section which states that the landlord is not opposed to the grant of a new tenancy to the tenant shall not have effect unless it sets out the landlord's proposals as to-

(a) the property to be comprised in the new tenancy (being either the whole or part of the property comprised in the current tenancy);

(b) the rent to be payable under the new tenancy; and

(c) the other terms of the new tenancy.

Tenant's request for a new tenancy

26-(1) A tenant's request for a new tenancy may be made where the current tenancy is a tenancy granted for a term of years certain exceeding one year, whether or not continued by section 24 of this Act, or granted for a term of years certain and thereafter from year to year.

(2) A tenant's request for a new tenancy shall be for a tenancy beginning with such date, not more than twelve nor less than six months after the making of the request, as may be specified therein:

Provided that the said date shall not be earlier than the date on which apart from this Act the current tenancy would come to an end by effluxion of time or could be brought to an end by notice to quit given by the tenant.

(3) A tenant's request for a new tenancy shall not have effect unless it is made by notice in the prescribed form given to the landlord and sets out the tenant's proposals as to the property to be comprised in the new tenancy (being either the whole or part of the property comprised in the current tenancy), as to the rent to be payable under the new tenancy and as to the other terms of the new tenancy.

(4) A tenant's request for a new tenancy shall not be made if the landlord has already given notice under the last foregoing section to terminate the current tenancy, or if the tenant has already given notice to quit or notice under the next following section; and no such notice shall be given by the landlord or the tenant after the making by the tenant of a request for a new tenancy.

(5) Where the tenant makes a request for a new tenancy in accordance with the foregoing provisions of this section, the current tenancy shall, subject to the provisions of

> sections 29B(4) and 36(2) of this Act and the provisions of Part IV of this Act as to the interim continuation of tenancies, terminate immediately before the date specified in the request for the beginning of the new tenancy.

(6) Within two months of the making of a tenant's request for a new tenancy the landlord may give notice to the tenant that he will oppose an application to the court for the grant of a new tenancy, and any such notice shall state on which of the grounds mentioned in section 30 of this Act the landlord will oppose the application.

Termination by tenant of tenancy for fixed term

27-(1) Where the tenant under a tenancy to which this Part of this Act applies, being a tenancy granted for a term of years certain, gives to the immediate landlord, not later than three months before the date on which apart from this Act the tenancy would come to an end by effluxion of time, a notice in writing that the tenant does not desire the tenancy to be continued, section 24 of this Act shall not have effect in relation to the tenancy, unless the notice is given before the tenant has been in occupation in right of the tenancy for one month.

(1A) Section 24 of this Act shall not have effect in relation to a tenancy for a term of years certain where the tenant is not in occupation of the property comprised in the tenancy at the time when, apart from this Act, the tenancy would come to an end by effluxion of time.

(2) A tenancy granted for a term of years certain which is continuing by virtue of section 24 of this Act shall not come to an end by reason only of the tenant ceasing to occupy the property comprised in the tenancy but may be brought to an end on any day by not less than three months' notice in writing given by the tenant to the immediate landlord, whether the notice is given after the date on which apart from this Act the tenancy would have come to an end or before that date, but not before the tenant has been in occupation in right of the tenancy for one month.

(3) Where a tenancy is terminated under subsection (2) above, any rent payable in respect of a period which begins before, and ends after, the tenancy is terminated shall be apportioned, and any rent paid by the tenant in excess of the amount apportioned to the period before termination shall be recoverable by him.

Renewal of tenancies by agreement

28 Where the landlord and tenant agree for the grant to the tenant of a future tenancy of the holding, or of the holding with other land, on terms and from a date specified in the agreement, the current tenancy shall continue until that date but no longer, and shall not be a tenancy to which this Part of this Act applies.

Applications to court

Order by court for grant of new tenancy or termination of current tenancy

29-(1) Subject to the provisions of this Act, on an application under section 24(1) of this Act, the court shall make an order for the grant of a new tenancy and accordingly for the termination of the current tenancy immediately before the commencement of the new tenancy.

(2) Subject to the following provisions of this Act, a landlord may apply to the court for an order for the termination of a tenancy to which this Part of this Act applies without the grant of a new tenancy-

(a) if he has given notice under section 25 of this Act that he is opposed to the grant of a new tenancy to the tenant; or

(b) if the tenant has made a request for a new tenancy in accordance with section 26 of this Act and the landlord has given notice under subsection (6) of that section.

(3) The landlord may not make an application under subsection (2) above if either the tenant or the landlord has made an application under section 24(1) of this Act.

(4) Subject to the provisions of this Act, where the landlord makes an application under subsection (2) above-

(a) if he establishes, to the satisfaction of the court, any of the grounds on which he is entitled to make the application in accordance with section 30 of this Act, the court shall make an order for the termination of the current tenancy in accordance with section 64 of this Act without the grant of a new tenancy; and

(b) if not, it shall make an order for the grant of a new tenancy and accordingly for the termination of the current tenancy immediately before the commencement of the new tenancy.

(5) The court shall dismiss an application by the landlord under section 24(1) of this Act if the tenant informs the court that he does not want a new tenancy.

(6) The landlord may not withdraw an application under subsection (2) above unless the tenant consents to its withdrawal.

Time limits for applications to court

29A-(1) Subject to section 29B of this Act, the court shall not entertain an application-

(a) by the tenant or the landlord under section 24(1) of this Act; or

(b) by the landlord under section 29(2) of this Act,

if it is made after the end of the statutory period.

(2) In this section and section 29B of this Act 'the statutory period' means a period ending-

(a) where the landlord gave a notice under section 25 of this Act, on the date specified in his notice; and

(b) where the tenant made a request for a new tenancy under section 26 of this Act, immediately before the date specified in his request.

(3) Where the tenant has made a request for a new tenancy under section 26 of this Act, the court shall not entertain an application under section 24(1) of this Act which is made before the end of the period of two months beginning with the date of the making of the request, unless the application is made after the landlord has given a notice under section 26(6) of this Act.

Agreements extending time limits

29B-(1) After the landlord has given a notice under section 25 of this Act, or the tenant has made a request under section 26 of this Act, but before the end of the statutory period, the landlord and tenant may agree that an application such as is mentioned in section 29A(1) of this Act may be made before the end of a period specified in the agreement which will expire after the end of the statutory period.

(2) The landlord and tenant may from time to time by agreement further extend the period for making such an application, but any such agreement must be made before the end of the period specified in the current agreement.

(3) Where an agreement is made under this section, the court may entertain an application such as is mentioned in section 29A(1) of this Act if it is made before the end of the period specified in the agreement.

(4) Where an agreement is made under this section, or two or more agreements are made under this section, the landlord's notice under section 25 of this Act or tenant's request under section 26 of this Act shall be treated as terminating the tenancy at the end of the period specified in the agreement or, as the case may be, at the end of the period specified in the last of those agreements.

Opposition by landlord to application for new tenancy

30-(1) The grounds on which a landlord may oppose an application under section 24(1) of this Act, or make an application under section 29(2) of this Act, are such of the following grounds as may be stated in the landlord's notice under section 25 of this Act or, as the case may be, under subsection (6) of section 26 thereof, that is to say-

(a) where under the current tenancy the tenant has any obligations as respects the repair and maintenance of the holding, that the tenant ought not to be granted a new tenancy in view of the state of repair of the holding, being a state resulting from the tenant's failure to comply with the said obligations;

(b) that the tenant ought not to be granted a new tenancy in view of his persistent delay in paying rent which has become due;

(c) that the tenant ought not to be granted a new tenancy in view of other substantial breaches by him of his obligations under the current tenancy, or for any other reason connected with the tenant's use or management of the holding;

(d) that the landlord has offered and is willing to provide or secure the provision of alternative accommodation for the tenant, that the terms on which the alternative accommodation is available are reasonable having regard to the terms of the current tenancy and to all other relevant circumstances, and that the accommodation and the time at which it will be available are suitable for the tenant's requirements (including the requirement to preserve goodwill) having regard to the nature and class of his business and to the situation and extent of, and facilities afforded by, the holding;

(e) where the current tenancy was created by the sub-letting of part only of the property comprised in a superior tenancy and the landlord is the owner of an interest in reversion expectant on the termination of that superior tenancy, that the aggregate of the rents reasonably obtainable on separate lettings of the holding and the remainder of that property would be substantially less than the rent reasonably obtainable on a letting of that property as a whole, that on the termination of the current tenancy the landlord requires possession of the holding for the purpose of letting or otherwise disposing of the said property as a whole, and that in view thereof the tenant ought not to be granted a new tenancy;

(f) that on the termination of the current tenancy the landlord intends to demolish or reconstruct the premises comprised in the holding or a substantial part of those premises or to carry out substantial work of construction on the holding or part thereof and that he could not reasonably do so without obtaining possession of the holding;

(g) subject as hereinafter provided, that on the termination of the current tenancy the landlord intends to occupy the holding for the purposes, or partly for the purposes, of a business to be carried on by him therein, or as his residence.

(1A) Where the landlord has a controlling interest in a company, the reference in subsection (1)(g) above to the landlord shall be construed as a reference to the landlord or that company.

(1B) Subject to subsection (2A) below, where the landlord is a company and a person has a controlling interest in the company, the reference in subsection (1)(g) above to the landlord shall be construed as a reference to the landlord or that person.

(2) The landlord shall not be entitled to oppose an application under section 24(1) of this Act, or make an application under section 29(2) of this Act, on the ground specified in paragraph (g) of the last foregoing subsection if the interest of the landlord, or an interest which has merged in that interest and but for the merger would be the interest of the landlord, was purchased or created after the beginning of the period of five years which ends with the termination of the current tenancy, and at all times since the purchase or creation thereof the holding has been comprised in a tenancy or successive tenancies of the description specified in subsection (1) of section 23 of this Act.

(2A) Subsection (1B) above shall not apply if the controlling interest was acquired after the beginning of the period of five years which ends with the termination of the current tenancy, and at all times since the acquisition of the controlling interest the holding has been comprised in a tenancy or successive tenancies of the description specified in section 23(1) of this Act.

(3) ...

Dismissal of application for new tenancy where landlord successfully opposes

31-(1) If the landlord opposes an application under subsection (1) of section 24 of this Act on grounds on which he is entitled to oppose it in accordance with the last foregoing section and establishes any of those grounds to the satisfaction of the court, the court shall not make an order for the grant of a new tenancy.

(2) Where the landlord opposes an application under section 24(1) of this Act, or makes an application under section 29(2) of this Act, on one or more of the grounds specified in section 30(1)(d) to (f) of this Act but establishes none of those grounds, and none of the other grounds specified in section 30(1) of this Act, to the satisfaction of the court, then if the court would have been satisfied on any of the grounds specified in section 30(1)(d) to (f) of this Act if the date of termination specified in the landlord's notice or, as the case may be, the date specified in the tenant's request for a new tenancy as the date from which the new tenancy is to begin, had been such later date as the court may determine, being a date not more than one year later than the date so specified-

(a) the court shall make a declaration to that effect, stating of which of the said grounds the court would have been satisfied as aforesaid and specifying the date determined by the court as aforesaid, but shall not make an order for the grant of a new tenancy;

(b) if, within fourteen days after the making of the declaration, the tenant so requires the court shall make an order substituting the said date for the date specified in the said landlord's notice or tenant's request, and thereupon that notice or request shall have effect accordingly.

Grant of new tenancy in some cases where section 30(1)(f) applies

31A-(1) Where the landlord opposes an application under section 24(1) of this Act on the ground specified in paragraph (f) of section 30(1) of this Act, or makes an application under section 29(2) of this Act on that ground, the court shall not hold that the landlord could not reasonably carry out the demolition, reconstruction or work of construction intended without obtaining possession of the holding if-

(a) the tenant agrees to the inclusion in the terms of the new tenancy of terms giving the landlord access and other facilities for carrying out the work intended and, given that access and those facilities, the landlord could reasonably carry out the work without obtaining possession of the holding and without interfering to a substantial extent or for a substantial time with the use of the holding for the purposes of the business carried on by the tenant; or

(b) the tenant is willing to accept a tenancy of an economically separable part of the holding and either paragraph (a) of this section is satisfied with respect to that part or possession of the remainder of the holding would be reasonably sufficient to enable the landlord to carry out the intended work.

(2) For the purposes of subsection (1) (b) of this section a part of a holding shall be deemed to be an economically separate part if, and only if, the aggregate of the rents which, after the completion of the intended work, would be reasonably obtainable on separate lettings of that part and the remainder of the premises affected by or resulting from the work would not be substantially less than the rent which would then be reasonably obtainable on a letting of those premises as a whole.

Property to be comprised in new tenancy

32-(1) Subject to the following provisions of this section, an order under section 29 of this Act for the grant of a new tenancy shall be an order for the grant of a new tenancy of the holding; and in the absence of agreement between the landlord and the tenant as to the property which constitutes the holding the court shall in the order designate that property by reference to the circumstances existing at the date of the order.

(1A) Where the court, by virtue of paragraph (b) of section 31A(1) of this Act, makes an order under section 29 of this Act for the grant of a new tenancy in a case where the tenant is willing to accept a tenancy of part of the holding, the order shall be an order for the grant of a new tenancy of that part only.

(2) The foregoing provisions of this section shall not apply in a case where the property comprised in the current tenancy includes other property besides the holding and the landlord requires any new tenancy ordered to be granted under section 29 of this Act to be a tenancy of the whole of the property comprised in the current tenancy; but in any such case-

(a) any order under the said section 29 for the grant of a new tenancy shall be an order for the grant of a new tenancy of the whole of the property comprised in the current tenancy, and

(b) references in the following provisions of this Part of this Act to the holding shall be construed as references to the whole of that property.

(3) Where the current tenancy includes rights enjoyed by the tenant in connection with the holding, those rights shall be included in a tenancy ordered to be granted under section 29 of this Act, except as otherwise agreed between the landlord and the tenant or, in default of such agreement, determined by the court.

Duration of new tenancy

33 Where on an application under this Part of this Act the court makes an order for the grant of a new tenancy, the new tenancy shall be such tenancy as may be agreed between the landlord and the tenant, or, in default of such an agreement, shall be such a tenancy as may be determined by the court to be reasonable in all the circumstances, being, if it is a tenancy for a term of years certain, a tenancy for a term not exceeding fifteen years, and shall begin on the coming to an end of the current tenancy.

Rent under new tenancy

34-(1) The rent payable under a tenancy granted by order of the court under this Part of this Act shall be such as may be agreed between the landlord and the tenant or as, in default of such agreement, may be determined by the court to be that at which, having regard to the terms of the tenancy (other than those relating to rent), the holding might reasonably be expected to be let in the open market by a willing lessor, there being disregarded-

(a) any effect on rent of the fact that the tenant has or his predecessors in title have been in occupation of the holding,

(b) any goodwill attached to the holding by reason of the carrying on thereat of the business of the tenant (whether by him or by a predecessor of his in that business),

(c) any effect on rent of an improvement to which this paragraph applies,

(d) in the case of a holding comprising licensed premises, any addition to its value attributable to the licence, if it appears to the court that having regard to the terms of the current tenancy and any other relevant circumstances the benefit of the licence belongs to the tenant.

(2) Paragraph (c) of the foregoing subsection applies to any improvement carried out by a person who at the time it was carried out was the tenant, but only if it was carried out otherwise than in pursuance of an obligation to his immediate landlord, and either it was carried out during the current tenancy or the following conditions are satisfied, that is to say-

(a) that it was completed not more than twenty-one years before the application to the court was made; and

(b) that the holding or any part of it affected by the improvement has at all times since the completion of the improvement been comprised in tenancies of the description specified in section 23(1) of this Act; and

(c) that at the termination of each of those tenancies the tenant did not quit.

(2A) If this Part of this Act applies by virtue of section 23(1A) of this Act, the reference in subsection (1)(d) above to the tenant shall be construed as including-

(a) a company in which the tenant has a controlling interest, or

(b) where the tenant is a company, a person with a controlling interest in the company.

(3) Where the rent is determined by the court the court may, if it thinks fit, further determine that the terms of the tenancy shall include such provision for varying the rent as may be specified in the determination.

(4) It is hereby declared that the matters which are to be taken into account by the court in determining the rent include any effect on rent of the operation of the provisions of the Landlord and Tenant (Covenants) Act 1995.

Other terms of new tenancy

35-(1) The terms of a tenancy granted by order of the court under this Part of this Act (other than terms as to the duration thereof and as to the rent payable thereunder), including, where different persons own interests which fulfil the conditions specified in section 44(1) of this Act in different parts of it, terms as to the apportionment of the rent, shall be such as may be agreed between the landlord and the tenant or as, in default of such agreement, may be determined by the court; and in determining those terms the court shall have regard to the terms of the current tenancy and to all relevant circumstances.

(2) In subsection (1) of this section the reference to all relevant circumstances includes (without prejudice to the generality of that reference) a reference to the operation of the provisions of the Landlord and Tenant (Covenants) Act 1995.

Carrying out of order for new tenancy

36-(1) Where under this Part of this Act the court makes an order for the grant of a new tenancy, then, unless the order is revoked under the next following subsection or the landlord and the tenant agree not to act upon the order, the landlord shall be bound to execute or make in favour of the tenant, and the tenant shall be bound to accept, a lease or agreement for a tenancy of the holding embodying the terms agreed between the landlord and the tenant or determined by the court in accordance with the foregoing provisions of this Part of this Act; and where the landlord executes or makes such a lease or agreement the tenant shall be bound, if so required by the landlord, to execute a counterpart or duplicate thereof.

(2) If the tenant, within fourteen days after the making of an order under this Part of this Act for the grant of a new tenancy, applies to the court for the revocation of the order the court shall revoke the order; and where the order is so revoked, then, if it is so agreed between the landlord and the tenant or determined by the court, the current tenancy shall continue, beyond the date at which it would have come to an end apart from this subsection, for such period as may be so agreed or determined to be necessary to afford to the landlord a reasonable opportunity for reletting or otherwise disposing of the premises which would have been comprised in the new tenancy; and while the current tenancy continues by virtue of this subsection it shall not be a tenancy to which this Part of this Act applies.

(3) Where an order is revoked under the last foregoing subsection any provision thereof as to payment of costs shall not cease to have effect by reason only of the revocation; but the court may, if it thinks fit, revoke or vary any such provision or, where no costs have been awarded in the proceedings for the revoked order, award such costs.

(4) A lease executed or agreement made under this section, in a case where the interest of the lessor is subject to a mortgage, shall be deemed to be one authorised by section 99 of the Law of Property Act 1925 (which confers certain powers of leasing on mortgagors in possession), and subsection (13) of that section (which allows those

powers to be restricted or excluded by agreement) shall not have effect in relation to such a lease or agreement.

Compensation where order for new tenancy precluded on certain grounds

37-(1) Subject to the provisions of this Act, in a case specified in subsection (1A), (1B) or (1C) below (a 'compensation case') the tenant shall be entitled on quitting the holding to recover from the landlord by way of compensation an amount determined in accordance with this section.

(1A) The first compensation case is where on the making of an application by the tenant under section 24(1) of this Act the court is precluded (whether by subsection (1) or subsection (2) of section 31 of this Act) from making an order for the grant of a new tenancy by reason of any of the grounds specified in paragraphs (e), (f) and (g) of section 30(1) of this Act (the 'compensation grounds') and not of any grounds specified in any other paragraph of section 30(1).

(1B) The second compensation case is where on the making of an application under section 29(2) of this Act the court is precluded (whether by section 29(4)(a) or section 31(2) of this Act) from making an order for the grant of a new tenancy by reason of any of the compensation grounds and not of any other grounds specified in section 30(1) of this Act.

(1C) The third compensation case is where-

(a) the landlord's notice under section 25 of this Act or, as the case may be, under section 26(6) of this Act, states his opposition to the grant of a new tenancy on any of the compensation grounds and not on any other grounds specified in section 30(1) of this Act; and

(b) either-

   (i) no application is made by the tenant under section 24(1) of this Act or by the landlord under section 29(2) of this Act; or

   (ii) such an application is made but is subsequently withdrawn.

(2) Subject to the following provisions of this section, compensation under this section shall be as follows, that is to say-

(a) where the conditions specified in the next following subsection are satisfied in relation to the whole of the holding it shall be the product of the appropriate multiplier and twice the rateable value of the holding,

(b) in any other case it shall be the product of the appropriate multiplier and the rateable value of the holding.

(3) The said conditions are-

(a) that, during the whole of the fourteen years immediately preceding the termination of the current tenancy, premises being or comprised in the holding have been occupied for the purposes of a business carried on by the occupier or for those and other purposes;

(b) that, if during those fourteen years there was a change in the occupier of the premises, the person who was the occupier immediately after the change was the successor to the business carried on by the person who was the occupier immediately before the change.

(3A) If the conditions specified in subsection (3) above are satisfied in relation to part of the holding but not in relation to the other part, the amount of compensation shall be the aggregate of sums calculated separately as compensation in respect of each part, and accordingly, for the purpose of calculating compensation in respect of a part any reference in this section to the holding shall be construed as a reference to that part.

(3B) Where section 44(1A) of this Act applies, the compensation shall be determined separately for each part and compensation determined for any part shall be recoverable only from the person who is the owner of an interest in that part which fulfils the conditions specified in section 44(1) of this Act.

(4) Where the court is precluded from making an order for the grant of a new tenancy under this Part of this Act in a compensation case, the court shall on the application of the tenant certify that fact.

(5) For the purposes of subsection (2) of this section the rateable value of the holding shall be determined as follows-

(a) where in the valuation list in force at the date on which the landlord's notice under section 25 or, as the case may be, subsection (6) of section 26 of this Act is given a value is then shown as the annual value (as hereinafter defined) of the holding, the rateable value of the holding shall be taken to be that value;

(b) where no such value is so shown with respect to the holding but such a value or such values is or are so shown with respect to premises comprised in or comprising the holding or part of it, the rateable value of the holding shall be taken to be such value as is found by a proper apportionment or aggregation of the value or values so shown;

(c) where the rateable value of the holding cannot be ascertained in accordance with the foregoing paragraphs of this subsection, it shall be taken to be the value which, apart from any exemption from assessment to rates, would on a proper assessment be the value to be entered in the said valuation list as the annual value of the holding;

and any dispute arising, whether in proceedings before the court or otherwise, as to the determination for those purposes of the rateable value of the holding shall be referred to the Commissioners of Inland Revenue for decision by the valuation officer.

An appeal shall lie to the Lands Tribunal from any decision of a valuation officer under this subsection, but subject thereto any such decision shall be final.

(5A) If part of the holding is domestic property, as defined in section 66 of the Local Government Finance Act 1988-

(a) the domestic property shall be disregarded in determining the rateable value of the holding under subsection (5) of this section; and

(b) if, on the date specified in subsection (5)(a) of this section, the tenant occupied the whole or any part of the domestic property, the amount of compensation to which he is entitled under subsection (1) of this section shall be increased by the addition of a sum equal to his reasonable expenses in removing from the domestic property.

(5B) Any question as to the amount of the sum referred to in paragraph (b) of subsection (5A) of this section shall be determined by agreement between the landlord and the tenant or, in default of agreement, by the court.

(5C) If the whole of the holding is domestic property, as defined in section 66 of the Local Government Finance Act 1988, for the purposes of subsection (2) of this section the rateable value of the holding shall be taken to be an amount equal to the rent at which it is estimated the holding might reasonably be expected to let from year to year if the tenant undertook to pay all usual tenant's rates and taxes and to bear the cost of the repairs and insurance and the other expenses (if any) necessary to maintain the holding in a state to command that rent.

(5D) The following provisions shall have effect as regards a determination of an amount mentioned in subsection (5C) of this section-

(a) the date by reference to which such a determination is to be made is the date on which the landlord's notice under section 25 or, as the case may be, subsection (6) of section 26 of this Act is given;

(b) dispute arising, whether in proceedings before the court or otherwise, as to such a determination shall be referred to the Commissioners of Inland Revenue for decision by a valuation officer;

(c) an appeal shall lie to the Lands Tribunal from such a decision, but subject to that, such a decision shall be final.

(5E) Any deduction made under paragraph 2A of Schedule 6 to the Local Government Finance Act 1988 (deduction from valuation of hereditaments used for breeding horses etc) shall be disregarded, to the extent that it relates to the holding, in determining the rateable value of the holding under subsection (5) of this section.

(6) The Commissioners of Inland Revenue may by statutory instrument make rules prescribing the procedure in connection with references under this section.

(7) In this section-

the reference to the termination of the current tenancy is a reference to the date of termination specified in the landlord's notice under section 25 of this Act or, as the case may be, the date specified in the tenant's request for a new tenancy as the date from which the new tenancy is to begin;

the expression 'annual value' means rateable value except that where the rateable value differs from the net annual value the said expression means net annual value;

the expression 'valuation officer' means any officer of the Commissioners of Inland Revenue for the time being authorised by a certificate of the Commissioners to act in relation to a valuation list.

(8) In subsection (2) of this section 'the appropriate multiplier' means such multiplier as the Secretary of State may by order made by statutory instrument prescribe and different multipliers may be so prescribed in relation to different cases.

(9) A statutory instrument containing an order under subsection (8) of this section shall be subject to annulment in pursuance of a resolution of either House of Parliament.

Compensation for possession obtained by misrepresentation

37A-(1) Where the court-

(a) makes an order for the termination of the current tenancy but does not make an order for the grant of a new tenancy, or

(b) refuses an order for the grant of a new tenancy,

and it is subsequently made to appear to the court that the order was obtained, or the court was induced to refuse the grant, by misrepresentation or the concealment of material facts, the court may order the landlord to pay to the tenant such sum as appears sufficient as compensation for damage or loss sustained by the tenant as the result of the order or refusal.

(2) Where-

(a) the tenant has quit the holding-

   (i) after making but withdrawing an application under section 24(1) of this Act; or

(ii) without making such an application; and

(b) it is made to appear to the court that he did so by reason of misrepresentation or the concealment of material facts,

the court may order the landlord to pay to the tenant such sum as appears sufficient as compensation for damage or loss sustained by the tenant as the result of quitting the holding.

Restriction on agreements excluding provisions of Part II

38-(1) Any agreement relating to a tenancy to which this Part of this Act applies (whether contained in the instrument creating the tenancy or not) shall be void (except as provided by section 38A of this Act) in so far as it purports to preclude the tenant from making an application or request under this Part of this Act or provides for the termination or the surrender of the tenancy in the event of his making such an application or request or for the imposition of any penalty or disability on the tenant in that event.

(2) Where-

(a) during the whole of the five years immediately preceding the date on which the tenant under a tenancy to which this Part of this Act applies is to quit the holding, premises being or comprised in the holding have been occupied for the purposes of a business carried on by the occupier or for those and other purposes, and

(b) if during those five years there was a change in the occupier of the premises, the person who was the occupier immediately after the change was the successor to the business carried on by the person who was the occupier immediately before the change,

any agreement (whether contained in the instrument creating the tenancy or not and whether made before or after the termination of that tenancy) which purports to exclude or reduce compensation under section 37 of this Act shall to that extent be void, so however that this subsection shall not affect any agreement as to the amount of any such compensation which is made after the right to compensation has accrued.

(3) In a case not falling within the last foregoing subsection the right to compensation conferred by section 37 of this Act may be excluded or modified by agreement.

(4) ...

Agreements to exclude provisions of Part II

38A-(1) The persons who will be the landlord and the tenant in relation to a tenancy to be granted for a term of years certain which will be a tenancy to which this Part of this Act applies may agree that the provisions of sections 24 to 28 of this Act shall be excluded in relation to that tenancy.

(2) The persons who are the landlord and the tenant in relation to a tenancy to which this Part of this Act applies may agree that the tenancy shall be surrendered on such date or in such circumstances as may be specified in the agreement and on such terms (if any) as may be so specified.

(3) An agreement under subsection (1) above shall be void unless-

(a) the landlord has served on the tenant a notice in the form, or substantially in the form, set out in Schedule 1 to the Regulatory Reform (Business Tenancies) (England and Wales) Order 2003 ("the 2003 Order"); and

(b) the requirements specified in Schedule 2 to that Order are met.

(4) An agreement under subsection (2) above shall be void unless-

(a) the landlord has served on the tenant a notice in the form, or substantially in the form, set out in Schedule 3 to the 2003 Order; and

(b) the requirements specified in Schedule 4 to that Order are met."

General and supplementary provisions

Saving for compulsory acquisitions

39-(1) [Repealed]

(2) If the amount of the compensation which would have been payable under section 37 of this Act if the tenancy had come to an end in circumstances giving rise to compensation under that section and the date at which the acquiring authority obtained possession had been the termination of the current tenancy exceeds the amount of the compensation payable under section 121 of the Lands Clauses Consolidation Act 1845, or section 20 of the Compulsory Purchase Act 1965, in the case of a tenancy to which this Part of this Act applies, that compensation shall be increased by the amount of the excess.

(3) Nothing in section 24 of this Act shall affect the operation of the said section 121.

Duty of tenants and landlords of business premises to give information to each other

40-(1) Where a person who is an owner of an interest in reversion expectant (whether immediately or not) on a tenancy of any business premises has served on the tenant a notice in the prescribed form requiring him to do so, it shall be the duty of the tenant to give the appropriate person in writing the information specified in subsection (2) below.

(2) That information is-

(a) whether the tenant occupies the premises or any part of them wholly or partly for the purposes of a business carried on by him;

(b) whether his tenancy has effect subject to any sub-tenancy on which his tenancy is immediately expectant and, if so-

    (i) what premises are comprised in the sub-tenancy;

    (ii) for what term it has effect (or, if it is terminable by notice, by what notice it can be terminated);

    (iii) what is the rent payable under it;

    (iv) who is the sub-tenant;

    (v) (to the best of his knowledge and belief) whether the sub-tenant is in occupation of the premises or of part of the premises comprised in the sub-tenancy and, if not, what is the sub-tenant's address;

    (vi) whether an agreement is in force excluding in relation to the sub-tenancy the provisions of sections 24 to 28 of this Act; and

    (vii) whether a notice has been given under section 25 or 26(6) of this Act, or a request has been made under section 26 of this Act, in relation to the sub-tenancy and, if so, details of the notice or request; and

(c) (to the best of his knowledge and belief) the name and address of any other person who owns an interest in reversion in any part of the premises.

(3) Where the tenant of any business premises who is a tenant under such a tenancy as is mentioned in section 26(1) of this Act has served on a reversioner or a reversioner's mortgagee in possession a notice in the prescribed form requiring him to do so, it shall be the duty of the person on whom the notice is served to give the appropriate person in writing the information specified in subsection (4) below.

(4) That information is-

(a) whether he is the owner of the fee simple in respect of the premises or any part of them or the mortgagee in possession of such an owner,

(b) if he is not, then (to the best of his knowledge and belief)-

    (i) the name and address of the person who is his or, as the case may be, his mortgagor's immediate landlord in respect of those premises or of the part in respect of which he or his mortgagor is not the owner in fee simple;

    (ii) for what term his or his mortgagor's tenancy has effect and what is the earliest date (if any) at which that tenancy is terminable by notice to quit given by the landlord; and

(iii) whether a notice has been given under section 25 or 26(6) of this Act, or a request has been made under section 26 of this Act, in relation to the tenancy and, if so, details of the notice or request;

(c) (to the best of his knowledge and belief) the name and address of any other person who owns an interest in reversion in any part of the premises; and

(d) if he is a reversioner, whether there is a mortgagee in possession of his interest in the premises and, if so, (to the best of his knowledge and belief) what is the name and address of the mortgagee.

(5) A duty imposed on a person by this section is a duty-

(a) to give the information concerned within the period of one month beginning with the date of service of the notice; and

(b) if within the period of six months beginning with the date of service of the notice that person becomes aware that any information which has been given in pursuance of the notice is not, or is no longer, correct, to give the appropriate person correct information within the period of one month beginning with the date on which he becomes aware.

(6) This section shall not apply to a notice served by or on the tenant more than two years before the date on which apart from this Act his tenancy would come to an end by effluxion of time or could be brought to an end by notice to quit given by the landlord.

(7) Except as provided by section 40A of this Act, the appropriate person for the purposes of this section and section 40A(1) of this Act is the person who served the notice under subsection (1) or (3) above.

(8) In this section-

'business premises' means premises used wholly or partly for the purposes of a business;

'mortgagee in possession' includes a receiver appointed by the mortgagee or by the court who is in receipt of the rents and profits, and 'his mortgagor' shall be construed accordingly;

'reversioner' means any person having an interest in the premises, being an interest in reversion expectant (whether immediately or not) on the tenancy;

'reversioner's mortgagee in possession' means any person being a mortgagee in possession in respect of such an interest; and

'sub-tenant' includes a person retaining possession of any premises by virtue of the Rent (Agriculture) Act 1976 or the Rent Act 1977 after the coming to an end of a sub-tenancy, and 'sub-tenancy' includes a right so to retain possession.

Duties in transfer cases

40A-(1) If a person on whom a notice under section 40(1) or (3) of this Act has been served has transferred his interest in the premises or any part of them to some other person and gives the appropriate person notice in writing-

(a) of the transfer of his interest; and

(b) of the name and address of the person to whom he transferred it,

on giving the notice he ceases in relation to the premises or (as the case may be) to that part to be under any duty imposed by section 40 of this Act.

(2) If-

(a) the person who served the notice under section 40(1) or (3) of this Act ('the transferor') has transferred his interest in the premises to some other person ('the transferee'); and

(b) the transferor or the transferee has given the person required to give the information notice in writing-

    (i) of the transfer; and

    (ii) of the transferee's name and address,

the appropriate person for the purposes of section 40 of this Act and subsection (1) above is the transferee.

(3) If-

(a) a transfer such as is mentioned in paragraph (a) of subsection (2) above has taken place; but

(b) neither the transferor nor the transferee has given a notice such as is mentioned in paragraph (b) of that subsection,

any duty imposed by section 40 of this Act may be performed by giving the information either to the transferor or to the transferee.

Proceedings for breach of duties to give information

40B A claim that a person has broken any duty imposed by section 40 of this Act may be made the subject of civil proceedings for breach of statutory duty; and in any such proceedings a court may order that person to comply with that duty and may make an award of damages.

Trusts

41-(1) Where a tenancy is held on trust, occupation by all or any of the beneficiaries under the trust, and the carrying on of a business by all or any of the beneficiaries, shall be treated for the purposes of section 23 of this Act as equivalent to occupation or the carrying on of a business by the tenant; and in relation to a tenancy to which this Part of this Act applies by virtue of the foregoing provisions of this subsection-

(a) references (however expressed) in this Part of this Act and in the Ninth Schedule to this Act to the business of, or to carrying on of business, use, occupation or enjoyment by, the tenant shall be construed as including references to the business of, or to carrying on of business, use, occupation or enjoyment by, the beneficiaries or beneficiary;

(b) the reference in paragraph (d) of subsection (1) of section 34 of this Act to the tenant shall be construed as including the beneficiaries or beneficiary; and

(c) a change in the persons of the trustees shall not be treated as a change in the person of the tenant.

(2) Where the landlord's interest is held on trust the references in paragraph (g) of subsection (1) of section 30 of this Act to the landlord shall be construed as including references to the beneficiaries under the trust or any of them; but, except in the case of a trust arising under a will or on the intestacy of any person, the reference in subsection (2) of that section to the creation of the interest therein mentioned shall be construed as including the creation of the trust.

Partnerships

41A-(1) The following provisions of this section shall apply where-

(a) a tenancy is held jointly by two or more persons (in this section referred to as the joint tenants); and

(b) the property comprised in the tenancy is or includes premises occupied for the purposes of a business; and

(c) the business (or some other business) was at some time during the existence of the tenancy carried on in partnership by all the persons who were then the joint tenants or by those and other persons and the joint tenants' interest in the premises was then partnership property; and

(d) the business is carried on (whether alone or in partnership with other persons) by one or some only of the joint tenants and no part of the property comprised in the tenancy is occupied, in right of the tenancy, for the purposes of a business carried on (whether alone or in partnership with other persons) by the other or others.

(2) In the following provisions of this section those of the joint tenants who for the time being carry on the business are referred to as the business tenants and the others as the other joint tenants.

(3) Any notice given by the business tenants which, had it been given by all the joint tenants, would have been-

(a) a tenant's request for anew tenancy made in accordance with section 26 of this Act; or

(b) a notice under subsection (1) or subsection (2) of section 27 of this Act; shall be treated as such if it states that it is given by virtue of this section and sets out the facts by virtue of which the persons giving it are the business tenants;

and references in those sections and in section 24A of this Act to the tenant shall be construed accordingly.

(4) A notice given by the landlord to the business tenants which, had it been given to all the joint tenants, would have been a notice under section 25 of this Act shall be treated as such a notice, and references in that section to the tenant shall be construed accordingly.

(5) An application under section 24(1) of this Act for a new tenancy may, instead of being made by all the joint tenants, be made by the business tenants alone; and where it is so made-

(a) this Part of this Act shall have effect, in relation to it, as if the references therein to the tenant included references to the business tenants alone; and

(b) the business tenants shall be liable, to the exclusion of the other joint tenants, for the payment of rent and the discharge of any other obligation under the current tenancy for any rental period beginning after the date specified in the landlord's notice under section 25 of this Act or, as the case my be, beginning on or after the date specified in their request for a new tenancy.

(6) Where the court makes an order under section 29 of this Act for the grant of a new tenancy it may order the grant to be made to the business tenants or to them jointly with the persons carrying on the business in partnership with them, and may order the grant to be made subject to the satisfaction, within a time specified by the order, of such conditions as to guarantors, sureties or otherwise as appear to the court equitable, having regard to the omission of the other joint tenants from the persons who will be the tenants under the new tenancy.

(7) The business tenants shall be entitled to recover any amount payable by way of compensation under section 37 or section 59 of this Act.

Groups of companies

42-(1) For the purposes of this section two bodies corporate shall be taken to be members of a group if and only if one is a subsidiary of the other or both are subsidiaries of the third body corporate or the same person has a controlling interest in both.

(2) Where a tenancy is held by a member of a group, occupation by another member of the group, and the carrying on of a business by another member of the group, shall be treated for the purposes of section 23 of this Act as equivalent to occupation or the carrying on of a business by the member of the group holding the tenancy; and in relation to a tenancy to which this Part of this Act applies by virtue of the foregoing provisions of this subsection-

(a) references (however expressed) in this Part of this Act and in the Ninth Schedule to this Act to the business of or to use occupation or enjoyment by the tenant shall be construed as including references to the business of or to use occupation or enjoyment by the said other member;

(b) the reference in paragraph (d) of subsection (1) of section 34 of this Act to the tenant shall be construed as including the said other member; and

(c) an assignment of the tenancy from one member of the group to another shall not be treated as a change in the person of the tenant.

(3) Where the landlord's interest is held by a member of a group-

(a) the reference in paragraph (g) of subsection (1) of section 30 of this Act to intended occupation by the landlord for the purposes of a business to be carried on by him shall be construed as including intended occupation by any member of the group for the purposes of a business to be carried on by that member; and

(b) the reference in subsection (2) of that section to the purchase or creation of any interest shall be construed as a reference to a purchaser from or creation by a person other than a member of the group.

Tenancies excluded from Part II

43-(1) This Part of this Act does not apply-

(a) to a tenancy of an agricultural holding which is a tenancy in relation to which the Agricultural Holdings Act 1986 applies or a tenancy which would be a tenancy of an agricultural holding in relation to which that Act applied if subsection (3) of section 2 of that Act did not have effect or, in a case where approval was given under subsection (1) of that section, if that approval had not been given;

(aa) to a farm business tenancy;

(b) to a tenancy created by a mining lease; or

(c) [Repealed]

(d) [Repealed]

(2) This Part of this Act does not apply to a tenancy granted by reason that the tenant was the holder of an office, appointment or employment from the grantor thereof and continuing only so long as the tenant holds the office, appointment or employment, or terminable by the grantor on the tenant's ceasing to hold it, or coming to an end at a time fixed by reference to the time at which the tenant ceases to hold it:

Provided that this subsection shall not have effect in relation to a tenancy granted after the commencement of this Act unless

the tenancy was granted by an instrument in writing which expressed the purpose for which the tenancy was granted.

(3) This Part of this Act does not apply to a tenancy granted for a term certain not exceeding six months unless-

(a) the tenancy contains provision for renewing the term or for extending it beyond six months from its beginning; or

(b) the tenant has been in occupation for a period which, together with any period during which any predecessor in the carrying on of the business carried on by the tenant was in occupation, exceeds twelve months.

Jurisdiction of county court to make declaration

43A Where the rateable value of the holding is such that the jurisdiction conferred on the court by any other provision of this Part of this Act is, by virtue of section 63 of this Act, exercisable by the county court, the county court shall have jurisdiction (but without prejudice to the jurisdiction of the High Court) to make any declaration as to any matter arising under this Part of this Act, whether or not any other relief is sought in the proceedings.

Meaning of 'the landlord,' in Part II, and provisions as to mesne landlords, etc

44-(1) Subject to subsections (1A) and (2) below, in this Part of this Act the expression 'the landlord' in relation to a tenancy (in this section referred to as 'the relevant tenancy'), means the person (whether or not he is the immediate landlord) who is the owner of that interest in the property comprised in the relevant tenancy which for the time being fulfils the following conditions, that is to say-

(a) that it is an interest in reversion expectant (whether immediately or not) on the termination of the relevant tenancy, and

(b) that it is either the fee simple or a tenancy which will not come to an end within fourteen months by effluxion of time and, if it is such a tenancy, that no notice has been given by virtue of which it will come to an end within fourteen months or any further time by which it may be continued under section 36(2) or section 64 of this Act, and is not itself in reversion expectant (whether immediately or not) on an interest which fulfils those conditions.

(1A) The reference in subsection (1) above to a person who is the owner of an interest such as is mentioned in that subsection is to be construed, where different persons own such interests in different parts of the property, as a reference to all those persons collectively.

(2) References in this Part of this Act to a notice to quit given by the landlord are references to a notice to quit given by the immediate landlord.

(3) The provisions of the Sixth Schedule to this Act shall have effect for the application of this Part of this Act to cases where the immediate landlord of the tenant is not the owner of the fee simple in respect of the holding.

45 [Repealed]

Interpretation of Part II

46-(1) In this Part of this Act-

'business' has the meaning assigned to it by subsection (2) of section 23 of this Act;

'current tenancy' means the tenancy under which the tenant holds for the time being;

'date of termination' has the meaning assigned to it by subsection (1) of section 25 of this Act;

subject to the provisions of section 32 of this Act, 'the holding' has the meaning assigned to it by subsection (3) of section 23 of this Act;

'interim rent' has the meaning given by section 24A(1) of this Act;

'mining lease' has the same meaning as in the Landlord and Tenant Act 1927.

(2) For the purposes of this Part of this Act, a person has a controlling interest in a company if, had he been a company, the other company would have been its subsidiary; and in this Part-

'company' has the meaning given by section 735 of the Companies Act 1985; and

'subsidiary' has the meaning given by section 736 of that Act.

PART III

COMPENSATION FOR IMPROVEMENTS

Time for making claims for compensation for improvements

47-(1) Where a tenancy is terminated by notice to quit, whether given by the landlord or by the tenant, or by a notice given by any person under Part I or Part II of this Act, the time for making a claim for compensation at the termination of the tenancy shall be a time falling within the period of three months beginning on the date on which the notice is given:

Provided that where the tenancy is terminated by a tenant's request for a new tenancy under section 26 of this Act, the said

time shall be a time falling within the period of three months beginning on the date on which the landlord gives notice, or (if he has not given such a notice) the latest date on which he could have given notice, under subsection (6) of the said section 26 or, as the case may be, paragraph (a) of subsection (4) of section 57 or paragraph (b) of subsection (1) of section 58 of this Act.

(2) Where a tenancy comes to an end by effluxion of time, the time for making such a claim shall be a time not earlier than six nor later than three months before the coming to an end of the tenancy.

(3) Where a tenancy is terminated by forfeiture or re-entry, the time for making such a claim shall be a time falling within the period of three months beginning with the effective date of the order of the court for the recovery of possession of the land comprised in the tenancy or, if the tenancy is terminated by re-entry without such an order, the period of three months beginning with the date of the re-entry.

(4) In the last foregoing subsection the reference to the effective date of an order is a reference to the date on which the order is to take effect according to the terms thereof or the date on which it ceases to be subject to appeal, whichever is the later.

(5) In subsection (1) of section 1 of the Act of 1927, for paragraphs (a) and (b) (which specify the time for making claims for compensation) there shall be substituted the words 'and within the time limited by section 47 of the Landlord and Tenant Act 1954'.

Amendments as to limitations on tenant's right to compensation

48-(1) So much of paragraph (b) of subsection (1) of section 2 of the Act of 1927 as provides that a tenant shall not be entitled to compensation in respect of any improvement made in pursuance of a statutory obligation shall not apply to any improvement begun after the commencement of this Act, but section 3 of the Act of 1927 (which enables a landlord to object to a proposed improvement) shall not have effect in relation to an improvement made in pursuance of a statutory obligation except so much thereof as-

(a) requires the tenant to serve on the landlord notice of his intention to make the improvement together with such a plan and specification as are mentioned in that section and to supply copies of the plan and specification at the request of any superior landlord; and

(b) enables the tenant to obtain at his expense a certificate from the landlord or the tribunal that the improvement has been duly executed.

(2) Paragraph (c) of the said subsection (1) (which provides that a tenant shall not be entitled to compensation in respect of any

improvement made less than three years before the termination of the tenancy) shall not apply to any improvement begun after the commencement of this Act.

(3) No notice shall be served after the commencement of this Act under paragraph (d) of the said subsection (1) (which excludes rights to compensation where the landlord serves on the tenant notice offering a renewal of the tenancy on reasonable terms).

Restrictions on contracting out

49 In section 9 of the Act of 1927 (which provides that Part I of that Act shall apply notwithstanding any contract to the contrary made after the date specified in that section) the proviso (which requires effect to be given to such a contract where it appears to the tribunal that the contract was made for adequate consideration) shall cease to have effect except as respects a contract made before the tenth day of December, nineteen hundred and fifty-three.

Interpretation of Part III

50 In this Part of this Act the expression 'Act of 1927' means the Landlord and Tenant Act 1927, the expression 'compensation' means compensation under Part I of that Act in respect of an improvement, and other expressions used in this Part of this Act and in the Act of 1927 have the same meanings in this Part of this Act as in that Act.

[Sections 51–54 not reproduced here.]

PART IV

MISCELLANEOUS AND SUPPLEMENTARY

Compensation for possession obtained by misrepresentation

55-...

Application to Crown

56-(1) Subject to the provisions of this and the four next following sections, Part II of this Act shall apply where there is an interest belonging to Her Majesty in right of the Crown or the Duchy of Lancaster or belonging to the Duchy of Cornwall, or belonging to a Government department or held on behalf of Her Majesty for the purposes of a Government department, in like manner as if that interest were an interest not so belonging or held.

(2) The provisions of the Eighth Schedule to this Act shall have effect as respects the application of Part II of this Act to cases where the interest

of the landlord belongs to Her Majesty in right of the Crown or the Duchy of Lancaster or to the Duchy of Cornwall.

(3) Where a tenancy is held by or on behalf of a Government department and the property comprised therein is or includes premises occupied for any purposes of a Government department, the tenancy shall be one to which Part II of this Act applies; and for the purposes of any provision of the said Part II or the Ninth Schedule to this Act which is applicable only if either or both of the following conditions are satisfied, that is to say-

(a) that any premises have during any period been occupied for the purposes of the tenant's business;

(b) that on any change of occupier of any premises the new occupier succeeded to the business of the former occupier,

the said conditions shall be deemed to be satisfied respectively, in relation to such a tenancy, if during that period or, as the case may be, immediately before and immediately after the change, the premises were occupied for the purposes of a Government department.

(4) The last foregoing subsection shall apply in relation to any premises provided by a Government department without any rent being payable to the department therefor as if the premises were occupied for the purposes of a Government department.

(5) The provisions of Parts III and IV of this Act, amending any other enactment which binds the Crown or applies to land belonging to Her Majesty in right of the Crown or the Duchy of Lancaster, or land belonging to the Duchy of Cornwall, or to land belonging to any Government department, shall bind the Crown or apply to such land.

(6) Sections 53 and 54 of this Act shall apply where the interest of the landlord, or any other interest in the land in question, belongs to Her Majesty in right of the Crown or the Duchy of Lancaster or to the Duchy of Cornwall, or belongs to a Government department or is held on behalf of Her Majesty for the purposes of a Government department, in like manner as if that interest were an interest not so belonging or held.

(7) Part I of this Act shall apply where-

(a) there is an interest belonging to Her Majesty in right of the Crown and that interest is under the management of the Crown Estate Commissioners; or

(b) there is an interest belonging to Her Majesty in right of the Duchy of Lancaster or belonging to the Duchy of Cornwall;

as if it were an interest not so belonging.

Modification on grounds of public interest of rights under Part II

57-(1) Where the interest of the landlord or any superior landlord in the property comprised in any tenancy belongs to or is held for the purposes of a Government department or is held by a local authority, statutory undertakers or a development corporation, the Minister or Board in charge of any Government department may certify that it is requisite for the purposes of the first-mentioned department, or, as the case may be, of the authority, undertakers or corporation, that the use or occupation of the property or a part thereof shall be changed by a specified date.

(2) A certificate under the last foregoing subsection shall not be given unless the owner of the interest belonging or held as mentioned in the last foregoing subsection has given to the tenant a notice stating-

(a) that the question of the giving of such a certificate is under consideration by the Minister or Board specified in the notice; and

(b) that if within twenty-one days of the giving of the notice the tenant makes to that Minister or Board representations in writing with respect to that question, they will be considered before the question is determined, and if the tenant makes any such representations within the said twenty-one days the Minister or Board shall consider them before determining whether to give the certificate.

(3) Where a certificate has been given under subsection (1) of this section in relation to any tenancy, then-

(a) if a notice given under subsection (1) of section 25 of this Act specifies as the date of termination a date not earlier than the date specified in the certificate and contains a copy of the certificate subsection (6) of that section shall not apply to the notice and no application for a new tenancy shall be made by the tenant under subsection (1) of section 24 of this Act;

(b) if such a notice specifies an earlier date as the date of termination and contains a copy of the certificate, then if the court makes an order under Part II of this Act for the grant of a new tenancy the new tenancy shall be for a term expiring not later than the date specified in the certificate and shall not be a tenancy to which Part II of this Act applies.

(4) Where a tenant makes a request for a new tenancy under section 26 of this Act, and the interest of the landlord or any superior landlord in the property comprised in the current tenancy belongs or is held as mentioned in subsection (1) of this section, the following provisions shall have effect-

(a) if a certificate has been given under the said subsection (1) in relation to the current tenancy, and within two months after the making of the request the landlord gives notice to the tenant that the certificate has been given and the notice contains a copy of the certificate, then-

(i) if the date specified in the certificate is not later than that specified in the tenant's request for a new tenancy, the tenant shall not make an application under section 24 of this Act for the grant of a new tenancy;

(ii) if, in any other case, the court makes an order under Part II of this Act for the grant of a new tenancy the new tenancy shall be for a term expiring not later than the date specified in the certificate and shall not be a tenant to which Part II of this Act applies;

(b) if no such certificate has been given but notice under subsection (2) of this section has been given before the making of the request or within two months thereafter, the request shall not have effect, without prejudice however, to the making of a new request when the Minister or Board has determined whether to give a certificate.

(5) Where application is made to the court under Part II of this Act for the grant of a new tenancy and the landlord's interest in the property comprised in the tenancy belongs or is held as mentioned in subsection (1) of this section, the Minister or Board in charge of any Government department may certify that it is necessary in the public interest that if the landlord makes an application in that behalf the court shall determine as a term of the new tenancy that is shall be terminable by six months' notice to quit given by the landlord.

Subsection (2) of this section shall apply in relation to a certificate under this subsection, and if notice under the said subsection (2) has been given to the tenant-

(a) the court shall not determine the application for the grant of a new tenancy until the Minister or Board has determined whether to give a certificate,

(b) if a certificate is given, the court shall on the application of the landlord determine as a term of the new tenancy that it shall be terminable as aforesaid, and section 25 of this Act shall apply accordingly.

(6) The foregoing provisions of this section shall apply to an interest held by a Health Authority or Special Health Authority as they apply to an interest held by a local authority but with the substitution, for the reference to the purposes of the authority, of a reference to the purposes of the National Health Service Act 1977.

(7) Where the interest of the landlord or any superior landlord in the property comprised in any tenancy belongs to the National Trust the Minister of Works may certify that it is requisite, for the purpose of securing that the property will as from a specified date be used or occupied in a manner better suited to the nature thereof, that the use or

occupation of the property should be changed; and subsections (2) to (4) of this section shall apply in relation to certificates under this subsection, and to cases where the interest of the landlord or any superior landlord belongs to the National Trust, as those subsections apply in relation to certificates under subsection (1) of this section and to cases where the interest of the landlord or any superior landlord belongs or is held as mentioned in that subsection.

(8) In this and the next following section the expression 'Government department' does not include the Commissioners of Crown Lands and the expression 'landlord' has the same meaning as in Part II of this Act; and in the last foregoing subsection the expression 'National Trust' means the National Trust for Places of Historic Interest or Natural Beauty.

Termination on special grounds of tenancies to which Part II applies

58-(1) Where the landlord's interest in the property comprised in any tenancy belongs or is held for the purposes of a Government department, and the Minister or Board in charge of any Government department certifies that for reasons of national security it is necessary that the use or occupation of the property should be discontinued or changed, then-

(a) if the landlord gives a notice under subsection (1) of section 25 of this Act containing a copy of the certificate, subsection (6) of that section shall not apply to the notice and no application for a new tenancy shall be made by the tenant under subsection (1) of section 24 of this Act;

(b) if (whether before or after the giving of the certificate) the tenant makes a request for a new tenancy under section 26 of this Act, and within two months after the making the request the landlord gives notice to the tenant that the certificate has been given and the notice contains a copy of the certificate-

   (i) the tenant shall not make an application under section 24 of this Act for the grant of a new tenancy, and

   (ii) if the notice specifies as the date on which the tenancy is to terminate a date earlier than that specified in the tenant's request as the date on which the new tenancy is to begin but neither earlier than six months from the giving of the notice nor earlier than the earliest date at which apart from this Act the tenancy would come to an end or could be brought to an end, the tenancy shall terminate on the date specified in the notice instead of that specified in the request.

(2) Where the landlord's interest in the property comprised in any tenancy belongs to or is held for the purposes of a Government department, nothing in this Act shall invalidate an agreement to the effect-

(a) that on the giving of such a certificate as is mentioned in the last foregoing subsection the tenancy may be terminated by notice to quit given by the landlord of such length as may be specified in the agreement, if the notice contains a copy of the certificate; and

(b) that after the giving of such a notice containing such a copy the tenancy shall not be one to which Part II of this Act applies.

(3) Where the landlord's interest in the property comprised in any tenancy is held by statutory undertakers, nothing in this Act shall invalidate an agreement to the effect-

(a) that where the Minister or Board in charge of a Government department certifies that possession of the property comprised in the tenancy or a part thereof is urgently required for carrying out repairs (whether on that property or elsewhere) which are needed for the proper operation of the landlord's undertaking, the tenancy may be terminated by notice to quit given by the landlord of such length as may be specified in the agreement, if the notice contains a copy of the certificate; and

(b) that after the giving of such a notice containing such a copy, the tenancy shall not be one to which Part II of this Act applies.

(4) Where the court makes an order under Part II of this Act for the grant of a new tenancy and the Minister or Board in charge of any Government department certifies that the public interest requires the tenancy to be subject to such a term as is mentioned in paragraph (a) or (b) of this subsection, as the case may be, then-

(a) if the landlord's interest in the property comprised in the tenancy belongs to or is held for the purposes of a Government department, the court shall on the application of the landlord determine as a term of the new tenancy that such an agreement as is mentioned in subsection (2) of this section and specifying such length of notice as is mentioned in the certificate shall be embodied in the new tenancy;

(b) if the landlord's interest in that property is held by statutory undertakers, the court shall on the application of the landlord determine as a term of the new tenancy that such an agreement as is mentioned in subsection (3) of this section and specifying such length of notice as is mentioned in the certificate shall be embodied in the new tenancy.

Compensation for exercise of powers under sections 57 and 58

59-(1) Where by virtue of any certificate given for the purposes of either of the two last foregoing sections or, subject to subsection (1A) below, section 60A below the tenant is precluded from obtaining an order for the grant of a new tenancy, or of a new tenancy for a term expiring later than a specified date, the tenant shall be entitled on quitting the premises to recover from the owner of the interest by virtue of which the certificate was given an amount by way of compensation, and subsections (2), (3) to (3B) and (5) to (7) of section 37 of this Act shall with the necessary modifications apply for the purposes of ascertaining the amount.

(1A) No compensation shall be recoverable under subsection (1) above where the certificate was given under section 60A below and either-

(a) the premises vested in the Welsh Development Agency under section 7 (property of Welsh Industrial Estates Corporation) or 8 (land held under Local Employment Act 1972) of the Welsh Development Agency Act 1975, or

(b) the tenant was not tenant of the premises when the said Agency acquired the interest by virtue of which the certificate was given.

(2) Subsections (2) and (3) of section 38 of this Act shall apply to compensation under this section as they apply to compensation under section 37 of this Act.

Special provisions as to premises in development or intermediate areas

60-(1) Where the property comprised in a tenancy consists of premises of which the Secretary of State or the Urban Regeneration Agency is the landlord, being premises situated in a locality which is either-

(a) a development area; or

(b) an intermediate area;

and the Secretary of State certifies that it is necessary or expedient for achieving the purpose mentioned in section 2(1) of the Local Employment Act 1972 that the use or occupation of the property should be changed, paragraphs (a) and (b) of subsection (1) of section 58 of this Act shall apply as they apply where such a certificate is given as is mentioned in that subsection.

(2) Where the court makes an order under Part II of this Act for the grant of a new tenancy of any such premises as aforesaid, and the Secretary of State certifies that it is necessary or expedient as aforesaid that the tenancy should be subject to a term, specified in the certificate, prohibiting or restricting the tenant from assigning the tenancy or sub-letting, charging or parting with possession of the premises or any part thereof or changing the use of the premises or any part thereof, the court shall determine that the terms of the tenancy shall include the terms specified in the certificate.

(3) In this section 'development area' and 'intermediate area' mean an area for the time being specified as a development area or, as the case may be, as an intermediate area by an order made, or having effect as if made, under section 1 of the Industrial Development Act 1982.

Welsh Development Agency premises

60A-(1) Where property comprised in a tenancy consists of premises of which the Welsh Development Agency is the landlord, and the Secretary of State certifies that it is necessary or expedient, for the purpose of providing employment appropriate to the needs of the area in which the premises are situated, that the use or occupation of the property should be changed, paragraphs (a) and (b) of section 58(l) above shall apply as they apply where such a certificate is given as is mentioned in that sub-section.

(2) Where the court makes an order under Part II of this Act for the grant of a new tenancy of any such premises as aforesaid, and the Secretary of State certifies that it is necessary or expedient as aforesaid that the tenancy should be subject to a term, specified in the certificate, prohibiting or restricting the tenant from assigning the tenancy or subletting, charging or parting with possession of the premises or any part of the premises or changing the use of the premises or any part of the premises, the court shall determine that the terms of the tenancy shall include the terms specified in the certificate.

60B–62 [Repealed]

Jurisdiction of court for purposes of Parts I and II and of Part I of Landlord and Tenant Act 1927

63-(1) Any jurisdiction conferred on the court by any provision of Part I of this Act shall be exercised by the county court.

(2) Any jurisdiction conferred on the court by any provision of Part II of this Act or conferred on the tribunal by Part I of the Landlord and Tenant Act 1927, shall, subject to the provisions of this section, be exercised, by the High Court or a county court.

(3) [Repealed]

(4) The following provisions shall have effect as respects transfer of proceedings from or to the High Court or the county court, that is to say-

(a) where an application is made to the one but by virtue of an Order under section 1 of the Courts and Legal Services Act 1990, cannot be entertained except by the other, the application shall not be treated as improperly made but any proceedings thereon shall be transferred to the other court;

(b) any proceedings under the provisions of Part II of this Act or of Part I of the Landlord and Tenant Act 1927, which are pending before one of those courts may by order of that court made on the application of any person interested be transferred to the other court, if it appears to the court making the order that it is desirable that the proceedings and any proceedings before the other court should both be entertained by the other court.

(5) In any proceedings where in accordance with the foregoing provisions of this section the county court exercises jurisdiction the powers of the judge of summoning one or more assessors under subsection (1) of section 63(1) of the County Courts Act 1984, may be exercised notwithstanding that no application is made in that behalf by any party to the proceedings.

(6) Where in any such proceedings an assessor is summoned by a judge under the said subsection (1)-

(a) he may, if so directed by the judge, inspect the land to which the proceedings relate without the judge and report to the judge in writing thereon;

(b) the judge may on consideration of the report and any observations of the parties thereon give such judgment or make such order in the proceedings as may be just;

(c) the remuneration of the assessor shall beat such rate as maybe determined by the Lord Chancellor with the approval of the Treasury and shall be defrayed out of moneys provided by Parliament.

(7) In this section the expression 'the holding'-

(a) in relation to proceedings under Part II of this Act, has the meaning assigned to it by subsection (3) of section 23 of this Act,

(b) in relation to proceedings under Part I of the Landlord and Tenant Act 1927, has the same meaning as in the said Part I.

(9) Nothing in this section shall prejudice the operation of section 41 of the County Courts Act 1984 (which relates to the removal into the High Court of proceedings commenced in a county court).

(10) In accordance with the foregoing provisions of this section, for section 21 of the Landlord and Tenant Act 1927, there shall be substituted the following section-

'The tribunal

21. The tribunal for the purposes of Part I of this Act shall be the court exercising jurisdiction in accordance with the provisions of section 63 of the Landlord and Tenant Act 1954'.

64-(1) In any case where-

(a) a notice to terminate a tenancy has been given under Part I or Part II of this Act or a request for a new tenancy has been made under Part II thereof, and

(b) an application to the court has been made under the said Part I or under section 24(1) or 29(2) of this Act as the case may be, and

(c) apart from this section the effect of the notice or request would be to terminate the tenancy before the expiration of the period of three months beginning with the date on which the application is finally disposed of,

the effect of the notice or request shall be to terminate the tenancy at the expiration of the said period of three months and not at any other time.

(2) The reference in paragraph (c) of subsection (1) of this section to the date on which an application is finally disposed of shall be construed as a reference to the earliest date by which the proceedings on the application (including any proceedings on or in consequence of an appeal) have been determined and any time for appealing or further appealing has expired, except that if the application is withdrawn or any appeal is abandoned the reference shall be construed as a reference to the date of the withdrawal or abandonment.

Provisions as to reversions

65-(1) Where by virtue of any provision of this Act a tenancy (in this sub-section referred to as 'the inferior tenancy') is continued for a period such as to extend to or beyond the end of the term of a superior tenancy, the superior tenancy shall, for the purposes of this Act and of any other enactment and of any rule of law, be deemed so long as it subsists to be an interest in reversion expectant upon the termination of the inferior tenancy and, if there is no intermediate tenancy, to be the interest in reversion immediately expectant upon the termination thereof.

(2) In the case of a tenancy continuing by virtue of any provision of this Act after the coming to an end of the interest in reversion immediately expectant upon the termination thereof, subsection (1) of section 139 of the Law of Property Act 1925 (which relates to the effect of the extinguishment of a reversion) shall apply as if references in the said subsection (1) to the surrender or merger of the reversion included references to the coming to an end of the reversion for any reason other than surrender or merger.

(3) Where by virtue of any provision of this Act a tenancy (in this subsection referred to as 'the continuing tenancy') is continued beyond the beginning of a reversionary tenancy which was granted (whether before or after the commencement of this Act) so as to begin on or after the date on which apart from this Act the continuing tenancy would have come to an end, the reversionary tenancy shall have effect as if it had been granted subject to the continuing tenancy.

(4) Where by virtue of any provision of this Act a tenancy (in this subsection referred to as 'the new tenancy') is granted for a period

beginning on the same date as a reversionary tenancy or for a period such as to extend beyond the beginning of the term of a reversionary tenancy, whether the reversionary tenancy in question was granted before or after the commencement of this Act, the reversionary tenancy shall have effect as if it had been granted subject to the new tenancy.

Provisions as to notices

66-(1) Any form of notice required by this Act to be prescribed shall be prescribed by regulations made by the Secretary of State by statutory instrument.

(2) Where the form of a notice to be served on persons of any description is to be prescribed for any of the purposes of this Act, the form to be prescribed shall include such an explanation of the relevant provisions of this Act as appears to the Secretary of State requisite for informing persons of that description of their rights and obligations under those provisions.

(3) Different forms of notice may be prescribed for the purposes of the operation of any provision of this Act in relation to different cases.

(4) Section 23 of the Landlord and Tenant Act 1927 (which relates to the service of notices) shall apply for the purposes of this Act.

(5) Any statutory instrument under this section shall be subject to annulment in pursuance of a resolution of either House of Parliament.

Provisions as to mortgagees in possession

67 Anything authorised or required by the provisions of this Act, other than subsection (3) of section 40, to be done at any time by, to or with the landlord, or a landlord of a specified description, shall, if at that time the interest of the landlord in question is subject to a mortgage and the mortgagee is in possession or a receiver appointed by the mortgagee or by the courts is in receipt of the rents and profits, be deemed to be authorised or required to be done by, to or with the mortgagee instead of that landlord.

68 [Not reproduced here]

Interpretation

69-(1) In this Act, the following expressions have the meanings hereby assigned to them respectively, that is to say-

'agricultural holding' has the same meaning as in the Agricultural Holdings Act 1986;

'development corporation' has the same meaning as in the New Towns Act 1946;

'farm business tenancy' has the same meaning as in the Agricultural Tenancies Act 1995;

'local authority' means any local authority within the meaning of the Town and Country Planning Act 1990, any National Park Authority, the Broads Authority or joint authority established by Part 4 of the Local Government Act 1985;

'mortgage' includes a charge or lien and 'mortgagor' and "mortgagee" shall be construed accordingly;

'notice to quit' means a notice to terminate a tenancy (whether a periodical tenancy or a tenancy for a term of years certain) given in accordance with the provisions (whether express or implied) of that tenancy;

'repairs' includes any work of maintenance, decoration or restoration, and references to repairing, to keeping or yielding up in repair and to state of repair shall be construed accordingly;

'statutory undertakers' has the same meaning as in the Town and Country

Planning Act 1990;

'tenancy' means a tenancy created either immediately or derivatively out of the freehold, whether by a lease or underlease, by an agreement for a lease or underlease or by a tenancy agreement or in pursuance of any enactment (including this Act), but does not include a mortgage term or any interest arising in favour of a mortgagor by his attorning tenant to his mortgagee, and references to the granting of a tenancy and to demised property shall be construed accordingly;

'terms', in relation to a tenancy, includes conditions.

(2) References in this Act to an agreement between the landlord and the tenant (except in section 17 and subsections (1) and (2) of section 38 thereof) shall be construed as references to an agreement in writing between them.

(3) Reference in this Act to an action for any relief shall be construed as including references to a claim for that relief by way of counterclaim in any proceedings.

Short title and citation, commencement and extent

70-(1) This Act may be cited as the Landlord and Tenant Act, 1954, and the Landlord and Tenant Act, 1927, and this Act may be cited together as the Landlord and Tenant Acts, 1927 and 1954.

(2) This Act shall come into operation on the first day of October, nineteen hundred and fifty-four.

(3) This Act shall not extend to Scotland or to Northern Ireland.

APPENDIX 4

COSTS OF LEASES ACT 1958

1 Costs of leases

Notwithstanding any custom to the contrary, a party to a lease shall, unless the parties thereto agree otherwise in writing, be under no obligation to pay the whole or any part of any other party's solicitor's costs of the lease.

2 Interpretation

In this Act—

(a) 'lease' includes an underlease and an agreement for a lease or underlease or for a tenancy or sub-tenancy;

(b) 'costs' includes fees, charges, disbursements (including stamp duty), expenses and remuneration.

3 Short Title

This Act may be cited as the Costs of Leases Act 1958.

APPENDIX 5

RECORDED DELIVERY SERVICE ACT 1962

1 Recorded delivery service to be an alternative to registered post

(1) Any enactment which requires or authorises a document or other thing to be sent by registered post (whether or not it makes any other provision in relation thereto) shall have effect as if it required or, as the case may be, authorised that thing to be sent by registered post or the recorded delivery service; and any enactment which makes any other provision in relation to the sending of a document or other thing by registered post or to a thing so sent shall have effect as if it made the like provision in relation to the sending of that thing by the recorded delivery service or, as the case may be, to a thing sent by that service.

(2) The Schedule to this Act shall have effect for the purpose of making consequential adaptations of the enactments therein mentioned.

(3) Subject to the following subsection [the Secretary of State] may by order make such amendments of any enactment contained in a local or private Act (being an enactment to which this Act applies) as appear to him to be necessary or expedient in consequence of subsection (1) of this section.

(4) Before making an order under this section,[the Secretary of State] shall, unless it appears to him to be impracticable to do so, consult with the person who promoted the Bill for the Act to which the order relates, or where it appears to [the Secretary of State] that some other person has succeeded to the promoter's interest in that Act, that other person.

(5) Any order under this section may be varied or revoked by a subsequent order thereunder, and the power to make any such order shall be exercisable by statutory instrument which shall be subject to annulment in pursuance of a resolution of either House of Parliament.

(6) This section shall not be construed as authorising the sending by the recorded delivery service of anything which under the Post Office Act 1953 or any instrument thereunder is not allowed to be sent by that service.

2 Application and interpretation

(1) Subject to the next following subsection, this Act applies to the following enactments, that is to say—

(a) the provisions of any Act (whether public general, local or private) passed before or in the same Session as this Act;

(b) the provisions of any Church Assembly Measure so passed;

(c) the provisions of any agricultural marketing scheme made under the Agricultural Marketing Act 1958, before the passing of this Act or having effect as if made under that Act;

and, in the case of a provision which has been applied by or under any other enactment passed, or any instrument made under any enactment passed, before or in the same Session as this Act, applies to that provision as so applied, subject, however, in the case of an instrument made after the passing of this Act to any contrary intention appearing therein; and references in this Act (except this section) to any enactment shall be construed accordingly.

(2) This Act does not apply—

(a) to subsection (2) of section nine of the Crown Proceedings Act 1947 (which enables proceedings to be brought against the Crown for loss of or damage to registered inland postal packets);

(b) to any enactment which, either as originally enacted or as amended by any subsequent enactment, requires or authorises a thing to be sent by the recorded delivery service as an alternative to registered post or makes provision in relation to a thing sent by that service;

(c) to the provisions of any Act of the Parliament of Northern Ireland or of any local or private Act which extends only to Northern Ireland.

(3) In this Act—

(a) references to sending a document or other thing include references to serving, executing, giving or delivering it or doing any similar thing;

(b) references to sending any thing by registered post include references to sending it by or in a registered letter or packet, whether the references are expressed in those terms or terms having the like effect and whether or not there is any mention of the post or prepayment;

(c) references to any thing sent by registered post or the recorded delivery service shall be construed accordingly; and

(d) references to a local Act include references to any Act confirming a provisional order or scheme.

3 Extent

(1) It is hereby declared that (subject to subsection (2) of the foregoing section) this Act extends to Northern Ireland.

(2) …

(3) This Act, so far as it amends any enactment which extends to the Isle of Man or to any of the Channel Islands, or which applies in relation to persons of or belonging to any such island, shall extend to that island or, as the case may be, shall apply in like manner in relation to those persons.

4 Short title

This Act may be cited as the Recorded Delivery Service Act 1962.

SCHEDULE

ADAPTATION OF ENACTMENTS

Section 1

1

Any reference, however worded—

(a) in any enactment the provisions of which apply to, or operate in consequence of the operation of, any enactment amended by section one of this Act; or

(b) in any enactment relating to the sending of documents or other things otherwise than by registered post or to documents or other things so sent;

to the registered post or to a registered letter or packet, shall be construed as including a reference to the recorded delivery service or to a letter or packet sent by that service; and any reference, however worded, in any such enactment to a Post Office receipt for a registered letter or to an acknowledgment of or certificate of delivery of a registered letter shall be construed accordingly.

2

The foregoing paragraph shall not be taken to prejudice the generality of subsection (1) of section one of this Act.

3, 4

…

5

The requirement imposed by subsection (4) of section nine of the Agricultural Marketing Act 1958 that every scheme under that Act shall be so framed as to secure that the notice mentioned in paragraph (b) of that subsection shall be served by registered post shall have effect as a requirement that that notice shall be served by registered post or by the recorded delivery service.

APPENDIX 6

CIVIL EVIDENCE ACT 1972

2 Rules of court with respect to expert reports and oral expert evidence

(1), (2) ...

(3) Notwithstanding any enactment or rule of law by virtue of which documents prepared for the purpose of pending or contemplated civil proceedings or in connection with the obtaining or giving of legal advice are in certain circumstances privileged from disclosure, provision may be made by rules of court—

(a) for enabling the court in any civil proceedings to direct, with respect to medical matters or matters of any other class which may be specified in the direction, that the parties or some of them shall each by such date as may be so specified (or such later date as may be permitted or agreed in accordance with the rules) disclose to the other or others in the form of one or more expert reports the expert evidence on matters of that class which he proposes to adduce as part of his case at the trial; and

(b) for prohibiting a party who fails to comply with a direction given in any such proceedings under rules of court made by virtue of paragraph (a) above from adducing in evidence ... except with the leave of the court, any statement (whether of fact or opinion) contained in any expert report whatsoever in so far as that statement deals with matters of any class specified in the direction.

(4) Provision may be made by rules of court as to the conditions subject to which oral expert evidence may be given in civil proceedings.

(5) Without prejudice to the generality of subsection (4) above, rules of court made in pursuance of that subsection may make provision for prohibiting a party who fails to comply with a direction given as mentioned in subsection (3)(b) above from adducing, except with the leave of the court, any oral expert evidence whatsoever with respect to matters of any class specified in the direction.

(6) Any rules of court made in pursuance of this section may make different provision for different classes of cases, for expert reports dealing with matters of different classes, and for other different circumstances.

(7) References in this section to an expert report are references to a written report by a person dealing wholly or mainly with matters on which he is (or would if living be) qualified to give expert evidence.

(8) Nothing in the foregoing provisions of this section shall prejudice the generality of ... [section 75 of the County Courts Act 1984], [section 144 of the Magistrates' Courts Act 1980] or any other enactment conferring power to make rules of court; and nothing in ... [section 75(2) of the County Courts Act 1984] or any other enactment restricting the matters with respect to which rules of court may be made shall prejudice the making of rules of court in pursuance of this section or the operation of any rules of court so made.

3 Admissibility of expert opinion and certain expressions of non-expert opinion

(1) Subject to any rules of court made in pursuance of ... this Act, where a person is called as a witness in any civil proceedings, his opinion on any relevant matter on which he is qualified to give expert evidence shall be admissible in evidence.

(2) It is hereby declared that where a person is called as a witness in any civil proceedings, a statement of opinion by him on any relevant matter on which he is not qualified to give expert evidence, if made as a way of conveying relevant facts personally perceived by him, is admissible as evidence of what he perceived.

(3) In this section 'relevant matter' includes an issue in the proceedings in question.

5 Interpretation, application to arbitrations etc and savings

[(1) In this Act 'civil proceedings' means civil proceedings, before any tribunal, in relation to which the strict rules of evidence apply, whether as a matter of law or by agreement, of the parties; and references to 'the court' shall be construed accordingly.]

[(2) The rules of court made for the purposes of the application of sections 2 and 4 of this Act to proceedings in the High Court apply, except in so far as their application is excluded by agreement, to proceedings before tribunals other than the ordinary courts of law, subject to such modifications as may be appropriate.

Any question arising as to what modifications are appropriate shall be determined, in default of agreement, by the tribunal.]

(3) Nothing in this Act shall prejudice—

(a) any power of a court, in any civil proceedings, to exclude evidence (whether by preventing questions from being put or otherwise) at its discretion; or

(b) the operation of any agreement (whenever made) between the parties to any civil proceedings as to the evidence which is to be admissible (whether generally or for any particular purpose) in those proceedings.

6 Short title, extent and commencement

(1) This Act may be cited as the Civil Evidence Act 1972.

(2) This Act shall not extend to Scotland or Northern Ireland.

(3) This Act, except sections ... 4(2) to (5), shall come into force on 1st January 1973, and sections ... 4(2) to (5) shall come into force on such day as the Lord Chancellor may by order made by statutory instrument appoint; and different days may be so appointed for different purposes or for the same purposes in relation to different courts or proceedings or otherwise in relation to different circumstances.

APPENDIX 7

COUNTY COURTS ACT 1984

[40 Transfer of proceedings to county court]

[(1) Where the High Court is satisfied that any proceedings before it are required by any provision of a kind mentioned in subsection (8) to be in a county court it shall—

(a) order the transfer of the proceedings to a county court; or

(b) if the court is satisfied that the person bringing the proceedings knew, or ought to have known, of that requirement, order that they be struck out.

(2) Subject to any such provision, the High Court may order the transfer of any proceedings before it to a county court.

(3) An order under this section may be made either on the motion of the High Court itself or on the application of any party to the proceedings.

(4) Proceedings transferred under this section shall be transferred to such county court as the High Court considers appropriate, having taken into account the convenience of the parties and that of any other persons likely to be affected and the state of business in the courts concerned.

(5) The transfer of any proceedings under this section shall not affect any right of appeal from the order directing the transfer.

(6) Where proceedings for the enforcement of any judgment or order of the High Court are transferred under this section—

(a) the judgment or order may be enforced as if it were a judgment or order of a county court; and

(b) subject to subsection (7), it shall be treated as a judgment or order of that court for all purposes.

(7) Where proceedings for the enforcement of any judgment or order of the High Court are transferred under this section—

(a) the powers of any court to set aside, correct, vary or quash a judgment or order of the High Court, and the enactments relating to appeals from such a judgment or order, shall continue to apply; and

(b) the powers of any court to set aside, correct, vary or quash a judgment or order of a county court, and the enactments relating to appeals from such a judgment or order, shall not apply.

(8) The provisions referred to in subsection (1) are any made—

(a) under section 1 of the Courts and Legal Services Act 1990; or

(b) by or under any other enactment.

(9) This section does not apply to family proceedings within the meaning of Part V of the Matrimonial and Family Proceedings Act 1984.]

41 Transfer to High Court by Order of High Court

(1) If at any stage in proceedings commenced in a county court or transferred to a county court under section 40, the High Court thinks it desirable that the proceedings, or any part of them, should be heard and determined in the High Court, it may order the transfer to the High Court of the proceedings or, as the case may be, of that part of them.

(2) The power conferred by subsection (1) is without prejudice to section 29 of the Supreme Court Act 1981 (power of High Court to issue prerogative orders) [but shall be exercised in relation to family proceedings (within the meaning of Part V of the Matrimonial and Family Proceedings Act 1984) in accordance with any directions given under section 37 of that Act (directions as to distribution and transfer of family business and proceedings)].

[(3) The power conferred by subsection (1) shall be exercised subject to any provision made—

(a) under section 1 of the Courts and Legal Services Act 1990; or

(b) by or under any other enactment.]

[42 Transfer to High Court by order of a county court]

[(1) Where a county court is satisfied that any proceedings before it are required by any provision of a kind mentioned in subsection (7) to be in the High Court, it shall—

(a) order the transfer of the proceedings to the High Court; or

(b) if the court is satisfied that the person bringing the proceedings knew, or ought to have known, of that requirement, order that they be struck out.

(2) Subject to any such provision, a county court may order the transfer of any proceedings before it to the High Court.

(3) An order under this section may be made either on the motion of the court itself or on the application of any party to the proceedings.

(4) The transfer of any proceedings under this section shall not affect any right of appeal from the order directing the transfer.

(5) Where proceedings for the enforcement of any judgment or order of a county court are transferred under this section—

(a) the judgment or order may be enforced as if it were a judgment or order of the High Court; and

(b) subject to subsection (6), it shall be treated as a judgment or order of that court for all purposes.

(6) Where proceedings for the enforcement of any judgment or order of a county court are transferred under this section—

(a) the powers of any court to set aside, correct, vary or quash a judgment or order of a county court, and the enactments relating to appeals from such a judgment or order, shall continue to apply; and

(b) the powers of any court to set aside, correct, vary or quash a judgment or order of the High Court, and the enactments relating to appeals from such a judgment or order, shall not apply.

(7) The provisions referred to in subsection (1) are any made—

(a) under section 1 of the Courts and Legal Services Act 1990; or

(b) by or under any other enactment.

(8) This section does not apply to family proceedings within the meaning of Part V of the Matrimonial and Family Proceedings Act 1984.]

APPENDIX 8

COMPANIES ACT 1985

287 Registered Office

[(1) A company shall at all times have a registered office to which all communications and notices may be addressed.

(2) On incorporation the situation of the company's registered office is that specified in the statement sent to the registrar under section 10.

(3) The company may change the situation of its registered office from time to time by giving notice in the prescribed form to the registrar.

(4) The change takes effect upon the notice being registered by the registrar, but until the end of the period of 14 days beginning with the date on which it is registered a person may validly serve any document on the company at its previous registered office.

(5) For the purposes of any duty of a company—

(a) to keep at its registered office, or make available for public inspection there, any register, index or other document, or

(b) to mention the address of its registered office in any document,

a company which has given notice to the registrar of a change in the situation of its registered office may act on the change as from such date, not more than 14 days after the notice is given, as it may determine.

(6) Where a company unavoidably ceases to perform at its registered office any such duty as is mentioned in subsection (5)(a) in circumstances in which it was not practicable to give prior notice to the registrar of a change in the situation of its registered office, but—

(a) resumes performance of that duty at other premises as soon as practicable, and

(b) gives notice accordingly to the registrar of a change in the situation of its registered office within 14 days of doing so,

it shall not be treated as having failed to comply with that duty.

(7) In proceedings for an offence of failing to comply with any such duty as is mentioned in subsection (5), it is for the person charged to show that by reason of the matters referred to in that subsection or subsection (6) no offence was committed.]

725 Service of documents

(1) A document may be served on a company by leaving it at, or sending it by post to, the company's registered office.

(2) Where a company registered in Scotland carries on business in England and Wales, the process of any court in England and Wales may be served on the company by leaving it at, or sending it by post to, the company's principal place of business in England and Wales, addressed to the manager or other head officer in England and Wales of the company.

(3) Where process is served on a company under subsection (2), the person issuing out the process shall send a copy of it by post to the company's registered office.

[736 'Subsidiary', 'holding company' and 'wholly owned subsidiary']

[(1) A company is a 'subsidiary' of another company, its 'holding company', if that other company—

(a) holds a majority of the voting rights in it, or

(b) is a member of it and has the right to appoint or remove a majority of its board of directors, or

(c) is a member of it and controls alone, pursuant to an agreement with other shareholders or members, a majority of the voting rights in it,

or if it is a subsidiary of a company which is itself a subsidiary of that other company.

(2) A company is a 'wholly-owned subsidiary' of another company if it has no members except that other and that other's wholly-owned subsidiaries or persons acting on behalf of that other or its wholly-owned subsidiaries.

(3) In this section 'company' includes any body corporate.]

APPENDIX 9

AGRICULTURAL HOLDINGS ACT 1986

1 Principal definitions

(1) In this Act 'agricultural holding' means the aggregate of the land (whether agricultural land or not) comprised in a contract of tenancy which is a contract for an agricultural tenancy, not being a contract under which the land is let to the tenant during his continuance in any office, appointment or employment held under the landlord.

(2) For the purposes of this section, a contract of tenancy relating to any land is a contract for an agricultural tenancy if, having regard to—

(a) the terms of the tenancy,

(b) the actual or contemplated use of the land at the time of the conclusion of the contract and subsequently, and

(c) any other relevant circumstances,

the whole of the land comprised in the contract, subject to such exceptions only as do not substantially affect the character of the tenancy, is let for use as agricultural land.

(3) A change in user of the land concerned subsequent to the conclusion of a contract of tenancy which involves any breach of the terms of the tenancy shall be disregarded for the purpose of determining whether a contract which was not originally a contract for an agricultural tenancy has subsequently become one unless it is effected with the landlord's permission, consent or acquiescence.

(4) In this Act 'agricultural land' means—

(a) land used for agriculture which is so used for the purposes of a trade or business, and

(b) any other land which, by virtue of a designation under section 109(1) of the Agriculture Act 1947, is agricultural land within the meaning of that Act.

(5) In this Act 'contract of tenancy' means a letting of land, or agreement for letting land, for a term of years or from year to year; and for the purposes of this definition a letting of land, or an agreement for letting land, which, by virtue of subsection (6) of section 149 of the Law of Property Act 1925, takes effect as such a letting of land or agreement for letting land as is mentioned in that subsection shall be deemed to be a letting of land or, as the case may be, an agreement for letting land, for a term of years.

2 Restriction on letting agricultural land for less than from year to year

(1) An agreement to which this section applies shall take effect, with the necessary modifications, as if it were an agreement for the letting of land for a tenancy from year to year unless the agreement was approved by the Minister before it was entered into.

(2) Subject to subsection (3) below, this section applies to an agreement under which—

(a) any land is let to a person for use as agricultural land for an interest less than a tenancy from year to year, or

(b) a person is granted a licence to occupy land for use as agricultural land,

if the circumstances are such that if his interest were a tenancy from year to year he would in respect of that land be the tenant of an agricultural holding.

(3) This section does not apply to an agreement for the letting of land, or the granting of a licence to occupy land—

(a) made (whether or not it expressly so provides) in contemplation of the use of the land only for grazing or mowing (or both) during some specified period of the year, or

(b) by a person whose interest in the land is less than a tenancy from year to year and has not taken effect as such a tenancy by virtue of this section.

(4) Any dispute arising as to the operation of this section in relation to any agreement shall be determined by arbitration under this Act.

3 Tenancies for two years or more to continue from year to year unless terminated by notice

(1) Subject to section 5 below, a tenancy of an agricultural holding for a term of two years or more shall, instead of terminating on the term date, continue (as from that date) as a tenancy from year to year, but otherwise on the terms of the original tenancy so far as applicable, unless—

(a) not less than one year nor more than two years before the term date a written notice has been given by either party to the other of his intention to terminate the tenancy, or

(b) section 4 below applies.

(2) A notice given under subsection (1) above shall be deemed, for the purposes of this Act, to be a notice to quit.

(3) This section does not apply to a tenancy which, by virtue of subsection (6) of section 149 of the Law of Property Act 1925, takes effect as such a term of years as is mentioned in that subsection.

(4) In this section 'term date', in relation to a tenancy granted for a term of years, means the date fixed for the expiry of that term.

4 Death of tenant before term date

(1) This section applies where—

(a) a tenancy such as is mentioned in subsection (1) of section 3 above is granted on or after 12th September 1984 to any person or persons,

(b) the person, or the survivor of the persons, dies before the term date, and

(c) no notice effective to terminate the tenancy on the term date has been given under that subsection.

(2) Where this section applies, the tenancy, instead of continuing as mentioned in section 3(1) above—

(a) shall, if the death is one year or more before the term date, terminate on that date, or

(b) shall, if the death is at any other time, continue (as from the term date) for a further period of twelve months, but otherwise on the terms of the tenancy so far as applicable, and shall accordingly terminate on the first anniversary of the term date.

(3) For the purposes of the provisions of this Act with respect to compensation any tenancy terminating in accordance with this section shall be deemed to terminate by reason of a notice to quit given by the landlord of the holding.

(4) In this section 'term date' has the same meaning as in section 3 above.

5 Restriction on agreements excluding effect of section 3

(1) Except as provided in this section, section 3 above shall have effect notwithstanding any agreement to the contrary.

(2) Where before the grant of a tenancy of an agricultural holding for a term of not less than two, and not more than five, years—

(a) the persons who will be the landlord and the tenant in relation to the tenancy agree that section 3 above shall not apply to the tenancy, and

(b) those persons make a joint application in writing to the Minister for his approval of that agreement, and

(c) the Minister notifies them of his approval,

section 3 shall not apply to the tenancy if it satisfies the requirements of subsection (3) below.

(2) A tenancy satisfies the requirements of this subsection if the contract of tenancy is in writing and it, or a statement endorsed upon it, indicates (in whatever terms) that section 3 does not apply to the tenancy.

APPENDIX 10

COURTS AND LEGAL SERVICES ACT 1990

1 Allocation of business between High Court and county courts

(1) The Lord Chancellor may by order make provision—

(a) conferring jurisdiction on the High Court in relation to proceedings in which county courts have jurisdiction;

(b) conferring jurisdiction on county courts in relation to proceedings in which the High Court has jurisdiction;

(c) allocating proceedings to the High Court or to county courts;

(d) specifying proceedings which may be commenced only in the High Court;

(e) specifying proceedings which may be commenced only in a county court;

(f) specifying proceedings which may be taken only in the High Court;

(g) specifying proceedings which may be taken only in a county court.

(2) Without prejudice to the generality of section 120(2), any such order may differentiate between categories of proceedings by reference to such criteria as the Lord Chancellor sees fit to specify in the order.

(3) The criteria so specified may, in particular, relate to—

(a) the value of an action (as defined by the order);

(b) the nature of the proceedings;

(c) the parties to the proceedings;

(d) the degree of complexity likely to be involved in any aspect of the proceedings; and

(e) the importance of any question likely to be raised by, or in the course of, the proceedings.

(4) An order under subsection (1)(b), (e) or (g) may specify one or more particular county courts in relation to the proceedings so specified.

(5) Any jurisdiction exercisable by a county court, under any provision made by virtue of subsection (4), shall be exercisable throughout England and Wales.

(6) Rules of court may provide for a matter—

(a) which is pending in one county court; and

(b) over which that court has jurisdiction under any provision made by virtue of subsection (4), to be heard and determined wholly or partly in another county court which also has jurisdiction in that matter under any such provision.

(7) Any such order may—

(a) amend or repeal any provision falling within subsection (8) and relating to—

> the jurisdiction, practice or procedure of the Supreme Court; or

> the jurisdiction, practice or procedure of any county court,

> so far as the Lord Chancellor considers it to be necessary, or expedient, in consequence of any provision made by the order; or

(b) make such incidental or transitional provision as the Lord Chancellor considers necessary, or expedient, in consequence of any provision made by the order.

(8) A provision falls within this subsection if it is made by any enactment other than this Act or made under any enactment.

(9) Before making any such order the Lord Chancellor shall consult the Lord Chief Justice, the Master of the Rolls, the President of the Family Division, the Vice-Chancellor and the Senior Presiding Judge (appointed under section 72).

(10) No such order shall be made so as to confer jurisdiction on any county court to hear any application for judicial review.

(11) For the purposes of this section the commencement of proceedings may include the making of any application in anticipation of any proceedings or in the course of any proceedings.

(12) The Lord Chancellor shall, within one year of the coming into force of the first order made under this section, and annually thereafter, prepare and lay before both Houses of Parliament a report as to the business of the Supreme Court and county courts.

120 Regulations and orders

(1) Any power to make orders or regulations conferred by this Act shall be exercisable by statutory instrument.

(2) Any such regulations or order may make different provision for different cases or classes of case.

(3) Any such regulations or order may contain such incidental, supplemental or transitional provisions or savings as the person making the regulations or order considers expedient.

(4) No instrument shall be made under section … 26(1), 37(10), 40(1), 58, [58(4),] 60, 89(5) or (7), 125(4)[, paragraph 24 of Schedule 4, paragraph 4] or 6 of Schedule 9 or paragraph 9(c) of Schedule 14 unless

a draft of the instrument has been approved by both Houses of Parliament.

(5) An Order in Council shall not be made in pursuance of a recommendation made under [Part I or Part IV of Schedule 4] unless a draft of the Order has been approved by both Houses of Parliament.

(6) Any other statutory instrument made under this Act other than one under section 124(3) shall be subject to annulment in pursuance of a resolution of either House of Parliament.

APPENDIX 11

LANDLORD AND TENANT (LICENSED PREMISES) ACT 1990

1 Licensed premises: application of Landlord and Tenant Act 1954 Part II

(1) In the Landlord and Tenant Act 1954 (in this section referred to as "the 1954 Act"), in section 43 (tenancies excluded from Part II), paragraph (d) of subsection (1) (which excludes tenancies of premises licensed for the sale of intoxicating liquor for consumption on the premises) shall cease to have effect in relation to any tenancy entered into on or after 11th July 1989, otherwise than in pursuance of a contract made before that date.

(2) If a tenancy—

(a) is of a description mentioned in paragraph (d) of subsection (1) of section 43 of the 1954 Act, and

(b) is in existence on 11th July 1992, and

(c) does not fall within subsection (1) above,

that paragraph shall cease to have effect in relation to the tenancy on and after 11th July 1992; and section 24(3)(b) of the 1954 Act (which, in certain cases, preserves the effect of a notice to quit given in respect of a tenancy which becomes one to which Part II of the 1954 Act applies) shall not have effect in the case of a tenancy which becomes one to which that Part applies by virtue of this subsection.

(3) In relation to a tenancy falling within subsection (2) above, before 11th July 1992 the following notices may be given and any steps may be taken in consequence thereof as if section 43(1)(d) of the 1954 Act had already ceased to have effect—

(a) a notice under section 25 of the 1954 Act (termination of tenancy by landlord) specifying as the date of termination 11th July 1992 or any later date;

(b) a notice under section 26 of the 1954 Act (tenant's request for a new tenancy) requesting a new tenancy beginning not earlier than that date; and

(c) a notice under section 27(1) of the 1954 Act (termination by tenant of tenancy for fixed term) stating that the tenant does not desire his tenancy to be continued.

(4) In this section "tenancy" has the same meaning as in Part II of the 1954 Act.

2 Short title, repeal, commencement and extent

(1) This Act may be cited as the Landlord and Tenant (Licensed Premises) Act 1990.

(2) Subject to subsections (1) and (2) of section 1 of this Act—

(a) section 43(1)(d) of the Landlord and Tenant Act 1954, and

(b) paragraph 5 of Schedule 2 to the Finance Act 1959 (which amended section 43 by substituting the present subsection (1)(d)),

are hereby repealed.

(3) This Act shall come into force at the end of the period of two months beginning with the day on which it is passed.

(4) This Act does not extend to Scotland or Northern Ireland.

AGRICULTURAL TENANCIES ACT 1995

1 Meaning of 'farm business tenancy'

(1) A tenancy is a 'farm business tenancy' for the purposes of this Act if—

(a) it meets the business conditions together with either the agriculture condition or the notice conditions, and

(b) it is not a tenancy which, by virtue of section 2 of this Act, cannot be a farm business tenancy.

(2) The business conditions are—

(a) that all or part of the land comprised in the tenancy is farmed for the purposes of a trade or business, and

(b) that, since the beginning of the tenancy, all or part of the land so comprised has been so farmed.

(3) The agriculture condition is that, having regard to—

(a) the terms of the tenancy,

(b) the use of the land comprised in the tenancy,

(c) the nature of any commercial activities carried on on that land, and

(d) any other relevant circumstances,

the character of the tenancy is primarily or wholly agricultural.

(4) The notice conditions are—

(a) that, on or before the relevant day, the landlord and the tenant each gave the other a written notice—

identifying (by name or otherwise) the land to be comprised in the tenancy or proposed tenancy, and

containing a statement to the effect that the person giving the notice intends that the tenancy or proposed tenancy is to be, and remain, a farm business tenancy, and

(b) that, at the beginning of the tenancy, having regard to the terms of the tenancy and any other relevant circumstances, the character of the tenancy was primarily or wholly agricultural.

(5) In subsection (4) above 'the relevant day' means whichever is the earlier of the following—

(a) the day on which the parties enter into any instrument creating the tenancy, other than an agreement to enter into a tenancy on a future date, or

(b) the beginning of the tenancy.

(6) The written notice referred to in subsection (4) above must not be included in any instrument creating the tenancy.

(7) If in any proceedings—

(a) any question arises as to whether a tenancy was a farm business tenancy at any time, and

(b) it is proved that all or part of the land comprised in the tenancy was farmed for the purposes of a trade or business at that time,

it shall be presumed, unless the contrary is proved, that all or part of the land so comprised has been so farmed since the beginning of the tenancy.

(8) Any use of land in breach of the terms of the tenancy, any commercial activities carried on in breach of those terms, and any cessation of such activities in breach of those terms, shall be disregarded in determining whether at any time the tenancy meets the business conditions or the agriculture condition, unless the landlord or his predecessor in title has consented to the breach or the landlord has acquiesced in the breach.

2 Tenancies which cannot be farm business tenancies

(1) A tenancy cannot be a farm business tenancy for the purposes of this Act if—

(a) the tenancy begins before 1st September 1995, or

(b) it is a tenancy of an agricultural holding beginning on or after that date with respect to which, by virtue of section 4 of this Act, the Agricultural Holdings Act 1986 applies.

(2) In this section "agricultural holding" has the same meaning as in the Agricultural Holdings Act 1986.

4 Agricultural Holdings Act 1986 not to apply in relation to new tenancies except in special cases

(1) The Agricultural Holdings Act 1986 (in this section referred to as 'the 1986 Act') shall not apply in relation to any tenancy beginning on or after 1st September 1995 (including any agreement to which section 2 of that Act would otherwise apply beginning on or after that date), except any tenancy of an agricultural holding which—

(a) is granted by a written contract of tenancy entered into before 1st September 1995 and indicating (in whatever terms) that the 1986 Act is to apply in relation to the tenancy,

(b) is obtained by virtue of a direction of an Agricultural Land Tribunal under section 39 or 53 of the 1986 Act,

(c) is granted (following a direction under section 39 of that Act) in circumstances falling within section 45(6) of that Act,

(d) is granted on an agreed succession by a written contract of tenancy indicating (in whatever terms) that Part IV of the 1986 Act is to apply in relation to the tenancy,

(e) is created by the acceptance of a tenant, in accordance with the provisions as to compensation known as the "Evesham custom" and set out in subsections (3) to (5) of section 80 of the 1986 Act, on the terms and conditions of the previous tenancy, or

(f) is granted to a person who, immediately before the grant of the tenancy, was the tenant of the holding, or of any agricultural holding which comprised the whole or a substantial part of the land comprised in the holding, under a tenancy in relation to which the 1986 Act applied ('the previous tenancy') and is so granted merely because a purported variation of the previous tenancy (not being an agreement expressed to take effect as a new tenancy between the parties) has effect as an implied surrender followed by the grant of the tenancy.

(2) For the purposes of subsection (1)(d) above, a tenancy ('the current tenancy') is granted on an agreed succession if, and only if—

(a) the previous tenancy of the holding or a related holding was a tenancy in relation to which Part IV of the 1986 Act applied, and

(b) the current tenancy is granted otherwise than as mentioned in paragraph (b) or (c) of subsection (1) above but in such circumstances that if—

Part IV of the 1986 Act applied in relation to the current tenancy, and

a sole (or sole surviving) tenant under the current tenancy were to die and be survived by a close relative of his,

the occasion on which the current tenancy is granted would for the purposes of subsection (1) of section 37 of the 1986 Act be taken to be an occasion falling within paragraph (a) or (b) of that subsection.

(3) In this section—

(a) 'agricultural holding' and 'contract of tenancy' have the same meaning as in the 1986 Act, and

(b) 'close relative' and 'related holding' have the meaning given by section 35(2) of that Act.

CIVIL EVIDENCE ACT 1995

1 Admissibility of hearsay evidence

(1) In civil proceedings evidence shall not be excluded on the ground that it is hearsay.

(2) In this Act—

(a) 'hearsay' means a statement made otherwise than by a person while giving oral evidence in the proceedings which is tendered as evidence of the matters stated; and

(b) references to hearsay include hearsay of whatever degree.

(3) Nothing in this Act affects the admissibility of evidence admissible apart from this section.

(4) The provisions of sections 2 to 6 (safeguards and supplementary provisions relating to hearsay evidence) do not apply in relation to hearsay evidence admissible apart from this section, notwithstanding that it may also be admissible by virtue of this section.

2 Notice of proposal to adduce hearsay evidence

(1) A party proposing to adduce hearsay evidence in civil proceedings shall, subject to the following provisions of this section, give to the other party or parties to the proceedings—

(a) such notice (if any) of that fact, and

(b) on request, such particulars of or relating to the evidence,

as is reasonable and practicable in the circumstances for the purpose of enabling him or them to deal with any matters arising from its being hearsay.

(2) Provision may be made by rules of court—

(a) specifying classes of proceedings or evidence in relation to which subsection (1) does not apply, and

(b) as to the manner in which (including the time within which) the duties imposed by that subsection are to be complied with in the cases where it does apply.

(3) Subsection (1) may also be excluded by agreement of the parties; and compliance with the duty to give notice may in any case be waived by the person to whom notice is required to be given.

(4) A failure to comply with subsection (1), or with rules under subsection (2)(b), does not affect the admissibility of the evidence but may be taken into account by the court—

(a) in considering the exercise of its powers with respect to the course of proceedings and costs, and

(b) as a matter adversely affecting the weight to be given to the evidence in accordance with section 4.

3 Power to call witness for cross-examination on hearsay statement

Rules of court may provide that where a party to civil proceedings adduces hearsay evidence of a statement made by a person and does not call that person as a witness, any other party to the proceedings may, with the leave of the court, call that person as a witness and cross-examine him on the statement as if he had been called by the first-mentioned party and as if the hearsay statement were his evidence in chief.

4 Considerations relevant to weighing of hearsay evidence

(1) In estimating the weight (if any) to be given to hearsay evidence in civil proceedings the court shall have regard to any circumstances from which any inference can reasonably be drawn as to the reliability or otherwise of the evidence.

(2) Regard may be had, in particular, to the following—

(a) whether it would have been reasonable and practicable for the party by whom the evidence was adduced to have produced the maker of the original statement as a witness;

(b) whether the original statement was made contemporaneously with the occurrence or existence of the matters stated;

(c) whether the evidence involves multiple hearsay;

(d) whether any person involved had any motive to conceal or misrepresent matters;

(e) whether the original statement was an edited account, or was made in collaboration with another or for a particular purpose;

(f) whether the circumstances in which the evidence is adduced as hearsay are such as to suggest an attempt to prevent proper evaluation of its weight.

5 Competence and credibility

(1) Hearsay evidence shall not be admitted in civil proceedings if or to the extent that it is shown to consist of, or to be proved by means of, a statement made by a person who at the time he made the statement was not competent as a witness.

For this purpose 'not competent as a witness' means suffering from such mental or physical infirmity, or lack of understanding, as would render a person incompetent as a witness in civil proceedings; but a child shall be treated as competent as a witness if he satisfies the requirements of section 96(2)(a) and (b) of the Children Act 1989 (conditions for reception of unsworn evidence of child).

(2) Where in civil proceedings hearsay evidence is adduced and the maker of the original statement, or of any statement relied upon to prove another statement, is not called as a witness—

(a) evidence which if he had been so called would be admissible for the purpose of attacking or supporting his credibility as a witness is admissible for that purpose in the proceedings; and

(b) evidence tending to prove that, whether before or after he made the statement, he made any other statement inconsistent with it is admissible for the purpose of showing that he had contradicted himself.

Provided that evidence may not be given of any matter of which, if he had been called as a witness and had denied that matter in cross-examination, evidence could not have been adduced by the cross-examining party.

6 Previous statements of witnesses

(1) Subject as follows, the provisions of this Act as to hearsay evidence in civil proceedings apply equally (but with any necessary modifications) in relation to a previous statement made by a person called as a witness in the proceedings.

(2) A party who has called or intends to call a person as a witness in civil proceedings may not in those proceedings adduce evidence of a previous statement made by that person, except—

(a) with the leave of the court, or

(b) for the purpose of rebutting a suggestion that his evidence has been fabricated.

This shall not be construed as preventing a witness statement (that is, a written statement of oral evidence which a party to the proceedings intends to lead) from being adopted by a witness in giving evidence or treated as his evidence.

(3) Where in the case of civil proceedings section 3, 4 or 5 of the Criminal Procedure Act 1865 applies, which make provision as to—

(a) how far a witness may be discredited by the party producing him,

(b) the proof of contradictory statements made by a witness, and

(c) cross-examination as to previous statements in writing,

this Act does not authorise the adducing of evidence of a previous inconsistent or contradictory statement otherwise than in accordance with those sections.

This is without prejudice to any provision made by rules of court under section 3 above (power to call witness for cross-examination on hearsay statement).

(4) Nothing in this Act affects any of the rules of law as to the circumstances in which, where a person called as a witness in civil proceedings is cross-examined on a document used by him to refresh his memory, that document may be made evidence in the proceedings.

(5) Nothing in this section shall be construed as preventing a statement of any description referred to above from being admissible by virtue of section 1 as evidence of the matters stated.

7 Evidence formerly admissible at common law

(1) The common law rule effectively preserved by section 9(1) and (2)(a) of the Civil Evidence Act 1968 (admissibility of admissions adverse to a party) is superseded by the provisions of this Act.

(2) The common law rules effectively preserved by section 9(1) and (2)(b) to (d) of the Civil Evidence Act 1968 that is, any rule of law whereby in civil proceedings—

(a) published works dealing with matters of a public nature (for example, histories, scientific works, dictionaries and maps) are admissible as evidence of facts of a public nature stated in them,

(b) public documents (for example, public registers, and returns made under public authority with respect to matters of public interest) are admissible as evidence of facts stated in them, or

(c) records (for example, the records of certain courts, treaties, Crown grants, pardons and commissions) are admissible as evidence of facts stated in them,

shall continue to have effect.

(3) The common law rules effectively preserved by section 9(3) and (4) of the Civil Evidence Act 1968, that is, any rule of law whereby in civil proceedings—

(a) evidence of a person's reputation is admissible for the purpose of proving his good or bad character, or

(b) evidence of reputation or family tradition is admissible—

    (i) for the purpose of proving or disproving pedigree or the existence of a marriage, or

    (ii) for the purpose of proving or disproving the existence of any public or general right or of identifying any person or thing,

shall continue to have effect in so far as they authorise the court to treat such evidence as proving or disproving that matter.

Where any such rule applies, reputation or family tradition shall be treated for the purposes of this Act as a fact and not as a statement or multiplicity of statements about the matter in question.

(4) The words in which a rule of law mentioned in this section is described are intended only to identify the rule and shall not be construed as altering it in any way.

8 Proof of statements contained in documents

(1) Where a statement contained in a document is admissible as evidence in civil proceedings, it may be proved—

(a) by the production of that document, or

(b) whether or not that document is still in existence, by the production of a copy of that document or of the material part of it,

authenticated in such manner as the court may approve.

(2) It is immaterial for this purpose how many removes there are between a copy and the original.

9 Proof of records of business or public authority

(1) A document which is shown to form part of the records of a business or public authority may be received in evidence in civil proceedings without further proof.

(2) A document shall be taken to form part of the records of a business or public authority if there is produced to the court a certificate to that effect signed by an officer of the business or authority to which the records belong.

For this purpose—

(a) a document purporting to be a certificate signed by an officer of a business or public authority shall be deemed to have been duly given by such an officer and signed by him; and

(b) a certificate shall be treated as signed by a person if it purports to bear a facsimile of his signature.

(3) The absence of an entry in the records of a business or public authority may be proved in civil proceedings by affidavit of an officer of the business or authority to which the records belong.

(4) In this section—

'records' means records in whatever form;

'business' includes any activity regularly carried on over a period of time, whether for profit or not, by any body (whether corporate or not) or by an individual;

'officer' includes any person occupying a responsible position in relation to the relevant activities of the business or public authority or in relation to its records; and

'public authority' includes any public or statutory undertaking, any government department and any person holding office under Her Majesty.

(5) The court may, having regard to the circumstances of the case, direct that all or any of the above provisions of this section do not apply in relation to a particular document or record, or description of documents or records.

11 Meaning of 'civil proceedings'

In this Act 'civil proceedings' means civil proceedings, before any tribunal, in relation to which the strict rules of evidence apply, whether as a matter of law or by agreement of the parties.

References to 'the court' and 'rules of court' shall be construed accordingly.

12 Provisions as to rules of court

(1) Any power to make rules of court regulating the practice or procedure of the court in relation to civil proceedings includes power to make such provision as may be necessary or expedient for carrying into effect the provisions of this Act.

(2) Any rules of court made for the purposes of this Act as it applies in relation to proceedings in the High Court apply, except in so far as their operation is excluded by agreement, to arbitration proceedings to which this Act applies, subject to such modifications as may be appropriate.

Any question arising as to what modifications are appropriate shall be determined, in default of agreement, by the arbitrator or umpire, as the case may be.

13 Interpretation

In this Act—

'civil proceedings' has the meaning given by section 11 and 'court' and 'rules of court' shall be construed in accordance with that section;

'document' means anything in which information of any description is recorded, and 'copy', in relation to a document, means anything onto which information recorded in the document has been copied, by whatever means and whether directly or indirectly;

'hearsay' shall be construed in accordance with section 1(2);

'oral evidence' includes evidence which, by reason of a defect of speech or hearing, a person called as a witness gives in writing or by signs;

'the original statement', in relation to hearsay evidence, means the underlying statement (if any) by—

(a) in the case of evidence of fact, a person having personal knowledge of that fact, or

(b) in the case of evidence of opinion, the person whose opinion it is; and

'statement' means any representation of fact or opinion, however made.

APPENDIX 14

LANDLORD AND TENANT ACT 1954 (DETERMINATION OF RATEABLE VALUE PROCEDURE) RULES 1954 (SI 1954/1255)

1 These Rules may be cited as the Landlord and Tenant (Determination of Rateable Value Procedure) Rules 1954, and shall come into operation on the first day of October, 1954.

2 (1) In these Rules—

'The Commissioners' means the Commissioners of Inland Revenue;

'The Act' means the Landlord and Tenant Act 1954, and other expressions have the same meaning as in that Act.

(2) The Interpretation Act 1889 shall apply to these Rules as it applies to an Act of Parliament.

3 (1) Any reference to the Commissioners of a dispute arising as to the determination of the rateable value of any holding for the purposes of Sections 37(2) and 63(2) of the Act, shall be in the form 'A' in the Schedule hereto, or in a form substantially to the like effect. A separate form shall be completed in respect of each holding.

(2) The said reference may be made either—

(a) by one of the parties, or

(b) jointly by two or more of the parties to the dispute:

Provided that, where the said reference is not made by all the parties jointly, the party or parties making the reference shall, on the same day as the reference is made, send a copy thereof to the other party, or parties, to the dispute.

4 The Commissioners shall, so soon as may be after the receipt of a reference, send a copy thereof to the Valuation Officer.

5 The Valuation Officer shall, upon receipt of the copy of the reference, inform the parties that the dispute has been referred to him for determination and that they may make representations to him on the matter in writing within twenty-eight days, or such longer time as he may in a particular case allow.

6 The Valuation Officer may require the parties to furnish him with such information as he may reasonably require for the proper determination of the rateable value of the holding.

7 The Valuation Officer may, before making his determination, invite all the parties to a meeting at his office or at such other place as he may think convenient.

8 The Valuation Officer shall so soon as may be determine the rateable value of the holding and shall send a notification of his determination to the Commissioners and to each of the parties together with a statement of their right of appeal to the Lands Tribunal under Section 37(5) of the Act. The notification of such determination shall be in the form 'B' in the Schedule hereto, and a separate notification shall be sent in respect of each holding.

SCHEDULE

FORMS 'A','B'

Regulations 3, 8

FORM 'A'

Landlord and Tenant Act 1954

Reference of a dispute arising as to the determination of the Rateable Value of any holding for the purposes of Section 37(2) or of Section 63(2).

To:— The Commissioners of Inland Revenue,
Somerset House,
London, WC2.

PART I (Applicable to all references).

I/We (see headnote to Part II of form) being a party/parties (see headnote to Part II of form) to a dispute which has arisen as to the determination for the purposes of Section [37(2)/63(2)] (see headnote to Part II of form) of the rateable value of a holding known as (Insert here address or situation, and such further particulars as may be necessary for the identification of the holding.) .... hereby refer the dispute for decision by a Valuation Officer.

(1)* (2)* (3)*

Signed ....

Capacity in which reference made (eg Tenant, Landlord, etc) Address
....

Date ....

Part II (Applicable where the reference is not made by all the parties to the dispute).

Note.—Where the reference is not made by all the parties, the party or parties making the reference should sign and complete the form in Part 1 above, and should give below the name or names of the other party or parties to the dispute, and should send a copy of this form, as completed, to the other party or parties.

Name(s) and address(es) of other party(ies)

(A) (B)

Name ....

Address ....

FORM 'B'

Landlord and Tenant Act 1954

Determination of Rateable Value

Whereas a dispute has arisen as to the determination for the purposes of Section [37(2)/63(2)] (delete as appropriate) of the rateable value of the holding described in the first column of the Schedule hereto.

Now I the undersigned being the Valuation Officer to whom the Commissioners of Inland Revenue have pursuant to Section 37(5) referred the dispute for determination hereby determine that for the said purposes the rateable value of the said holding shall be the amount set out in the second column of the said Schedule.

THE SCHEDULE above referred to

Description of Holding   Rateable Value as Determined

(The description will follow that in 'A'.)

Dated this .... day of ......, 19 ....

Signed ....

Valuation Officer

for ....

Official Address ....

Any party who is dissatisfied with the foregoing determination may appeal to the Lands Tribunal by giving written notice of such appeal to the Registrar of the Lands Tribunal within 21 days from the date hereof.

APPENDIX 15

LANDLORD AND TENANT ACT 1954 (APPROPRIATE MULTIPLIER) ORDER 1990

LANDLORD AND TENANT ACT 1954 (APPROPRIATE MULTIPLIER) ORDER 1990 (SI 1990, No 363)

1 This Order may be cited as the Landlord and Tenant Act 1954 (Appropriate Multiplier) Order 1990 and shall come into force on 1st April 1990.

2 In this Order references to section 37 are references to section 37 of the Landlord and Tenant Act 1954 and references to the 1989 Act are to the Local Government and Housing Act 1989.

3 Where the date which (apart from paragraph 4 of Schedule 7 to the 1989 Act) is relevant for determining the rateable value of the holding under section 37(5) is before 1st April 1990, the appropriate multiplier for the purposes of section 37(2) is 3.

4 Where the date which (apart from paragraph 4 of Schedule 7 to the 1989 Act) is relevant for determining the rateable value of the holding under section 37(5) is on or after 1st April 1990, the appropriate multiplier for the purposes of section 37(2) is-

(a) 1, except in a case specified in (b) below, and

(b) 8 in a case where section 37 has effect with the modification specified in paragraph 4(2) of Schedule 7 to the 1989 Act.

APPENDIX 16

LANDLORD AND TENANT ACT 1954, PART 2 (NOTICES) REGULATIONS 2004

The Landlord and Tenant Act 1954, Part 2 (Notices) Regulations 2004 (SI 2004, No 1005)

Made	*30th March 2004*
Laid before Parliament	*6th April 2004*
Coming into force	*1st June 2004*

The First Secretary of State, as respects England, and the National Assembly for Wales, as respects Wales, in exercise of the powers conferred by section 66 of the Landlord and Tenant Act 1954 [1] (including that section as it has effect as mentioned in section 22(5) of the Leasehold Reform Act 1967), and of all other powers enabling them in that behalf, hereby make the following Regulations:

Citation and commencement

1 These Regulations may be cited as the Landlord and Tenant Act 1954, Part 2 (Notices) Regulations 2004 and shall come into force on 1st June 2004.

Interpretation

2 - (1) In these Regulations -

'the Act' means the Landlord and Tenant Act 1954[2]; and

'the 1967 Act' means the Leasehold Reform Act 1967[3].

(2) Any reference in these Regulations to a numbered form (in whatever terms) is a reference to the form bearing that number in Schedule 2 to these Regulations or a form substantially to the same effect.

Prescribed forms, and purposes for which they are to be used.

3 The form with the number shown in column (1) of Schedule 1 to these Regulations is prescribed for use for the purpose shown in the corresponding entry in column (2) of that Schedule.

Revocation of Regulations

4 The Landlord and Tenant Act 1954, Part 2 (Notices) Regulations 1983[4] and the Landlord and Tenant Act 1954, Part 2 (Notices) (Amendment) Regulations 1989[5] are hereby revoked.

Signed by authority of the First Secretary of State

Keith Hill

Minister of State, Office of the Deputy Prime Minister

16th March 2004

Signed on behalf of the National Assembly for Wales

D. Elis- Thomas
Presiding Officer of the National Assembly

30th March 2004

SCHEDULE 1

Regulations 2(2) and 3

PRESCRIBED FORMS, AND PURPOSES FOR WHICH THEY ARE TO BE USED

(1) (2)

Form number   Purpose for which to be used

1   Ending a tenancy to which Part 2 of the Act applies, where the landlord is not opposed to the grant of a new tenancy (notice under section 25 of the Act).

2   Ending a tenancy to which Part 2 of the Act applies, where -

(a) the landlord is opposed to the grant of a new tenancy (notice under section 25 of the Act); and

(b) the tenant is not entitled under the 1967 Act to buy the freehold or an extended lease.

3   Tenant's request for a new tenancy of premises where Part 2 of the Act applies (notice under section 26 of the Act).

4   Landlord's notice activating tenant's duty under section 40(1) of the Act to give information as to his or her occupation of the premises and as to any sub-tenancies.

5   Tenant's notice activating duty under section 40(3) of the Act of reversioner or reversioner's mortgagee in possession to give information about his or her interest in the premises.

6   Withdrawal of notice given under section 25 of the Act ending a tenancy to which Part 2 of the Act applies (notice under section 44 of, and paragraph 6 of Schedule 6 to, the Act).

7   Ending a tenancy to which Part 2 of the Act applies, where the landlord is opposed to the grant of a new tenancy but where the tenant may be entitled under the 1967 Act to buy the freehold or an extended lease (notice under section 25 of the Act and paragraph 10 of Schedule 3 to the 1967 Act).

8   Ending a tenancy to which Part 2 of the Act applies, where:

(a) the notice under section 25 of the Act contains a copy of a certificate given under section 57 of the Act that the use or occupation of the property or part of it is to be changed by a specified date;

(b) the date of termination of the tenancy specified in the notice is not earlier than the date specified in the certificate; and

(c) the tenant is not entitled under the 1967 Act to buy the freehold or an extended lease.

9   Ending a tenancy to which Part 2 of the Act applies, where:

(a) the notice under section 25 of the Act contains a copy of a certificate given under section 57 of the Act that the use or occupation of the property or part of it is to be changed at a future date;

(b) the date of termination of the tenancy specified in the notice is earlier than the date specified in the certificate;

(c) the landlord opposes the grant of a new tenancy; and

(d) the tenant is not entitled under the 1967 Act to buy the freehold or an extended lease.

10   Ending a tenancy to which Part 2 of the Act applies, where:

(a) the notice under section 25 of the Act contains a copy of a certificate given under section 57 of the Act that the use or occupation of the property or part of it is to be changed at a future date;

(b) the date of termination of the tenancy specified in the notice is earlier than the date specified in the certificate;

(c) the landlord does not oppose the grant of a new tenancy; and

(d) the tenant is not entitled under the 1967 Act to buy the freehold or an extended lease.

11   Ending a tenancy to which Part 2 of the Act applies, where the notice under section 25 of the Act contains a copy of a certificate given under section 58 of the Act that for reasons of national security it is necessary that the use or occupation of the property should be discontinued or changed.

12   Ending a tenancy to which Part 2 of the Act applies, where -

(a) the notice under section 25 of the Act contains a copy of a certificate given under section 58 of the Act (as applied by section 60 of the Act) that it is necessary or expedient for achieving the purpose mentioned in section 2(1) of the Local Employment Act 1972[6] that the use or occupation of the property should be changed; and

(b) the tenant is not entitled under the 1967 Act to buy the freehold or an extended lease.

13   Ending a tenancy to which Part 2 of the Act applies, where:

(a) the notice under section 25 of the Act contains a copy of a certificate given under section 57 of the Act that the use or occupation of the property or part of it is to be changed by a specified date; and

(b) the date of termination of the tenancy specified in the notice is not earlier than the date specified in the certificate; and

(c) the tenant may be entitled under the 1967 Act to buy the freehold or an extended lease.

14 Ending a tenancy to which Part 2 of the Act applies, where:

(a) the notice under section 25 of the Act contains a copy of a certificate given under section 57 of the Act that the use or occupation of the property or part of it is to be changed at a future date;

(b) the date of termination of the tenancy specified in the notice is earlier than the date specified in the certificate; and

(c) the tenant may be entitled under the 1967 Act to buy the freehold or an extended lease the landlord opposes the grant of a new tenancy.

15 Ending a tenancy to which Part 2 of the Act applies, where:

(a) the notice under section 25 of the Act contains a copy of a certificate given under section 58 of the Act (as applied by section 60 of the Act) that it is necessary or expedient for achieving the purpose mentioned in section 2(1) of the Local Employment Act 1972[7] that the use or occupation of the property should be changed; and

(b) the tenant may be entitled under the 1967 Act to buy the freehold or an extended lease the landlord opposes the grant of a new tenancy.

16 Ending a tenancy of Welsh Development Agency premises where -

(a) the notice under section 25 of the Act contains a copy of a certificate given under section 58 of the Act (as applied by section 60A of the Act) that it is necessary or expedient, for the purposes of providing employment appropriate to the needs of the area in which the premises are situated, that the use or occupation of the property should be changed; and

(b) the tenant is not entitled under the 1967 Act to buy the freehold or an extended lease.

17 Ending a tenancy of Welsh Development Agency premises where:

(a) the notice under section 25 of the Act contains a copy of a certificate given under section 58 of the Act (as applied by section 60A of the Act) that it is necessary or expedient, for the purposes of providing employment appropriate to the needs of the area in which the premises are situated, that the use or occupation of the property should be changed; and

(b) the tenant may be entitled under the 1967 Act to buy the freehold or an extended lease.

SCHEDULE 2

Regulation 2(2)
PRESCRIBED FORMS

Form 1

LANDLORD'S NOTICE ENDING A BUSINESS TENANCY WITH
PROPOSALS FOR A NEW ONE

Section 25 of the Landlord and Tenant Act 1954

IMPORTANT NOTE FOR THE LANDLORD: If you are willing to
grant a new tenancy, complete this form and send it to the tenant. If
you wish to oppose the grant of a new tenancy, use form 2 in Schedule
2 to the Landlord and Tenant Act 1954, Part 2 (Notices) Regulations
2004 or, where the tenant may be entitled to acquire the freehold or an
extended lease, form 7 in that Schedule, instead of this form.

To: (*insert name and address of tenant*)

From: (*insert name and address of landlord*)

    1 This notice applies to the following property: (*insert address or
description of property*).

    2 I am giving you notice under section 25 of the Landlord and
Tenant Act 1954 to end your tenancy on (*insert date*).

    3 I am not opposed to granting you a new tenancy. You will find
my proposals for the new tenancy, which we can discuss, in the
Schedule to this notice.

    4 If we cannot agree on all the terms of a new tenancy, either you
or I may ask the court to order the grant of a new tenancy and settle
the terms on which we cannot agree.

    5 If you wish to ask the court for a new tenancy you must do so by
the date in paragraph 2, unless we agree in writing to a later date and
do so before the date in paragraph 2.

    6 Please send all correspondence about this notice to:

Name:

Address:

Signed: Date:

*[Landlord] *[On behalf of the landlord] *[Mortgagee] *[On behalf of
the mortgagee]

*(*delete if inapplicable*)

SCHEDULE

LANDLORD'S PROPOSALS FOR A NEW TENANCY

(attach or insert proposed terms of the new tenancy)

IMPORTANT NOTE FOR THE TENANT

This Notice is intended to bring your tenancy to an end. If you want to continue to occupy your property after the date specified in paragraph 2 you must act quickly. If you are in any doubt about the action that you should take, get advice immediately from a solicitor or a surveyor.

The landlord is prepared to offer you a new tenancy and has set out proposed terms in the Schedule to this notice. You are not bound to accept these terms. They are merely suggestions as a basis for negotiation. In the event of disagreement, ultimately the court would settle the terms of the new tenancy.

It would be wise to seek professional advice before agreeing to accept the landlord's terms or putting forward your own proposals.

NOTES

The sections mentioned below are sections of the Landlord and Tenant Act 1954, as amended, (most recently by the Regulatory Reform (Business Tenancies) (England and Wales) Order 2003).

Ending of tenancy and grant of new tenancy

This notice is intended to bring your tenancy to an end on the date given in paragraph 2. Section 25 contains rules about the date that the landlord can put in that paragraph.

However, your landlord is prepared to offer you a new tenancy and has set out proposals for it in the Schedule to this notice (section 25(8)). You are not obliged to accept these proposals and may put forward your own.

If you and your landlord are unable to agree terms either one of you may apply to the court. You may not apply to the court if your landlord has already done so (section 24(2A)). If you wish to apply to the court you must do so by the date given in paragraph 2 of this notice, unless you and your landlord have agreed in writing to extend the deadline (sections 29A and 29B).

The court will settle the rent and other terms of the new tenancy or those on which you and your landlord cannot agree (sections 34 and 35). If you apply to the court your tenancy will continue after the date shown in paragraph 2 of this notice while your application is being considered (section 24).

If you are in any doubt about what action you should take, get advice immediately from a solicitor or a surveyor.

Negotiating a new tenancy

Most tenancies are renewed by negotiation. You and your landlord may agree in writing to extend the deadline for making an application to the court while negotiations continue. Either you or your landlord can ask the court to fix the rent that you will have to pay while the tenancy continues (sections 24A to 24D).

You may only stay in the property after the date in paragraph 2 (or if we have agreed in writing to a later date, that date), if by then you or the landlord has asked the court to order the grant of a new tenancy.

If you do try to agree a new tenancy with your landlord remember:

that your present tenancy will not continue after the date in paragraph 2 of this notice without the agreement in writing mentioned above, unless you have applied to the court or your landlord has done so, and

that you will lose your right to apply to the court once the deadline in paragraph 2 of this notice has passed, unless there is a written agreement extending the deadline.

Validity of this notice

The landlord who has given you this notice may not be the landlord to whom you pay your rent (sections 44 and 67). This does not necessarily mean that the notice is invalid.

If you have any doubts about whether this notice is valid, get advice immediately from a solicitor or a surveyor.

Further information

An explanation of the main points to consider when renewing or ending a business tenancy, 'Renewing and Ending Business Leases: a Guide for Tenants and Landlords', can be found at www.odpm.gov.uk. Printed copies of the explanation, but not of this form, are available from 1st June 2004 from Free Literature, PO Box 236, Wetherby, West Yorkshire, LS23 7NB (0870 1226 236).

Form 2

LANDLORD'S NOTICE ENDING A BUSINESS TENANCY AND REASONS FOR REFUSING A NEW ONE

Section 25 of the Landlord and Tenant Act 1954

IMPORTANT NOTE FOR THE LANDLORD: If you wish to oppose the grant of a new tenancy on any of the grounds in section 30(1) of the Landlord and Tenant Act 1954, complete this form and send it to the tenant. If the tenant may be entitled to acquire the freehold or an extended lease, use form 7 in Schedule 2 to the Landlord and Tenant Act 1954, Part 2 (Notices) Regulations 2004 instead of this form.

To: (*insert name and address of tenant*)

From: (*insert name and address of landlord*)

1 This notice relates to the following property: (*insert address or description of property*).

2 I am giving you notice under section 25 of the Landlord and Tenant Act 1954 to end your tenancy on (*insert date*).

3 I am opposed to the grant of a new tenancy.

4 You may ask the court to order the grant of a new tenancy. If you do, I will oppose your application on the ground(s) mentioned in paragraph(s)* of section 30(1) of that Act. I draw your attention to the Table in the Notes below, which sets out all the grounds of opposition.

*(*insert letter(s) of the paragraph(s) relied on*)

5 If you wish to ask the court for a new tenancy you must do so before the date in paragraph 2 unless, before that date, we agree in writing to a later date.

6 I can ask the court to order the ending of your tenancy without granting you a new tenancy. I may have to pay you compensation if I have relied only on one or more of the grounds mentioned in paragraphs (e), (f) and (g) of section 30(1). If I ask the court to end your tenancy, you can challenge my application.

7 Please send all correspondence about this notice to:

Name:

Address:

Signed: Date:

*[Landlord] *[On behalf of the landlord] *[Mortgagee] *[On behalf of the mortgagee]

(*delete if inapplicable*)

IMPORTANT NOTE FOR THE TENANT

This notice is intended to bring your tenancy to an end on the date specified in paragraph 2.

Your landlord is not prepared to offer you a new tenancy. You will not get a new tenancy unless you successfully challenge in court the grounds on which your landlord opposes the grant of a new tenancy.

If you want to continue to occupy your property you must act quickly. The notes below should help you to decide what action you now need to take. If you want to challenge your landlord's refusal to renew your tenancy, get advice immediately from a solicitor or a surveyor.

NOTES

The sections mentioned below are sections of the Landlord and Tenant Act 1954, as amended (most recently by the Regulatory Reform (Business Tenancies) (England and Wales) Order 2003).

Ending of your tenancy

This notice is intended to bring your tenancy to an end on the date given in paragraph 2. Section 25 contains rules about the date that the landlord can put in that paragraph.

Your landlord is not prepared to offer you a new tenancy. If you want a new tenancy you will need to apply to the court for a new tenancy and successfully challenge the landlord's grounds for opposition (see the section below headed *'Landlord's opposition to new tenancy'*). If you wish to apply to the court you must do so before the date given in paragraph 2 of this notice, unless you and your landlord have agreed in writing, before that date, to extend the deadline (sections 29A and 29B).

If you apply to the court your tenancy will continue after the date given in paragraph 2 of this notice while your application is being considered (section 24). You may not apply to the court if your landlord has already done so (section 24(2A) and (2B)).

You may only stay in the property after the date given in paragraph 2 (or such later date as you and the landlord may have agreed in writing) if before that date you have asked the court to order the grant of a new tenancy or the landlord has asked the court to order the ending of your tenancy without granting you a new one.

If you are in any doubt about what action you should take, get advice immediately from a solicitor or a surveyor.

Landlord's opposition to new tenancy

If you apply to the court for a new tenancy, the landlord can only oppose your application on one or more of the grounds set out in section 30(1). If you match the letter(s) specified in paragraph 4 of this notice with those in the first column in the Table below, you can see from the second column the ground(s) on which the landlord relies.

Paragraph of section 30(1)   Grounds

(a) Where under the current tenancy the tenant has any obligations as respects the repair and maintenance of the holding, that the tenant ought not to be granted a new tenancy in view of the state of repair of the holding, being a state resulting from the tenant's failure to comply with the said obligations.

(b) That the tenant ought not to be granted a new tenancy in view of his persistent delay in paying rent which has become due.

(c) That the tenant ought not to be granted a new tenancy in view of other substantial breaches by him of his obligations under the current tenancy, or for any other reason connected with the tenant's use or management of the holding.

(d) That the landlord has offered and is willing to provide or secure the provision of alternative accommodation for the tenant, that the terms on which the alternative accommodation is available are reasonable having regard to the terms of the current tenancy and to all other relevant circumstances, and that the accommodation and the time at which it will be available are suitable for the tenant's requirements (including the requirement to preserve goodwill) having regard to the nature and class of his business and to the situation and extent of, and facilities afforded by, the holding.

(e) Where the current tenancy was created by the sub-letting of part only of the property comprised in a superior tenancy and the landlord is the owner of an interest in reversion expectant on the termination of that superior tenancy, that the aggregate of the rents reasonably obtainable on separate lettings of the holding and the remainder of that property would be substantially less than the rent reasonably obtainable on a letting of that property as a whole, that on the termination of the current tenancy the landlord requires possession of the holding for the purposes of letting or otherwise disposing of the said property as a whole, and that in view thereof the tenant ought not to be granted a new tenancy.

(f) That on the termination of the current tenancy the landlord intends to demolish or reconstruct the premises comprised in the holding or a substantial part of those premises or to carry out substantial work of construction on the holding or part thereof and that he could not reasonably do so without obtaining possession of the holding.

(g) On the termination of the current tenancy the landlord intends to occupy the holding for the purposes, or partly for the purposes, of a business to be carried on by him therein, or as his residence.

In this Table 'the holding' means the property that is the subject of the tenancy.

In ground (e), 'the landlord is the owner an interest in reversion expectant on the termination of that superior tenancy' means that the landlord has an interest in the property that will entitle him or her, when your immediate landlord's tenancy comes to an end, to exercise certain rights and obligations in relation to the property that are currently exercisable by your immediate landlord.

If the landlord relies on ground (f), the court can sometimes still grant a new tenancy if certain conditions set out in section 31A are met.

If the landlord relies on ground (g), please note that 'the landlord' may have an extended meaning. Where a landlord has a controlling interest in a company then either the landlord or the company can rely on ground (g). Where the landlord is a company and a person has a controlling interest in that company then either of them can rely on ground (g) (section 30(1A) and (1B)). A person has a 'controlling interest' in a company if, had he been a company, the other company would have been its subsidiary (section 46(2)).

The landlord must normally have been the landlord for at least five years before he or she can rely on ground (g).

Compensation

If you cannot get a new tenancy solely because one or more of grounds (e), (f) and (g) applies, you may be entitled to compensation under section 37. If your landlord has opposed your application on any of the other grounds as well as (e), (f) or (g) you can only get compensation if the court's refusal to grant a new tenancy is based solely on one or more of grounds (e), (f) and (g). In other words, you cannot get compensation under section 37 if the court has refused your tenancy on *other* grounds, even if one or more of grounds (e), (f) and (g) also applies.

If your landlord is an authority possessing compulsory purchase powers (such as a local authority) you may be entitled to a disturbance payment under Part 3 of the Land Compensation Act 1973.

Validity of this notice

The landlord who has given you this notice may not be the landlord to whom you pay your rent (sections 44 and 67). This does not necessarily mean that the notice is invalid.

If you have any doubts about whether this notice is valid, get advice immediately from a solicitor or a surveyor.

Further information

An explanation of the main points to consider when renewing or ending a business tenancy, 'Renewing and Ending Business Leases: a Guide for Tenants and Landlords', can be found at www.odpm.gov.uk. Printed copies of the explanation, but not of this form, are available from 1st June 2004 from Free Literature, PO Box 236, Wetherby, West Yorkshire, LS23 7NB (0870 1226 236).

Form 3

TENANT'S REQUEST FOR A NEW BUSINESS TENANCY
Section 26 of the Landlord and Tenant Act 1954

To (*insert name and address of landlord*):

From (*insert name and address of tenant*):

1 This notice relates to the following property: (*insert address or description of property*).

2 I am giving you notice under section 26 of the Landlord and Tenant Act 1954 that I request a new tenancy beginning on (*insert date*).

3 You will find my proposals for the new tenancy, which we can discuss, in the Schedule to this notice.

4 If we cannot agree on all the terms of a new tenancy, either you or I may ask the court to order the grant of a new tenancy and settle the terms on which we cannot agree.

5 If you wish to ask the court to order the grant of a new tenancy you must do so by the date in paragraph 2, unless we agree in writing to a later date and do so before the date in paragraph 2.

6 You may oppose my request for a new tenancy only on one or more of the grounds set out in section 30(1) of the Landlord and Tenant Act 1954. You must tell me what your grounds are within two months of receiving this notice. If you miss this deadline you will not be able to oppose renewal of my tenancy and you will have to grant me a new tenancy.

7 Please send all correspondence about this notice to:

Name:

Address:

Signed: Date:

*[Tenant] *[On behalf of the tenant] (*delete whichever is inapplicable*)

SCHEDULE

TENANT'S PROPOSALS FOR A NEW TENANCY
(*attach or insert proposed terms of the new tenancy*)

IMPORTANT NOTE FOR THE LANDLORD

This notice requests a new tenancy of your property or part of it. If you want to oppose this request you must act quickly.

Read the notice and all the Notes carefully. It would be wise to seek professional advice.

NOTES

The sections mentioned below are sections of the Landlord and Tenant Act 1954, as amended (most recently by the Regulatory Reform (Business Tenancies) (England and Wales) Order 2003)

Tenant's request for a new tenancy

This request by your tenant for a new tenancy brings his or her current tenancy to an end on the day before the date mentioned in paragraph 2 of this notice. Section 26 contains rules about the date that the tenant can put in paragraph 2 of this notice.

Your tenant can apply to the court under section 24 for a new tenancy. You may apply for a new tenancy yourself, under the same section, but not if your tenant has already served an application. Once an application has been made to the court, your tenant's current tenancy will continue after the date mentioned in paragraph 2 while the application is being considered by the court. Either you or your tenant can ask the court to fix the rent which your tenant will have to pay whilst the tenancy continues (sections 24A to 24D). The court will settle any terms of a new tenancy on which you and your tenant disagree (sections 34 and 35).

Time limit for opposing your tenant's request

If you do not want to grant a new tenancy, you have two months from the making of your tenant's request in which to notify him or her that you will oppose any appli-cation made to the court for a new tenancy. You do not need a special form to do this, but the notice must be in writing and it must state on which of the grounds set out in section 30(1) you will oppose the application. If you do not use the same wording of the ground (or grounds), as set out below, your notice may be ineffective.

If there has been any delay in your seeing this notice, you may need to act very quickly. If you are in any doubt about what action you should take, get advice immediately from a solicitor or a surveyor.

Grounds for opposing tenant's application

If you wish to oppose the renewal of the tenancy, you can do so by opposing your tenant's application to the court, or by making your own application to the court for termination without renewal. However, you can only oppose your tenant's application, or apply for termination without renewal, on one or more of the grounds set out in section 30(1). These grounds are set out below. You will only be able to rely on the ground(s) of opposition that you have mentioned in your written notice to your tenant.

In this Table 'the holding' means the property that is the subject of the tenancy.

Paragraph of section 30(1)   Grounds

(a) Where under the current tenancy the tenant has any obligations as respects the repair and maintenance of the holding, that the tenant ought not to be granted a new tenancy in view of the state of repair of the holding, being a state resulting from the tenant's failure to comply with the said obligations.

(b) That the tenant ought not to be granted a new tenancy in view of his persistent delay in paying rent which has become due.

(c) That the tenant ought not to be granted a new tenancy in view of other substantial breaches by him of his obligations under the current tenancy, or for any other reason connected with the tenant's use or management of the holding.

(d) That the landlord has offered and is willing to provide or secure the provision of alternative accommodation for the tenant, that the terms on which the alternative accommodation is available are reasonable having regard to the terms of the current tenancy and to all other relevant circumstances, and that the accommodation and the time at which it will be available are suitable for the tenant's requirements (including the requirement to preserve goodwill) having regard to the nature and class of his business and to the situation and extent of, and facilities afforded by, the holding.

(e) Where the current tenancy was created by the sub-letting of part only of the property comprised in a superior tenancy and the landlord is the owner of an interest in reversion expectant on the termination of that superior tenancy, that the aggregate of the rents reasonably obtainable on separate lettings of the holding and the remainder of that property would be substantially less than the rent reasonably obtainable on a letting of that property as a whole, that on the termination of the current tenancy the landlord requires possession of the holding for the purposes of letting or otherwise disposing of the said property as a whole, and that in view thereof the tenant ought not to be granted a new tenancy.

(f) That on the termination of the current tenancy the landlord intends to demolish or reconstruct the premises comprised in the holding or a substantial part of those premises or to carry out substantial work of construction on the holding or part thereof and that he could not reasonably do so without obtaining possession of the holding.

(g) On the termination of the current tenancy the landlord intends to occupy the holding for the purposes, or partly for the purposes, of a business to be carried on by him therein, or as his residence.

Compensation

If your tenant cannot get a new tenancy solely because one or more of grounds (e), (f) and (g) applies, he or she is entitled to compensation under section 37. If you have opposed your tenant's application on any of the other grounds mentioned in section 30(1), as well as on one or more of grounds (e), (f) and (g), your tenant can only get compensation if the court's refusal to grant a new tenancy is based solely on ground (e), (f) or (g). In other words, your tenant cannot get compensation under section 37 if the court has refused the tenancy on *other* grounds, even if one or more of grounds (e), (f) and (g) also applies.

If you are an authority possessing compulsory purchase powers (such as a local authority), your tenant may be entitled to a disturbance payment under Part 3 of the Land Compensation Act 1973.

Negotiating a new tenancy

Most tenancies are renewed by negotiation and your tenant has set out proposals for the new tenancy in paragraph 3 of this notice. You are not obliged to accept these proposals and may put forward your own. You and your tenant may agree in writing to extend the deadline for making an application to the court while negotiations continue. Your tenant may not apply to the court for a new tenancy until two months have passed from the date of the making of the request contained in this notice, unless you have already given notice opposing your tenant's request as mentioned in paragraph 6 of this notice (section 29A(3)).

If you try to agree a new tenancy with your tenant, remember:

> that one of you will need to apply to the court before the date in paragraph 2 of this notice, unless you both agree to extend the period for making an application.

> that any such agreement must be in writing and must be made before the date in paragraph 2 (sections 29A and 29B).

Validity of this notice

The tenant who has given you this notice may not be the person from whom you receive rent (sections 44 and 67). This does not necessarily mean that the notice is invalid.

If you have any doubts about whether this notice is valid, get advice immediately from a solicitor or a surveyor.

Further information

An explanation of the main points to consider when renewing or ending a business tenancy, 'Renewing and Ending Business Leases: a Guide for Tenants and Landlords', can be found at www.odpm.gov.uk. Printed copies of the explanation, but not of this form, are available from 1st June 2004 from Free Literature, PO Box 236, Wetherby, West Yorkshire, LS23 7NB (0870 1226 236).

Form 4

LANDLORD'S REQUEST FOR INFORMATION ABOUT OCCUPATION AND SUB-TENANCIES

Section 40(1) of the Landlord and Tenant Act 1954

To: (*insert name and address of tenant*)

From: (*insert name and address of landlord*)

1 This notice relates to the following premises: (*insert address or description of premises*)

2 I give you notice under section 40(1) of the Landlord and Tenant Act 1954 that I require you to provide information -

(a) by answering questions (1) to (3) in the Table below;

(b) if you answer 'yes' to question (2), by giving me the name and address of the person or persons concerned;

(c) if you answer 'yes' to question (3), by also answering questions (4) to (10) in the Table below;

(d) if you answer 'no' to question (8), by giving me the name and address of the sub-tenant; and

(e) if you answer 'yes' to question (10), by giving me details of the notice or request.

TABLE

(1) Do you occupy the premises or any part of them wholly or partly for the purposes of a business that is carried on by you?

(2) To the best of your knowledge and belief, does any other person own an interest in reversion in any part of the premises?

(3) Does your tenancy have effect subject to any sub-tenancy on which your tenancy is immediately expectant?

(4) What premises are comprised in the sub-tenancy?

(5) For what term does it have effect or, if it is terminable by notice, by what notice can it be terminated?

(6) What is the rent payable under it?

(7) Who is the sub-tenant?

(8) To the best of your knowledge and belief, is the sub-tenant in occupation of the premises or of part of the premises comprised in the sub-tenancy?

(9) Is an agreement in force excluding, in relation to the sub-tenancy, the provisions of sections 24 to 28 of the Landlord and Tenant Act 1954?

(10) Has a notice been given under section 25 or 26(6) of that Act, or has a request been made under section 26 of that Act, in relation to the sub-tenancy?

3 You must give the information concerned in writing and within the period of one month beginning with the date of service of this notice.

4 Please send all correspondence about this notice to:

Name:

Address:

Signed: Date:

*[Landlord] *[on behalf of the landlord] *delete whichever is inapplicable

IMPORTANT NOTE FOR THE TENANT

This notice contains some words and phrases that you may not understand. The Notes below should help you, but it would be wise to seek professional advice, for example, from a solicitor or surveyor, before responding to this notice.

Once you have provided the information required by this notice, you must correct it if you realise that it is not, or is no longer, correct. This obligation lasts for six months from the date of service of this notice, but an exception is explained in the next paragraph. If you need to correct information already given, you must do so within one month of becoming aware that the information is incorrect.

The obligation will cease if, after transferring your tenancy, you notify the landlord of the transfer and of the name and address of the person to whom your tenancy has been transferred.

If you fail to comply with the requirements of this notice, or the obligation mentioned above, you may face civil proceedings for breach of the statutory duty that arises under section 40 of the Landlord and Tenant Act 1954. In any such proceedings a court may order you to comply with that duty and may make an award of damages.

NOTES

The sections mentioned below are sections of the Landlord and Tenant Act 1954, as amended, (most recently by the Regulatory Reform (Business Tenancies) (England and Wales) Order 2003).

Purpose of this notice

Your landlord (or, if he or she is a tenant, possibly your landlord's landlord) has sent you this notice in order to obtain information about your occupation and that of any sub-tenants. This information may be relevant to the taking of steps to end or renew your business tenancy.

Time limit for replying

You must provide the relevant information within one month of the date of service of this notice (section 40(1), (2) and (5)).

Information required

You do not have to give your answers on this form; you may use a separate sheet for this purpose. The notice requires you to provide, in writing, information in the form of answers to questions (1) to (3) in the Table above and, if you answer 'yes' to question (3), also to provide information in the form of answers to questions (4) to (10) in that Table. Depending on your answer to question (2) and, if applicable in your case, questions (8) and (10), you must also provide the information referred to in paragraph 2(b), (d) and (e) of this notice. Question (2) refers to a person who owns an interest in reversion. You should answer 'yes' to this question if you know or believe that there is a person who receives, or is entitled to receive, rent in respect of any part of the premises (other than the landlord who served this notice).

When you answer questions about sub-tenants, please bear in mind that, for these purposes, a sub-tenant includes a person retaining possession of premises by virtue of the Rent (Agriculture) Act 1976 or the Rent Act 1977 after the coming to an end of a sub-tenancy, and 'sub-tenancy' includes a right so to retain possession (section 40(8)).

You should keep a copy of your answers and of any other information provided in response to questions (2), (8) or (10) above.

If, once you have given this information, you realise that it is not, or is no longer, correct, you must give the correct information within one month of becoming aware that the previous information is incorrect. Subject to the next paragraph, your duty to correct any information that you have already given continues for six months after you receive this notice (section 40(5)). You should give the correct information to the landlord who gave you this notice unless you receive notice of the transfer of his or her interest, and of the name and address of the person to whom that interest has been transferred. In that case, the correct information must be given to that person.

If you transfer your tenancy within the period of six months referred to above, your duty to correct information already given will cease if you notify the landlord of the transfer and of the name and address of the person to whom your tenancy has been transferred.

If you do not provide the information requested, or fail to correct information that you have provided earlier, after realising that it is not, or is no longer, correct, proceedings may be taken against you and you may have to pay damages (section 40B).

If you are in any doubt about the information that you should give, get immediate advice from a solicitor or a surveyor.

Validity of this notice

The landlord who has given you this notice may not be the landlord to whom you pay your rent (sections 44 and 67). This does not necessarily mean that the notice is invalid.

If you have any doubts about whether this notice is valid, get advice immediately from a solicitor or a surveyor.

Further information

An explanation of the main points to consider when renewing or ending a business tenancy, 'Renewing and Ending Business Leases: a Guide for Tenants and Landlords', can be found at www.odpm.gov.uk. Printed copies of the explanation, but not of this form, are available from 1st June 2004 from Free Literature, PO Box 236, Wetherby, West Yorkshire, LS23 7NB (0870 1226 236).

Form 5

TENANT'S REQUEST FOR INFORMATION FROM LANDLORD OR LANDLORD'S MORTGAGEE ABOUT LANDLORD'S INTEREST

Section 40(3) of the Landlord and Tenant Act 1954

To: (*insert name and address of reversioner or reversioner's mortgagee in possession [see the first note below]*)

From: (*insert name and address of tenant*)

1 This notice relates to the following premises: (*insert address or description of premises*)

2 In accordance with section 40(3) of the Landlord and Tenant Act 1954 I require you -

(a) to state in writing whether you are the owner of the fee simple in respect of the premises or any part of them or the mortgagee in possession of such an owner,

(b) if you answer 'no' to (a), to state in writing, to the best of your knowledge and belief -

   (i) the name and address of the person who is your or, as the case may be, your mortgagor's immediate landlord in respect of the premises or of the part in respect of which you are not, or your mortgagor is not, the owner in fee simple;

   (ii) for what term your or your mortgagor's tenancy has effect and what is the earliest date (if any) at which that tenancy is terminable by notice to quit given by the landlord; and

   (iii) whether a notice has been given under section 25 or 26(6) of the Landlord and Tenant Act 1954, or a request has been made under section 26 of that Act, in relation to the tenancy and, if so, details of the notice or request;

(c) to state in writing, to the best of your knowledge and belief, the name and address of any other person who owns an interest in reversion in any part of the premises;

(d) if you are a reversioner, to state in writing whether there is a mortgagee in possession of your interest in the premises; and

(e) if you answer 'yes' to (d), to state in writing, to the best of your knowledge and belief, the name and address of the mortgagee in possession.

3 You must give the information concerned within the period of one month beginning with the date of service of this notice.

4 Please send all correspondence about this notice to:

Name:

Address:

Signed: Date:

*[Tenant] *[on behalf of the tenant] (*delete whichever is inapplicable*)

IMPORTANT NOTE FOR LANDLORD OR LANDLORD'S MORTGAGEE

This notice contains some words and phrases that you may not understand. The Notes below should help you, but it would be wise to seek professional advice, for example, from a solicitor or surveyor, before responding to this notice.

Once you have provided the information required by this notice, you must correct it if you realise that it is not, or is no longer, correct. This obligation lasts for six months from the date of service of this notice, but an exception is explained in the next paragraph. If you need to correct information already given, you must do so within one month of becoming aware that the information is incorrect.

The obligation will cease if, after transferring your interest, you notify the tenant of the transfer and of the name and address of the person to whom your interest has been transferred.

If you fail to comply with the requirements of this notice, or the obligation mentioned above, you may face civil proceedings for breach of the statutory duty that arises under section 40 of the Landlord and Tenant Act 1954. In any such proceedings a court may order you to comply with that duty and may make an award of damages.

NOTES

The sections mentioned below are sections of the Landlord and Tenant Act 1954, as amended (most recently by the Regulatory Reform (Business Tenancies) (England and Wales) Order 2003)

Terms used in this notice

The following terms, which are used in paragraph 2 of this notice, are defined in section 40(8):

'mortgagee in possession' includes a receiver appointed by the mortgagee or by the court who is in receipt of the rents and profits;

'reversioner' means any person having an interest in the premises, being an interest in reversion expectant (whether immediately or not) on the tenancy; and

'reversioner's mortgagee in possession' means any person being a mortgagee in possession in respect of such an interest.

Section 40(8) requires the reference in paragraph 2(b) of this notice to your mortgagor to be read in the light of the definition of 'mortgagee in possession'.

A mortgagee (mortgage lender) will be 'in possession' if the mortgagor (the person who owes money to the mortgage lender) has failed to comply with the terms of the mortgage. The mortgagee may then be entitled to receive rent that would normally have been paid to the mortgagor.

The term 'the owner of the fee simple' means the freehold owner.

The term 'reversioner' includes the freehold owner and any intermediate landlord as well as the immediate landlord of the tenant who served this notice.

Purpose of this notice and information required

This notice requires you to provide, in writing, the information requested in paragraph 2(a) and (c) of the notice and, if applicable in your case, in paragraph 2(b), (d) and (e). You do not need to use a special form for this purpose.

If , once you have given this information, you realise that it is not, or is no longer, correct, you must give the correct information within one month of becoming aware that the previous information is incorrect. Subject to the last paragraph in this section of these Notes, your duty to correct any information that you have already given continues for six months after you receive this notice (section 40(5)).

You should give the correct information to the tenant who gave you this notice unless you receive notice of the transfer of his or her interest, and of the name and address of the person to whom that interest has been transferred. In that case, the correct information must be given to that person.

If you do not provide the information requested, or fail to correct information that you have provided earlier, after realising that it is not, or is no longer, correct, proceedings may be taken against you and you may have to pay damages (section 40B).

If you are in any doubt as to the information that you should give, get advice immediately from a solicitor or a surveyor.

If you transfer your interest within the period of six months referred to above, your duty to correct information already given will cease if you notify the tenant of that transfer and of the name and address of the person to whom your interest has been transferred.

Time limit for replying

You must provide the relevant information within one month of the date of service of this notice (section 40(3), (4) and (5)).

Validity of this notice

The tenant who has given you this notice may not be the person from whom you receive rent (sections 44 and 67). This does not necessarily mean that the notice is invalid.

If you have any doubts about the validity of the notice, get advice immediately from a solicitor or a surveyor.

Further information

An explanation of the main points to consider when renewing or ending a business tenancy, 'Renewing and Ending Business Leases: a

Guide for Tenants and Landlords', can be found at www.odpm.gov.uk. Printed copies of the explanation, but not of this form, are available from 1st June 2004 from Free Literature, PO Box 236, Wetherby, West Yorkshire, LS23 7NB (0870 1226 236).

Form 6

LANDLORD'S WITHDRAWAL OF NOTICE TERMINATING TENANCY

Section 44 of, and paragraph 6 of Schedule 6 to, the Landlord and Tenant Act 1954

To: (*insert name and address of tenant*)

From: (*insert name and address of landlord*)

1 This notice is given under section 44 of, and paragraph 6 of Schedule 6 to, the Landlord and Tenant Act 1954 ('the 1954 Act').

2 It relates to the following property: (*insert address or description of property*)

3 I have become your landlord for the purposes of the 1954 Act.

4 I withdraw the notice given to you by (*insert name of former landlord*), terminating your tenancy on (*insert date*).

5 Please send any correspondence about this notice to:

Name:

Address:

Signed: Date:

*[Landlord] *[on behalf of the landlord] (*delete whichever is inapplicable*)

IMPORTANT NOTE FOR THE TENANT

If you have any doubts about the validity of this notice, get advice immediately from a solicitor or a surveyor.

NOTES

The sections and Schedule mentioned below are sections of, and a Schedule to, the Landlord and Tenant Act 1954, as amended (most recently by the Regulatory Reform (Business Tenancies) (England and Wales) Order 2003).

Purpose of this notice

You were earlier given a notice bringing your tenancy to an end, but there has now been a change of landlord. This new notice is given to you by your new landlord and withdraws the earlier notice, which now has no effect. However, the new landlord can, if he or she wishes, give you a fresh notice with the intention of bringing your tenancy to an end (section 44 and paragraph 6 of Schedule 6).

Validity of this notice

The landlord who has given you this notice may not be the landlord to whom you pay your rent (sections 44 and 67). This does not necessarily mean that the notice is invalid.

If you have any doubts about whether this notice is valid, get advice immediately from a solicitor or a surveyor. If this notice is *not* valid, the original notice will have effect. Your tenancy will end on the date given in that notice (stated in paragraph 4 of this notice).

Further information

An explanation of the main points to consider when renewing or ending a business tenancy, 'Renewing and Ending Business Leases: a Guide for Tenants and Landlords', can be found at www.odpm.gov.uk Printed copies of the explanation, but not of this form, are available from 1st June 2004 from Free Literature, PO Box 236, Wetherby, West Yorkshire, LS23 7NB (0870 1226 236).

Form 7

LANDLORD'S NOTICE ENDING A BUSINESS TENANCY (WITH REASONS FOR REFUSING A NEW TENANCY) WHERE THE LEASEHOLD REFORM ACT 1967 MAY APPLY

Section 25 of the Landlord and Tenant Act 1954 and paragraph 10 of Schedule 3 to the Leasehold Reform Act 1967

IMPORTANT NOTE FOR THE LANDLORD: Use this form where you wish to oppose the grant of a new tenancy, and the tenant may be entitled to acquire the freehold or an extended lease. Complete this form and send it to the tenant. If you are opposed to the grant of a new tenancy, and the tenant is not entitled to acquire the freehold or an extended lease, use form 2 in Schedule 2 to the Landlord and Tenant Act 1954, Part 2 (Notices) Regulations 2004 instead of this form.

To: (*insert name and address of tenant*)

From: (*insert name and address of landlord*)

    1 This notice relates to the following property: (*insert address or description of property*)

    2 I am giving you notice under section 25 of the Landlord and Tenant Act 1954 to end your tenancy on (*insert date*).

    3 I am opposed to the grant of a new tenancy.

    4 You may ask the court to order the grant of a new tenancy. If you do, I will oppose your application on the ground(s) mentioned in paragraph(s)* of section 30(1) of that Act. I draw your attention to the Table in the Notes below, which sets out all the grounds of opposition.

* (*insert letter(s) of the paragraph(s) relied on*)

5 If you wish to ask the court for a new tenancy you must do so by the date in paragraph 2 unless, before that date, we agree in writing to a later date

6 I can ask the court to order the ending of your tenancy without granting you a new tenancy. I may have to pay you compensation if I have relied only on one or more of the grounds mentioned in paragraph (e), (f) and (g) of section 30(1). If I ask the court to end your tenancy, you can challenge my application.

7 If you have a right under Part 1 of the Leasehold Reform Act 1967 to acquire the freehold or an extended lease of property comprised in the tenancy, notice of your desire to have the freehold or an extended lease cannot be given more than two months after the service of this notice. If you have that right, and give notice of your desire to have the freehold or an extended lease within those two months, this notice will not operate, and I may take no further proceedings under Part 2 of the Landlord and Tenant Act 1954.

*8 If you give notice of your desire to have the freehold or an extended lease, I will be entitled to apply to the court under section 17/section 18** of the Leasehold Reform Act 1967, and propose to do so. If I am successful I may have to pay you compensation. (**delete the reference to section 17 or section 18, as the circumstances require)

OR

*8 If you give notice of your desire to have the freehold or an extended lease, I will be entitled to apply to the court under section 17/section 18** of the Leasehold Reform Act 1967, but do not propose to do so. (**delete the reference to section 17 or section 18, as the circumstances require)

OR

*8 If you give notice of your desire to have the freehold or an extended lease, I will not be entitled to apply to the court under section 17 or section 18 of the Leasehold Reform Act 1967.

* DELETE TWO versions of this paragraph, as the circumstances require

*9 I know or believe that the following persons have an interest superior to your tenancy or to be the agent concerned with the property on behalf of someone who has such an interest (insert names and addresses):

* delete if inapplicable

10 Please send all correspondence about this notice to:

Name:

Address:

Signed: Date:

*[Landlord] *[On behalf of the landlord] *[Mortgagee] *[On behalf of the mortgagee]

(*delete if inapplicable)

IMPORTANT NOTE FOR THE TENANT

This Notice is intended to bring your tenancy to an end on the date specified in paragraph 2.

Your landlord is not prepared to offer you a new tenancy. You will not get a new tenancy unless you successfully challenge in court the grounds on which your landlord opposes the grant of a new tenancy.

If you want to continue to occupy your property you must act quickly. The notes below should help you to decide what action you now need to take. If you want to challenge your landlord's refusal to renew your tenancy, get advice immediately from a solicitor or a surveyor.

NOTES

Unless otherwise stated, the sections mentioned below are sections of the Landlord and Tenant Act 1954, as amended, (most recently by the Regulatory Reform (Business Tenancies) (England and Wales) Order 2003)

Ending of your tenancy

This notice is intended to bring your tenancy to an end on the date given in paragraph 2. Section 25 contains rules about the date that the landlord can put in paragraph 2 of this notice.

Your landlord is not prepared to offer you a new tenancy. If you want a new tenancy you will need to apply to the court for a new tenancy and successfully challenge the landlord's opposition (see the section below headed 'Landlord's opposition to new tenancy'). If you wish to apply to the court you must do so before the date given in paragraph 2 of this notice, unless you and your landlord have agreed in writing, before that date, to extend the deadline (sections 29A and 29B).

If you apply to the court your tenancy will continue after the date given in paragraph 2 of this notice while your application is being considered (section 24). You may not apply to the court if your landlord has already done so (section 24(2A) and (2B)).

You may only stay in the property after the date given in paragraph 2 (or such later date as you and the landlord may have agreed in writing) if before that date you have asked the court to order the grant of a new tenancy or the landlord has asked the court to order the ending of your tenancy without granting you a new one.

If you are in any doubt about what action you should take, get advice immediately from a solicitor or a surveyor.

Landlord's opposition to new tenancy

If you apply to the court for a new tenancy, the landlord can only oppose your application on one or more of the grounds set out in section 30(1). If you match the letter(s) specified in paragraph 4 of the notice with those in the first column in the Table below, you can see from the second column the ground(s) on which the landlord relies.

Paragraph of section 30(1)　　　Grounds

(a) Where under the current tenancy the tenant has any obligations as respects the repair and maintenance of the holding, that the tenant ought not to be granted a new tenancy in view of the state of repair of the holding, being a state resulting from the tenant's failure to comply with the said obligations.

(b) That the tenant ought not to be granted a new tenancy in view of his persistent delay in paying rent which has become due.

(c) That the tenant ought not to be granted a new tenancy in view of other substantial breaches by him of his obligations under the current tenancy, or for any other reason connected with the tenant's use or management of the holding.

(d) That the landlord has offered and is willing to provide or secure the provision of alternative accommodation for the tenant, that the terms on which the alternative accommodation is available are reasonable having regard to the terms of the current tenancy and to all other relevant circumstances, and that the accommodation and the time at which it will be available are suitable for the tenant's requirements (including the requirement to preserve goodwill) having regard to the nature and class of his business and to the situation and extent of, and facilities afforded by, the holding.

(e) Where the current tenancy was created by the sub-letting of part only of the property comprised in a superior tenancy and the landlord is the owner of an interest in reversion expectant on the termination of that superior tenancy, that the aggregate of the rents reasonably obtainable on separate lettings of the holding and the remainder of that property would be substantially less than the rent reasonably obtainable on a letting of that property as a whole, that on the termination of the current tenancy the landlord requires possession of the holding for the purposes of letting or otherwise disposing of the said property as a whole, and that in view thereof the tenant ought not to be granted a new tenancy.

(f) That on the termination of the current tenancy the landlord intends to demolish or reconstruct the premises comprised in the holding or a substantial part of those premises or to carry out substantial work of construction on the holding or part thereof and that he could not reasonably do so without obtaining possession of the holding.

(g) On the termination of the current tenancy the landlord intends to occupy the holding for the purposes, or partly for the purposes, of a business to be carried on by him therein, or as his residence.

In this Table 'the holding' means the property that is the subject of the tenancy.

In ground (e), 'the landlord is the owner an interest in reversion expectant on the termination of that superior tenancy' means that the landlord has an interest in the property that will entitle him or her, when your immediate landlord's tenancy comes to an end, to exercise certain rights and obligations in relation to the property that are currently exercisable by your immediate landlord.

If the landlord relies on ground (f), the court can sometimes still grant a new tenancy if certain conditions set out in section 31A are met.

If the landlord relies on ground (g), please note that 'the landlord' may have an extended meaning. Where a landlord has a controlling interest in a company then either the landlord or the company can rely on ground (g). Where the landlord is a company and a person has a controlling interest in that company then either of them can rely on ground (g) (section 30(1A) and (1B)). A person has a 'controlling interest' in a company if, had he been a company, the other company would have been its subsidiary (section 46(2)).

The landlord must normally have been the landlord for at least five years before he or she can rely on ground (g).

Rights under the Leasehold Reform Act 1967

If the property comprised in your tenancy is a house, as defined in section 2 of the Leasehold Reform Act 1967 ('the 1967 Act'), you may have the right to buy the freehold of the property or an extended lease. If the house is for the time being let under two or more tenancies, you will not have that right if your tenancy is subject to a sub-tenancy and the sub-tenant is himself or herself entitled to that right.

You will have that right if all the following conditions are met:

(i)   your lease was originally granted for a term of more than 35 years, or was preceded by such a lease which was granted or assigned to you; and

(ii)   your lease is of the whole house; and

(iii) your lease is at a low rent. If your tenancy was entered into before 1 April 1990 (or later if you contracted before that date to enter into the tenancy) 'low rent' means that your present annual rent is less than two-thirds of the rateable value of your house as assessed either on 23 March 1965, or on the first day of the term in the case of a lease granted to commence after 23 March 1965; and the property had a rateable value other than nil when the tenancy began or at any time before 1 April 1990. If your tenancy was granted on or after 1 April 1990, 'low rent' means that the present annual rent is not more than £1,000 in London or £250 elsewhere; and

(iv)   you have been occupying the house (or any part of it) as your only or main residence (whether or not it has been occupied for other purposes) either for the whole of the last two years, or for a total of two years in the last ten years; and

(v)   the rateable value of your house was at one time within certain limits.

Claiming your rights under the 1967 Act

If you have a right to buy the freehold or an extended lease and wish to exercise it you must serve the appropriate notice on the landlord. A special form is prescribed for this purpose; it is Form 1 as set out in the Schedule to the Leasehold Reform (Notices) (Amendment) (England) Regulations 2002 (SI 2002/1715) or, if the property is in Wales, the Leasehold Reform (Notices) (Amendment) (Wales) Regulations 2002 (SI 2002/3187) (W.303). Subject to the two exceptions mentioned below, you must serve the notice claiming to buy the freehold or an extended lease within two months after the date of service of this notice. The first exception is where, within that two-month period, you apply to the court to order the grant of a new tenancy. In that case your claim to buy the freehold or an extended lease must be made when you make the application to the court. The second exception is where the landlord agrees in writing to your claim being made after the date on which it should have been made.

There are special rules about the service of notices. If there has been any delay in your seeing this notice, you may need to act very quickly.

If you are in any doubt about your rights under the 1967 Act or what action you should take, get advice immediately from a solicitor or a surveyor.

Landlord's opposition to claims under the 1967 Act

If your landlord acquired his or her interest in the house not later than 18 February 1966 he or she can object to your claim to buy the freehold or an extended lease on the grounds that he or she needs to occupy the house or that the house is needed for occupation by a member of his or her family. This objection will be under section 18 of the 1967 Act.

If you claim an extended lease, your landlord can object under section 17 of the 1967 Act on the grounds that he or she wishes to redevelop the property.

You will be able to tell from paragraph 8 of this notice whether your landlord intends to apply to the court and, if so, whether for the purposes of occupation or redevelopment of the house.

Compensation

If you cannot get a new tenancy solely because one or more of grounds (e), (f) and (g) in section 30(1) applies, you may be entitled to compensation under section 37. If your landlord has opposed your application on any of the other grounds as well as (e), (f) or (g) you can only get compensation if the court's refusal to grant a new tenancy is based solely on one or more of grounds (e), (f) and (g). In other words, you cannot get compensation under section 37 if the court has refused your tenancy on other grounds, even if one or more of grounds (e), (f) and (g) also applies.

If your landlord is an authority possessing compulsory purchase powers (such as a local authority) you may be entitled to a disturbance payment under Part 3 of the Land Compensation Act 1973.

If you have a right under the 1967 Act to buy the freehold or an extended lease but the landlord is able to obtain pos-session of the premises, compensation is payable under section 17(2) or section 18(4) of the 1967 Act. Your solicitor or surveyor will be able to advise you about this.

Negotiations with your landlord

If you try to buy the property by agreement or negotiate an extended lease with the landlord, remember:

that your present tenancy will not be extended under the 1954 Act after the date in paragraph 2 of this notice unless you agree in writing to extend the deadline for applying to the court under the 1954 Act or you (or the landlord) has applied to the court before that date (sections 29, 29A and 29B), and

that you may lose your right to serve a notice claiming to buy the freehold or an extended lease under the 1967 Act if you do not observe the two-month time limit referred to in the note headed *Claiming your rights under the 1967 Act.*

Validity of this notice

The landlord who has given you this notice may not be the landlord to whom you pay your rent (sections 44 and 67). This does not necessarily mean that the notice is invalid.

If you have any doubts about whether this notice is valid, get advice immediately from a solicitor or a surveyor.

Further information

An explanation of the main points to consider when renewing or ending a business tenancy, 'Renewing and Ending Business Leases: a Guide for Tenants and Landlords', can be found at www.odpm.gov.uk. Printed copies of the explanation, but not of this form, are available from 1st June 2004 from Free Literature, PO Box 236, Wetherby, West Yorkshire, LS23 7NB (0870 1226 236).

Form 8

NOTICE ENDING A BUSINESS TENANCY ON PUBLIC INTEREST GROUNDS

Sections 25 and 57 of the Landlord and Tenant Act 1954

IMPORTANT NOTE FOR THE LANDLORD: Use this form if you have a section 57 certificate, but where the tenant may be entitled to acquire the freehold or an extended lease, use form 13 in Schedule 2 to the Landlord and Tenant Act 1954, Part 2 (Notices) Regulations 2004 instead of this form.

To: (*insert name and address of tenant*)

From: (*insert name and address of landlord*)

1 This notice relates to the following property: (*insert address or description of property*)

2 I am giving you notice under section 25 of the Landlord and Tenant Act 1954 ('the 1954 Act') to end your tenancy on (*insert date*).

3 A certificate has been given by (*state the title of the Secretary of State on whose authority the certificate was issued or, if the certificate was issued by the National Assembly for Wales, insert* 'the National Assembly for Wales') under section 57 of the 1954 Act that the use or occupation of all or part of the property should be changed by (*insert date*). A copy of the certificate appears in the Schedule to this notice.

4 Please send all correspondence about this notice to:

Name:

Address:

Signed: Date:

[Landlord] [On behalf of the landlord] *[Mortgagee] *[On behalf of the mortgagee]

(*delete if inapplicable*)

SCHEDULE

CERTIFICATE UNDER SECTION 57

(*attach or insert a copy of the section 57 certificate*)

IMPORTANT NOTE FOR THE TENANT

This notice is intended to bring your tenancy to an end on the date specified in paragraph 2.

The landlord is not prepared to offer you a new tenancy because it has been certified that the occupation or use of the premises should be changed no later than the date specified in paragraph 2. The date by which the change must have taken place is specified in paragraph 3.

NOTES

The sections mentioned below are sections of the Landlord and Tenant Act 1954, as amended (most recently by the Regulatory Reform (Business Tenancies) (England and Wales) Order 2003)

Ending of your tenancy

This notice is intended to bring your tenancy to an end on the date stated in paragraph 2 of the notice.

Your landlord is both giving you notice that your current tenancy will end on the date stated in paragraph 2 of this notice and drawing attention to a certificate under section 57 that would prevent you from applying to the court for a new tenancy.

Usually, tenants who have tenancies under Part 2 of the Landlord and Tenant Act 1954 can apply to the court for a new tenancy. However, the effect of the section 57 certificate that it is requisite that the use or occupation of all or part of the property should be changed by a certain date, is to prevent the tenant from making an application to the court for a new tenancy.

Compensation

Because the court cannot order the grant of a new tenancy, you may be entitled to compensation when you leave the property (section 59). If your landlord is an authority possessing compulsory purchase powers (such as a local authority) you may also be entitled to a disturbance payment under Part 3 of the Land Compensation Act 1973.

Validity of this notice

The landlord who has given you this notice may not be the landlord to whom you pay your rent (sections 44 and 67). This does not necessarily mean that the notice is invalid.

If you have any doubts about whether this notice is valid, get advice immediately from a solicitor or a surveyor.

Further information

An explanation of the main points to consider when renewing or ending a business tenancy, 'Renewing and Ending Business Leases: a Guide for Tenants and Landlords', can be found at www.odpm.gov.uk. Printed copies of the explanation, but not of this form, are available from 1st June from Free Literature, PO Box 236, Wetherby, West Yorkshire, LS23 7NB (0870 1226 236).

Form 9

NOTICE ENDING A BUSINESS TENANCY WHERE A CHANGE IS REQUIRED AT A FUTURE DATE AND THE LANDLORD OPPOSES A NEW TENANCY

Sections 25 and 57 of the Landlord and Tenant Act 1954

IMPORTANT NOTE FOR THE LANDLORD: Use this form if you have a section 57 certificate and you wish to oppose the grant of a new tenancy, for the period between the end of the current tenancy and the date given in the section 57 certificate, on any of the grounds in section 30(1) of the Landlord and Tenant Act 1954.

If you are willing to grant a new tenancy for that period, use form 10 in Schedule 2 to the Landlord and Tenant Act 1954, Part 2 (Notices) Regulations 2004 instead of this form.

If the tenant may be entitled to acquire the freehold or an extended lease, use form 14 in that Schedule, instead of this form or form 10.

To: (*insert name and address of tenant*)

From: (*insert name and address of landlord*)

1 This notice relates to the following property: (*insert address or description of property*)

2 I am giving you notice under section 25 of the Landlord and Tenant Act 1954 ('the 1954 Act') to end your tenancy on (*insert date*).

3 A certificate has been given by (*state the title of the Secretary of State on whose authority the certificate was issued or, if the certificate was issued by the National Assembly for Wales, insert* 'the National Assembly for Wales') under section 57 of the 1954 that the use or occupation of all or part of the property should be changed by (*insert date*). A copy of the certificate appears in the Schedule to this notice.

4 I do not intend to grant you a new tenancy between the end of your current tenancy and the date specified in the section 57 certificate.

5 You may ask the court to order the grant of a new tenancy for a term ending not later than the date specified in the section 57 certificate. If you do, I will oppose your application on the ground(s) mentioned in paragraph(s)* of section 30(1) of the Act. I draw your attention to the Table in the Notes below, which sets out all the grounds of opposition.

*(*insert letter(s) of the paragraph(s) relied on*)

6 If you wish to ask the court for a new tenancy you must do so by the date in paragraph 2 unless, before that date, we agree in writing to a later date.

7 I can ask the court to order the ending of your tenancy without granting you a new tenancy. If I do, you can challenge my application.

8 Please send all correspondence about this notice to:

Name:

Address:

Signed: Date:

*[Landlord] *[On behalf of the landlord] *[Mortgagee] *[On behalf of the mortgagee]
(*delete if inapplicable)

IMPORTANT NOTE FOR THE TENANT

This Notice is intended to bring your tenancy to an end on the date specified in paragraph 2.

A certificate has been given that it is requisite that occupation or use of the premises should be changed by the date specified in paragraph 3 of this notice.

Your landlord has indicated that he will oppose your application for a new tenancy (if you decide to make one). You will not get a new tenancy unless you successfully challenge in court the grounds on which your landlord opposes the grant of a new tenancy.

If you want to continue to occupy your property you must act quickly. The notes below should help you to decide what action you now need to take. If you want to challenge your landlord's refusal to renew your tenancy, get advice immediately from a solicitor or a surveyor.

NOTES

The sections mentioned below are sections of the Landlord and Tenant Act 1954, as amended (most recently by the Regulatory Reform (Business Tenancies) (England and Wales) Order 2003)

Ending of your tenancy

This notice is intended to bring your tenancy to an end on the date specified in paragraph 2 of the notice.

Claiming a new tenancy

Your landlord is not prepared to offer you a new tenancy for a limited period pending the effect of the section 57 certificate (see the section below headed *'Effect of section 57 certificate'*). If you want a new tenancy for this period you will need to apply to the court for a new tenancy and successfully challenge the landlord's opposition (see the section below headed *'Landlord's opposition to new tenancy'*).

If you wish to apply to the court you must do so before the date specified in paragraph 2 of this notice, unless you and your landlord have agreed in writing, before that date, to extend the deadline (sections 29A and 29B). However, before you take that step, read carefully the section below headed '*Effect of section 57 certificate*'.

If you apply to the court your tenancy will continue after the date specified in paragraph 2 of this notice while your application is being considered (section 24).

If you are in any doubt about what action you should take, get advice immediately from a solicitor or a surveyor.

Landlord's opposition to new tenancy

If you apply to the court for a new tenancy, the landlord can only oppose your application on one or more of the grounds set out in section 30(1). If you match the letter(s) specified in paragraph 5 of the notice with those in the first column in the Table below, you can see from the second column the ground(s) on which the landlord relies.

Paragraph of section 30(1)   Grounds

(a) Where under the current tenancy the tenant has any obligations as respects the repair and maintenance of the holding, that the tenant ought not to be granted a new tenancy in view of the state of repair of the holding, being a state resulting from the tenant's failure to comply with the said obligations.

(b) That the tenant ought not to be granted a new tenancy in view of his persistent delay in paying rent which has become due.

(c) That the tenant ought not to be granted a new tenancy in view of other substantial breaches by him of his obligations under the current tenancy, or for any other reason connected with the tenant's use or management of the holding.

(d) That the landlord has offered and is willing to provide or secure the provision of alternative accommodation for the tenant, that the terms on which the alternative accommodation is available are reasonable having regard to the terms of the current tenancy and to all other relevant circumstances, and that the accommodation and the time at which it will be available are suitable for the tenant's requirements (including the requirement to preserve goodwill) having regard to the nature and class of his business and to the situation and extent of, and facilities afforded by, the holding.

(e) Where the current tenancy was created by the sub-letting of part only of the property comprised in a superior tenancy and the landlord is the owner of an interest in reversion expectant on the termination of that superior tenancy, that the aggregate of the rents reasonably obtainable on separate lettings of the holding and the remainder of that property would be substantially less than the rent reasonably obtainable on a letting of that property as a whole, that on the termination of the current tenancy the landlord requires possession of the holding for the purposes of letting or otherwise disposing of the said property as a whole, and that in view thereof the tenant ought not to be granted a new tenancy.

(f) That on the termination of the current tenancy the landlord intends to demolish or reconstruct the premises comprised in the holding or a substantial part of those premises or to carry out substantial work of construction on the holding or part thereof and that he could not reasonably do so without obtaining possession of the holding.

(g) On the termination of the current tenancy the landlord intends to occupy the holding for the purposes, or partly for the purposes, of a business to be carried on by him therein, or as his residence.

In this Table 'the holding' means the property that is the subject of the tenancy.

In ground (e), 'the landlord is the owner an interest in reversion expectant on the termination of that superior tenancy' means that the landlord has an interest in the property that will entitle him, when your immediate landlord's tenancy comes to an end, to exercise certain rights and obligations in relation to the property that are currently exercisable by your immediate landlord.

If the landlord relies on ground (f), the court can sometimes still grant a new tenancy if certain conditions set out in section 31A are met.

If the landlord relies on ground (g), please note that 'the landlord' may have an extended meaning. Where a landlord has a controlling interest in a company then either the landlord or the company can rely on ground (g). Where the landlord is a company and a person has a controlling interest in that company then either of them can rely on ground (g) (section 30(1A) and (1B)). A person has a 'controlling interest' in a company if, had he been a company, the other company would have been its subsidiary (section 46(2)).

The landlord must normally have been the landlord for at least five years before he or she can rely on ground (g).

Effect of section 57 certificate

A copy of a certificate issued under section 57 appears in the Schedule to this notice. The effect of the certificate is that, even if you are successful in challenging your landlord's opposition to the grant of a new tenancy, and the court orders the grant of a new tenancy, the new tenancy must end not later than the date specified in the certificate (section 57(3)(b)). Any new tenancy will not be a tenancy to which Part II of the 1954 Act applies (section 57(3)(b)).

Compensation

If you cannot get a new tenancy solely because one or more of grounds (e), (f) and (g) applies, you may be entitled to compensation under section 37. If your landlord has opposed your application on any of the other grounds as well as (e), (f) or (g) you can only get compensation if the court's refusal to grant a new tenancy is based solely on one or more of grounds (e), (f) and (g). In other words, you cannot get compensation under section 37 if the court has refused your tenancy on other grounds, even if one or more of grounds (e), (f) and (g) also applies.

If the court orders the grant of a new tenancy, you may be entitled to compensation under section 59 when you leave the property (on or before the date specified in the section 57 certificate).

If your landlord is an authority possessing compulsory purchase powers (such as a local authority) you may be entitled to a disturbance payment under Part 3 of the Land Compensation Act 1973.

Validity of this notice

The landlord who has given you this notice may not be the landlord to whom you pay your rent (sections 44 and 67). This does not necessarily mean that the notice is invalid.

If you have any doubts about whether this notice is valid, get advice immediately from a solicitor or a surveyor.

Further information

An explanation of the main points to consider when renewing or ending a business tenancy, 'Renewing and Ending Business Leases: a Guide for Tenants and Landlords', can be found at www.odpm.gov.uk. Printed copies of the explanation, but not of this form, are available from 1st June 2004 from Free Literature, PO Box 236, Wetherby, West Yorkshire, LS23 7NB (0870 1226 236).

Form 10

NOTICE ENDING A BUSINESS TENANCY WHERE A CHANGE IS REQUIRED AT A FUTURE DATE AND THE LANDLORD DOES NOT OPPOSE A NEW TENANCY

Sections 25 and 57 of the Landlord and Tenant Act 1954

IMPORTANT NOTE FOR THE LANDLORD: Use this form if you have a section 57 certificate and you are willing to grant a new tenancy for the period between the end of the current tenancy and the date given in the section 57 certificate.

If you wish to oppose the grant of a new tenancy for that period on any of the grounds in section 30(1) of the Landlord and Tenant Act 1954, use form 9 in Schedule 2 to the Landlord and Tenant Act 1954, Part 2 (Notices) Regulations 2004 instead of this form.

If the tenant may be entitled to acquire the freehold or an extended lease, use form 14 in that Schedule, instead of this form or form 9.

To: (*insert name and address of tenant*)

From: (*insert name and address of landlord*)

1 This notice relates to the following property: (*insert address or description of property*)

2 I am giving you notice under section 25 of the Landlord and Tenant Act 1954 ('the 1954 Act') to end your tenancy on (*insert date*).

3 A certificate has been given by (*state the title of the Secretary of State, Minister or Board on whose authority the certificate was issued or, if the certificate was issued by the National Assembly for Wales, insert* 'the National Assembly for Wales') under section 57 of the 1954 Act that the use or occupation of all or part of the property should be changed by (*insert date*). A copy of the certificate appears in Schedule 1 to this notice.

4 If you apply to the court under Part 2 of the 1954 Act for the grant of a new tenancy, I will not oppose your application. However, the court can only order the grant of a new tenancy for a term ending not later than the date in paragraph 3.

5 You will find my proposals for the new tenancy, which we can discuss, in Schedule 2 to this notice.

6 If we cannot agree on all the terms of a new tenancy, either you or I may ask the court to order the grant of a new tenancy and settle the terms on which we cannot agree.

7 Please send all correspondence about this notice to:

Name:

Address:

Signed: Date:

*[Landlord] *[On behalf of the landlord] *[Mortgagee] *[On behalf of the mortgagee]

(**delete if inapplicable*)

SCHEDULE 1

CERTIFICATE UNDER SECTION 57
(*attach or insert a copy of the section 57 certificate*)

SCHEDULE 2

LANDLORD'S PROPOSALS FOR A NEW TENANCY
(*attach or insert proposed terms of the new tenancy*)

IMPORTANT NOTE FOR THE TENANT
This notice is intended to bring your tenancy to an end on the date specified in paragraph 2.

A certificate has been issued that it is requisite that occupation or use of the premises should be changed by the date specified in paragraph 3.

However, the landlord is prepared to offer you a new tenancy for the whole or part of the period between the dates in paragraphs 2 and 3 of the notice. You will find his or her proposed terms in Schedule 2 to this notice. You are not bound to accept these terms. They are merely suggestions as a basis for negotiation. In the event of disagreement, ultimately the court would settle the terms of the new tenancy.

It would be wise to seek professional advice before agreeing to accept the landlord's terms or putting forward your own proposals.

If you want to continue to occupy your property you must act quickly. The notes below should help you to decide what action you now need to take.

NOTES

The sections mentioned below are sections of the Landlord and Tenant Act 1954, as amended (most recently by the Regulatory Reform (Business Tenancies) (England and Wales) Order 2003)

Ending of your tenancy

This notice is intended to bring your tenancy to an end on the date specified in paragraph 2 of the notice.

A certificate has been given under section 57 and a copy appears in Schedule 1 to this notice. The certificate states that it is requisite that occupation or use of the premises should be changed by the date specified in paragraph 3 of the notice.

However, your landlord is prepared to offer you a new tenancy, for the whole or part of the period between the dates specified in paragraphs 2 and 3 of the notice. You will find his or her proposals in Schedule 2 to this notice. You are not obliged to accept these proposals and may put forward your own.

Claiming a new tenancy

If you and your landlord are unable to agree terms, you may apply to the court (unless the landlord has already made his or her own application to the court (section 24(2A)). However, before you take that step, read carefully the section below headed '*Effect of section 57 certificate*'.

An application to the court must be made by the date set out in paragraph 2, unless you and your landlord have agreed in writing, before that date, to extend the deadline (sections 29A and 29B). Otherwise, you will lose the right to renew the tenancy.

If you apply to the court, your tenancy will continue after the date shown in paragraph 2 of this notice while your application is being considered (section 24). Either you or your landlord can ask the court to fix the rent that you will have to pay while the tenancy continues (section 24A and B). The terms of any new tenancy not agreed between you and the landlord will be settled by the court (section 25).

If you are in any doubt about the action that you should take, get advice immediately from a solicitor or a surveyor.

Effect of section 57 certificate

The effect of the section 57 certificate is that, if the court orders the grant of a new tenancy, the new tenancy must end not later than the date specified in the certificate (section 57(3)(b)).

Any new tenancy will not be a tenancy to which Part 2 of the 1954 Act applies (section 57(3)(b)).

Compensation

You may be entitled to compensation under section 59 when you leave the property (on or before the date specified in the section 57 certificate).

If your landlord is an authority possessing compulsory purchase powers (such as a local authority) you may be entitled to a disturbance payment under Part 3 of the Land Compensation Act 1973.

Validity of this notice

The landlord who has given you this notice may not be the landlord to whom you pay your rent (sections 44 and 67). This does not necessarily mean that the notice is invalid.

If you have any doubts about whether this notice is valid, get advice immediately from a solicitor or a surveyor.

Further information

An explanation of the main points to consider when renewing or ending a business tenancy, 'Renewing and Ending Business Leases: a Guide for Tenants and Landlords', can be found at www.odpm.gov.uk. Printed copies of the explanation, but not of this form, are available from 1st June 2004 from Free Literature, PO Box 236, Wetherby, West Yorkshire, LS23 7NB (0870 1226 236).

Form 11

NOTICE ENDING A BUSINESS TENANCY ON GROUNDS OF NATIONAL SECURITY AND WITHOUT THE OPTION TO RENEW

Sections 25 and 58 of the Landlord and Tenant Act 1954

To: (*insert name and address of tenant*)

From: (*insert name and address of landlord*)

1 This notice relates to the following property: (*insert address or description of property*)

2 I am giving you notice under section 25 of the Landlord and Tenant Act 1954 to end your tenancy on (*insert date*).

3 A certificate has been given by (*state the title of the Secretary of State, Minister or Board on whose authority the certificate was issued or, if the certificate was issued by the National Assembly for Wales, insert* 'the National Assembly for Wales') under section 58 of the 1954 Act that it is necessary for reasons of national security that the use or occupation of the property should be discontinued or changed. A copy of the certificate appears in the Schedule to this notice.

4 The certificate prevents me from granting you a new tenancy. It also means that you will not be able to make an application to the court under section 24(1) of the Landlord and Tenant Act 1954 for the grant of a new tenancy.

5 Please send all correspondence about this notice to:

Name:

Address:

Signed: Date:

*[Landlord] *[On behalf of the landlord] *[Mortgagee] *[On behalf of the mortgagee]

(*delete if inapplicable*)

SCHEDULE

CERTIFICATE UNDER SECTION 58

(*attach or insert a copy of the section 58 certificate*)

IMPORTANT NOTE FOR THE TENANT

This notice is intended to bring your tenancy to an end on the date specified in paragraph 2.

The national security certificate referred to in paragraph 3 of this notice means that the landlord cannot grant you a new tenancy, and the court cannot order the grant of a new tenancy.

You may be entitled to compensation. You may wish to seek professional advice in connection with this notice.

NOTES

The sections mentioned below are sections of the Landlord and Tenant Act 1954, as amended, (most recently by the Regulatory Reform (Business Tenancies) (England and Wales) Order 2003)

Ending of your tenancy

This notice is intended to bring your tenancy to an end on the date shown in paragraph 2 of the notice. Section 25 contains rules about the date that the landlord can put in that paragraph.

Tenants under tenancies to which Part II of the Landlord and Tenant Act 1954 applies can normally apply to the court for the grant of a new tenancy. However, a certificate has been given that it is necessary for reasons of national security that the use or occupation of the property should be discontinued or changed (section 58). The combined effect of this notice and the certificate is that you will be unable to apply to the court for the grant of a new tenancy.

Compensation

You may be entitled to compensation under section 59 when you leave the property (on or before the date specified in the section 58 certificate).

You may also be entitled to a disturbance payment under Part 3 of the Land Compensation Act 1973.

Validity of notice

The landlord who has given you this notice may not be the landlord to whom you pay your rent (sections 44 and 67). This does not necessarily mean that the notice is invalid.

If you have any doubts about whether this notice is valid, get advice immediately from a solicitor or a surveyor.

Further information

An explanation of the main points to consider when renewing or ending a business tenancy, 'Renewing and Ending Business Leases: a Guide for Tenants and Landlords', can be found at www.odpm.gov.uk. Printed copies of the explanation, but not of this form, are available from 1st June 2004 from Free Literature, PO Box 236, Wetherby, West Yorkshire, LS23 7NB (0870 1226 236).

Form 12

NOTICE ENDING A BUSINESS TENANCY WHERE THE PROPERTY IS REQUIRED FOR REGENERATION

Sections 25, 58 and 60 of the Landlord and Tenant Act 1954

IMPORTANT NOTE FOR THE LANDLORD: Use this form if you have a certificate under section 58 (as applied by section 60), but if the tenant may be entitled to acquire the freehold or an extended lease, use form 15 in Schedule 2 to the Landlord and Tenant Act 1954, Part 2 (Notices) Regulations 2004 instead of this form.

To: (*insert name and address of tenant*)

From: (*insert name and address of landlord*)

1 This notice relates to the following property, which is situated in an area for the time being specified as a development area or intermediate area by an order made, or having effect as if made, under section 1 of the Industrial Development Act 1982: (*insert address or description of property*)

2 I am giving you notice under section 25 of the Landlord and Tenant Act 1954 ('the 1954 Act') to end your tenancy on (*insert date*).

3 A certificate has been given by (*state the title of the Secretary of State, Minister or Board on whose authority the certificate was issued*) that it is necessary or expedient for the purpose mentioned in section 2(1) of the Local Employment Act 1972 that the use or occupation of the property should be changed. A copy of the certificate appears in the Schedule to this notice.

4 The certificate prevents me from granting you a new tenancy. It also means that you will not be able to make an application to the court under section 24(1) of the 1954 Act for the grant of a new tenancy.

5 Please send all correspondence about this notice to:

Name:

Address:

Signed: Date:

*[Landlord] *[On behalf of the landlord]
(*delete if inapplicable*)

SCHEDULE

CERTIFICATE UNDER SECTION 58
(*attach or insert a copy of the section 58 certificate*)

IMPORTANT NOTE FOR THE TENANT

This Notice is intended to bring your tenancy to an end on the date specified in paragraph 2.

The certificate referred to in paragraph 3 of this notice means that the landlord cannot grant you a new tenancy, and the court cannot order the grant of a new tenancy.

You may wish to seek professional advice in connection with this notice.

NOTES

The sections mentioned below are sections of the Landlord and Tenant Act 1954, as amended (most recently by the Regulatory Reform (Business Tenancies) (England and Wales) Order 2003).

Ending of your tenancy

This notice is intended to bring your tenancy to an end. Section 25 contains rules about the date that the landlord can put in paragraph 2 of this notice.

Your landlord is both giving you notice that your current tenancy will end on the date stated in paragraph 2 of this notice and drawing attention to a certificate under section 58 (as applied by section 60) that would prevent you from applying to the court for a new tenancy.

Usually, tenants who have tenancies under Part II of the Landlord and Tenant Act 1954 can apply to the court for a new tenancy. However, where a Government Minister has certified that it is necessary or expedient for the purpose mentioned in section 2(1) of the Local Employment Act 1972 that the use or occupation of the property should be changed, the landlord may prevent the tenant from making an application to the court for a new tenancy.

Validity of this notice

The landlord who has given you this notice may not be the landlord to whom you pay your rent (sections 44 and 67). This does not necessarily mean that the notice is invalid.

If you have any doubts about whether this notice is valid, get advice immediately from a solicitor or a surveyor.

Further information

An explanation of the main points to consider when renewing or ending a business tenancy, 'Renewing and Ending Business Leases: a Guide for Tenants and Landlords', can be found at www.odpm.gov.uk. Printed copies of the explanation, but not of this form, are available from 1st June 2004 from Free Literature, PO Box 236, Wetherby, West Yorkshire, LS23 7NB (0870 1226 236).

Form 13

NOTICE ENDING A BUSINESS TENANCY ON PUBLIC INTEREST GROUNDS WHERE THE LEASEHOLD REFORM ACT 1967 MAY APPLY

Sections 25 and 57 of the Landlord and Tenant Act 1954

Paragraph 10 of Schedule 3 to the Leasehold Reform Act 1967

IMPORTANT NOTE FOR THE LANDLORD

This form *must* be used (instead of Form 8 in Schedule 2 to the Landlord and Tenant Act 1954, Part 2 (Notices) Regulations 2004) if -

(a) no previous notice terminating the tenancy has been given under section 4 or 25 of the Landlord and Tenant Act 1954 Act or under paragraph 4(1) of Schedule 10 to the Local Government and Housing Act 1989; and

(b) the tenancy is of a house as defined for the purposes of Part 1 of the Leasehold Reform Act 1967 ('the 1967 Act'); and

(c) the tenancy is a long tenancy at a low rent within the meaning of the 1967 Act; and

(d) the tenant is not a company or other artificial person.

To: (*insert name and address of tenant*)

From: (*insert name and address of landlord*)

1 This notice relates to the following property: (*insert address or description of property*)

2 I am giving you notice under sections 25 of the Landlord and Tenant Act 1954 ('the 1954 Act') to end your tenancy on (*insert date*).

3 A certificate has been given by (*state the title of the Secretary of State, Minister or Board on whose authority the certificate was issued or, if the certificate was issued by the National Assembly for Wales, insert* 'the National Assembly for Wales') under section 57 of the 1954 Act that the use or occupation of all or part of the property should be changed by (*insert date*). A copy of the certificate appears in the Schedule to this notice.

4 If you have a right under Part 1 of the Leasehold Reform Act 1967 to acquire the freehold or an extended lease of property comprised in the tenancy, notice of your desire to have the freehold or an extended lease cannot be given more than two months after the service of this notice. If you have that right, and give notice of your desire to have the freehold or an extended lease within those two months, this notice will not operate, and I may take no further proceedings under Part 2 of the 1954 Act.

*5 If you give notice of your desire to have the freehold or an extended lease, I will be entitled to apply to the court under section 17 of the Leasehold Reform Act 1967, and propose to do so. If I am successful I may have to pay you compensation.

OR

*5 If you give notice of your desire to have the freehold or an extended lease, I will be entitled to apply to the court under section 17 of the Leasehold Reform Act 1967, but do not propose to do so.

OR

*5 If you give notice of your desire to have the freehold or an extended lease, I will not be entitled to apply to the court under section 17 of the Leasehold Reform Act 1967.

* DELETE TWO *versions of this paragraph, as the circumstances require*

*6 I know or believe that the following persons have an interest superior to your tenancy or to be the agent concerned with the property on behalf of someone who has such an interest (*insert names and addresses*):

delete if inapplicable

7 Please send all correspondence about this notice to:

Name:

Address:

Signed:Date:

*[Landlord] *[On behalf of the landlord] *[Mortgagee] *[On behalf of the mortgagee]

(*delete if inapplicable*)

SCHEDULE

CERTIFICATE UNDER SECTION 57
(*attach or insert a copy of the section 57 certificate*)

IMPORTANT NOTE FOR THE TENANT
This Notice is intended to bring your tenancy to an end on the date specified in paragraph 2.
The landlord is not prepared to offer you a new lease because it has been certified that it is requisite that occupation or use of the premises should be changed.

NOTES
Unless otherwise stated, the sections mentioned below are sections of the Landlord and Tenant Act 1954, as amended (most recently by the Regulatory Reform (Business Tenancies) (England and Wales) Order 2003)

Ending of your tenancy
This notice is intended to bring your tenancy to an end on the date stated in paragraph 2 of the notice.

Your landlord is both giving you notice that your current tenancy will end on the date stated in paragraph 2 of this notice and drawing attention to a certificate under section 57 that would prevent you from applying to the court for a new tenancy.

Usually, tenants who have tenancies under Part II of the Landlord and Tenant Act 1954 can apply to the court for a new tenancy. However, it has been certified that it is requisite that the use or occupation of all or part of the property should be changed by a certain date, the landlord may prevent the tenant from making an application to the court for a new tenancy.

Rights under the Leasehold Reform Act 1967

If the property comprised in your tenancy is a house, as defined in section 2 of the Leasehold Reform Act 1967 ('the 1967 Act'), you may have the right to buy the freehold of the property or to get an extended lease. If the house is for the time being let under two or more tenancies, you will not have that right if your tenancy is subject to a sub-tenancy and the sub-tenant is himself or herself entitled to that right.

You will have that right if all the following conditions are met:

(i)   your lease was originally granted for a term of more than 35 years, or was preceded by such a lease which was granted or assigned to you; and

(ii)   your lease is of the whole house; and

(iii) your lease is at a low rent. If your tenancy was entered into before 1 April 1990 (or later if you contracted before that date to enter into the tenancy) 'low rent' means that your present annual rent is less than two-thirds of the rateable value of your house as assessed either on 23 March 1965, or on the first day of the term in the case of a lease granted to commence after 23 March 1965; and the property had a rateable value other than nil when the tenancy began or at any time before 1 April 1990. If your tenancy was granted on or after 1 April 1990, 'low rent' means that the present annual rent is not more than £1,000 in London or £250 elsewhere; *and*

(iv)   you have been occupying the house (or any part of it) as your only or main residence (whether or not it has been occupied for other purposes) either for the whole of the last two years, or for a total of two years in the last ten years; *and*

(v)   the rateable value of your house was at one time within certain limits.

However, if you have a right to buy the freehold or to get an extended lease, you will not be able to exercise it in this case because of the certificate that has been given under section 57. That is the effect of section 28 of the 1967 Act.

Compensation

Because the court cannot order the grant of a new tenancy, you are entitled to compensation when you leave the property (section 59).

If you have a right under the 1967 Act to buy the freehold or to get an extended lease but you cannot exercise that right because of the section 57 certificate, compensation will be payable under section 17(2) of the 1967 Act.

You cannot, however, get compensation under both the 1954 Act and the 1967 Act. The compensation payable under the 1967 Act is likely to be greater than that payable under the 1954 Act. In order to be able to claim compensation under the 1967 Act you must serve the appropriate notice on the landlord. A special form is prescribed for this purpose; it is Form 1 as set out in the Schedule to the Leasehold Reform (Notices) (Amendment) (England) Regulations 2002 (SI 2002/1715), or if the property is in Wales, the Leasehold Reform (Notices) (Amendment) (Wales) Regulations 2002 (SI 2002/3187) (W.303). Subject to the exception mentioned below, you must serve the notice claiming to buy the freehold or to get an extended lease within two months after the date of service of this notice. The exception is where the landlord agrees in writing to your claim being made after the date on which it should have been made.

If there has been any delay in your seeing this notice you may need to act very quickly. If you are in any doubt about the action that you should take, get advice immediately from a solicitor or a surveyor.

If your landlord is an authority possessing compulsory purchase powers (such as a local authority) you may also be entitled to a disturbance payment under Part 3 of the Land Compensation Act 1973.

Validity of this notice

The landlord who has given you this notice may not be the landlord to whom you pay your rent (sections 44 and 67). This does not necessarily mean that the notice is invalid.

If you have any doubts about whether this notice is valid, get advice immediately from a solicitor or a surveyor.

Further information

An explanation of the main points to consider when renewing or ending a business tenancy, 'Renewing and Ending Business Leases: a Guide for Tenants and Landlords', can be found at www.odpm.gov.uk. Printed copies of the explanation, but not of this form, are available from 1st June 2004 from Free Literature, PO Box 236, Wetherby, West Yorkshire, LS23 7NB (0870 1226 236).

An explanation of the rights of leaseholders to buy the freehold or to have an extended lease, 'Residential Long Leaseholders – A Guide to Your Rights and Responsibilities', can be found at www.odpm.gov.uk.

Printed copies of the explanation, but not of this form, are available from 1st June 2004 from Free Literature, PO Box 236, Wetherby, West Yorkshire, LS23 7NB (0870 1226 236).

Form 14

NOTICE ENDING A BUSINESS TENANCY ON PUBLIC INTEREST GROUNDS WHERE A CHANGE IS REQUIRED AT A FUTURE DATE AND WHERE THE LEASEHOLD REFORM ACT 1967 MAY APPLY

Sections 25 and 57 of the Landlord and Tenant Act 1954

Paragraph 10 of Schedule 3 to the Leasehold Reform Act 1967

IMPORTANT NOTE FOR THE LANDLORD

This form *must* be used (instead of Form 9 or 10 in Schedule 2 to the Landlord and Tenant Act 1954, Part 2 (Notices) Regulations 2004) if -

(a) no previous notice terminating the tenancy has been given under section 4 or 25 of the Landlord and Tenant Act 1954 or under paragraph 4(1) of Schedule 10 to the Local Government and Housing Act 1989; and

(b) the tenancy is of a house as defined for the purposes of Part 1 of the Leasehold Reform Act 1967 ('the 1967 Act'); and

(c) the tenancy is a long tenancy at a low rent within the meaning of the 1967 Act; and

(d) the tenant is not a company or other artificial person.

To: (*insert name and address of tenant*)

From: (*insert name and address of landlord*)

1 This notice relates to the following property: (*insert address or description of property*)

2 I am giving you notice under sections 25 of the Landlord and Tenant Act 1954 ('the 1954 Act') to end your tenancy on (*insert date*).

*3 If you apply to the court under Part 2 of the 1954 Act for the grant of a new tenancy, I will not oppose your application.

OR* *DELETE ONE version of this paragraph, as the circumstances require.*

3 If you apply to the court under Part 2 of the 1954 Act for the grant of a new tenancy, I will oppose your application on the ground(s) mentioned in paragraph(s) of section 30(1) of the 1954 Act. I draw your attention to the Table in the Notes below, which sets out all the grounds of opposition.

* (*insert letter(s) of the paragraph(s) relied on*)

4 A certificate has been given by (*state the title of the Secretary of State, Minister or Board on whose authority the certificate was issued or, if the certificate was issued by the National Assembly for Wales, insert 'the*

National Assembly for Wales') under section 57 of the 1954 Act that the use or occupation of all or part of the property should be changed by (*insert date*). A copy of the certificate appears in the Schedule to this notice.

5 If you have a right under Part 1 of the Leasehold Reform Act 1967 to acquire the freehold or an extended lease of property comprised in the tenancy, notice of your desire to have the freehold or an extended lease cannot be given more than two months after the service of this notice. If you have that right, and give notice of your desire to have the freehold or an extended lease within those two months, this notice will not operate, and I may take no further proceedings under Part II of the Landlord and Tenant Act 1954.

**6 If you give notice of your desire to have the freehold or an extended lease, I will be entitled to apply to the court under section 17 of the Leasehold Reform Act 1967, and propose to do so. If I am successful I may have to pay you compensation.

OR

**6 If you give notice of your desire to have the freehold or an extended lease, I will be entitled to apply to the court under section 17 of the Leasehold Reform Act 1967, but do not propose to do so.

OR

**6 If you give notice of your desire to have the freehold or an extended lease, I will not be entitled to apply to the court under section 17 of the Leasehold Reform Act 1967.

** *DELETE TWO versions of this paragraph, as the circumstances require*

*7 I know or believe that the following persons have an interest superior to your tenancy or to be the agent concerned with the property on behalf of someone who has such an interest (*insert names and addresses*):

*(*delete if inapplicable*)

8 Please send all correspondence about this notice to:

Name:

Address:

Signed: Date:

*[Landlord] *[On behalf of the landlord] *[Mortgagee] *[On behalf of the mortgagee]

(*delete if inapplicable*)

SCHEDULE

CERTIFICATE UNDER SECTION 57

(attach or insert a copy of the section 57 certificate)

IMPORTANT NOTE FOR THE TENANT

This Notice is intended to bring your tenancy to an end on the date specified in paragraph 2.

Your landlord may have indicated in paragraph 3 that he will oppose your application for a new tenancy (if you decide to make one). You will not get a new tenancy unless you successfully challenge in court the grounds indicated in paragraph 3 on which your landlord opposes the grant of a new tenancy.

It has been certified that it is requisite that occupation or use of the premises should be changed by the date specified in paragraph 4.

If you want to continue to occupy your property you must act quickly. The notes below should help you to decide what action you now need to take. If you are unsure about what you should do, get advice immediately from a solicitor or a surveyor.

NOTES

Unless otherwise stated, the sections mentioned below are sections of the Landlord and Tenant Act 1954, as amended (most recently by the Regulatory Reform (Business Tenancies) (England and Wales) Order 2003)

Ending of your tenancy

This notice is intended to bring your tenancy to an end on the date stated in paragraph 2 of the notice.

Claiming a new tenancy

If you wish to apply to the court for a new tenancy you must do so by the date set out in paragraph 2 of this notice, unless you and your landlord have agreed in writing, before that date, to extend the deadline (sections 29A and 29B). However, before you take that step, read carefully the section below headed '*Effect of section 57 certificate*'.

If you apply to the court, your tenancy will continue after the date shown in paragraph 2 of this notice while your application is being considered (section 24).

If you are in any doubt about what action you should take, get advice immediately from a solicitor or a surveyor.

Landlord's opposition to claim for a new tenancy

If paragraph 3 of this notice indicates that your landlord is opposed to the grant of a new tenancy, you will not get a new tenancy unless you apply to the court and successfully challenge the ground(s) of your landlord's opposition.

If you apply to the court for a new tenancy, the landlord can only oppose your application on one or more of the grounds set out in section 30(1). If you match the letter(s) specified in paragraph 3 of this notice with those in the first column in the Table below, you can see from the second column the ground(s) on which the landlord relies.

Paragraph of section 30(1)   Grounds

(a) Where under the current tenancy the tenant has any obligations as respects the repair and maintenance of the holding, that the tenant ought not to be granted a new tenancy in view of the state of repair of the holding, being a state resulting from the tenant's failure to comply with the said obligations.

(b) That the tenant ought not to be granted a new tenancy in view of his persistent delay in paying rent which has become due.

(c) That the tenant ought not to be granted a new tenancy in view of other substantial breaches by him of his obligations under the current tenancy, or for any other reason connected with the tenant's use or management of the holding.

(d) That the landlord has offered and is willing to provide or secure the provision of alternative accommodation for the tenant, that the terms on which the alternative accommodation is available are reasonable having regard to the terms of the current tenancy and to all other relevant circumstances, and that the accommodation and the time at which it will be available are suitable for the tenant's requirements (including the requirement to preserve goodwill) having regard to the nature and class of his business and to the situation and extent of, and facilities afforded by, the holding.

(e) Where the current tenancy was created by the sub-letting of part only of the property comprised in a superior tenancy and the landlord is the owner of an interest in reversion expectant on the termination of that superior tenancy, that the aggregate of the rents reasonably obtainable on separate lettings of the holding and the remainder of that property would be substantially less than the rent reasonably obtainable on a letting of that property as a whole, that on the termination of the current tenancy the landlord requires possession of the holding for the purposes of letting or otherwise disposing of the said property as a whole, and that in view thereof the tenant ought not to be granted a new tenancy.

(f) That on the termination of the current tenancy the landlord intends to demolish or reconstruct the premises comprised in the holding or a substantial part of those premises or to carry out substantial work of construction on the holding or part thereof and that he could not reasonably do so without obtaining possession of the holding.

(g) On the termination of the current tenancy the landlord intends to occupy the holding for the purposes, or partly for the purposes, of a business to be carried on by him therein, or as his residence.

In the Table 'the holding' means the property that is the subject of the tenancy.

In ground (e), 'the landlord is the owner an interest in reversion expectant on the termination of that superior tenancy' means that the landlord has an interest in the property that will entitle him, when your immediate landlord's tenancy comes to an end, to exercise certain rights and obligations in relation to the property that are currently exercisable by your immediate landlord.

If ground (f) is specified, the court can sometimes still grant a new tenancy if certain conditions set out in section 31A of the 1954 Act can be met.

If ground (g) is specified, please note that 'the landlord' may have an extended meaning. Where a landlord has a controlling interest in a company then either the landlord or the company can rely on ground (g). Where the landlord is a company and a person has a controlling interest in that company then either of them can rely on ground (g) (section 30(1A) and (1B)). A person has a 'controlling interest' in a company if, had he been a company, the other company would have been its subsidiary (section 46(2)).

The landlord must normally have been the landlord for at least five years before he or she can use ground (g).

Effect of section 57 certificate

A copy of a certificate issued under section 57 appears in the Schedule to this notice. The effect of the certificate is that, even if you are successful in challenging your landlord's opposition to the grant of a new tenancy, and the court orders the grant of a new tenancy, the new tenancy must end not later than the date specified in the certificate (section 57(3)(b)).

Any new tenancy will not be a tenancy to which Part 2 of the 1954 Act applies (section 57(3)(b)).

Rights under the Leasehold Reform Act 1967

If the property comprised in your tenancy is a house, as defined in section 2 of the Leasehold Reform Act 1967 ('the 1967 Act'), you may have the right to buy the freehold of the property or to get an extended lease. If the house is for the time being let under two or more tenancies, you will not have that right if your tenancy is subject to a sub-tenancy and the sub-tenant is himself or herself entitled to that right.

You will have that right if *all* the following conditions are met:

(i) your lease was originally granted for a term of more than 35 years, or was preceded by such a lease which was granted or assigned to you; *and*

(ii)   your lease is of the whole house; *and*

(iii) your lease is at a low rent. If your tenancy was entered into before 1 April 1990 (or later if you contracted before that date to enter into the tenancy) 'low rent' means that your present annual rent is less than two-thirds of the rateable value of your house as assessed either on 23 March 1965, or on the first day of the term in the case of a lease granted to commence after 23 March 1965; and the property had a rateable value other than nil when the tenancy began or at any time before 1 April 1990. If your tenancy was granted on or after 1 April 1990, 'low rent' means that the present annual rent is not more than £1,000 in London or £250 elsewhere; *and*

(iv) you have been occupying the house (or any part of it) as your only or main residence (whether or not it has been occupied for other purposes) either for the whole of the last two years, or for a total of two years in the last ten years; *and*

(v)   the rateable value of your house was at one time within certain limits.

However, if you have a right to buy the freehold or to get an extended lease, you will not be able to exercise it in this case because of the certificate that has been given under section 57. That is the effect of section 28 of the 1967 Act.

Compensation

If you cannot get a new tenancy solely because one or more of grounds (e), (f) and (g) applies, you may be entitled to compensation under section 37. If your landlord has opposed your application on any of the other grounds as well as (e), (f) or (g) you can only get compensation if the court's refusal to grant a new tenancy is based solely on one or more of grounds (e), (f) and (g). In other words, you cannot get compensation under section 37 if the court has refused your tenancy on *other* grounds, even if one or more of grounds (e), (f) and (g) also applies.

If the court orders the grant of a new tenancy, you may be entitled to compensation under section 59.

If you have a right under the 1967 Act to buy the freehold or to get an extended lease but you cannot exercise that right because of the section 57 certificate, compensation will be payable under that Act.

You cannot, however, get compensation under both the 1954 Act and the 1967 Act. The compensation payable under the 1967 Act is likely to be greater than that payable under the 1954 Act. In order to be able to claim compensation under the 1967 Act you must serve the appropriate notice on the landlord. A special form is prescribed for this purpose; it is Form 1 as set out in the Schedule to the Leasehold Reform (Notices) (Amendment) (England) Regulations 2002 (S.I.

2002/1715), or if the property is in Wales, the Leasehold Reform (Notices) (Amendment) (Wales) Regulations 2002 (SI 2002/3187) (W.303). Subject to the exception mentioned below, you must serve the notice claiming to buy the freehold or to get an extended lease within two months after the date of service of this notice. The exception is where the landlord agrees in writing to your claim being made after the date on which it should have been made.

If there has been any delay in your seeing this notice you may need to act very quickly. If you are in any doubt about what action you should take, get advice immediately from a solicitor or a surveyor.

If your landlord is an authority possessing compulsory purchase powers (such as a local authority) you may be entitled to a disturbance payment under Part 3 of the Land Compensation Act 1973.

Validity of this notice

The landlord who has given you this notice may not be the landlord to whom you pay your rent (sections 44 and 67). This does not necessarily mean that the notice is invalid.

If you have any doubts about whether this notice is valid, get advice immediately from a solicitor or a surveyor.

Further information

An explanation of the main points to consider when renewing or ending a business tenancy, 'Renewing and Ending Business Leases: a Guide for Tenants and Landlords', can be found at www.odpm.gov.uk. Printed copies of the explanation, but not of this form, are available from 1st June 2004 from Free Literature, PO Box 236, Wetherby, West Yorkshire, LS23 7NB (0870 1226 236).

An explanation of the rights of leaseholders to buy the freehold or to have an extended lease, 'Residential Long Leaseholders – A Guide to Your Rights and Responsibilities', can be found at www.odpm.gov.uk. Printed copies of the explanation, but not of this form, are available from 1st June 2004 from Free Literature, PO Box 236, Wetherby, West Yorkshire, LS23 7NB (0870 1226 236).

Form 15

NOTICE ENDING A BUSINESS TENANCY WHERE THE PROPERTY IS REQUIRED FOR REGENERATION AND THE LEASEHOLD REFORM ACT 1967 MAY APPLY

Sections 25, 58 and 60 of the Landlord and Tenant Act 1954

Paragraph 10 of Schedule 3 to the Leasehold Reform Act 1967

IMPORTANT NOTE FOR THE LANDLORD

This form *must* be used (instead of Form 12 in Schedule 2 to the Landlord and Tenant Act 1954, Part 2 (Notices) Regulations 2004) if -

(a) no previous notice terminating the tenancy has been given under section 4 or 25 of the Landlord and Tenant Act 1954 or under paragraph 4(1) of Schedule 10 to the Local Government and Housing Act 1989; and

(b) the tenancy is of a house as defined for the purposes of Part 1 of the Leasehold Reform Act 1967 ('the 1967 Act'); and

(c) the tenancy is a long tenancy at a low rent within the meaning of the 1967 Act; and

(d) the tenant is not a company or other artificial person.

To: (*insert name and address of tenant*)

From: (*insert name and address of landlord*)

1 This notice relates to the following property, which is situated in an area for the time being specified as a development area or intermediate area by an order made, or having effect as if made, under section 1 of the Industrial Development Act 1982: (*insert address or description of property*)

2 I am giving you notice under section 25 of the Landlord and Tenant Act 1954 ('the 1954 Act') to end your tenancy on (*insert date*).

3 A certificate has been given by (*state the title of the Secretary of State, Minister or Board on whose authority the certificate was issued*) under section 58 of the 1954 Act (as applied by section 60 of that Act) that it is necessary or expedient for the purpose mentioned in section 2(1) of the Local Employment Act 1972 that the use or occupation of the property should be changed. A copy of the certificate appears in the Schedule to this notice.

4 The certificate prevents me from granting you a new tenancy. It also means that you will not be able to make an application to the court under section 24(1) of the 1954 Act for the grant of a new tenancy.

5 If you have a right under Part 1 of the Leasehold Reform Act 1967 to acquire the freehold or an extended lease of property comprised in the tenancy, notice of your desire to have the freehold or an extended lease cannot be given more than two months after the service of this notice. If you have that right, and give notice of your desire to have the freehold or an extended lease within those two months, this notice will not operate, and I may take no further proceedings under Part 2 of the 1954 Act.

*6 If you give notice of your desire to have the freehold or an extended lease, I will be entitled to apply to the court under section 17 of the Leasehold Reform Act 1967, and propose to do so. If I am successful I may have to pay you compensation.

OR

*6 If you give notice of your desire to have the freehold or an extended lease, I will be entitled to apply to the court under section 17 of the Leasehold Reform Act 1967, but do not propose to do so.

OR

*6 If you give notice of your desire to have the freehold or an extended lease, I will not be entitled to apply to the court under section 17 of the Leasehold Reform Act 1967.

* DELETE TWO *versions of this paragraph, as the circumstances require*

**7 I know or believe that the following persons have an interest superior to your tenancy or to be the agent concerned with the property on behalf of someone who has such an interest (*insert names and addresses*):

**(*delete if inapplicable*)

8 Please send all correspondence about this notice to:

Name:

Address:

Signed: Date:

*[Landlord] *[On behalf of the landlord] (*delete if inapplicable*)

SCHEDULE

CERTIFICATE UNDER SECTION 58
(*attach or insert a copy of the section 58 certificate*)

IMPORTANT NOTE FOR THE TENANT
This notice is intended to bring your tenancy to an end on the date specified in paragraph 2.

A Government Minister has decided that it is necessary or expedient that occupation or use of the premises should be changed.

It would be wise to seek professional advice.

NOTES
Unless otherwise stated, the sections mentioned below are sections of the Landlord and Tenant Act 1954, as amended (most recently by the Regulatory Reform (Business Tenancies) (England and Wales) Order 2003).

Ending of your tenancy
This notice is intended to bring your tenancy to an end on the date stated in paragraph 2 of the notice.

Your landlord is both giving you notice that your current tenancy will end on the date stated in paragraph 2 of this notice and drawing attention to a certificate under section 58 (as applied by section 60) that would prevent you from applying to the court for a new tenancy.

Usually, tenants who have tenancies under Part II of the Landlord and Tenant Act 1954 can apply to the court for a new tenancy. However, where a Government Minister has certified that it is necessary or expedient for the purpose mentioned in section 2(1) of the Local Employment Act 1972 that the use or occupation of the property should be changed, the landlord may prevent the tenant from making an application to the court for a new tenancy.

Rights under the Leasehold Reform Act 1967

If the property comprised in your tenancy is a house, as defined in section 2 of the Leasehold Reform Act 1967 ('the 1967 Act'), you may have the right to buy the freehold of the property or to get an extended lease. If the house is for the time being let under two or more tenancies, you will not have that right if your tenancy is subject to a sub-tenancy and the sub-tenant is himself or herself entitled to that right.

You will have that right if *all* the following conditions are met:

(i)   your lease was originally granted for a term of more than 35 years, or was preceded by such a lease which was granted or assigned to you; *and*

(ii) your lease is of the whole house; *and*

(iii) your lease is at a low rent. If your tenancy was entered into before 1 April 1990 (or later if you contracted before that date to enter into the tenancy) 'low rent' means that your present annual rent is less than two-thirds of the rateable value of your house as assessed either on 23 March 1965, or on the first day of the term in the case of a lease granted to commence after 23 March 1965; and the property had a rateable value other than nil when the tenancy began or at any time before 1 April 1990. If your tenancy was granted on or after 1 April 1990, 'low rent' means that the present annual rent is not more than £1,000 in London or £250 elsewhere; *and*

(iv) you have been occupying the house (or any part of it) as your only or main residence (whether or not it has been occupied for other purposes) either for the whole of the last two years, or for a total of two years in the last ten years; *and*

(v)   the rateable value of your house was at one time within certain limits.

However, if you have a right to buy the freehold or to get an extended lease, you will not be able to exercise it in this case because of the certificate that has been given. That is the effect of section 28 of the 1967 Act.

Compensation

If you have a right under the 1967 Act to buy the freehold or to get an extended lease but you cannot exercise that right because of the certificate, compensation will be payable under that Act.

In order to be able to claim compensation under the 1967 Act you must serve the appropriate notice on the landlord. A special form is prescribed for this purpose; it is Form 1 as set out in the Schedule to the Leasehold Reform (Notices) (Amendment) (England) Regulations 2002 (SI 2002/1715). Subject to the exception mentioned below, you must serve the notice claiming to buy the freehold or to get an extended lease within two months after the date of service of this notice. The exception is where the landlord agrees in writing to your claim being made after the date on which it should have been made.

If there has been any delay in your seeing this notice you may need to act very quickly. If you are in any doubt about what steps you should take, get advice immediately from a solicitor or a surveyor.

Validity of this notice

The landlord who has given you this notice may not be the landlord to whom you pay your rent (sections 44 and 67). This does not necessarily mean that the notice is invalid.

If you have any doubts about whether this notice is valid, get advice immediately from a solicitor or a surveyor.

Further information

An explanation of the main points to consider when renewing or ending a business tenancy, 'Renewing and Ending Business Leases: a Guide for Tenants and Landlords', can be found at www.odpm.gov.uk. Printed copies of the explanation, but not of this form, are available from 1st June 2004 from Free Literature, PO Box 236, Wetherby, West Yorkshire, LS23 7NB (0870 1226 236).

An explanation of the rights of leaseholders to buy the freehold or to have an extended lease, 'Residential Long Leaseholders - A Guide to Your Rights and Responsibilities", can be found at www.odpm.gov.uk. Printed copies of the explanation, but not of this form, are available from 1st June 2004 from Free Literature, PO Box 236, Wetherby, West Yorkshire, LS23 7NB (0870 1226 236).

Form 16

NOTICE ENDING A BUSINESS TENANCY OF WELSH DEVELOPMENT AGENCY PREMISES WHERE THE PROPERTY IS REQUIRED FOR EMPLOYMENT PURPOSES

Sections 25, 58 and 60A of the Landlord and Tenant Act 1954

IMPORTANT NOTE

This form must *not* be used if -

(a) no previous notice terminating the tenancy has been given under section 4 or 25 of the Landlord and Tenant Act 1954, or under paragraph 4(1) of Schedule 10 to the Local Government and Housing Act 1989, and

(b) the tenancy is of a house as defined for the purposes of Part 1 of the Leasehold Reform Act 1967, and

(c) the tenancy is a long tenancy at a low rent within the meaning of that Act, and

(d) the tenant is not a company or other artificial person.

If (a) to (d) apply, use form 17 in Schedule 2 to the Landlord and Tenant Act 1954, Part 2 (Notices) Regulations 2004 instead of this form.

To: (*insert name and address of tenant*)

From: (*insert name and address of landlord*)

1 This notice relates to the following property, of which you are the tenant: (*insert address or description of property*)

2 We give you notice under section 25 of the Landlord and Tenant Act 1954 ("the 1954 Act") to end your tenancy on: (*insert date*)

3 A certificate has been given by the National Assembly for Wales under section 58 of the 1954 Act (as applied by section 60A of that Act) that it is necessary or expedient, for the purposes of providing employment appropriate to the needs of the area in which the premises are situated, that the use or occupation of the property should be changed. A copy of the certificate appears in the Schedule to this notice.

4 The certificate prevents us from granting you a new tenancy. It also means that you will not be able to make an application to the court under section 24(1) of the 1954 Act for the grant of a new tenancy. However, you may be entitled to compensation.

5 Please send all correspondence about this notice to:

Name:

Address:

Signed: Date:

*[Landlord] *[On behalf of the landlord]

(*delete if inapplicable*)

SCHEDULE

CERTFICATE UNDER SECTION 58

(attach or insert a copy of the section 58 certificate)

IMPORTANT NOTE FOR THE TENANT

This notice is intended to bring your tenancy to an end on the date specified in paragraph 2 above.

The certificate referred to in paragraph 3 above means that the landlord cannot grant you a new tenancy, and the court cannot order the grant of a new tenancy. However, you may be entitled to compensation.

It would be wise to seek professional advice immediately in connection with this notice.

NOTES

Unless otherwise stated, the sections mentioned below are sections of the Landlord and Tenant Act 1954, as amended (most recently by the Regulatory Reform (Business Tenancies) (England and Wales) Order 2003 (SI 2003/3096))

Ending of your tenancy

   1 This notice is intended to bring your tenancy to an end on the date specified in paragraph 2 of this notice. Section 25 contains rules about the date that the landlord can put in that paragraph.

   2 Your landlord is both giving you notice that your tenancy will end on the date specified in paragraph 2 of this notice and drawing attention, in paragraph 3 of this notice, to a certificate given by the National Assembly for Wales under section 58 (as applied by section 60A) that would prevent you from applying to the court for a new tenancy under Part II of the Landlord and Tenant Act 1954.

   3 Usually, tenants who have tenancies under Part II of the Landlord and Tenant Act 1954 can apply to the court for a new tenancy. However, where the National Assembly for Wales has certified that it is necessary or expedient, for the purposes of providing employment appropriate to the needs of the area in which the premises are situated, that the use or occupation of the property should be changed, the landlord may prevent the tenant from making an application to the court for a new tenancy.

Compensation

   4 You will be entitled to compensation under section 59 when you leave the property UNLESS:

(a) the premises vested in the Welsh Development Agency under section 7 or 8 of the Welsh Development Agency Act 1975; *or*

(b) you were not the tenant of the premises when the Welsh Development Agency acquired the interest by virtue of which the certificate referred to in paragraph 3 of this notice was given.

5 You may also be entitled to a disturbance payment under Part 3 of the Land Compensation Act 1973.

Validity of this notice

6 The landlord who has given you this notice may not be the landlord to whom you pay your rent (sections 44 and 67). This does not necessarily mean that the notice is invalid.

7 If you have any doubts about whether this notice is valid, get advice immediately from a solicitor or a surveyor.

Further information

8 An explanation of the main points to consider when renewing or ending a business tenancy, "Renewing and Ending Business Leases: a Guide for Tenants and Landlords", can be found at www.odpm.gov.uk Printed copies of the explanation, but not of this form, are available from 1st June 2004 from Free Literature, PO Box 236, Wetherby, West Yorkshire, LS23 7NB (0870 1226 236).

Form 17

NOTICE ENDING A BUSINESS TENANCY OF WELSH DEVELOPMENT AGENCY PREMISES WHERE THE PROPERTY IS REQUIRED FOR EMPLOYMENT PURPOSES AND THE LEASEHOLD REFORM ACT 1967 MAY APPLY

Sections 25, 58 and 60A of the Landlord and Tenant Act 1954

Paragraph 10 of Schedule 3 to the Leasehold Reform Act 1967

IMPORTANT NOTE

This form *must* be used (instead of Form 16 in Schedule 2 to the Landlord and Tenant Act 1954, Part 2 (Notices) Regulations 2004) if -

(a) no previous notice terminating the tenancy has been given under section 4 or 25 of the Landlord and Tenant Act 1954 Act or under paragraph 4(1) of Schedule 10 to the Local Government and Housing Act 1989; and

(b) the tenancy is of a house as defined for the purposes of Part 1 of the Leasehold Reform Act 1967; and

(c) the tenancy is a long tenancy at a low rent within the meaning of the 1967 Act; and

(d) the tenant is not a company or other artificial person.

To: (*insert name and address of tenant*)

From: (*insert name and address of landlord*)

1 This notice relates to the following property, of which you are the tenant: (*insert address or description of property*):

2 We give you notice under section 25 of the Landlord and Tenant Act 1954 ("the 1954 Act") to end your tenancy on: (*insert date*)

3 A certificate has been given by the National Assembly for Wales under section 58 of the 1954 Act (as applied by section 60A of that Act) that it is necessary or expedient, for the purposes of providing employment appropriate to the needs of the area in which the premises are situated, that the use or occupation of the property should be changed. A copy of the certificate appears in the Schedule to this notice.

4 The certificate prevents us from granting you a new tenancy. It also means that you will not be able to make an application to the court under section 24(1) of the 1954 Act for the grant of a new tenancy. However, you may be entitled to compensation.

5 If you have a right under Part 1 of the Leasehold Reform Act 1967 ("the 1967 Act") to acquire the freehold or to get an extended lease of property comprised in the tenancy, notice of your desire to have the freehold or an extended lease cannot be given more than two months after the service of this notice. If you have that right, and give notice of your desire to have the freehold or an extended lease within those two months, this notice will not operate, and we may take no further proceedings under Part II of the 1954 Act.

*6 If you give notice of your desire to have the freehold or an extended lease, we will be entitled to apply to the court under section 17 of the 1967 Act, and propose to do so. If we are successful we may have to pay you compensation.

OR

*6 If you give notice of your desire to have the freehold or an extended lease, we will be entitled to apply to the court under section 17 of the 1967 Act, but do not propose to do so.

OR

*6 If you give notice of your desire to have the freehold or an extended lease, we will not be entitled to apply to the court under section 17 of the 1967 Act.

*(DELETE TWO *versions of paragraph 6, as the circumstances require*)

**7 We know or believe that the following persons have an interest superior to your tenancy or to be the agent concerned with the property on behalf of someone who has such an interest (*insert names and addresses*):

**(*delete if inapplicable*)

8 Please send all correspondence about this notice to:

Name:

Address:

Signed: Date:

*[Landlord] *[On behalf of the landlord]

(*delete if inapplicable*)

SCHEDULE

CERTFICATE UNDER SECTION 58

(attach or insert a copy of the section 58 certificate)

IMPORTANT NOTE FOR THE TENANT

This notice is intended to bring your tenancy to an end on the date specified in paragraph 2 above.

The National Assembly for Wales has certified that it is necessary or expedient that occupation or use of the premises should be changed.

It would be wise to seek professional advice immediately in connection with this notice.

NOTES

Unless otherwise stated, the sections mentioned below are sections of the Landlord and Tenant Act 1954, as amended, (most recently by the Regulatory Reform (Business Tenancies) (England and Wales) Order 2003 (SI 2003/3096)).

Ending of your tenancy

1 This notice is intended to bring your tenancy to an end on the date specified in paragraph 2 of this notice. Section 25 contains rules about the date that the landlord can put in that paragraph.

2 Your landlord is both giving you notice that your tenancy will end on the date specified in paragraph 2 of this notice and drawing attention, in paragraph 3 of this notice, to a certificate given by the National Assembly for Wales under section 58 (as applied by section 60A) that would prevent you from applying to the court for a new tenancy under Part II of the Landlord and Tenant Act 1954.

3 Usually, tenants who have tenancies under Part II of the Landlord and Tenant Act 1954 can apply to the court for a new tenancy. However, where the National Assembly for Wales has certified that it is necessary or expedient, for the purposes of providing employment appropriate to the needs of the area in which the premises are situated, that the use or occupation of the property should be changed, the landlord may prevent the tenant from making an application to the court for a new tenancy under that Part II.

4 However, the Leasehold Reform Act 1967 ("the 1967 Act") may also apply in your case. If it does, you may be able to buy the freehold of the property or get an extended lease under that Act (see *Rights under the 1967 Act*: notes 5 to 7 below and *Claiming your rights under the 1967 Act*: notes 8 and 9 below). If you claim an extended lease your landlord may still be able to get possession of the property (see *Landlord's opposition to claims under the 1967 Act*: note 10 below). If he does, you may be able to get compensation (see *Compensation*: notes 11 to 14 below). The amount of any compensation will depend on the

steps you have taken and under which Act (it is likely to be greater under the 1967 Act). If you have any doubt about what you should do, get professional advice immediately.

Rights under the 1967 Act

5 If the property comprised in your tenancy is a house, as defined in section 2 of the 1967 Act, you may have the right to buy the freehold of the property or to get an extended lease.

6 If the house is for the time being let under two or more tenancies, you will not have that right if your tenancy is subject to a sub-tenancy and the sub-tenant is himself or herself entitled to that right.

7 You will have that right if *all* the following conditions (i) - (v) are met:

(i)   your lease was originally granted for a term of more than 35 years, or was preceded by such a lease which was granted or assigned to you; *and*

(ii) your lease is of the whole house; *and*

(iii) (where applicable) your lease is at a low rent. If your tenancy was entered into before 1 April 1990 (or later if you contracted before that date to enter into the tenancy) "low rent" means that your present annual rent is less than two-thirds of the rateable value of your house as assessed either on 23 March 1965, or on the first day of the term in the case of a lease granted to commence after 23 March 1965, and the property had a rateable value other than nil when the tenancy began or any time before 1 April 1990. If your tenancy was granted on or after 1 April 1990, "low rent" means that the present annual rent is not more than £250; *and*

(iv) you have been occupying the house (or any part of it) as your only or main residence (whether or not it has been occupied for other purposes) either for the whole of the last two years, or for a total of two years in the last ten years; *and*

(v)   the rateable value of your house was at one time within certain limits.

Claiming your rights under the 1967 Act

8 If you have the right to buy the freehold or to get an extended lease and wish to exercise it, you must serve the appropriate notice on the landlord. A special form is prescribed for this purpose; it is Form 1 as set out in the Schedule to the Leasehold Reform (Notices) (Amendment) (Wales) Regulations 2002 (SI 2002/3187)(W.303). Subject to the exception mentioned below, you must serve the notice claiming to buy the freehold or to get an extended lease within two months after the date of service of this notice. The exception is where the landlord agrees in writing to your claim being made after the date on which it should have been made.

9 There are special rules about the service of notices. If there has been any delay in your seeing this notice you may need to act very quickly. If you are in any doubt about what you should do, get advice immediately from a solicitor or a surveyor.

Landlord's opposition to claims under the 1967 Act

10 If you claim a right under the 1967 Act, your landlord can object under section 17 of the 1967 Act on the grounds that he wishes to redevelop the property. Paragraph 6 of the notice will tell you whether the landlord believes he has the right to apply to the court under section 17 and whether or not he proposes to do so.

Compensation

11 Because the court cannot order the grant of a new tenancy under the 1954 Act in your case, you may be entitled to compensation under the 1954 Act when you leave the property. You will not be entitled to such compensation if either:

(a) the premises were vested in the Welsh Development Agency under section 7 or 8 of the Welsh Development Agency Act 1975; or

(b) you were not the tenant of the premises when the Agency acquired the interest by virtue of which the certificate referred to in paragraph 3 of this notice was given.

12 You may be entitled to a disturbance payment under Part 3 of the Land Compensation Act 1973.

13 If you have a right under the 1967 Act to buy the freehold or to get an extended lease of your premises but the landlord is able to obtain possession of the premises (see *Landlord's opposition to claims under the 1967 Act*: note 10 above), compensation under the 1967 Act is payable. This is normally higher than compensation under the 1954 Act. Your professional adviser will be able to advise you on this.

14 In order to be able to claim compensation under the 1967 Act you must serve the appropriate notice on the landlord within the stated time limit (see *Claiming your Rights under the 1967 Act*: notes 8 and 9 above).

Validity of this notice

15 The landlord who has given you this notice may not be the landlord to whom you pay your rent (sections 44 and 67). This does not necessarily mean that the notice is invalid.

16 If you have any doubts about whether this notice is valid, get advice immediately from a solicitor or a surveyor.

Further information

17 An explanation of the main points to consider when renewing or ending a business tenancy, "Renewing and Ending Business Leases: a Guide for Tenants and Landlords", can be found at www.odpm.gov.uk Printed copies of the explanation, but not of this

form, are available from 1st June 2004 from Free Literature, PO Box 236, Wetherby, West Yorkshire, LS23 7NB (0870 1226 236).

18. An explanation of the rights of leaseholders to buy the freehold or to have an extended lease, "Residential Long Leaseholders – A Guide to Your Rights and Responsibilities", can be found at www.odpm.gov.uk. Printed copies of the explanation, but not of this form, are available from Free Literature, PO Box 236, Wetherby, West Yorkshire, LS23 7NB (0870 1226 236).

EXPLANATORY NOTE

(This note is not part of the Regulations)

These Regulations replace the Landlord and Tenant Act 1954, Part 2 (Notices) Regulations 1983.

Regulation 3 of these Regulations prescribes the form of various notices relevant to business tenancies. The prescribed forms are set out in Schedule 2. Forms that are substantially to the same effect as those prescribed may be used (regulation 2(2)).

The purposes for which the prescribed forms are to be used are specified in Schedule 1.

The forms prescribed by these Regulations reflect amendments to Part II of the Landlord and Tenant Act 1954 made by the Regulatory Reform (Business Tenancies) (England and Wales) Order 2003 (SI 2003/3096).

Regulation 4 revokes the Landlord and Tenant Act 1954, Part 2 (Notices) Regulations 1983 and the Landlord and Tenant Act 1954, Part 2 (Notices) (Amendment) Regulations 1989.

A full regulatory impact assessment has not been produced for this instrument, as it has no impact on the costs of businesses, charities or voluntary bodies.

Notes:

[1] 1954 c. 56. The functions of the Secretary of State under section 66 (including that section as it has effect as mentioned in section 22(5) of the Leasehold Reform Act 1967) are, so far as exercisable in relation to Wales, transferred to the National Assembly for Wales by article 2 of, and Schedule 1 to, the National Assembly for Wales (Transfer of Functions) Order 1999 (SI 1999/672), to which there are amendments not relevant to these Regulations.

[2] For amendments relevant to these Regulations, see the Regulatory Reform (Business Tenancies) (England and Wales) Order 2003 (S.I. 2003/3096).

[3] 1967 c 88. Amendments to Schedule 3 relevant to these Regulations are made by SI 2003/3096, Schedule 5, paragraphs 10 to13.

[4] SI 1983/133.

[5] SI 1989/1548.

[6] 1972 c 5. Section 2(1) was repealed by the Industry Act 1972 (c 63), except as applied by section 60(1) of the Landlord and Tenant Act 1954; *see* Part 1 of Schedule 4 to the Industry Act 1972. Its application continues by virtue of paragraph 2(a) of Part 2 of Schedule 2 to the Industrial Development Act 1982 (c 52).

[7] 1972 c 5. Section 2(1) was repealed by the Industry Act 1972 (c 63), except as applied by section 60(1) of the Landlord and Tenant Act 1954; *see* Part 1 of Schedule 4 to the Industry Act 1972. Its application continues by virtue of paragraph 2(a) of Part 2 of Schedule 2 to the Industrial Development Act 1982 (c 52).

APPENDIX 17

REGULATORY REFORM (BUSINESS TENANCIES) (ENGLAND AND WALES) ORDER 2003

SCHEDULE 1

Article 22(2)

FORM OF NOTICE THAT SECTIONS 24 TO 28 OF THE LANDLORD AND TENANT ACT 1954 ARE NOT TO APPLY TO A BUSINESS TENANCY

To:

_____

_____

_____

[Name and address of tenant]

From:

_____

_____

_____

[Name and address of landlord]

IMPORTANT NOTICE

You are being offered a lease without security of tenure. Do not commit yourself to the lease unless you have read this message carefully and have discussed it with a professional adviser.

Business tenants normally have security of tenure – the right to stay in their business premises when the lease ends.

If you commit yourself to the lease you will be giving up these important legal rights.

- You will have **no right** to stay in the premises when the lease ends.
- Unless the landlord chooses to offer you another lease, you will need to leave the premises.
- You will be unable to claim compensation for the loss of your business premises, unless the lease specifically gives you this right.
- If the landlord offers you another lease, you will have no right to ask the court to fix the rent.

It is therefore important to get professional advice – from a qualified surveyor, lawyer or accountant – before agreeing to give up these rights.

If you want to ensure that you can stay in the same business premises when the lease ends, you should consult your adviser about another form of lease that does not exclude the protection of the Landlord and Tenant Act 1954.

If you receive this notice at least 14 days before committing yourself to the lease, you will need to sign a simple declaration that you have received this notice and have accepted its consequences, before signing the lease.

But if you do not receive at least 14 days notice, you will need to sign a 'statutory' declaration. To do so, you will need to visit an independent solicitor (or someone else empowered to administer oaths).

Unless there is a special reason for committing yourself to the lease sooner, you may want to ask the landlord to let you have at least 14 days to consider whether you wish to give up your statutory rights. If you then decided to go ahead with the agreement to exclude the protection of the Landlord and Tenant Act 1954, you would only need to make a simple declaration, and so you would not need to make a separate visit to an independent solicitor.

SCHEDULE 2

Article 22(2)

REQUIREMENTS FOR A VALID AGREEMENT THAT SECTIONS 24 TO 28 OF THE LANDLORD AND TENANT ACT 1954 ARE NOT TO APPLY TO A BUSINESS TENANCY

1. The following are the requirements referred to in section 38A(3)(b) of the Act.

2. Subject to paragraph 4, the notice referred to in section 38A(3)(a) of the Act must be served on the tenant not less than 14 days before the tenant enters into the tenancy to which it applies, or (if earlier) becomes contractually bound to do so.

3. If the requirement in paragraph 2 is met, the tenant, or a person duly authorised by him to do so, must, before the tenant enters into the tenancy to which the notice applies, or (if earlier) becomes contractually bound to do so, make a declaration in the form, or substantially in the form, set out in paragraph 7.

4. If the requirement in paragraph 2 is not met, the notice referred to in section 38A(3)(a) of the Act must be served on the tenant before the tenant enters into the tenancy to which it applies, or (if earlier) becomes contractually bound to do so, and the tenant, or a person duly authorised by him to do so, must before that time make a statutory declaration in the form, or substantially in the form, set out in paragraph 8.

5. A reference to the notice and, where paragraph 3 applies, the declaration or, where paragraph 4 applies, the statutory declaration must be contained in or endorsed on the instrument creating the tenancy.

6. The agreement under section 38A(1) of the Act, or a reference to the agreement, must be contained in or endorsed upon the instrument creating the tenancy.

7. The form of declaration referred to in paragraph 3 is as follows -

I

_____

(*name of declarant*) of

_____

(*address*) declare that -

    1. I/

_____

(*name of tenant*) propose(s) to enter into a tenancy of premises at

_____

(*address of premises*) for a term commencing on

_____

    2. I/The tenant propose(s) to enter into an agreement with

_____

(*name of landlord*) that the provisions of sections 24 to 28 of the Landlord and Tenant Act 1954 (security of tenure) shall be excluded in relation to the tenancy.

    3. The landlord has, not less than 14 days before I/the tenant enter(s) into the tenancy, or (if earlier) become(s) contractually bound to do so served on me/the tenant a notice in the form, or substantially in the form, set out in Schedule 1 to the Regulatory Reform (Business Tenancies) (England and Wales) Order 2003. The form of notice set out in that Schedule is reproduced below.

    4. I have/The tenant has read the notice referred to in paragraph 3 above and accept(s) the consequences of entering into the agreement referred to in paragraph 2 above.

    5. (*as appropriate*) I am duly authorised by the tenant to make this declaration.

DECLARED this

_____

day of

_____

.

To:

_____

_____

_____

[*Name and address of tenant*]

From:

_____

_____

_____

[*Name and address of landlord*]

IMPORTANT NOTICE

<u>**You are being offered a lease without security of tenure. Do not commit yourself to the lease unless you have read this message carefully and have discussed it with a professional adviser.**</u>

Business tenants normally have security of tenure – the right to stay in their business premises when the lease ends.

<u>**If you commit yourself to the lease you will be giving up these important legal rights.**</u>

- You will have **no right** to stay in the premises when the lease ends.

- Unless the landlord chooses to offer you another lease, you will need to leave the premises.

- You will be unable to claim compensation for the loss of your business premises, unless the lease specifically gives you this right.

- If the landlord offers you another lease, you will have no right to ask the court to fix the rent.

It is therefore important to get professional advice – from a qualified surveyor, lawyer or accountant – before agreeing to give up these rights.

If you want to ensure that you can stay in the same business premises when the lease ends, you should consult your adviser about another form of lease that does not exclude the protection of the Landlord and Tenant Act 1954.

If you receive this notice at least 14 days before committing yourself to the lease, you will need to sign a simple declaration that you have received this notice and have accepted its consequences, before signing the lease.

But if you do not receive at least 14 days notice, you will need to sign a 'statutory' declaration. To do so, you will need to visit an independent solicitor (or someone else empowered to administer oaths).

Unless there is a special reason for committing yourself to the lease sooner, you may want to ask the landlord to let you have at least 14 days to consider whether you wish to give up your statutory rights. If you then decided to go ahead with the agreement to exclude the protection of the Landlord and Tenant Act 1954, you would only need to make a simple declaration, and so you would not need to make a separate visit to an independent solicitor.

8. The form of statutory declaration referred to in paragraph 4 is as follows -

I

_____

(*name of declarant*) of

_____

(*address*) do solemnly and sincerely declare that -

1. I

_____

(*name of tenant*) propose(s) to enter into a tenancy of premises at

_____

(*address of premises*) for a term commencing on

_____

.

2. I/The tenant propose(s) to enter into an agreement with (name of landlord) that the provisions of sections 24 to 28 of the Landlord and Tenant Act 1954 (security of tenure) shall be excluded in relation to the tenancy.

3. The landlord has served on me/the tenant a notice in the form, or substantially in the form, set out in Schedule 1 to the Regulatory Reform (Business Tenancies) (England and Wales) Order 2003. The form of notice set out in that Schedule is reproduced below.

4. I have/The tenant has read the notice referred to in paragraph 3 above and accept(s) the consequences of entering into the agreement referred to in paragraph 2 above.

5. (*as appropriate*) I am duly authorised by the tenant to make this declaration.

To:

_____

_____

_____

[*Name and address of tenant*]

From:

_____

_____

_____

[*Name and address of landlord*]

IMPORTANT NOTICE

You are being offered a lease without security of tenure. Do not commit yourself to the lease unless you have read this message carefully and have discussed it with a professional adviser.

Business tenants normally have security of tenure – the right to stay in their business premises when the lease ends.

If you commit yourself to the lease you will be giving up these important legal rights.

- You will have **no right** to stay in the premises when the lease ends.

- Unless the landlord chooses to offer you another lease, you will need to leave the premises.

- You will be unable to claim compensation for the loss of your business premises, unless the lease specifically gives you this right.

- If the landlord offers you another lease, you will have no right to ask the court to fix the rent.

It is therefore important to get professional advice – from a qualified surveyor, lawyer or accountant – before agreeing to give up these rights.

If you want to ensure that you can stay in the same business premises when the lease ends, you should consult your adviser about another form of lease that does not exclude the protection of the Landlord and Tenant Act 1954.

If you receive this notice at least 14 days before committing yourself to the lease, you will need to sign a simple declaration that you have received this notice and have accepted its consequences, before signing the lease.

But if you do not receive at least 14 days notice, you will need to sign a 'statutory' declaration. To do so, you will need to visit an independent solicitor (or someone else empowered to administer oaths).

Unless there is a special reason for committing yourself to the lease sooner, you may want to ask the landlord to let you have at least 14 days to consider whether you wish to give up your statutory rights. If you then decided to go ahead with the agreement to exclude the protection of the Landlord and Tenant Act 1954, you would only need to make a simple declaration, and so you would not need to make a separate visit to an independent solicitor.

AND I make this solemn declaration conscientiously believing the same to be true and by virtue of the Statutory Declaration Act 1835.

DECLARED at

_____

this

_____

day of

_____

.

Before me

(*signature of person before whom declaration is made*)

A commissioner for oaths or a solicitor empowered to administer oaths or (*as appropriate*)

SCHEDULE 3

Article 22(2)

FORM OF NOTICE THAT AN AGREEMENT TO SURRENDER A BUSINESS TENANCY IS TO BE MADE

To:

_____

_____

_____

[*Name and address of tenant*]

From:

_____

_____

_____

[*Name and address of landlord*]

IMPORTANT NOTICE FOR TENANT

Do no commit yourself to any agreement to surrender your lease unless you have read this message carefully and discussed it with a professional adviser.

Normally, you have the right to renew your lease when it expires. By committing yourself to an agreement to surrender, **you will be giving up this important statutory right.**

- You will **not** be able to continue occupying the premises beyond the date provided for under the agreement for surrender, **unless** the landlord chooses to offer you a further term (in which case you would lose the right to ask the court to determine the new rent). You will need to leave the premises.

- You will be unable to claim compensation for the loss of your business premises, unless the lease or agreement for surrender gives you this right.

A qualified surveyor, lawyer or accountant would be able to offer you professional advice on your options.

You do not have to commit yourself to the agreement to surrender your lease unless you want to.

If you receive this notice at least 14 days before committing yourself to the agreement to surrender, you will need to sign a simple declaration that you have received this notice and have accepted its consequences, before signing the agreement to surrender.

But if you do not receive at least 14 days notice, you will need to sign a 'statutory' declaration. To do so, you will need to visit an independent solicitor (or someone else empowered to administer oaths).

Unless there is a special reason for committing yourself to the lease sooner, you may want to ask the landlord to let you have at least 14 days to consider whether you wish to give up your statutory rights. If you then decided to go ahead with the agreement to end your lease, you would only need to make a simple declaration, and so you would not need to make a separate visit to an independent solicitor.

SCHEDULE 4

Article 22(2)

REQUIREMENTS FOR A VALID AGREEMENT TO SURRENDER A BUSINESS TENANCY

1. The following are the requirements referred to in section 38A(4)(b) of the Act.

2. Subject to paragraph 4, the notice referred to in section 38A(4)(a) of the Act must be served on the tenant not less than 14 days before the tenant enters into the agreement under section 38A(2) of the Act, or (if earlier) becomes contractually bound to do so.

3. If the requirement in paragraph 2 is met, the tenant or a person duly authorised by him to do so, must, before the tenant enters into the agreement under section 38A(2) of the Act, or (if earlier) becomes contractually bound to do so, make a declaration in the form, or substantially in the form, set out in paragraph 6.

4. If the requirement in paragraph 2 is not met, the notice referred to in section 38A(4)(a) of the Act must be served on the tenant before the tenant enters into the agreement under section 38A(2) of the Act, or (if earlier) becomes contractually bound to do so, and the tenant, or a person duly authorised by him to do so, must before that time make a statutory declaration in the form, or substantially in the form, set out in paragraph 7.

5. A reference to the notice and, where paragraph 3 applies, the declaration or, where paragraph 4 applies, the statutory declaration must be contained in or endorsed on the instrument creating the agreement under section 38A(2).

6. The form of declaration referred to in paragraph 3 is as follows -

I

_____

(*Name of declarant*) of

_____

(*Address*) declare that -

   1. I have/

_____

(*Name of tenant*) has a tenancy of premises at

_____

(*Address of premises*) for a term commencing on

.

   2. I/The tenant propose(s) to enter into an agreement with

_____

(*name of landlord*) to surrender the tenancy on a date or in circumstances specified in the agreement.

   3. The landlord has not less than 14 days before I/the tenant enter(s) into the agreement referred to in paragraph 2 above, or (if earlier) become(s) contractually bound to do so, served on me/the tenant a notice in the form, or substantially in the form, set out in Schedule 3 to Regulatory Reform (Business Tenancies) (England and Wales) Order 2003. The form of notice set out in that Schedule is reproduced below.

   4. I have/The tenant has read the notice referred to in paragraph 3 above and accept(s) the consequences of entering into the agreement referred to in paragraph 2 above.

   5. (*as appropriate*) I am duly authorised by the tenant to make this declaration.

DECLARED this

_____

day of

_____

To:

_____

_____

_____

[*Name and address of tenant*]

From:

_____

_____

_____

[*Name and address of landlord*]

IMPORTANT NOTICE FOR TENANT

Do no commit yourself to any agreement to surrender your lease unless you have read this message carefully and discussed it with a professional adviser.

Normally, you have the right to renew your lease when it expires. By committing yourself to an agreement to surrender, **you will be giving up this important statutory right.**

- You will **not** be able to continue occupying the premises beyond the date provided for under the agreement for surrender, **unless** the landlord chooses to offer you a further term (in which case you would lose the right to ask the court to determine the new rent). You will need to leave the premises.

- You will be unable to claim compensation for the loss of your business premises, unless the lease or agreement for surrender gives you this right.

A qualified surveyor, lawyer or accountant would be able to offer you professional advice on your options.

You do not have to commit yourself to the agreement to surrender your lease unless you want to.

If you receive this notice at least 14 days before committing yourself to the agreement to surrender, you will need to sign a simple declaration that you have received this notice and have accepted its consequences, before signing the agreement to surrender.

But if you do not receive at least 14 days notice, you will need to sign a 'statutory' declaration. To do so, you will need to visit an independent solicitor (or someone else empowered to administer oaths).

Unless there is a special reason for committing yourself to the lease sooner, you may want to ask the landlord to let you have at least 14 days to consider whether you wish to give up your statutory rights. If you then decided to go ahead with the agreement to end your lease, you would only need to make a simple declaration, and so you would not need to make a separate visit to an independent solicitor.

7. The form of statutory declaration referred to in paragraph 4 is as follows-

I

(*Name of declarant*) of

(*Address*) do solemnly and sincerely declare that -

1. I have/

(*Name of tenant*) has a tenancy of premises at

(*Address of premises*) for a term commencing on

.

2. I/The tenant propose(s) to enter into an agreement with

(*name of landlord*) to surrender the tenancy on a date or in circumstances specified in the agreement.

3. The landlord has served on me/the tenant a notice in the form, or substantially in the form, set out in Schedule 3 to the Regulatory Reform (Business Tenancies) (England and Wales) Order 2003. The form of notice set out in that Schedule is reproduced below.

4. I have/The tenant has read the notice referred to in paragraph 3 above and accept(s) the consequences of entering into the agreement referred to in paragraph 2 above.

5. (*as appropriate*) I am duly authorised by the tenant to make this declaration.

To:

[*Name and address of tenant*]

From:

[*Name and address of landlord*]

IMPORTANT NOTICE FOR TENANT

Do no commit yourself to any agreement to surrender your lease unless you have read this message carefully and discussed it with a professional adviser.

Normally, you have the right to renew your lease when it expires. By committing yourself to an agreement to surrender, **you will be giving up this important statutory right.**

- You will **not** be able to continue occupying the premises beyond the date provided for under the agreement for surrender, **unless** the landlord chooses to offer you a further term (in which case you would lose the right to ask the court to determine the new rent). You will need to leave the premises.

- You will be unable to claim compensation for the loss of your business premises, unless the lease or agreement for surrender gives you this right.

A qualified surveyor, lawyer or accountant would be able to offer you professional advice on your options.

You do not have to commit yourself to the agreement to surrender your lease unless you want to.

If you receive this notice at least 14 days before committing yourself to the agreement to surrender, you will need to sign a simple declaration that you have received this notice and have accepted its consequences, before signing the agreement to surrender.

But if you do not receive at least 14 days notice, you will need to sign a 'statutory' declaration. To do so, you will need to visit an independent solicitor (or someone else empowered to administer oaths).

Unless there is a special reason for committing yourself to the lease sooner, you may want to ask the landlord to let you have at least 14 days to consider whether you wish to give up your statutory rights. If you then decided to go ahead with the agreement to end your lease, you would only need to make a simple declaration, and so you would not need to make a separate visit to an independent solicitor.

AND I make this solemn declaration conscientiously believing the same to be true and by virtue of the Statutory Declarations Act 1835

DECLARED at

_____

this

_____

day of

_____

.

Before me (*signature of person before whom declaration is made*)

A commissioner for oaths or a solicitor empowered to administer oaths *or* (*as appropriate*)

APPENDIX 18

CPR PART 56

I LANDLORD AND TENANT CLAIMS

Scope and interpretation

56.1 (1) In this Section of this Part 'landlord and tenant claim' means a claim under –

(a) the Landlord and Tenant Act 1927;

(b) the Leasehold Property (Repairs) Act 1938;

(c) the Landlord and Tenant Act 1954;

(d) the Landlord and Tenant Act 1985; or

(e) the Landlord and Tenant Act 1987.

(2) A practice direction may set out special provisions with regard to any particular category of landlord and tenant claim.

Starting the claim

56.2 (1) The claim must be started in the county court for the district in which the land is situated unless paragraph (2) applies or an enactment provides otherwise.

(2) The claim may be started in the High Court if the claimant files with his claim form a certificate stating the reasons for bringing the claim in that court verified by a statement of truth in accordance with rule 22.1(1).

(3) The practice direction refers to circumstances which may justify starting the claim in the High Court.

Claims for a new tenancy under section 24 and for the termination of a tenancy under section 29(2) of the Landlord and Tenant Act 1954

56.3 (1) This rule applies to a claim for a new tenancy under section 24 and to a claim for the termination of a tenancy under section 29(2) of the 1954 Act.

(2) In this rule –

(a) 'the 1954 Act' means the Landlord and Tenant Act 1954;

(b) 'an unopposed claim' means a claim for a new tenancy under section 24 of the 1954 Act in circumstances where the grant of a new tenancy is not opposed;

(c) 'an opposed claim' means a claim for –

    (i) a new tenancy under section 24 of the 1954 Act in circumstances where the grant of a new tenancy is opposed; or

    (ii) the termination of a tenancy under section 29(2) of the 1954 Act.

(3) Where the claim is an unopposed claim –

(a) the claimant must use the Part 8 procedure, but the following rules do not apply –

    (i)   rule 8.5; and

    (ii) rule 8.6;

(b) the claim form must be served within 2 months after the date of issue and rules 7.5 and 7.6 are modified accordingly; and

(c) the court will give directions about the future management of the claim following receipt of the acknowledgment of service.

(4) Where the claim is an opposed claim –

(a) the claimant must use the Part 7 procedure; but

(b) the claim form must be served within 2 months after the date of issue, and rules 7.5 and 7.6 are modified accordingly.

(The practice direction to this Part contains provisions about evidence, including expert evidence in opposed claims.)

II MISCELLANEOUS PROVISIONS ABOUT LAND

Scope

56.4 A practice direction may set out special provisions with regard to claims under the following enactments –

(a) the Chancel Repairs Act 1932;

(b) the Leasehold Reform Act 1967;

(c) the Access to Neighbouring Land Act 1992;

(d) the Leasehold Reform, Housing and Urban Development Act 1993; and

(e) the Commonhold and Leasehold Reform Act 2002.

APPENDIX 19

CPR PD 56

PRACTICE DIRECTION – LANDLORD AND TENANT CLAIMS AND MISCELLANEOUS PROVISIONS ABOUT LAND

THIS PRACTICE DIRECTION SUPPLEMENTS PART 56
SECTION I – LANDLORD AND TENANT CLAIMS

1.1   In this section of this practice direction –

(1) 'the 1927 Act' means the Landlord and Tenant Act 1927;

(2) 'the 1954 Act' means the Landlord and Tenant Act 1954;

(3) 'the 1985 Act' means the Landlord and Tenant Act 1985; and

(4) 'the 1987 Act' means the Landlord and Tenant Act 1987.

56.2 – STARTING THE CLAIM

2.1   Subject to paragraph 2.1A, the claimant in a landlord and tenant claim must use the Part 8 procedure as modified by Part 56 and this practice direction.

2.1A   Where the landlord and tenant claim is a claim for –

(1) a new tenancy under section 24 of the 1954 Act in circumstances where the grant of a new tenancy is opposed; or

(2) the termination of a tenancy under section 29(2) of the 1954 Act,

the claimant must use the Part 7 procedure as modified by Part 56 and this practice direction.

2.2   Except where the county court does not have jurisdiction, landlord and tenant claims should normally be brought in the county court. Only exceptional circumstances justify starting a claim in the High Court.

2.3   If a claimant starts a claim in the High Court and the court decides that it should have been started in the county court, the court will normally either strike the claim out or transfer it to the county court on its own initiative. This is likely to result in delay and the court will normally disallow the costs of starting the claim in the High Court and of any transfer.

2.4   Circumstances which may, in an appropriate case, justify starting a claim in the High Court are if –

(1) there are complicated disputes of fact; or

(2) there are points of law of general importance.

2.5   The value of the property and the amount of any financial claim may be relevant circumstances, but these factors alone will not normally justify starting the claim in the High Court.

2.6   A landlord and tenant claim started in the High Court must be brought in the Chancery Division.

CLAIMS FOR A NEW TENANCY UNDER SECTION 24 AND TERMINATION OF A TENANCY UNDER SECTION 29(2) OF THE 1954 ACT

3.1   This paragraph applies to a claim for a new tenancy under section 24 and termination of a tenancy under section 29(2) of the 1954 Act where rule 56.3 applies and in this paragraph –

(1) 'an unopposed claim' means a claim for a new tenancy under section 24 of the 1954 Act in circumstances where the grant of a new tenancy is not opposed;

(2) 'an opposed claim' means a claim for –

(a) a new tenancy under section 24 of the 1954 Act in circumstances where the grant of a new tenancy is opposed; or

(b) the termination of a tenancy under section 29(2) of the 1954 Act; and

(3) 'grounds of opposition' means –

(a) the grounds specified in section 30(1) of the 1954 Act on which a landlord may oppose an application for a new tenancy under section 24(1) of the 1954 Act or make an application under section 29(2) of the 1954 Act; or

(b) any other basis on which the landlord asserts that a new tenancy ought not to be granted.

Precedence of claim forms where there is more than one application to the court under section 24(1) or section 29(2) of the 1954 Act

3.2   Where more than one application to the court under section 24(1) or section 29(2) of the 1954 Act is made, the following provisions shall apply –

(1) once an application to the court under section 24(1) of the 1954 Act has been served on a defendant, no further application to the court in respect of the same tenancy whether under section 24(1) or section 29(2) of the 1954 Act may be served by that defendant without the permission of the court;

(2) if more than one application to the court under section 24(1) of the 1954 Act in respect of the same tenancy is served on the same day, any landlord's application shall stand stayed until further order of the court;

(3) if applications to the court under both section 24(1) and section 29(2) of the 1954 Act in respect of the same tenancy are

served on the same day, any tenant's application shall stand stayed until further order of the court; and

(4) if a defendant is served with an application under section 29(2) of the 1954 Act ('the section 29(2) application') which was issued at a time when an application to the court had already been made by that defendant in respect of the same tenancy under section 24(1) of the 1954 Act ('the section 24(1) application'), the service of the section 29(2) application shall be deemed to be a notice under rule 7.7 requiring service or discontinuance of the section 24(1) application within a period of 14 days after the service of the section 29(2) application.

Defendant where the claimant is the tenant making a claim for a new tenancy under section 24 of the 1954 Act

3.3   Where a claim for a new tenancy under section 24 of the 1954 Act is made by a tenant, the person who, in relation to the claimant's current tenancy, is the landlord as defined in section 44 of the 1954 Act must be a defendant.

Contents of the claim form in all cases

3.4   The claim form must contain details of –

(1) the property to which the claim relates;

(2) the particulars of the current tenancy (including date, parties and duration), the current rent (if not the original rent) and the date and method of termination;

(3) every notice or request given or made under sections 25 or 26 of the 1954 Act; and

(4) the expiry date of –

    (a) the statutory period under section 29A(2) of the 1954 Act; or

    (b) any agreed extended period made under section 29B(1) or 29B(2) of the 1954 Act.

Claim form where the claimant is the tenant making a claim for a new tenancy under section 24 of the 1954 Act

3.5   Where the claimant is the tenant making a claim for a new tenancy under section 24 of the 1954 Act, in addition to the details specified in paragraph 3.4, the claim form must contain details of –

(1) the nature of the business carried on at the property;

(2) whether the claimant relies on section 23(1A), 41 or 42 of the 1954 Act and, if so, the basis on which he does so;

(3) whether the claimant relies on section 31A of the 1954 Act and, if so, the basis on which he does so;

(4) whether any, and if so what part, of the property comprised in the tenancy is occupied neither by the claimant nor by a person

employed by the claimant for the purpose of the claimant's business;

(5) the claimant's proposed terms of the new tenancy; and

(6) the name and address of –

(a) anyone known to the claimant who has an interest in the reversion in the property (whether immediate or in not more than 15 years) on the termination of the claimant's current tenancy and who is likely to be affected by the grant of a new tenancy; or

(b) if the claimant does not know of anyone specified by sub-paragraph (6)(a), anyone who has a freehold interest in the property.

3.6   The claim form must be served on the persons referred to in paragraph 3.5(6)(a) or (b) as appropriate.

Claim form where the claimant is the landlord making a claim for a new tenancy under section 24 of the 1954 Act

3.7   Where the claimant is the landlord making a claim for a new tenancy under section 24 of the 1954 Act, in addition to the details specified in paragraph 3.4, the claim form must contain details of –

(1) the claimant's proposed terms of the new tenancy;

(2) whether the claimant is aware that the defendant's tenancy is one to which section 32(2) of the 1954 Act applies and, if so, whether the claimant requires that any new tenancy shall be a tenancy of the whole of the property comprised in the defendant's current tenancy or just of the holding as defined by section 23(3) of the 1954 Act; and

(3) the name and address of –

(a) anyone known to the claimant who has an interest in the reversion in the property (whether immediate or in not more than 15 years) on the termination of the claimant's current tenancy and who is likely to be affected by the grant of a new tenancy; or

(b) if the claimant does not know of anyone specified by sub-paragraph (3)(a), anyone who has a freehold interest in the property.

3.8   The claim form must be served on the persons referred to in paragraph 3.7(3)(a) or (b) as appropriate.

Claim form where the claimant is the landlord making an application for the termination of a tenancy under section 29(2) of the 1954 Act

3.9   Where the claimant is the landlord making an application for the termination of a tenancy under section 29(2) of the 1954 Act, in addition to the details specified in paragraph 3.4, the claim form must contain –

(1) the claimant's grounds of opposition;

(2) full details of those grounds of opposition; and

(3) the terms of a new tenancy that the claimant proposes in the event that his claim fails.

Acknowledgment of service where the claim is an unopposed claim and where the claimant is the tenant

3.10 Where the claim is an unopposed claim and the claimant is the tenant, the acknowledgment of service is to be in form N210 and must state with particulars –

(1) whether, if a new tenancy is granted, the defendant objects to any of the terms proposed by the claimant and if so –

    (a) the terms to which he objects; and

    (b) the terms that he proposes in so far as they differ from those proposed by the claimant;

(2) whether the defendant is a tenant under a lease having less than 15 years unexpired at the date of the termination of the claimant's current tenancy and, if so, the name and address of any person who, to the knowledge of the defendant, has an interest in the reversion in the property expectant (whether immediate or in not more than 15 years from that date) on the termination of the defendant's tenancy;

(3) the name and address of any person having an interest in the property who is likely to be affected by the grant of a new tenancy; and

(4) if the claimant's current tenancy is one to which section 32(2) of the 1954 Act applies, whether the defendant requires that any new tenancy shall be a tenancy of the whole of the property comprised in the claimant's current tenancy.

Acknowledgment of service where the claim is an unopposed claim and the claimant is the landlord

3.11 Where the claim is an unopposed claim and the claimant is the landlord, the acknowledgment of service is to be in form N210 and must state with particulars –

(1) the nature of the business carried on at the property;

(2) if the defendant relies on section 23(1A), 41 or 42 of the 1954 Act, the basis on which he does so;

(3) whether any, and if so what part, of the property comprised in the tenancy is occupied neither by the defendant nor by a person employed by the defendant for the purpose of the defendant's business;

(4) the name and address of –

    (a) anyone known to the defendant who has an interest in the reversion in the property (whether immediate or in not more than 15 years) on the termination of the defendant's current tenancy and who is likely to be affected by the grant of a new tenancy; or

(b) if the defendant does not know of anyone specified by sub-paragraph (4)(a), anyone who has a freehold interest in the property; and

(5) whether, if a new tenancy is granted, the defendant objects to any of the terms proposed by the claimant and, if so –

(a) the terms to which he objects; and

(b) the terms that he proposes in so far as they differ from those proposed by the claimant.

Acknowledgment of service and defence where the claim is an opposed claim and where the claimant is the tenant

3.12 Where the claim is an opposed claim and the claimant is the tenant –

(1) the acknowledgment of service is to be in form N9; and

(2) in his defence the defendant must state with particulars –

(a) the defendant's grounds of opposition;

(b) full details of those grounds of opposition;

(c) whether, if a new tenancy is granted, the defendant objects to any of the terms proposed by the claimant and if so –

(i) the terms to which he objects; and

(ii) the terms that he proposes in so far as they differ from those proposed by the claimant;

(d) whether the defendant is a tenant under a lease having less than 15 years unexpired at the date of the termination of the claimant's current tenancy and, if so, the name and address of any person who, to the knowledge of the defendant, has an interest in the reversion in the property expectant (whether immediately or in not more than 15 years from that date) on the termination of the defendant's tenancy;

(e) the name and address of any person having an interest in the property who is likely to be affected by the grant of a new tenancy; and

(f) if the claimant's current tenancy is one to which section 32(2) of the 1954 Act applies, whether the defendant requires that any new tenancy shall be a tenancy of the whole of the property comprised in the claimant's current tenancy.

Acknowledgment of service and defence where the claimant is the landlord making an application for the termination of a tenancy under section 29(2) of the 1954 Act

3.13　Where the claim is an opposed claim and the claimant is the landlord –

(1)　the acknowledgment of service is to be in form N9; and

(2)　in his defence the defendant must state with particulars –

    (a)　whether the defendant relies on section 23(1A), 41 or 42 of the 1954 Act and, if so, the basis on which he does so;

    (b)　whether the defendant relies on section 31A of the 1954 Act and, if so, the basis on which he does so; and

    (c)　the terms of the new tenancy that the defendant would propose in the event that the claimant's claim to terminate the current tenancy fails.

Evidence in an unopposed claim

3.14　Where the claim is an unopposed claim, no evidence need be filed unless and until the court directs it to be filed.

Evidence in an opposed claim

3.15　Where the claim is an opposed claim, evidence (including expert evidence) must be filed by the parties as the court directs and the landlord shall be required to file his evidence first.

Grounds of opposition to be tried as a preliminary issue

3.16　Unless in the circumstances of the case it is unreasonable to do so, any grounds of opposition shall be tried as a preliminary issue.

Applications for interim rent under section 24A to 24D of the 1954 Act

3.17　Where proceedings have already been commenced for the grant of a new tenancy or the termination of an existing tenancy, the claim for interim rent under section 24A of the 1954 Act shall be made in those proceedings by –

(1)　the claim form;

(2)　the acknowledgment of service or defence; or

(3)　an application on notice under Part 23.

3.18　Any application under section 24D(3) of the 1954 Act shall be made by an application on notice under Part 23 in the original proceedings.

3.19　Where no other proceedings have been commenced for the grant of a new tenancy or termination of an existing tenancy or where such proceedings have been disposed of, an application for interim rent under section 24A of the 1954 Act shall be made under the procedure in Part 8 and the claim form shall include details of –

(1) the property to which the claim relates;

(2) the particulars of the relevant tenancy (including date, parties and duration) and the current rent (if not the original rent);

(3) every notice or request given or made under sections 25 or 26 of the 1954 Act;

(4) if the relevant tenancy has terminated, the date and mode of termination; and

(5) if the relevant tenancy has been terminated and the landlord has granted a new tenancy of the property to the tenant –

    (a) particulars of the new tenancy (including date, parties and duration) and the rent; and

    (b) in a case where section 24C(2) of the 1954 Act applies but the claimant seeks a different rent under section 24C(3) of that Act, particulars and matters on which the claimant relies as satisfying section 24C(3).

OTHER CLAIMS UNDER PART II OF THE 1954 ACT

4.1 The mesne landlord to whose consent a claim for the determination of any question arising under paragraph 4(3) of Schedule 6 to the 1954 Act shall be made a defendant to the claim.

4.2 If any dispute as to the rateable value of any holding has been referred under section 37(5) of the 1954 Act to the Commissioners of Inland Revenue for decision by a valuation officer, any document purporting to be a statement of the valuation officer of his decision is admissible as evidence of the matters contained in it.

CLAIM FOR COMPENSATION FOR IMPROVEMENTS UNDER PART I OF THE 1927 ACT

5.1 This paragraph applies to a claim under Part I of the 1927 Act.

The claim form

5.2 The claim form must include details of:

(1) the nature of the claim or the matter to be determined;

(2) the property to which the claim relates;

(3) the nature of the business carried on at the property;

(4) particulars of the lease or agreement for the tenancy including:

    (a) the names and addresses of the parties to the lease or agreement;

    (b) its duration;

    (c) the rent payable;

    (d) details of any assignment or other devolution of the lease or agreement;

(5) the date and mode of termination of the tenancy;

(6) if the claimant has left the property, the date on which he did so;

(7) particulars of the improvement or proposed improvement to which the claim relates; and

(8) if the claim is for payment of compensation, the amount claimed.

5.3   The court will fix a date for a hearing when it issues the claim form.

Defendant

5.4   The claimant's immediate landlord must be a defendant to the claim.

5.5   The defendant must immediately serve a copy of the claim form and any document served with it and of his acknowledgment of service on his immediate landlord. If the person so served is not the freeholder, he must serve a copy of these documents on his landlord and so on from landlord to landlord.

Evidence

5.6   Evidence need not be filed – with the claim form or acknowledgment of service.

Certification under section 3 of the 1927 Act

5.7   If the court intends to certify under section 3 of the 1927 Act that an improvement is a proper improvement or has been duly executed, it shall do so by way of an order.

Compensation under section 1 or 8 of the 1927 Act

5.8   A claim under section 1(1) or 8(1) of the 1927 Act must be in writing, signed by the claimant, his solicitor or agent and include details of –

(1) the name and address of the claimant and of the landlord against whom the claim is made;

(2) the property to which the claim relates;

(3) the nature of the business carried on at the property;

(4) a concise statement of the nature of the claim;

(5) particulars of the improvement, including the date when it was completed and costs; and

(6) the amount claimed.

5.9   A mesne landlord must immediately serve a copy of the claim on his immediate superior landlord. If the person so served is not the freeholder, he must serve a copy of the document on his landlord and so on from landlord to landlord.

(Paragraphs 5.8 and 5.9 provide the procedure for making claims under section 1(1) and 8(1) of the 1927 Act – these 'claims' do not, at this stage, relate to proceedings before the court)

TRANSFER TO LEASEHOLD VALUATION TRIBUNAL UNDER 1985 ACT

6.1　If a question is ordered to be transferred to a leasehold valuation tribunal for determination under section 31C of the 1985 Act the court will:

(1)　send notice of the transfer to all parties to the claim; and

(2)　send to the leasehold valuation tribunal:

　　(a)　copies certified by the district judge of all entries in the records of the court relating to the question;

　　(b)　the order of transfer; and

　　(c)　all documents filed in the claim relating to the question.

(Paragraph 6.1 no longer applies to proceedings in England but continues to apply to proceedings in Wales.)

Claim form

8.2　The claim form must:

(1)　identify the property to which the claim relates and give details to show that section 25 of the 1987 Act applies;

(2)　give details of the claimants to show that they constitute the requisite majority of qualifying tenants;

(3)　state the names and addresses of the claimants and of the landlord of the property, or, if the landlord cannot be found or his identity ascertained, the steps taken to find him or ascertain his identity;

(4)　state the name and address of:

　　(a)　the person nominated by the claimants for the purposes of Part III of the 1987 Act; and

　　(b)　every person known to the claimants who is likely to be affected by the application, including (but not limited to), the other tenants of flats contained in the property (whether or not they could have made a claim), any mortgagee or superior landlord of the landlord, and any tenants' association (within the meaning of section 29 of the 1985 Act); and

(5)　state the grounds of the claim.

Notice under section 27

8.3　A copy of the notice served on the landlord under section 27 of the 1987 Act must accompany the claim form unless the court has dispensed with the requirement to serve a notice under section 27(3) of the 1987 Act.

Defendants

8.4   The landlord of the property (and the nominated person, if he is not a claimant) must be defendants.

Service

8.5   A copy of the claim form must be served on each of the persons named by the claimant under paragraph 8.2(4)(b) together with a notice that he may apply to be made a party.

Payment into court by nominated person

8.6   If the nominated person pays money into court in accordance with an order under section 33(1) of the 1987 Act, he must file a copy of the certificate of the surveyor selected under section 33(2)(a) of that Act.

CLAIM FOR AN ORDER VARYING LEASES UNDER THE 1987 ACT

9.1   This paragraph applies to a claim for an order under section 38 or section 40 of the 1987 Act.

Claim form

9.2   The claim form must state:

(1) the name and address of the claimant and of the other current parties to the lease or leases to which the claim relates;

(2) the date of the lease or leases, the property to which they relate, any relevant terms and the variation sought;

(3) the name and address of every person known to the claimant who is likely to be affected by the claim, including (but not limited to), the other tenants of flats contained in premises of which the relevant property forms a part, any previous parties to the lease, any mortgagee or superior landlord of the landlord, any mortgagee of the claimant and any tenants' association (within the meaning of section 29 of the 1985 Act); and

(4) the grounds of the claim.

Defendants

9.3   The other current parties to the lease must be defendants.

Service

9.4 A copy of the claim form must be served on each of the persons named under paragraph 9.2(3).

9.5 If the defendant knows of or has reason to believe that another person or persons are likely to be affected by the variation, he must serve a copy of the claim form on those persons, together with a notice that they may apply to be made a party.

Defendant's application to vary other leases

9.6 If a defendant wishes to apply to vary other leases under section 36 of the 1987 Act:

(1) he must make the application in his acknowledgment of service;

(2) paragraphs 9.2 to 9.5 apply as if the defendant were the claimant; and

(3) Part 20 does not apply.

(Paragraphs 9.1–9.6 no longer apply to proceedings in England but continue to apply to proceedings in Wales.)

SERVICE OF DOCUMENTS IN CLAIMS UNDER THE 1987 ACT

10.1 All documents must be served by the parties.

10.2 If a notice is to be served in or before a claim under the 1987 Act, it must be served –

(1) in accordance with section 54; and

(2) in the case of service on a landlord, at the address given under section 48(1).

SECTION II – MISCELLANEOUS PROVISIONS ABOUT LAND ACCESS TO NEIGHBOURING LAND ACT 1992

11.1 The claimant must use the Part 8 procedure.

11.2 The claim form must set out:

(1) details of the dominant and servient land involved and whether the dominant land includes or consists of residential property;

(2) the work required;

(3) why entry to the servient land is required with plans (if applicable);

(4) the names and addresses of the persons who will carry out the work;

(5) the proposed date when the work will be carried out; and

(6) what (if any) provision has been made by way of insurance in the event of possible injury to persons or damage to property arising out of the proposed work.

11.3   The owner and occupier of the servient land must be defendants to the claim.

CHANCEL REPAIRS ACT 1932

12.1   The claimant in a claim to recover the sum required to put a chancel in proper repair must use the Part 8 procedure.

12.2   A notice to repair under section 2 of the Chancel Repairs Act 1932 must –

(1) state –

   (a) the responsible authority by whom the notice is given;

   (b) the chancel alleged to be in need of repair;

   (c) the repairs alleged to be necessary; and

   (d) the grounds on which the person to whom the notice is addressed is alleged to be liable to repair the chancel; and

(2) call upon the person to whom the notice is addressed to put the chancel in proper repair.

12.3   The notice must be served in accordance with Part 6.

LEASEHOLD REFORM ACT 1967

13.1   In this paragraph a section or schedule referred to by number means the section or schedule so numbered in the Leasehold Reform Act 1967.

13.2   If a tenant of a house and premises wishes to pay money into court under sections 11(4), 13(1) or 13(3) –

(1) he must file in the office of the appropriate court an application notice containing or accompanied by evidence stating –

   (a) the reasons for the payment into court;

   (b) the house and premises to which the payment relates;

   (c) the name and address of the landlord; and

   (d) so far as they are known to the tenant, the name and address of every person who is or may be interested in or entitled to the money;

(2) on the filing of the witness statement the tenant must pay the money into court and the court will send notice of the payment to the landlord and every person whose name and address are given in the witness statement;

(3) any subsequent payment into court by the landlord under section 11(4) must be made to the credit of the same account as the payment into court by the tenant and sub-paragraphs (1) and (2) will apply to the landlord as if he were a tenant; and

(4) the appropriate court for the purposes of paragraph (a) is the county court for the district in which the property is situated or, if

the payment into court is made by reason of a notice under section 13(3), any other county court as specified in the notice.

13.3   If an order is made transferring an application to a leasehold valuation tribunal under section 21(3), the court will:

(1) send notice of the transfer to all parties to the application; and

(2) send to the tribunal copies of the order of transfer and all documents filed in the proceedings.

(Paragraph 13.3 no longer applies to proceedings in England but continues to apply to proceedings in Wales)

13.4   A claim under section 17 or 18 for an order for possession of a house and premises *must be made in accordance with Part 55*.

13.5   In a claim under section 17 or 18, the defendant must:

(1) immediately after being served with the claim form, serve on every person in occupation of the property or part of it under an immediate or derivative sub-tenancy, a notice informing him of the claim and of his right under paragraph 3(4) of Schedule 2 take part in the hearing of the claim with the permission of the court; and

(2) within 14 days after being served with the claim form, file a defence stating the ground, if any, on which he intends to oppose the claim and giving particulars of every such sub-tenancy.

13.6   An application made to the High Court under section 19 or 27 shall be assigned to the Chancery Division.

LEASEHOLD REFORM, HOUSING AND URBAN DEVELOPMENT ACT 1993

14.1   In this paragraph:

(1) 'the 1993 Act' means the Leasehold Reform, Housing and Urban Development Act 1993; and

(2) a section or schedule referred to by number means the section or schedule so numbered in the 1993 Act.

14.2   If a claim is made under section 23(1) by a person other than the reversioner:

(1) on the issue of the claim form in accordance with Part 8, the claimant must send a copy to the reversioner; and

(2) the claimant must promptly inform the reversioner either:

    (a) of the court's decision; or

    (b) that the claim has been withdrawn.

14.3   Where an application is made under section 26(1) or (2) or section 50(1) or (2):

(1) it must be made by the issue of a claim form in accordance with the Part 8 procedure which need not be served on any other party; and

(2) the court may grant or refuse the application or give directions for its future conduct, including the addition as defendants of such persons as appear to have an interest in it.

14.4   An application under section 26(3) must be made by the issue of a claim form in accordance with the Part 8 procedure and:

(1) the claimants must serve the claim form on any person who they know or have reason to believe is a relevant landlord, giving particulars of the claim and the hearing date and informing that person of his right to be joined as a party to the claim;

(2) the landlord whom it is sought to appoint as the reversioner must be a defendant, and must file an acknowledgment of service;

(3) a person on whom notice is served under paragraph (1) must be joined as a defendant to the claim if he gives notice in writing to the court of his wish to be added as a party, and the court will notify all other parties of the addition.

14.5   If a person wishes to pay money into court under section 27(3), section 51(3) or paragraph 4 of Schedule 8 –

(1) he must file in the office of the appropriate court an application notice containing or accompanied by evidence stating –

(a) the reasons for the payment into court;

(b) the interest or interests in the property to which the payment relates or where the payment into court is made under section 51(3), the flat to which it relates;

(c) details of any vesting order;

(d) the name and address of the landlord; and

(e) so far as they are known to the tenant, the name and address of every person who is or may be interested in or entitled to the money;

(2) on the filing of the witness statement the money must be paid into court and the court will send notice of the payment to the landlord and every person whose name and address are given in the witness statement;

(3) any subsequent payment into court by the landlord must be made to the credit of same account as the earlier payment into court;

(4) the appropriate court for the purposes of paragraph (1) is –

(a) where a vesting order has been made, the county court that made the order; or

(b) where no such order has been made, the county court in whose district the property is situated.

14.6   If an order is made transferring an application to a leasehold valuation tribunal under section 91(4), the court will:

(1) send notice of the transfer to all parties to the application; and

(2) send to the tribunal copies of the order of transfer and all documents filed in the proceedings.

(Paragraph 14.6 no longer applies to proceedings in England but continues to apply to proceedings in Wales.)

14.7   If a relevant landlord acts independently under Schedule 1, paragraph 7, he is entitled to require any party to claims under the 1993 Act (as described in paragraph 7(1)(b) of Schedule 1) to supply him, on payment of the reasonable costs of copying, with copies of all documents which that party has served on the other parties to the claim.

TRANSFER TO LEASEHOLD VALUATION TRIBUNAL UNDER THE COMMONHOLD AND LEASEHOLD REFORM ACT 2002

15.1   If a question is ordered to be transferred to a leasehold valuation tribunal for determination under paragraph 3 of Schedule 12 to the Commonhold and Leasehold Reform Act 2002 the court will –

(1) send notice of the transfer to all parties to the claim; and

(2) send to the leasehold valuation tribunal –

(a) the order of transfer; and

(b) all documents filed in the claim relating to the question.

(Paragraph 15.1 applies to proceedings in England but does not apply to proceedings in Wales.)

APPENDIX 20

LANDLORD'S COUNTERNOTICE

LANDLORD AND TENANT ACT 1954 SECTION 26(6)

To   (name of tenant)

of   (address)

I, (name of landlord), of (address), received on (insert date of receipt) your request for a new tenancy of (insert address of property).

I GIVE YOU NOTICE that I will oppose your application to the court for a new tenancy on the following ground(s) contained in paragraph(s) (insert paragraph letter(s)) of s 30(1) of the Landlord and Tenant Act 1954.

Dated:

Signed:
(signature of (or on behalf of) the landlord)

[as solicitor/agents for (name of landlord)]

Name of landlord:

Address of landlord:

[(name and address of agents)]

APPENDIX 21

JOINT APPLICATION TO THE COURT TO ACCOMPANY A CONSENT ORDER

Joint application

Claim no..

In the .... County Court

In the matter of the Landlord and Tenant Act 1954

In the matter of the premises known as

Between:

Tenant

Applicant

- and -

Landlord

Respondent

Joint Application

We [tenant] and [landlord] jointly apply to the court for an order in the terms of the draft consent order attached.

We have each taken independent legal advice before agreeing to the terms of the proposed order.

Dated this day of

Solicitors' certificate

We certify that we have each advised the applicant whom we represent on the suitability of the proposed procedure and terms set out in the draft consent order.

Solicitors for the tenant   Solicitors for the landlord

To: The District Judge of the court

Note: This procedure is suitable for those landlords and tenants who have decided, following the receipt of professional advice, that they wish to resolve certain matters relating to the tenant's application for a new business tenancy by arbitration or independent expert determination rather than through the courts. Landlord and tenant must each receive independent legal advice on the consequences of these procedures and their lawyers must sign the certificate on the application form.

APPENDIX 22

REFERRAL OF ALL OUTSTANDING ISSUES TO ARBITRATION

Version 1: Arbitration

Claim no..

In the .... County Court

In the matter of the Landlord and Tenant Act 1954

In the matter of the premises known as

Between:
Tenant
Applicant
- and -
Landlord
Respondent

Consent Order

Upon the joint application of the parties by their respective solicitors and upon reading the parties agreed terms

And by consent

It is ordered that:

1. The duration of the new tenancy shall be [a term commencing on the .... and ending on ....] [determined in accordance with Section 33 of the said Act, by a third party under the provisions of Part 2 of the schedule to this order].

2. The terms of the new tenancy (other than as to the duration thereof and as to the rent payable thereunder) shall be [in the form previously agreed between the parties, and set out in Part 1 of the schedule to this order] [such terms as have been previously agreed between the parties and are set out in Part 1 of the schedule to this order together with such other terms as shall be determined in accordance with Section 35 of the said Act by a third party under the provisions of Part 2 of the schedule to this order] [determined in accordance with Section 35 of the said Act by a third party under the provisions of Part 2 of the schedule to this order].

3. The initial rent payable under the new tenancy shall be [£.........per year] [determined by a third party under the provisions of Part 2 of the schedule to this order in accordance with

Section 34 of the said Act [and as if the new tenancy were to commence on the date of his determination]]*.

4. Pursuant to Section 24A of the said Act, the interim rent payable from [.........] for so long as the current tenancy continues by virtue of Sections 24 and 64 of the said Act shall be [at the rate of £......... per year] [at the same rate as is agreed or determined in respect of the new tenancy under paragraph 3 above] [determined in accordance with Section 24A of the said Act by a third party under the provisions of Part 2 of the schedule to this order].

And it is further ordered that all further proceedings in this action be stayed upon the terms agreed between the parties and set out in the schedule to this order to save that:

a. Either party shall have liberty to apply to the court for the purpose of carrying the said agreed terms into effect.

b. When all the terms for the new tenancy have been finally determined in accordance with the provisions of the schedule to this order and/or agreed either party shall have liberty to apply for an order pursuant to Section 29 of the said Act for the grant of a new tenancy on those terms.

c. On the filing of a Notice of Discontinuance by the applicant the current tenancy shall cease and determine on the expiration of three months from the date of filing of the said notice with the court.

Dated

Solicitors for the tenant   Solicitors for the landlord

* If an interim rent application has been made as a separate action, this paragraph will need to be incorporated in a separate consent order with an amended Schedule.

Schedule

Part 1 [agreed terms]

Part 2

A. The matters referred to in paragraphs [1][2][3] and [4] of the consent order ('the Substantive Issues') shall be determined by an independent third party acting as an arbitrator in accordance with the Arbitration Act 1996. [Unless otherwise agreed the parties shall be bound by their respective Claim Form, Particulars of Claim, Acknowledgement of Service or Statements of Case lodged with the court ('the Statements of Case') [but the arbitrator shall have the power to allow either party to depart from its Statements of Case].] [The parties shall not be bound by their respective Claim Form, Particulars of Claim, Acknowledgement of Service or Statements of Case lodged with the court].

B. The parties shall endeavour to make a joint appointment of the arbitrator within [ ] days from the date of the consent order failing which either party may thereafter apply to the president for the time being of the [RICS] [Law Society] to make the appointment.

C. The arbitrator shall make a single award ('the Award') determining all the Substantive Issues and where any of the Substantive Issues are agreed between the parties during the course of the arbitration proceedings, the arbitrator will incorporate their agreement in the award. The Substantive Issues do not include, for this purpose, any issue solely related to costs. The arbitrator will make a separate award on costs unless otherwise agreed by both parties.

D. The Substantive Issues shall be finally determined on the earliest date by which the arbitration proceedings on the Substantive Issues (including any proceedings on or in consequence of any application or appeal under Sections 67, 68 or 69 of the Arbitration Act 1996) have been determined and any time for making any such application or appeal or further application or appeal has expired without an application for extension of that time having been made.

E. If Notice of Discontinuance is filed by the applicant with the court, the applicant will forthwith notify the respondent and the arbitrator and any arbitration proceedings concerning the duration, terms or initial rent payable for the new tenancy will cease. The applicant will be liable for the arbitrator's fees and the respondent's costs (to be referred to detailed assessment if not agreed) in relation to the arbitration of these matters not withstanding any order of the arbitrator to the contrary.

F. If the respondent withdraws its application for the determination of a rent payable pursuant to Section 24A of the Landlord and Tenant Act 1954, the respondent will forthwith notify the applicant and the arbitrator and any arbitration proceedings concerning this matter shall cease. The respondent will be liable to pay the arbitrator's fees and the applicant's costs (to be referred to detailed assessment if not agreed) of the arbitration of this matter notwithstanding any order of the arbitrator to the contrary.

APPENDIX 23

EXPERT DETERMINATION ON RENT AND, IF NECESSARY, ARBITRATION ON INTERIM RENT

Claim no..

In the .... County Court

In the matter of the Landlord and Tenant Act 1954

In the matter of the premises known as

Between:
Tenant
Applicant
- and -
Landlord
Respondent

Consent Order

Upon the joint application of the parties by their respective solicitors and upon reading the parties agreed terms

And by consent

It is ordered that:

1. The duration of the new tenancy shall be a term commencing on the .... and ending on ....

2. The terms of the new tenancy (other than as to the duration thereof and as to the rent payable thereunder) shall be in the form previously agreed between the parties, and set out in Part 1 of the schedule to this order.

3. The initial rent payable under the new tenancy shall be determined by a third party under the provisions of Part 2 of the schedule to this order in accordance with Section 34 of the said Act [and as if the new tenancy were to commence on the date of his determination].

4. Pursuant to Section 24A of the said Act, the rent payable from [.........] for so long as the current tenancy continues by virtue of Section 24 of the said Act shall be [at the rate of £.........per year] [at the same rate as is agreed or determined in respect of the new tenancy under paragraph 3 above] [determined in accordance with Section 24A of the said Act by a third party under the provisions of Part 2 of the schedule to this order].

And it is further ordered that all further proceedings in this action be stayed upon the terms agreed between the parties and set out in the schedule to this order save that:

a. Either party shall have liberty to apply to the court for the purpose of carrying the said agreed terms into effect.

b. When all the terms of the new tenancy have been finally determined in accordance with the provisions of the schedule to this order either party shall have liberty to apply for an order pursuant to Section 29 of the said Act for the grant of a new tenancy on those terms.

c. On the filing of a Notice of Discontinuance by the applicant the applicant's tenancy shall cease and determine on the expiration of three months from the date of filing of the said notice with the court.

Dated

Solicitors for the tenant   Solicitors for the landlord

Schedule

Part 1 [Agreed Terms]

Part 2

A. The matter referred to in paragraph 3 of the consent order ('the Initial Rent') shall be determined [first] by an independent surveyor acting as an expert and not an arbitrator who shall give both parties a reasonable opportunity to make written representations to him which he shall take into account in reaching his determination but which shall not be binding on him. [The independent surveyor shall have power to decide how his fees shall be borne as between the parties but otherwise each party shall bear its own costs of the determination of the Initial Rent.] [The independent surveyor shall have power to decide how his fees and the parties' own costs shall be borne as between the parties.] [Each side shall bear its own costs and one half of the independent surveyor's fees of the determination of the Initial Rent.]

B. [The matter referred to in paragraph 4 of the consent order ('the Interim Rent') shall then be decided by the independent surveyor acting as an arbitrator in accordance with the Arbitration Act 1996.]

C. The parties shall endeavour to make a joint appointment of the independent surveyor within [ ] days from the date of the consent order failing which either party may apply to the president for the time being of the [RICS] [Law Society] to make the appointment.

D. [Unless otherwise agreed the parties shall be bound by their respective Claim Form, Particulars of Claim, Acknowledgement of

Service or Statements of Case lodged with the court ('the Statements of Case' [but the independent surveyor shall have power to allow either party to depart from its Statements of Case]] [The parties shall not be bound by their respective Claim Form, Particulars of Claim, Acknowledgement of Service or Statements of Case lodged with the court].

E. The Initial Rent shall be finally determined on the date of the independent surveyor's determination. Unless the parties otherwise agree the independent surveyor will then proceed to make an Award on the Interim Rent. [The Interim Rent shall be finally determined on the earliest date by which the arbitration proceedings on the Interim Rent (including any proceedings on or in consequence of any application or appeal under Sections 67, 68 or 69 of the Arbitration Act 1996) have been determined and any time for making such application or appeal or further application or appeal has expired without an application for extension of that time having been made.]

F. If Notice of Discontinuance is filed by the applicant with the court the applicant will forthwith notify the respondent and the independent surveyor and the independent surveyor will take no further steps to determine the Initial Rent. The applicant will be liable for the independent surveyor's fees in respect of the determination of the Initial Rent [and for the respondent's costs of the determination of the Initial Rent, such costs to be referred to detailed assessment if not agreed] not withstanding any direction of the independent surveyor to the contrary.

G. [If the respondent withdraws its application for the determination of the Interim Rent, the respondent will forthwith notify the applicant and the independent surveyor will take no further steps to determine the Interim Rent. The respondent will be liable for the independent surveyor's fees [and for the applicant's costs] in relation to the arbitration of the Interim Rent [such costs to be referred to detailed assessment if not agreed] notwithstanding any direction of the independent surveyor to the contrary.]

APPENDIX 24

ARBITRATION ON TERMS FOLLOWED, IF NECESSARY, BY EXPERT DETERMINATION ON INITIAL RENT AND ARBITRATION ON INTERIM RENT

Claim no...

In the ………………………... County Court

In the matter of the Landlord and Tenant Act 1954

In the matter of the premises known as

Between:
Tenant
Applicant
- and -
Landlord
Respondent

Consent order

Upon the joint application of the parties by their respective solicitors and upon reading the parties agreed terms

And by consent

It is ordered that:

1. The duration of the new tenancy shall be [a term commencing on ……… and ending on ………] [determined in accordance with Section 33 of the said Act, by a third party under the provisions of Part 2 of the schedule to this order].

2. The terms of the new tenancy (other than as to the duration thereof and as to the rent payable thereunder) shall be [in the form previously agreed between the parties and set out in Part 1 of the schedule to this order] [such terms as have been previously agreed between the parties and are set out in Part 1 of the schedule to this order together with such other terms as shall be determined in accordance with Section 35 of the said Act by a third party under the provisions of Part 2 of the schedule to this order] [determined in accordance with Section 35 of the said Act, by a third party under the provisions of Part 2 of the schedule to this order].

3. The initial rent payable under the new tenancy shall be [£ ……… per year] [determined by a third party under the provisions of Part

2 of the schedule to this order in accordance with Section 34 of the said Act [and as if the new tenancy were to commence on the date of his determination]].

4. Pursuant to Section 24A of the said Act, the rent payable from [.........] for so long as the current tenancy continues by virtue of Sections 24 and 64 of the said Act shall be [at the rate of £ .... per year] [at the same rate as is agreed or determined in respect of the new tenancy under paragraph 3 above] [determined in accordance with Section 24A of the said Act, by a third party under the provisions of Part 2 of the schedule to this order]*

And it is further ordered that all further proceedings in this action be stayed upon the terms agreed between the parties and set out in the schedule to this order save that:

a. Either party shall have liberty to apply to the court for the purpose of carrying the said agreed terms into effect.

b. When all the terms for the new tenancy have been finally determined and/or agreed in accordance with the provisions of the schedule to this order either party shall have liberty to apply for an order pursuant to Section 29 of the said Act for the grant of a new tenancy on those terms.

c. On the filing of a Notice of Discontinuance by the applicant the applicant's tenancy shall cease and determine on the expiration of three months from the date of filing of the said notice with the court.

Dated

Solicitors for the tenant   Solicitors for the landlord

*If an interim rent application has been made as a separate action, this paragraph will need to be incorporated in a separate consent order with an amended schedule.

Schedule

Part 1 [Agreed Terms]

Part 2

A. The matters referred to in paragraphs [1] [and] [2] of the consent order ('the Substantive Issues') shall be determined by an independent third party acting as an arbitrator in accordance with the Arbitration Act 1996 ('the Arbitrator').

B. The parties shall endeavour to make a joint appointment of the arbitrator within [ ] days from the date of the consent order failing which either party may apply to the president for the time being of the [RICS] [Law Society] to make the appointment.

C. The arbitrator shall make a single award ('the Award') determining all the Substantive Issues and where any of the Substantive Issues are agreed between the parties during the course of the arbitration proceedings, the arbitrator will incorporate their agreement in the award. The Substantive Issues do not include, for this purpose, any issue solely related to costs. The arbitrator will make a separate award on costs unless otherwise agreed by both parties.

D. The Substantive Issues shall be finally determined on the earliest date by which the arbitration proceedings on the Substantive Issues (including any proceedings on or in consequence of any application or appeal under Sections 67, 68 or 69 of the Arbitration Act 1996) have been determined and any time for making any such application or appeal or further application or appeal has expired without an application for extension of that time having been made.

E. The parties shall endeavour to agree the matters referred to in paragraphs [3] [and] [4] of the order ('the Rental Issues') within 28 days (or such longer period as they may agree in writing) from agreement or final determination of the Substantive Issues.

F. In default of agreement on the Rental Issues within the time referred to above either party may apply to the president for the time being of the [RICS] [Law Society] for the appointment of an independent surveyor ('the Surveyor') to determine the Rental Issues.

G. The matter referred to in paragraph 3 of the consent order ('the Initial Rent') shall be determined by the surveyor acting as expert and not as arbitrator who shall give both parties a reasonable opportunity to make written representations to him which he shall take into account in reaching his determination but which shall not be binding on him. [The surveyor shall have power to decide how his fees shall be borne as between the parties but otherwise each party shall bear its own costs of the determination of the Initial Rent.] [The surveyor shall have power to decide how his fees and the parties' own costs shall be borne as between the parties.] [Each side shall bear its own costs and one half of the surveyor's fees of the determination of the Initial Rent.]

H. The Initial Rent shall be finally determined on the date of the surveyor's determination. Unless the parties otherwise agree the surveyor will then proceed to decide the matter referred to in paragraph 4 of the consent order ('the Interim Rent') acting as an arbitrator in accordance with the Arbitration Act 1996. The Interim Rent shall be finally determined on the earliest date by which the arbitration proceedings on the Interim Rent (including any proceedings on or in consequence of any application or appeal under Sections 67, 68 or 69 of the Arbitration Act 1996) have been determined and any time for making any such application or appeal or further application or appeal has expired without an application for extension of that time having been made.

I.   In relation to the determination of the matters referred to in paragraphs [1] [2] [3] and [4] of the consent order [unless otherwise agreed the parties shall be bound by their respective Claim Form, Particulars of Claim, Acknowledgement of Service or Statements of Case lodged with the Court ('the Statements of Case') [but the independent third party shall have power to allow either party to depart from its Statements of Case]] [the parties shall not be bound by their respective Claim Form, Particulars of Claim, Acknowledgement of Service or Statements of Case lodged with the court].

J.   If Notice of Discontinuance is filed by the applicant with the court, the applicant will forthwith notify the arbitrator or the surveyor as the case may be and any arbitration proceedings shall cease, and any surveyor who has been appointed shall take no further action, in relation to the matters referred to in paragraphs [1] [2] and [3] of the order. The applicant will be liable for the arbitrator and the surveyor's fees [and for the other party's costs to be referred to detailed assessment if not agreed] of determining these matters notwithstanding any order of the arbitrator or direction of the surveyor to the contrary.

K.   If the respondent withdraws its application for the determination of a rent payable pursuant to Section 24A of the Landlord and Tenant Act 1954, the respondent will forthwith notify the applicant and the surveyor and any arbitration proceedings concerning this matter shall cease. The respondent will be liable to pay the fees of the surveyor and the applicant's costs of the arbitration of this matter (such costs to be referred to detailed assessment if not agreed) notwithstanding any order of the surveyor to the contrary.

APPENDIX 25

EXPERT DETERMINATION ON TEXT OF LEASE

Claim no..

In the .... County Court

In the matter of the Landlord and Tenant Act 1954

In the matter of the premises known as

Between:
Tenant
Applicant
- and -
Landlord
Respondent

Consent Order

Upon the joint application of the parties by their respective solicitors and upon reading the parties agreed terms

And by consent

It is ordered that:

1. The duration of the new tenancy shall be a term commencing on the .... and ending on ....
2. The terms of the new tenancy (other than as to the duration thereof and as to the rent payable thereunder) shall be in accordance with the heads of terms previously agreed between the parties as set out in Part I of the schedule and shall be given effect in a form of lease which shall be agreed between the parties or determined in accordance with the provisions of Part 2 of the schedule to this order.
3. The initial rent payable under the new tenancy shall be £ .... per year
4. Pursuant to Section 24A of the said Act, the rent payable from [.........] [for so long as the current tenancy continues by virtue of Section 24 of the said Act] [from .... to ....] shall be [at the rate of £ .... per year].

And it is further ordered that all further proceedings in this action be stayed upon the terms agreed between the parties and set out in the schedule to this order save that:

a. Either party shall have liberty to apply to the court for the purpose of carrying the said agreed terms into effect.

b. Either party shall have liberty to apply for an order pursuant to Section 29 of the said Act for the grant of a new tenancy in a form of Lease which has been finally determined in accordance with the provisions of the schedule to this order.

c. On the filing of a Notice of Discontinuance by the applicant the applicant's tenancy shall cease and determine on the expiration of three months from the date of filing of the said Notice with the court.

Dated

Solicitors for the tenant   Solicitors for the landlord

Schedule

Part 1 [Heads of Terms]

Part 2

A. The heads of terms set out in Part 1 of this schedule shall be incorporated in a form of lease which shall be determined by an independent third party who shall be a solicitor and who shall act as an expert and not an arbitrator who shall give both parties a reasonable opportunity to make written representations to him which he shall take into account in reaching his determination but which shall not be binding on him. [The independent expert shall have power to decide how his fees shall be borne as between the parties but otherwise each party shall bear its own costs of his determination.] [The independent expert shall have power to decide how his fees and the parties own costs shall be borne as between the parties.] [Each side shall bear its own costs and one half of the independent expert's fees of the determination.]

B. The parties shall endeavour to make a joint appointment of the independent expert within [ ] days from the date of the consent order failing which either party may apply to the president for the time being of the [RICS] [Law Society] to make the appointment.

C. [Unless otherwise agreed the parties shall be bound by their respective Claim Form, Particulars of Claim, Acknowledgement of Service or Statements of Case lodged with the court ('the Statements of Case') but the independent expert shall have power to allow either party to depart from its Statements of Case.] [The parties shall not be bound by their respective Claim Form, Particulars of Claim, Acknowledgement of Service or Statements of Case lodged with the court.]

D. The said form of lease shall be finally determined on the date of the independent expert's determination.

E. If Notice of Discontinuance is filed by the applicant with the court, the applicant will forthwith notify the respondent and independent expert and the independent expert will take no further action. The party filing such notice shall be liable for the independent expert's fees [and for the other party's costs to be referred to detailed assessment if not agreed] notwithstanding any direction of the independent expert to the contrary.

APPENDIX 26

FORMS UNDER THE LANDLORD AND TENANT ACT 1927

Form 1

Tenant's notice of proposal to make improvements

LANDLORD AND TENANT ACT 1927 SECTION 3(1)

NOTICE OF INTENTION TO MAKE IMPROVEMENTS

To   (name of landlord)

of   (address)

Details of lease:

Date:

Parties:

Premises:

THIS NOTICE is given under the Landlord and Tenant Act 1927 and relates to the Premises, of which you are the landlord.

I, (name of tenant), of (address), GIVE YOU NOTICE that I intend to make the improvements to the Premises described in the schedule to this notice and in the plan and specification annexed to this notice and that I intend to proceed with the making of these improvements unless, within 3 months after service of this notice, I receive notice of objection from you.

[Any correspondence about this notice, and any notices that you may wish to serve on me relating to the subject matter of this notice, should be sent to my agent, who is authorised to accept service of notices on my behalf at the address given below.]

SCHEDULE
(describe the proposed improvements)

Dated:

Signed:

(signature of (or on behalf of) the tenant)
[as agents for (name of tenant)
(name and address of agents)]

Form 2 – Landlord's notice objecting to improvements proposed by the tenant

LANDLORD AND TENANT ACT 1927 SECTION 3(1)

NOTICE OBJECTING TO PROPOSED IMPROVEMENTS

To   (name of tenant)

of   (address)

Details of lease:

Date:

Parties:

Premises:

I, (name of landlord) of (address) GIVE YOU NOTICE that I object to [such of] the proposed improvements described in your notice dated (date) [as are specified in the schedule to this notice].

[SCHEDULE
(particulars of the improvements objected to)]

Dated:

Signed:

(signature of, or on behalf of, the landlord)
[as agents for (name of landlord)
(name and address of agents)]

Form 3 – Landlord's notice of consent to proposed improvements

LANDLORD AND TENANT ACT 1927

NOTICE OF CONSENT TO IMPROVEMENTS

To   (name of tenant)

of   (address)

Details of lease:

Date:

Parties:

Premises:

I, (name of landlord), of (address), GIVE YOU NOTICE that I consent to the making of the improvements at the Premises mentioned in your notice dated (date).

Dated:

Signed:

(signature of, or on behalf of, the landlord)
[as agents for (name of landlord)
(name and address of agents)]

Form 4 – Landlord's notice consenting to proposed improvements subject to modifications

LANDLORD AND TENANT ACT 1927

NOTICE OF CONSENT TO IMPROVEMENTS SUBJECT TO MODIFICATIONS

To   (name of tenant)

of   (address)

Details of lease:

Date:

Parties:

Premises:

I, (name of landlord), of (address), GIVE YOU NOTICE that, subject to the modifications shown in the amended plan and specification annexed to this notice, I consent to the making of the improvements at the Premises described in your notice dated (date).

Save to the extent that I have given my consent above, I object to the improvements proposed in your notice.

Dated:

Signed:

(signature of, or on behalf of, the landlord)

[as agents for (name of landlord)

(name and address of agents)]

(annex amended plan and specification)

Form 5 – Landlord's notice offering to execute improvements himself in consideration of an increase in rent

LANDLORD AND TENANT ACT 1927 SECTION 3(1)

NOTICE OFFERING TO EXECUTE IMPROVEMENTS IN CONSIDERATION OF AN INCREASED RENT

To   (name of tenant)

of   (address)

Details of lease:

Date:

Parties:

Premises:

I, (name of landlord), of (address), GIVE YOU NOTICE that I offer to execute at the Premises the improvements described in your notice dated (date) in consideration of the rent of the Premises being increased to £......... exclusive of VAT per year, or of such increase being made in the rent as the tribunal may determine.

Dated:

Signed:

(signature of, or on behalf of, the landlord)
[as agents for (name of landlord)
(name and address of agents)]

Form 6 – Landlord's certificate that improvements have been executed

LANDLORD AND TENANT ACT 1927 SECTION 3(6)

CERTIFICATE OF EXECUTION OF IMPROVEMENTS

To   (name of tenant)

of   (address)

Details of lease:

Date:

Parties:

Premises:

I, (name of landlord), of (address), CERTIFY that the improvements in the Premises described in your notice dated (date) have been duly executed.

Dated:

Signed:

(signature of, or on behalf of, the landlord)
[as agents for (name of landlord)
(name and address of agents)]

Form 7 – Tenant's notice of claim for compensation for improvements

LANDLORD AND TENANT ACT 1927

NOTICE OF CLAIM FOR COMPENSATION

To   (name of landlord)

of   (address)

Details of lease:

Date:

Parties:

Premises:

I, (name of tenant), of (address), GIVE YOU NOTICE that I claim to be entitled to compensation, on quitting the Premises on the termination of my tenancy, for the improvements particulars of which are set out in the schedule below, which improvements have been made by [me (or as appropriate) my predecessors in title (or as appropriate) me and my predecessors in title] and will add to the letting value of the premises at the termination of my tenancy

[Any correspondence about this notice, and any notices that you may wish to serve on me relating to the subject matter of this notice, should be sent to my agent, who is authorised to accept service of notices on my behalf at the address given below.]

SCHEDULE

(describe the improvements made, state by whom made, when made, the cost of them and the amount of compensation claimed)

Dated:

Signed:

(signature of, or on behalf of, the tenant)
[as agents for (name of tenant)
(name and address of agents)]

Form 8 – Mesne landlord's notice to his head landlord of a notice of claim received from the tenant

LANDLORD AND TENANT ACT 1927 SECTION 8(1)

NOTICE OF COMPENSATION CLAIM RECEIVED

To   (name of head landlord)

of   (address)

Details of lease:

Date:

Parties:

Premises:

I, (name of mesne landlord), of (address), GIVE YOU NOTICE that I have received from (name of tenant), of (address), who is my tenant of the Premises, [a notice (or as appropriate) notices] dated (date(s)) [respectively] under the Landlord and Tenant Act 1927, claiming (set out details of the claim or claims) [a copy (or as appropriate) copies] of which, together with copies of the plan[s] and specifications referred to in the notice[s], [is (or as appropriate) are] enclosed.

Dated:

Signed:

(signature of, or on behalf of, the mesne landlord)

[as agents for (name of mesne landlord)

(name and address of agents)]

Form 9 – Mesne landlord's notice to his head landlord claiming as compensation the amount that he has paid or is liable to pay for improvements made by a tenant

LANDLORD AND TENANT ACT 1927 SECTION 8(1)

NOTICE OF COMPENSATION CLAIM RECEIVED

To   (name of head landlord)

of   (address)

Details of lease:

Date:

Parties:

Premises:

I, (name of mesne landlord), of (address), GIVE YOU NOTICE that I have paid or am liable to pay to (name of tenant) of (address) ('the Tenant') the sum of £......... as compensation pursuant to the Landlord and Tenant Act 1927 for improvements made by him to the Premises. I claim to be entitled to the sum of £......... from you at the end of my term, which will expire on (date) as compensation for the improvements in like manner and on the same conditions as if I had myself made the improvements, which are described in the notice from the Tenant to me dated (date), a copy of which was sent to you on (date).

Dated:

Signed:

(signature of, or on behalf of, the mesne landlord)

[as agents for (name of mesne landlord) (name and address of agents)]

INDEX